Lecture Notes of the Institute for Computer Sciences, Social Informatics and Telecommunications Engineering 614

The LNICST series publishes ICST's conferences, symposia and workshops.

LNICST reports state-of-the-art results in areas related to the scope of the Institute.

The type of material published includes

- Proceedings (published in time for the respective event)
- Other edited monographs (such as project reports or invited volumes)

LNICST topics span the following areas:

- General Computer Science
- E-Economy
- E-Medicine
- Knowledge Management
- Multimedia
- Operations, Management and Policy
- Social Informatics
- Systems

Sanjay Goel · Ersin Uzun · Mengjun Xie ·
Sumantra Sarkar
Editors

Digital Forensics and Cyber Crime

15th EAI International Conference, ICDF2C 2024
Dubrovnik, Croatia, October 9–10, 2024
Proceedings, Part II

Springer

Editors
Sanjay Goel
University of Albany
Albany, NY, USA

Ersin Uzun
Rochester Institute of Technology
Rochester, NY, USA

Mengjun Xie
University of Tennessee at Chattanooga
Chattanooga, TN, USA

Sumantra Sarkar
Binghamton University
Binghamton, NY, USA

ISSN 1867-8211 ISSN 1867-822X (electronic)
Lecture Notes of the Institute for Computer Sciences, Social Informatics and Telecommunications Engineering
ISBN 978-3-031-89359-9 ISBN 978-3-031-89360-5 (eBook)
https://doi.org/10.1007/978-3-031-89360-5

This Springer imprint is published by the registered company Springer Nature Switzerland AG
The registered company address is: Gewerbestrasse 11, 6330 Cham, Switzerland

Preface

We are delighted to introduce the proceedings of the fifteenth edition of the European Alliance for Innovation (EAI) International Conference on Digital Forensics & Cyber Crime (ICDF2C 2024), held in Dubrovnik, Croatia. This conference brought together researchers, developers, and practitioners around the world who are exploring, producing, and applying scientific knowledge to the broad area of Digital Forensics and Cyber Crime. This year's conference focused on emerging topics including the use of Artificial Intelligence and Machine Learning in digital forensics as well as adversary engagement and threat intelligence for cyber security.

The technical program of ICDF2C 2024 consisted of 40 papers out of 90 submissions covering a selection of aspects of the field. The conference sessions were grouped according to the main topics being discussed: Artificial Intelligence & Security; Multimedia Forensics; Intrusion Detection; Intrusion and Fraud Detection; Large Language Models, Advances in Security and Forensics; Advances in Security and Forensics; Security Analytics, Threat Intelligence, Multimedia Forensics; and Generative AI, Emerging Threats. Apart from the high-quality technical paper presentations, the technical program also featured keynote speeches by Ivan Martinovic from the University of Oxford and Srdjan Capkun from ETH Zurich.

We sincerely appreciate the constant support and guidance of the steering chairs Sanjay Goel and Pavel Gladyshev. It was also a great pleasure to work with such an excellent organizing committee team for their hard work in organizing and supporting the conference. In particular, the Technical Program Committee, led by our TPC Co-Chairs, Ersin Uzun, Mengjun Xie, and Sumantra Sarkar, completed the review process of technical papers and made a high-quality technical program. We are also grateful to the Conference Manager, Radka Vasileiadis, for her support and to all the authors who submitted their papers to the ICDF2C conference.

We strongly believe that the ICDF2C conference provides a good forum for all researchers, developers, and practitioners to discuss all science and technology aspects relevant to digital forensics and cybercrime, as indicated by the contributions presented in this volume.

Sanjay Goel
Ersin Uzun
Mengjun Xie

Organization

Steering Committee

Sanjay Goel	University at Albany, SUNY, USA
Pavel Gladyshev	University College Dublin, Ireland

Organizing Committee

General Chair

Sanjay Goel	University at Albany, SUNY, USA

General Co-chair

Dragan Peraković	University of Zagreb, Croatia

TPC Chair and Co-chairs

Alan Dennis	Indiana University, USA
Mengjun Xie	University of Tennessee at Chattanooga, USA
Ersin Uzun	Rochester Institute of Technology, USA
Sumantra Sarkar	Binghamton University, SUNY, USA

Local Chair

Petra Zoric	University of Zagreb, Croatia

Workshops Chair

Justin Pelletier	Rochester Institute of Technology, USA

Publicity and Social Media Chair

Sakshi Singh

Publications Chair

Mengjun Xie
Ersin Uzun

Web Chair

Lakshika Vaishnav

Panels Chair

Ivan Cvitić	University of Zagreb, Croatia

Tutorials and Workshop Chair

Justin Pelletier

Technical Program Committee

Allen Johnston	University of Alabama, USA
Merrill Warkentin	Mississippi State University, USA
Raj Sharman	University at Buffalo, SUNY, USA
Raymond Choo	University of Texas, San Antonio, USA
Marko Periša	University of Zagreb, Croatia
Aleksandar Jevremović	Singidunum University, Serbia
Andrii Shalaginov	Kristiania University College, Norway
Raffaele Olivieri	University of Messina, Italy
Marko Krstic	Regulatory Agency for Electronic Communications and Postal Services, Serbia
Hussam Al Hamadi	University of Dubai, UAE
Wathiq Mansoor	University of Dubai, UAE
Husameldin Mukhtar	University of Dubai, UAE
Munir Majdalawieh	Zayed University, UAE
Maher Alaraj	Zayed University, UAE
Jun Dai	Worcester Polytechnic Institute, USA
Xiaoyan Sun	Worcester Polytechnic Institute, USA
Bo Luo	University of Kansas, USA
Haitao Xu	Zhejiang University, China
Xing Gao	University of Delaware, USA
Meng Han	Zhejiang University, China
Yudi Prayudi	Universitas Islam Indonesia, Indonesia

Kyounggon Kim	Naif Arab University for Security Sciences, Saudi Arabia
Bo Chen	Michigan Technological University, USA
Glenn Dardick	ADSFL, USA
Ahmed Hamza	Rochester Institute of Technology, USA
Umit Karabiyik	Purdue University, USA
Joseph Bodden	Ivy Tech Community College, USA
Khair Eddin Sabri	University of Jordan, Jordan
Travis Lee	Tennessee Technological University, USA
Andy Green	Kennesaw State University, USA
Nick Suppiah	Kennesaw State University, USA
Qun Wang	San Francisco State University, USA
Stig F. Mjølsnes	NTNU, Norway
Hannan Azhar	Canterbury Christ Church University, UK
Neil Rowe	U.S. Naval Postgraduate School, USA
Petr Matousek	Brno University of Technology, Czech Republic
Jan Pluskal	Brno University of Technology, Czech Republic
Kathryn Seigfried-Spellar	Purdue University, USA
Brajendra Panda	University of Arkansas, USA

Contents – Part II

Contents – Part I

Intrusion Detection

Intrusion and Fraud Detection

Large Language Models, Advances in Security and Forensics

Security Analytics, Threat Intelligence, Multimedia Forensics

Assessing Threats: Security Boundary and Side-Channel Attack Detection in the Metaverse

Ruiyuan Yang, Guohao Li, Li Yang(✉), Hao Zhang, Jiangyu Wang, and Anyuan Sang

School of Computer Science and Technology, Xidian University, Xi'an 08544, China
yangli@xidian.edu.cn

Abstract. In the era of ubiquitous connectivity, the metaverse faces numerous cybersecurity risks. Current metaverse security research primarily focuses on authentication and privacy, with less emphasis on detecting intrusions. There are currently no effective methods to detect specific threats such as security boundary (TDSC'19) and side-channel attacks (USENIX Security'23) in the metaverse. Additionally, most intrusion detection systems are only effective against known attacks and struggle to handle new threats or correlate alerts effectively. To address these issues, we introduce an metaverse system intrusion detection scheme. Our scheme utilize metaverse system logs and isolation forest for anomaly detection, which does not require labeled data, thereby enabling the identification of attacks targeting metaverse applications, even if the attacks are previously unknown. Additionally, we use a provenance graph to establish causal relationships between system entities and to sequence events before and after an attack, aiding in alert correlation and attack scenario reconstruction. The scheme's effectiveness has been evaluated in a real-world environment, and we have successfully replicated security boundary and side-channel attacks. Experimental results demonstrate that the system can identify potential malicious activities with 99% accuracy and successfully reconstruct attack paths.

Keywords: Metaverse Security · Intrusion detection · Isolation forest · Provenance graph · Attack Reconstruction

1 Introduction

The metaverse [31] represents the next generation of the internet, a space where virtual and real environments converge. However, like any emerging technology, the metaverse faces a range of security challenges. Incorporating technologies such as Virtual Reality (VR) [1,26], Augmented Reality (AR) [11,22], blockchain, and Artificial Intelligence (AI), the metaverse offers users unprecedented immersive experiences and interactivity. Users can participate in various

S. Goel et al. (Eds.): ICDF2C 2024, LNICST 614, pp. 3–23, 2025.
https://doi.org/10.1007/978-3-031-89360-5_1

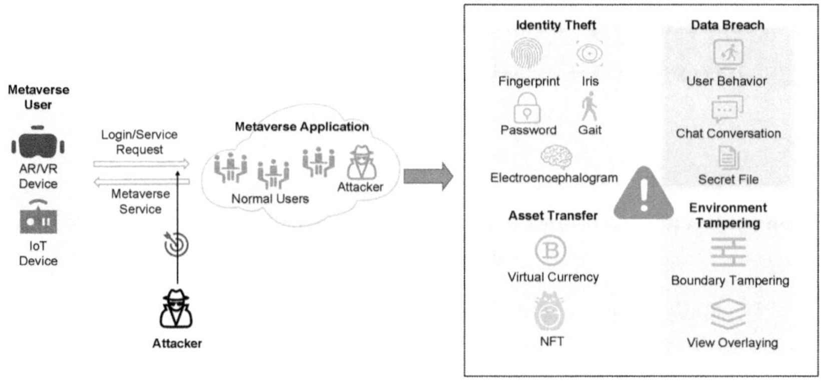

Fig. 1. Summary of attack scenarios in metaverse applications.

activities such as socializing, entertainment, work, education, and commerce through their digital representations, known as virtual avatars. As the metaverse develops, many existing issues in internet applications have re-emerged, including data breach, identity theft, and malware. Additionally, the metaverse introduces new threats such as virtual asset theft, physical harm, fake identity, and social engineering within virtual spaces, as shown in Fig. 1.

Distinct from traditional network threats, new types of attacks targeting the metaverse have more covert and profound implications for user privacy and physical safety. For instance, the "Big Brother" attack, identified and made public by ReasonLabs in 2022, exploits VR devices set to Developer Mode to remotely record the user's headset screen. This malware targets Android-based headsets such as Meta Quest and HTC Vive, compromising user privacy by transmitting VR sessions to the attacker [21]. In the metaverse, attackers utilize a broad range of data, including performance counters, head movements, and gait information, to infer sensitive details such as environmental context, keyboard inputs, and true identities [13,24,32]. In multiplayer environments, these attacks not only reveal users' geographic locations but also enable the secret observation of activities within their private virtual spaces [22,30]. Additionally, some attacks directly endanger user safety by altering virtual settings or resources, distorting users' perception of physical space, and potentially causing physical harm due to compromised immersive experiences [3,11].

Some research efforts [2,7,10,17,18,28,29] have targeted attack detection within the metaverse environment. However, there are no detection methods yet for the attacks in [7,18], and existing methods suffer from generalization issues as they cannot detect unknown attacks and are unable to identify attackers. In this paper, we propose an novel attack detection scheme intended to enhance the security of user interactions and preserve the confidentiality of user data within virtual environments. Our methodology makes extensive use of metaverse system logs including HoloLens and VR system logs. These logs serve as a detailed archive of system activities, which are crucial for constructing event timelines and understanding attackers' strategies. By integrating the sophisticated techniques of isolation forests and provenance graphs, our approach achieves high-efficiency and precision in the detection of cyber threats. The contributions of our work are summarized as follows:

- We systematically review metaverse attack detection methods, revealing their theoretical foundations and practical advantages and limitations in Sect. 2.2. Through comparative analysis, we summarize technology trends, providing a theoretical basis and technical reference for further enhancing metaverse security. To the best of our knowledge, this is the first attempt to leverage metaverse system logs to address security attacks within metaverse applications.
- We propose a metaverse intrusion detection scheme capable of identifying potential malicious nodes through methods based on isolation forest, and we introduce the concept of threat inference based on provenance graph into the metaverse ecosystem for the detection of covert attacks in metaverse applications.
- Utilizing real-world data, we have conducted experimental evaluations to assess the effectiveness of our proposed solution. Our approach has been implemented on AR/VR sensing devices, with security boundary attacks [3] on VR systems carried out on the PICO 4, and side-channel attacks [32] executed on AR systems using the HoloLens 2. Experimental results demonstrate that the system can accurately identify potential malicious activities with 99% accuracy and successfully reconstruct attack paths.

2 Related Work and Analysis

Metaverse applications provide immersive experiences for users, involving substantial amounts of private data, which could make them targets for attackers. Due to the intrinsic blend of virtual and real-world elements in the metaverse, attacks within these applications can not only disrupt the immersive experience but also impact the physical reality. Therefore, it is crucial to ensure the security and privacy of metaverse applications. Section 2.1 discusses security and privacy issues within metaverse applications and Sect. 2.2 briefly describes existing detection techniques for metaverse attacks.

2.1 Security and Privacy Issues in Metaverse Applications

As a bridge between reality and the virtual, metaverse applications [19] offer users a variety of virtual services and immersive experiences. Users can interact within these applications through virtual avatars, as shown in Fig. 2. Metaverse applications include various types:

- Virtual Social Applications: Users can create virtual identities, establish social networks, and interact with others through chat and media sharing.
- Virtual Business Applications: Users can use virtual currencies to purchase goods or services and participate in virtual investments and trading markets.

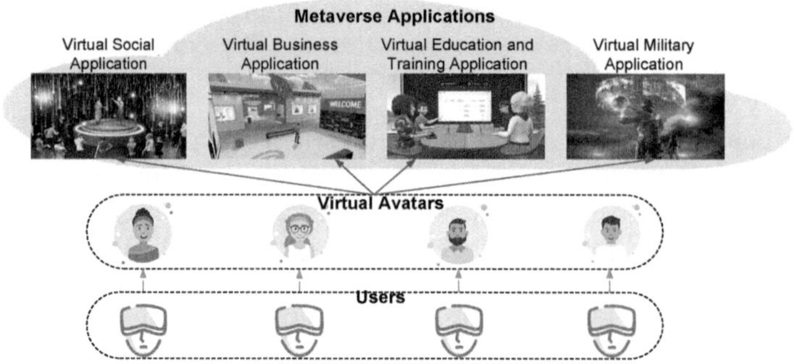

Fig. 2. User interaction in metaverse applications through virtual avatars.

- Virtual Education and Training Applications: Users can engage in virtual learning and training, acquiring knowledge and skills through simulated experiments and role-playing.
- Virtual Entertainment and Gaming Applications: Users can participate in virtual racing, role-playing games, and other immersive activities.
- Virtual Military Applications: Users can undergo virtual military training in diverse battlefield environments, facilitating tactical training and simulated warfare in a secure setting.

These applications enable extensive user participation and experience within the virtual environment through diverse functionalities.

Compared to traditional applications, the metaverse offers a more realistic and immersive user interaction. As a result, metaverse applications necessitate the collection of substantial user data [4]. This vast amount of privacy data renders the metaverse an attractive target for network attacks. Concurrently, the unique features of immersion and presence in the metaverse contribute significantly to the occurrence of attacks in this space. Immersion refers to the user's isolation from the real world, perceiving the external world through settings in the virtual environment; tampering with the virtual environment can affect the physical reality. Presence denotes the user's subjective experience of being present in the virtual environment; alterations to the virtual environment can disrupt the user's sense of presence, resulting in an unfavorable virtual experience. Moreover, due to the sense of presence, certain attacks may cause physical, psychological, and emotional harm to users, such as dizziness, fatigue, and nausea [20].

Due to its complexity and openness, metaverse applications are prone to numerous potential security vulnerabilities. These vulnerabilities present various risks, posing significant threats to the security of the metaverse. The complexity is reflected in the interconnectivity of multiple components, systems, and networks, which expands the attack surface and enables attackers to exploit various vulnerabilities to infiltrate systems, steal information, or cause other damage. The openness of the metaverse allows anyone to create and upload content and interact with other users. This means that attackers can easily masquerade as legitimate users, engaging in social engineering attacks such as impersonating others, spreading false information, or enticing users to click on malicious links and download malware.

2.2 Detection of Attacks in the Metaverse

Currently, only a limited number of studies have proposed detection schemes for attacks in the Metaverse. This section introduces the state-of-the-art related work, thereby exploring the research gaps that we aim to address.

Odeleye et al. [18] presented the first VR intrusion detection system designed to enhance user experiences in VR applications by mitigating frame rate reduction caused by malicious attacks. The system employs machine learning to provide early warnings of attacks based on certain system metrics (such as average frame rate and latency variations), without considering causality between attack events. Han et al. [7] and Nkoro et al. [17] advanced Metaverse intrusion detection using deep learning and used cybersecurity IoT datasets. The former combines KPCA for feature extraction with CNNs for attack recognition, targeting metaverse-IoT communications. The latter proposes an explainable DNN to manage network intrusions within metaverse learning environments.

Some studies developed network attack detection frameworks that collect data from simulated metaverse environments to mitigate network threats. Valluripally et al. [28] developed an abnormal event monitoring tool for VR learning environments, utilizing attack tree to model and describe security risks and potential attack paths. However, the attack tree is a static model, constructed only once, and thus unable to fully capture the dynamic nature of the system and cover new threats occurring in real-time. Bütün et al. [2] focused on user plane reasoning techniques to detect network attacks in the metaverse by monitoring and classifying user network behavior based on traffic features. Its drawback is the need for continuous updates and adjustments to the detection model to adapt to new attack types and evolving Metaverse network structures. Kuo et al. [10] proposed the wormhole detection with sequential probability ratio (WD-SPRT) method for wormhole attacks in the metaverse. This method employs sequential probability ratio analysis to continuously monitor network traffic, efficiently detecting anomalies with a low false-positive rate, making it well-suited for sensor-rich metaverse environments. However, the significant computational resources required by WD-SPRT may limit its applicability in large-scale or real-time networks. Erfan et al. [5] designed a CDA-enabled approach to detect and mitigate eclipse attacks launched on lightweight nodes or gateways in Metaverse networks.

For all the aforementioned efforts, zero-day attacks remain an unresolved challenge. Truong et al. [27] presented MetaCIDS, a Collaborative Intrusion Detection (CID) framework using federated learning and blockchain technology to enable Metaverse devices to collaboratively detect and respond to network threats, effectively identifying zero-day attacks.

Table 1. Summary of related works

Ref	Contribution	Method Type	Data	Zero-day Attack Detection	Attack Reconstruction
[18]	Proposed the first VR intrusion detection system to detect an ongoing attack	Machine learning	VR test environment framerate data	no	no
[29], [28]	Proposed a monitoring method to detect security and privacy attacks that disrupt User Immersive Experience in VRLE applications	Machine learning and statistical analysis techniques	Attack simulations data		
[7]	Proposed a hybrid machine and deep learning-based model to detect twelve classes of IoT attacks in metaverse IoT networks	CNN	BoT-IoT [9], ToN-IoT [14]		
[2]	Outlined a workflow integrating user-plane machine learning for real-time IoT cyberattack detection in the metaverse ecosystem	Random forest	Real-world test data		
[10]	Designed a scheme to overcome the wormhole attack problem	Statistics sequential probability ratio test	Network data generated by a simulation environment		
[5]	Designed a CDA-enabled approach to detect eclipse attacks in metaverse networks	Community detection algorithm (CDA)	Network data generated by a simulation environment		
[17]	Focused on the detection of diverse cyberattack types encountered by learning platforms	Deep neural network (DNN)	EdgeIIoT [6], CICIoT [16], UNSW-NB15 [15]		
[27]	Designed a semi-supervised model for multi-class intrusion detection and zero-day attack detection	Semi-supervised model, blockchain and federated learning	CSE-CIC-IDS [23], CIC-IDS [23], NSL-KDD [25], UNSW-NB1[[15]	yes	

Table 1 summarizes previous research in Metaverse attack detection. As shown, current efforts focus solely on network data and overlook Metaverse system log data. This study pioneers the use of system log data for attack detection. Existing researches often fail to detect zero-day attacks and cannot effectively trace and reconstruct attack scenarios. To address these gaps, this work introduces a scheme that combines unsupervised learning algorithms with attack reconstruction methods using provenance graphs.

3 Threat Model

Consistent with the majority of prior work that utilizes system audit logs for attack detection [8], we assume the system audit is not compromised, and the collected log data is complete and trustworthy. And we assumed the adversary has the capability to compromise the target machine in some fashion, allowing for user-land post-exploitation.

The metaverse side-channel and security boundary attacks [3,32] target data unique to user interaction data and security boundary data in the metaverse. Such attacks present novel and pressing threats, expanding our understanding of the threat models faced by emerging metaverse systems. We provide solutions for the detection and resistance of these threats. Figure 3 presents the attack scenarios considered in this paper. Metaverse applications process vast amounts of valuable user data, making them potential targets for attackers. Additionally, malicious applications can manipulate output data to mislead users. Such threats potentially cause user discomfort, and even manipulate users' movements, leading to physical harm.

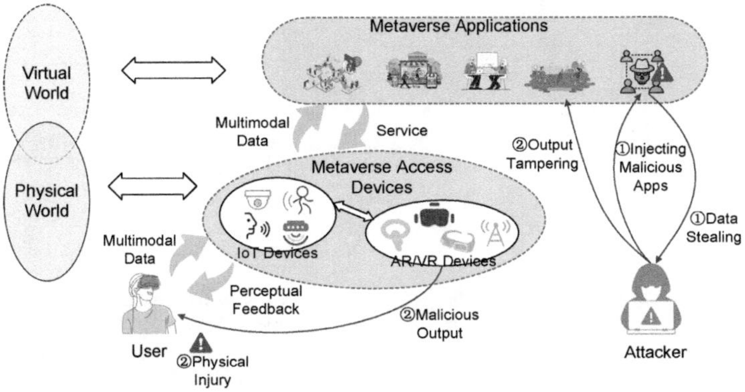

Fig. 3. Attack in the metaverse applications.

4 System Design

Our study leverages metaverse logs (system-level audit logs), applying unsupervised learning to unearth anomalies indicative of zero-day attacks, and utilizes provenance graphs for coherent attack reconstruction.

4.1 Overview

Figure 4 illustrates the architecture, consisting of two components: anomaly detection based on the isolation forest algorithm and attack reconstruction based on the provenance graph. The anomaly detection component based on the isolation forest algorithm collects metaverse log data (AR/VR system data) for anomaly detection. Data preprocessing involves normalization, feature selection, and data encoding operations. Key features are extracted from the logs, and the isolation forest algorithm, utilizing clustering techniques, identifies anomalous instances in the encoded data, generating anomaly alerts. The attack reconstruction component based on the provenance graph employs causality-based provenance graph construction techniques to build a provenance graph from metaverse log data. Anomaly nodes in the provenance graph are labeled using anomaly alert information. Recognizable features summarizing the attack methods and steps in metaverse applications are derived. Known attack features are used to classify and confirm the identified anomaly nodes, establishing associations to reconstruct the attack process comprehensively. This enables a thorough understanding of potential security incidents or attacks.

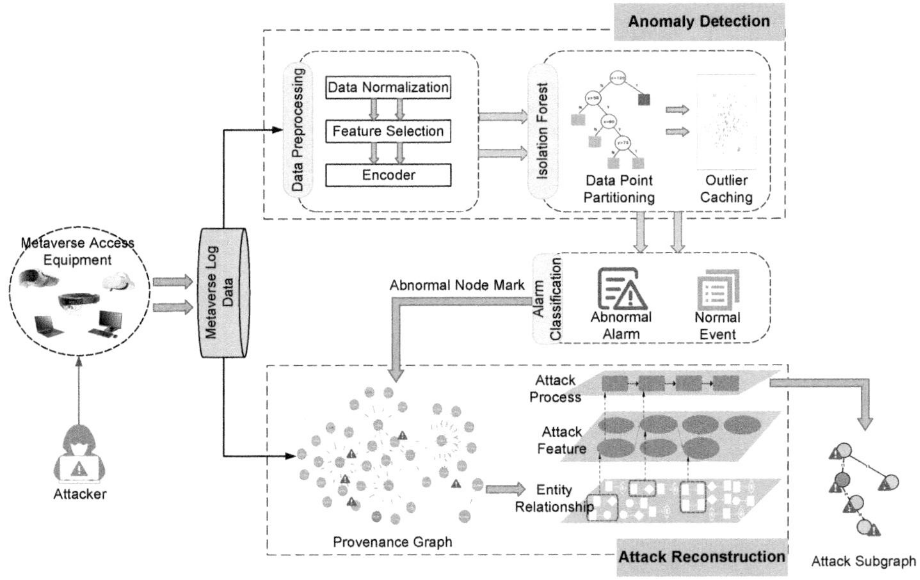

Fig. 4. Architecture of the implementation plan.

4.2 Anomaly Detection

Data Preprocessing. Log data from metaverse systems (AR/VR) provide detailed records crucial for detecting unusual or potentially suspicious activities, thereby identifying potential security threats. The quality of the data significantly impacts the model's predictive accuracy and the capability of generalization. The dataset, however, contains redundancies and invalid entries among categorical and numerical features. To enhance model accuracy, preprocessing steps are undertaken prior to training. These include normalizing data, selecting key features, and encoding these features into a vector matrix. Specifically, duplicate entries are removed by retaining only the first instance, and only essential features such as process names, filenames, and network addresses are retained. This streamlined dataset is then encoded into an attribute feature vector matrix for analysis.

Anomaly Detection Based on Isolation Forest. Anomalous data typically constitute a small proportion of the entire dataset. The isolation forest algorithm [12] is chosen, which uses clustering techniques to identify anomalous instances within encoded data. In the isolation forest algorithm, the dataset $D = \{x_1, x_2, \ldots, x_n\}$ is utilized to train the model. The core of the algorithm involves constructing multiple random trees to rapidly isolate anomalies, which can be mathematically expressed as shown in Eq. 1:

$$\mathrm{s}(x, n) = 2^{-\frac{E(h(x))}{c(n)}} \tag{1}$$

Here, $s(x, n)$ represents the anomaly score, x is the data instance, n is the number of samples, $E(h(x))$ is the average path length of x across all trees, and $c(n)$ is the normalization factor.

To handle large-scale data, we propose an improved method based on chunk processing. Specifically, the dataset D is divided into k subsets $\{D_1, D_2, \cdots, D_k\}$, each of which is used to independently train distinct isolation forest models $\{IF_1, IF_2, \ldots, IF_k\}$. The anomaly score function for each isolation forest model is denoted as $s_i x$. The training and prediction process of the models are described as follows:

- Data Chunking: The dataset D is evenly divided into k subsets D_i;
- Model Training: Each subset D_i is independently trained with the isolation forest anomaly detection model IF_i, using random feature sampling functions;
- Anomaly Prediction: Each model IF_i predicts anomalies for its corresponding subset D_i, outputting the anomaly scores $s_i x$;
- Result Aggregation: The prediction results from all subsets are aggregated to form a comprehensive anomaly score vector $S = \bigcup_{i=1}^{k} s_i(D_i)$.

4.3 Attack Reconstruction

This section explores an attack reconstruction model employing provenance graphs, which integrate spatial and temporal data to resist tampering and preserve execution histories, enhancing the detection of prolonged and covert attacks. These graphs are generated from metaverse log data using causality-based construction techniques. To bridge the semantic gap between low-level log data and high-level user actions, it is essential to develop semantic mappings. This involves mining causal dependencies among system entities within audit logs, including processes, files, and network connections. The mappings relate these entities to actions like process creation, file operations, and network activities.

The metaverse provenance graph is defined as $G =< S, O, E, T >$, where S represents the set of subjects (processes), O represents the set of objects (files, network connections), E represents the relationships among entities, including operations such as create, fork, read, write, sendmsg, link, and T represents timestamps. In this graph, entities are represented as vertices and their interactions as directed edges, allowing for multiple relational edges between two vertices at different times.

Using anomaly detection modules, anomalies identified within the provenance graphs are annotated, with nodes connected to these anomalous nodes considered attack-related and subjected to further analysis to ascertain the alert associations.

In this study, anomaly detection techniques annotate anomalies within provenance graphs, considering nodes connected to anomalous nodes as potentially attack-related, thereby warranting further scrutiny to determine the nature of alerts.

The framework employs attack rules to map low-level audit logs to high-level attack stages, emphasizing not only the steps involved in an attack but also the prerequisites. These rules incorporate causal relationships and information flows between stages, enhancing the understanding of connections across different phases of an attack. The attack model comprises seven stages: (1) initial compromise, characterized by remote connections from untrusted IP addresses; (2) establish flood, involving command and control (CnC) communications for further instructions; (3) privilege escalation, where attackers gain broader permissions using root access; (4) accessing sensitive files, triggering alerts when whitelisted files are accessed; (5) lateral movement; (6) mission completion, involving spawning of processes for malicious activities; (7) cleanup, removing locally downloaded malicious code.

In attack detection, each event information is matched against the prerequisites (such as generated entities and their states, edge relationships, and information flow directions) to determine if it constitutes an attack event. Using label propagation, matched prerequisites are efficiently spread across the graph, avoiding redundant traversals. Labels corresponding to each attack stage are propagated as follows:

- If a source node src is labeled for a particular attack stage, the target node $sink_k$ inherits this label: $sink.step_i = src.step_i$. If not, $sink.step_i$ retains its original label.
- For a system event $(src, r, sink)$ corresponding to the jth stage of an attack rule, the target node's label is updated: $sink.step_j = 1$.

This label propagation marks all nodes involved in the attack within the provenance graph.

Table 2. Devices details

Device	Detail
Computer	16G Memory, i5-10210U
Mobile Workstation	64G Memory, i9-13900HX
HoloLens	Windows Holographic 23H1 for arm64-based mixed reality devices
PICO	PICO4

To reconstruct the attack scenario, both forward and backward analyses are utilized. The backward analysis identifies the intrusion point, while the forward analysis traces the complete attack pathway. Traversal is guided by the attack rules, prioritizing nodes with one or more stage labels as likely attack-related. Backward analysis traces from an alert back to the intrusion point, whereas forward analysis progresses beyond the intrusion point, focusing on nodes with multiple attack labels to delineate the complete attack path and deduce related threat events.

5 Evaluation

Our experimental evaluation was conducted within authentic attack scenarios, exploring the applicability of the scheme as a detection system for real-world metaverse attacks. We evaluate each component of the method as well as its overall performance to demonstrate its effectiveness in detecting anomalies from large-scale system log data.

5.1 Hardware Configuration

The devices utilized by the system are summarized in Table 2. Attacks targeting VR systems are implemented on PICO, whereas attacks targeting AR systems are carried out on HoloLens. The HoloLens operates independently, while the PICO utilizes the PICO Streaming Assistant and SteamVR for streaming operations with a computer. SteamVR is an application that manages VR hardware, and PICO can utilize services provided by SteamVR, such as Chaperone.

5.2 Attack DataSet

Metaverse attack detection is a nascent field lacking open-source datasets for detection and forensic analysis. To address this gap, our scheme replicated covert attacks in VR and AR environments to generate a dataset of audit logs from VR and AR system logs.

Metaverse System Audit Log Collection. Audit logs are collected from various head-mounted devices and hosts, stored in the format prescribed by their respective data collection systems. We utilized these system audit logs to extract operations related to files, processes, and network connection events, as well as the relationships among these operations. Traditional operating systems like Windows and Linux provide comprehensive logging capabilities, in contrast to metaverse devices such as Magic Leap One and Microsoft HoloLens, which operate on Magic Leap OS and Windows Holographic OS, respectively. Oculus and HTC Vive depend on PC connections and primarily use Windows OS. Our data collection comprises audit logs from hosts running Windows OS and streaming with PICO using Event Tracing for Windows (ETW), as well as AR logs from HoloLens via Windows Device Portal, capturing both regular and attack activities. Figure 5 shows a log example from HoloLens, with process log data presented in Fig. 6. Figure 7 illustrates a log from a VR device connected to a PC running Windows OS. Due to space constraints, only select key portions of the log examples are presented.


```
{
  "ActivityId": "00000000-0000-0000-0000-000000000000",
  "FileKey": "18446688588971643248",
  "FileObject": "18446641861160012512",
  "ID": 16,
  "Irp": "18446641861245812088",
  "IssuingThreadId": "200",
  "Keyword": "9223372036854776000",
  "Level": 4,
  "ProcessId": 4,
  "ProviderName": "Microsoft-Windows-Kernel-File",
  "RelatedActivityId":
    "00000000-0000-0000-0000-000000000000",
  "TaskName": "Write",
  "Timestamp": "133512375782718610"
}
```


Fig. 5. AR system log data.


```
{
  "CPUUsage": 0,
  "ImageName": "svchost.exe",
  "PageFileUsage": 3313664,
  "PrivateWorkingSet": 2670592,
  "ProcessId": 2800,
  "SessionId": 0,
  "TotalCommit": 3534848,
  "UserName": "NT AUTHORITY\\NETWORK SERVICE"
}
```


Fig. 6. AR system process data.

```
{
  "@timestamp": "2024-01-11T07:59:18.192Z",
  "@metadata": {
    "name": "DESKTOP-R7S9KG0", "type": "winlogbeat"
  },
  "winlog": {
    "channel": "Security", "api": "wineventlog",
    "provider_name": "Microsoft-Windows-Security-Auditing",
    "record_id": 1891507311,
    "computer_name": "DESKTOP-R7S9KG0",
    "task": "Filtering Platform Connection",
    "event_data": {
      "Application": "\\device\\harddiskvolume3\\java\\jdk
    -17\\bin\\java.exe",
      "SourceAddress": "127.0.0.1",
      "DestAddress": "127.0.0.1", "ProcessID": "19668",
      "opcode": "Information", "event_id": "5156",
    },
    "event": {
      "action": "Filtering Platform Connection",
      "created": "2024-01-11T07:59:19.624Z",
      "code": "5156", "kind": "event",
      "provider": "Microsoft-Windows-Security-Auditing",
      "outcome": "success"
    }
  }
}
```


Fig. 7. VR system log data.

Attacks. We validated our detection system using the metaverse security boundary attacks from [3] and the metaverse side-channel attacks from [32] as representatives of covert metaverse attacks. Malicious software for the security boundary attack is deployed on hosts connected to VR devices, while software for the side-channel attack is deployed on HoloLens. Audit log collection is initiated prior to the onset of these attacks to capture logs containing attack activities.

Fig. 8. Example of the execution of a metaverse security boundary attack.

The following details the attacks. Metaverse security boundary attacks refer to threats that exploit the distinctive features of immersive VR environments and user vulnerabilities, leading to malicious alterations of virtual spaces that can inflict physical or psychological harm on users. The attack begins by infiltrating the target computer to deploy malicious code. This code then executes

Fig. 9. Example of the execution of a metaverse side-channel attack.

commands to manipulate the boundary configuration files and initiate instances of OpenVR. As a result, the boundary is compromised, which can lead to adverse effects such as dizziness, collisions, falls, and threats to user safety. Figure 8 demonstrates an example of this attack in practice. Metaverse side-channel attacks are defined as attacks in which a malicious application, without requiring special permissions, infers sensitive information from other concurrent applications or user interactions with the device. During AR/VR interactions, the malicious application operates in the background to collect leakage vectors such as CPU and GPU frame rates, which are stored in the HoloLens application folder and subsequently transmitted to the attacker. The variations in these performance counters are related to the sensitive information, enabling the attacker to infer this information from the observed counter values. Figure 9 presents a practical example of such an attack.

Benign Data. We also utilized benign audit data streams, running attack-unrelated programs such as browsers, various Windows service processes, and other AR applications on HoloLens. Before the attack, benign operations will run for a period on the host and sensing devices, and these benign operations will continue during the attack phase.

In total, the dataset contains 5620565 system audit logs (51.81 GB). The dataset includes four attack types, detailed in Table 3.

Table 3. Statistics of ground truth for attack campaigns

Attack Campaign	Devices	Attack Event Num
Boundary Expansion Attack	Computer, Mobile Workstation and PICO4	5
Boundary Movement Attack		5
Directional Disorientation Attack		5
Metaverse Side-channel Attack	HoloLens	14

We applied the data preprocessing steps to the dataset for the standardization of data from different sources, retaining the required fields; meanwhile, duplicate records were removed to prevent common records from biasing the model detection. The effects of dataset preprocessing are shown in Table 4. After normalization, the dataset size decreased from 51.81 GB to 0.72 GB. Removing duplicates further reduced it from 5,620,565 records to 261,256, culminating in a size of approximately 0.06 GB.

Table 4. Dataset preprocessing

Reduction Type	Original	Reduced	Reduction Rate
Dataset Size	51.81 GB	0.72 GB	98.61%
Record Count	5620565 records	261256 records	95.35%

5.3 Effectiveness of Anomaly Detection

This section primarily evaluates the anomaly detection model based on the isolation forest algorithm, assessing the effectiveness of detection in terms of accuracy and recall, and then studying the impact of different parameters on the model.

Accuracy: As demonstrated by Eq. 2, it denotes the proportion of correctly identified categories out of the total number of classifications.

$$\text{Accuracy} = \frac{TP + TN}{TP + FP + TN + FN} \tag{2}$$

Recall: As illustrated by Eq. 3, it represents the proportion of actual attacks that were accurately identified.

$$\text{Recall} = \frac{TP}{TP + FN} \tag{3}$$

Given that the log data originates from metaverse devices, and no prior studies have examined such data, the evaluation will focus solely on this model's effectiveness without comparative analysis.

By default, we use the following parameter values for the system: n_estimators = 300, contamination = 0.01 and N = 1. Here, n_estimators is the number of trees in the forest, contamination is the expected proportion of outliers in the dataset, and N is the number of chunks the dataset is divided into. Preliminary experiments show that the parameter n_estimators has a minimal impact on performance, hence it will not be discussed in detail here.

As shown in Fig. 10a, we find that the number of data chunks (N) has a negligible impact on the model's accuracy. However, we also note that as the contamination value increases, there is a slight downward trend in model accuracy. This is because when a higher proportion of anomalies is set, the model tends to predict more instances as anomalies, thereby affecting the accuracy. As illustrated in Fig. 10b, with the same N value, a larger contamination value corresponds to a higher recall rate. A higher contamination ratio means that the algorithm adopts a more lenient standard when deciding whether an instance is an anomaly. From the experiments, the recall rate of the detection model can reach 0.95, indicating that nearly all anomalies can be detected, which is extremely important for subsequent attack reconstruction.

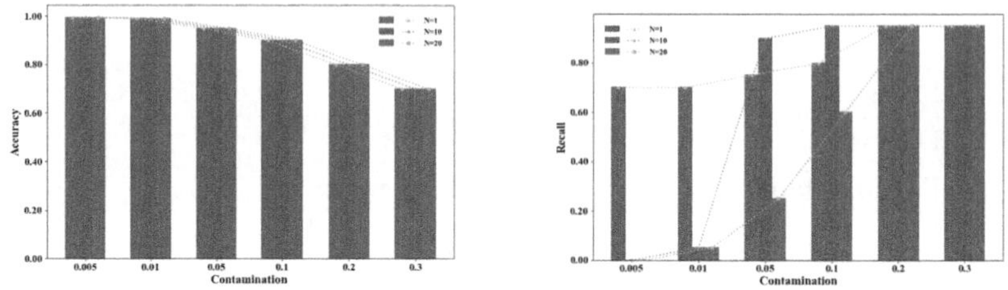

(a) Accuracy with different parameters (b) Recall with different parameters

Fig. 10. Accuracy and recall with different parameters.

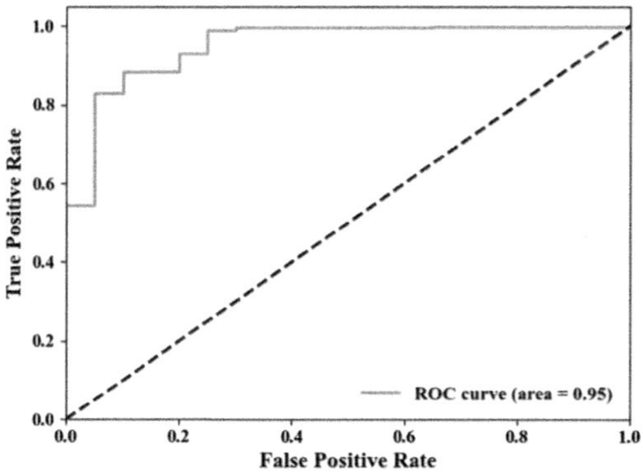

Fig. 11. ROC curve for the production dataset.

The Receiver Operating Characteristic (ROC) curve illustrates the performance of a classifier by depicting the relationship between the True Positive Rate (TPR) and the False Positive Rate (FPR) across various threshold settings. As demonstrated in Fig. 11, under the default parameter settings, the Area Under the Curve (AUC) value is 0.95, indicating that the model exhibits excellent performance in anomaly detection.

5.4 Effectiveness of Attack Reconstruction

This study has identified four attack scenarios within the dataset, in which the detection system has captured all intrusion points and key files. In this section, we provide a detailed description of the attack pathways captured by the detection system. In these scenarios that include attack pathways, rectangles represent files, diamonds represent network connections, and ellipses represent processes.

Figure 12 illustrates the disorientation attack scenario. Here, the point of intrusion is an untrusted IP address where the attacker executes the initial penetration. Subsequently, the attacker executes a malicious program, creates the file "chaperone_info.vrchap", and spawns a new malicious process "disorientation.exe". Figure 13a depicts the boundary expansion attack scenario. The attacker carries out the initial penetration, communicating with an untrusted IP address. Following this, the attacker invokes a command prompt to create "chaperone_info.vrchap" and spawns a new process. Figure 13b describes the boundary movement attack, starting with an initial breach via an untrusted IP and leading to the creation of "chaperone_info.vrchap" and the launching of "moveChaperone.exe" via a command prompt. Figure 14 portrays the metaverse side-channel attack where the attacker runs a malicious program, generating and writing to multiple files, then communicates with an untrusted IP for potential data exfiltration. In the attack scenarios detected in this study, the attacker has collected sensitive files, but has not yet transmitted the data.

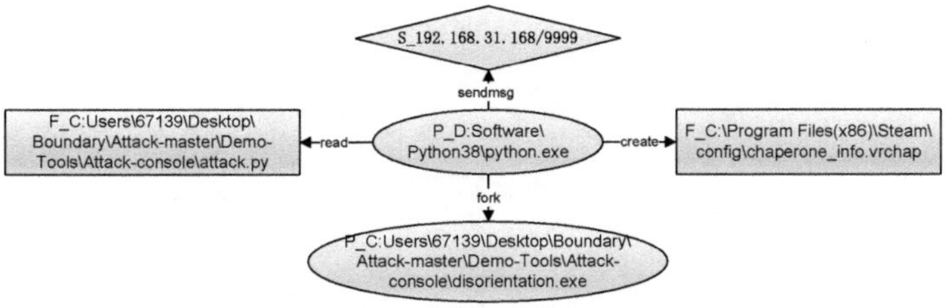

Fig. 12. Disorientation attack scenario.

6 Discussion

In real-time attack detection, it is essential to focus on the key characteristics of specific attacks. For security boundary attacks involving file tampering, monitoring changes in the hash values of boundary files is an effective defense. Once security boundaries are set, the system should monitor these files and alert users to any unexpected hash changes. For side-channel attacks, characterized by frequent file read-write operations, the system should closely monitor for suspicious, persistent data writing in system logs. By analyzing log data in real-time and setting appropriate thresholds, the system can detect anomalies and quickly alert users, enhancing security and providing a dynamic, responsive defense mechanism.

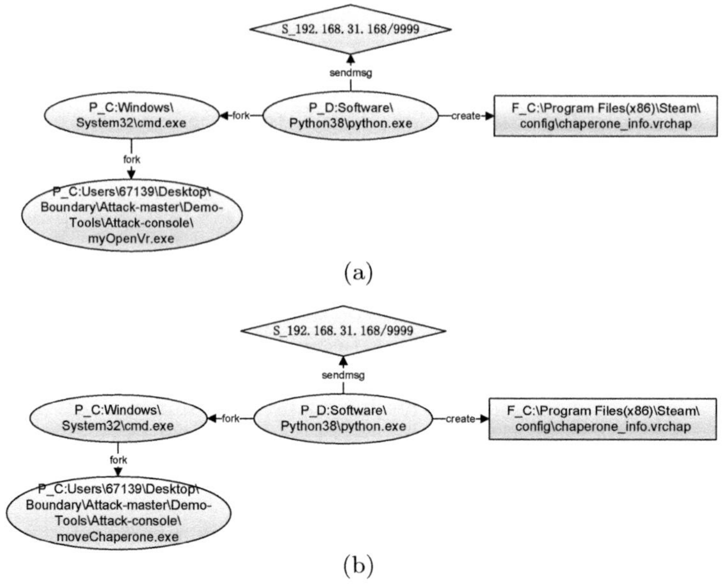

Fig. 13. Boundary attack scenarios. Figure a is the boundary expansion attack scenario and Figure b is the boundary movement attack scenario.

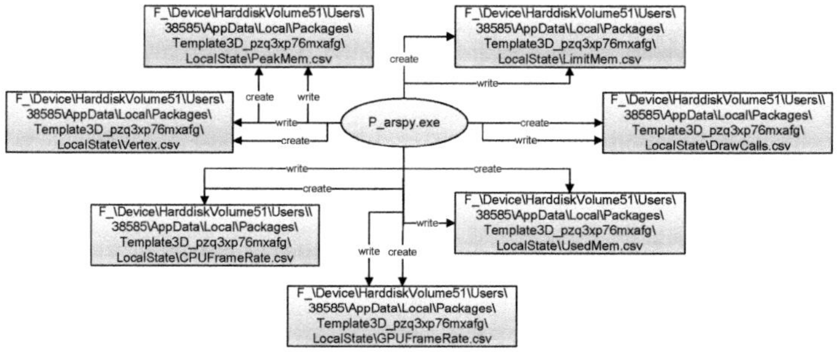

Fig. 14. Metaverse side-channel attack scenario.

7 Conclusion and Future Works

In this paper, we introduce a novel metaverse intrusion detection scheme designed to identify specific attacks targeting metaverse applications, such as side-channel attacks and security boundary attacks. Our approach leverages system log data from the metaverse to reconstruct the attack pathways. While existing systems have addressed metaverse attack detection, they typically focus on single attack types and overlook the replication of attack scenarios. We employ an isolation forest algorithm, which does not require labeled data, thereby facilitating the discovery of previously unidentified attacks. Our system gathers data from the metaverse, and utilizes a provenance graph model to trace various attack types. For anomaly detection, We have tested our system in real-world scenarios, where it has successfully identified malicious activities. Our future work will aim to maintain its effectiveness across a broader spectrum of attack scenarios. Additionally, our innovative use of metaverse log data for attack detection opens up new possibilities, including the integration of traffic data for a more thorough analysis of attacks. To address system performance concerns, our method employs a limited set of detection features to reduce overhead. We have also implemented redundancy elimination measures to control data volume, which have proven effective in our current setup. However, system-level auditing in real-time systems may introduce significant performance overhead, necessitating further investigation. Our method has not been extensively evaluated under real-time constraints. Future work will focus on extending our detection methods to real-time systems and comprehensively assessing their performance impact in these environments.

Acknowledgement. This research was supported in part by the National Key R&D Program of China (2023YFB3106900), the National Natural Science Foundation of China (62072359, 62072352).

References

1. Al Ali, T., Alfulaiti, S., Abuzour, M., Almaqahami, S., Ikuesan, R.: Digital forensic in a virtual world: a case of metaverse and VR. In: ECCWS 2023 22nd European Conference on Cyber Warfare and Security, no. 1, pp. 12–21 (2023)
2. Bütün, B., Akem, A.T.J., Gucciardo, M., Fiore, M.: Fast detection of cyberattacks on the metaverse through user-plane inference. In: 2023 IEEE International Conference on Metaverse Computing, Networking and Applications (MetaCom), pp. 350–354 (2023)
3. Casey, P., Baggili, I., Yarramreddy, A.: Immersive virtual reality attacks and the human joystick. IEEE Trans. Dependable Secure Comput. **18**(2), 550–562 (2019)
4. Di Pietro, R., Cresci, S.: Metaverse: security and privacy issues. In: 2021 Third IEEE International Conference on Trust, Privacy and Security in Intelligent Systems and Applications (TPS-ISA), pp. 281–288 (2021)
5. Erfan, F., Bellaiche, M., Halabi, T.: Community detection algorithm for mitigating eclipse attacks on blockchain-enabled metaverse. In: 2023 IEEE International Conference on Metaverse Computing, Networking and Applications (MetaCom), pp. 403–407 (2023)
6. Ferrag, M.A., Friha, O., Hamouda, D., Maglaras, L., Janicke, H.: Edge-IIoTset: a new comprehensive realistic cyber security dataset of IoT and IIoT applications for centralized and federated learning. IEEE Access **10**, 40281–40306 (2022)
7. Gaber, T., Awotunde, J.B., Torky, M., Ajagbe, S.A., Hammoudeh, M., Li, W.: Metaverse-ids: deep learning-based intrusion detection system for metaverse-IoT networks. Internet Things **24**, 100977 (2023)
8. Han, X., Pasquier, T., Bates, A., Mickens, J., Seltzer, M.: Unicorn: runtime provenance-based detector for advanced persistent threats. In: Network and Distributed Systems Security (NDSS) Symposium, pp. 1–18 (2020)
9. Koroniotis, N., Moustafa, N., Sitnikova, E., Turnbull, B.: Towards the development of realistic botnet dataset in the internet of things for network forensic analytics: Bot-IoT dataset. Future Gener. Comput. Syst. **100**, 779–796 (2019)

10. Kuo, S.Y., Tseng, F.H., Chou, Y.H.: Metaverse intrusion detection of wormhole attacks based on a novel statistical mechanism. Future Gener. Comput. Syst. **143**, 179–190 (2023)
11. Lebeck, K., Ruth, K., Kohno, T., Roesner, F.: Securing augmented reality output. In: 2017 IEEE Symposium on Security and Privacy (SP), pp. 320–337 (2017)
12. Liu, F.T., Ting, K.M., Zhou, Z.H.: Isolation forest. In: 2008 Eighth IEEE International Conference on Data Mining, pp. 413–422 (2008)
13. Meng, Y., Zhan, Y., Li, J., Du, S., Zhu, H., Shen, X.S.: De-anonymization attacks on metaverse. In: IEEE INFOCOM 2023-IEEE Conference on Computer Communications, pp. 1–10 (2023)
14. Moustafa, N.: A new distributed architecture for evaluating AI-based security systems at the edge: network TON_IoT datasets. Sustain. Cities Soc. **72**, 102994 (2021)
15. Moustafa, N., Slay, J.: UNSW-NB15: a comprehensive data set for network intrusion detection systems (UNSW-NB15 network data set). In: 2015 Military Communications and Information Systems Conference (MilCIS), pp. 1–6 (2015)
16. Neto, E., Dadkhah, S., Ferreira, R., Zohourian, A., Lu, R., Ghorbani, A.A.: CICIoT 2023: a real-time dataset and benchmark for large-scale attacks in IoT environment. Sensors **23**(13), 5941 (2023)
17. Nkoro, E.C., Nwakanma, C.I., Lee, J.M., Kim, D.S.: Detecting cyberthreats in metaverse learning platforms using an explainable DNN. Internet Things **25**, 101046 (2024)
18. Odeleye, B., Loukas, G., Heartfield, R., Spyridonis, F.: Detecting framerate-oriented cyber attacks on user experience in virtual reality (2021)
19. Park, S.M., Kim, Y.G.: A metaverse: taxonomy, components, applications, and open challenges. IEEE Access **10**, 4209–4251 (2022)
20. Qamar, S., Anwar, Z., Afzal, M.: A systematic threat analysis and defense strategies for the metaverse and extended reality systems. Comput. Secur. **128**, 103127 (2023)
21. ReasonLabs: Big brother: New malware records your VR sessions (2022). https://reasonlabs.com/research/big-brother. Accessed 01 Jul 2024
22. Shang, J., Chen, S., Wu, J., Yin, S.: ARSpy: breaking location-based multi-player augmented reality application for user location tracking. IEEE Trans. Mob. Comput. **21**(2), 433–447 (2020)
23. Sharafaldin, I., Lashkari, A.H., Ghorbani, A.A., et al.: Toward generating a new intrusion detection dataset and intrusion traffic characterization. ICISSp **1**, 108–116 (2018)
24. Slocum, C., Zhang, Y., Abu-Ghazaleh, N., Chen, J.: Going through the motions:{AR/VR} keylogging from user head motions. In: 32nd USENIX Security Symposium (USENIX Security 23), pp. 159–174 (2023)
25. Tavallaee, M., Bagheri, E., Lu, W., Ghorbani, A.A.: A detailed analysis of the KDD CUP 99 data set. In: 2009 IEEE Symposium on Computational Intelligence for Security and Defense Applications, pp. 1–6 (2009)
26. Trimananda, R., Le, H., Cui, H., Ho, J.T., Shuba, A., Markopoulou, A.: {OVRseen}: auditing network traffic and privacy policies in oculus {VR}. In: 31st USENIX Security Symposium (USENIX security 22), pp. 3789–3806 (2022)
27. Truong, V.T., Le, L.B.: MetaCIDS: privacy-preserving collaborative intrusion detection for metaverse based on blockchain and online federated learning. IEEE Open J. Comput. Soc. 253–266 (2023)

28. Valluripally, S., et al.: Detection of security and privacy attacks disrupting user immersive experience in virtual reality learning environments. IEEE Trans. Serv. Comput. **16**(4), 2559–2574 (2022)
29. Valluripally, S., Gulhane, A., Hoque, K.A., Calyam, P.: Modeling and defense of social virtual reality attacks inducing cybersickness. IEEE Trans. Dependable Secure Comput. **19**(6), 4127–4144 (2021)
30. Vondráček, M., Baggili, I., Casey, P., Mekni, M.: Rise of the metaverse's immersive virtual reality malware and the man-in-the-room attack & defenses. Comput. Secur. **127**, 102923 (2023)
31. Wang, Y., et al.: A survey on metaverse: fundamentals, security, and privacy. IEEE Commun. Surv. Tutorials **25**(1), 319–352 (2022)
32. Zhang, Y., Slocum, C., Chen, J., Abu-Ghazaleh, N.: It's all in your head (set): side-channel attacks on {AR/VR} systems. In: 32nd USENIX Security Symposium (USENIX Security 23), pp. 3979–3996 (2023)

EG-SAN: Evolving Graph Self-attention Networks for Detecting Illicit Activities in Cryptocurrency

Bo Cui[1,2(✉)] and Jia Zhang[1,2]

[1] Engineering Research Center of Ecological Big Data, Ministry of Education, Beijing, China
32209187@mail.imu.edu.cn
[2] College of Computer Science, Inner Mongolia University, Hohhot, China
cscb@imu.edu.cn

Abstract. In recent years, illicit activities in cryptocurrency transactions have posed a severe threat to financial systems and society. Current detection methods mainly rely on machine learning and graph neural networks but often overlook the dynamic evolution of transaction graphs over time. To address this, we propose a novel Evolutionary Graph Self-Attention Network (EG-SAN) that can simultaneously capture the spatial relationships among nodes as well as their temporal evolution features through a joint self-attention mechanism across structural and temporal dimensions. Specifically, the graph attention network aggregates features from node neighborhoods in the graph data, while gated recurrent units dynamically update its layer weights to capture the evolution of the graph over the temporal dimension. Subsequently, a self-attention mechanism further optimizes these weights, enabling the model to more accurately reflect the salient features of the data at different time steps. We evaluate EG-SAN on a Bitcoin transaction dataset, and the results demonstrate its superiority over existing state-of-the-art methods. Further application to graph datasets from other domains also confirms the effectiveness and robustness of EG-SAN, showcasing its broad application potential.

Keywords: Cryptocurrencies · Illicit activities · Anomaly detection · Graph neural networks · Self-attention mechanism

1 Introduction

Financial fraud, particularly money laundering [16], remains a major challenge for the global economy in the context of cryptocurrency transactions. The inherent anonymity and decentralized nature of cryptocurrencies make them an ideal vehicle for perpetrating fraud and illicit activities. Although traditional machine learning methods are effective to some extent, they often struggle to accurately detect fraudulent behavior due to the complex and dynamic nature of the cryptocurrency transaction environment. On the other hand, high-quality

S. Goel et al. (Eds.): ICDF2C 2024, LNICST 614, pp. 24–38, 2025.
https://doi.org/10.1007/978-3-031-89360-5_2

publicly available financial transaction datasets are relatively scarce, partly due to privacy considerations, which has limited the development of robust anomaly detection models for transactions. However, with the rise of internet finance, some datasets with graph structures revealing complex transaction relationships (e.g., Elliptic [18]) have provided new opportunities for fraud transaction detection. Although the complexity and high dimensionality of graph-structured data pose challenges for traditional machine learning methods, graph neural networks (GNN) have been proven to be an effective solution because they adeptly leverage the structural information in graphs. Nevertheless, most GNN models, such as GCN [10] and GAT [22], primarily focus on static graphs, whereas the dynamic nature of graphs is more crucial for many real-world applications such as financial transactions. Although previous works have attempted to introduce dynamism into the models by using recurrent neural network (RNN), typically long short-term memory (LSTM) [15], this strategy often hampers performance when new nodes are added.

The attention mechanism has proven effective in various machine learning tasks, such as natural language processing, computer vision, and recommender systems [27]. Mimicking the human attention process can help models more efficiently process complex input data, thereby improving model performance. However, despite the remarkable achievements of the attention mechanism in multiple domains, its application in detecting anomalous blockchain transaction data remains limited. Therefore, this paper proposes a novel model called the Evolutionary Graph Self-Attention Network (EG-SAN) for anomaly detection in blockchain transaction networks. EG-SAN applies the self-attention mechanism across both structural neighborhood and temporal dynamic dimensions to efficiently generate dynamic node representations. In the structural dimension, it leverages GATs to aggregate features from node neighborhoods in each time snapshot, while in the temporal dimension, it dynamically updates the GAT layer weights using GRU to capture the evolution of the graph over time. Further, it optimizes these time-sensitive historical weights through the self-attention mechanism, enabling the model to adjust the weights according to the relative importance of graph features at different time steps. We evaluate the proposed EG-SAN model on an authoritative cryptocurrency dataset, and the results demonstrate its significant superiority over state-of-the-art baseline methods in detecting illicit transactions. To validate the model's generalizability, we apply it to graph datasets from other domains, and the experimental results consistently confirm its effectiveness and robustness. This work provides a novel and effective solution for tasks such as cryptocurrency anomaly detection, offering theoretical significance and broad application prospects. The main contributions of this paper are summarized as follows:

- We propose a new model called EG-SAN that jointly employs self-attention mechanisms for structural neighborhood and temporal dynamics for anomaly detection in cryptocurrency transaction networks.
- By introducing a self-attention mechanism to optimize time-sensitive historical weights, the model can adjust weights according to the relative importance

of graph features at different time steps, improving detection accuracy and efficiency.
- We evaluate the EG-SAN model on an authoritative cryptocurrency dataset, and its performance significantly outperforms existing state-of-the-art methods.
- We apply the EG-SAN model to graph datasets from other domains, and the experimental results confirm its effectiveness and robustness, demonstrating its broad application potential.

The rest of the paper is organized as follows: Sect. 2 describes related work and the gaps in our knowledge. Section 3 introduces our model and its architecture. Section 4 explains our experiments, results, and analysis. Section 5 concludes the work.

2 Related Works

Our work involves the latest advancements in anomaly detection concerning traditional machine learning methods, the representation learning of static and dynamic graphs, as well as self-attention structures.

2.1 Traditional Methods

In the early stages, the primary tools were rule-based, operating based on rules derived from mean and standard deviation [11]. This expert-developed approach was widely used due to its straightforward rules and easy codability. Rule-based systems rely on structured and constrained data to ensure performance, but they face challenges when dealing with large datasets containing various types of data.

On the other hand, traditional anomaly detection methods such as distance-based methods [1,5], classification-based methods [3], and statistical methods [14] often encounter difficulties in fully utilizing the time and network structure information of blockchain transaction data. Distance-based methods, such as k-nearest neighbors and local outlier factor, identify anomalies by calculating the distance or similarity between data points. In [19], the AnoScore algorithm was designed, which is based on robust statistical bias measures to detect anomalies and identify various suspicious money laundering behavior patterns. However, these methods may not be able to fully exploit the complexity of blockchain data.

In classification-based methods, like the least squares Support Vector Machine classifier [2], while they can learn complex patterns and structures from large amounts of data, further optimization and adjustment may be warranted when dealing with specific characteristics of blockchain transaction data.

2.2 Graph Neural Network Approaches

GCN have been utilized for detecting anomalous behaviors such as money laundering [24]. In [17], a method for dynamically updating model parameters was proposed to capture the temporal properties of the Bitcoin transaction dataset. Dou et al. [4] proposed CARE-GNN, which enhances the GNN aggregation process against disguises through three unique modules. The robustness of this model is crucial for improving the performance of GCN in anomaly detection. Lian Yu et al. [28] proposed a graph-based method that improves the precision and recall of anomaly transaction detection by combining an enhanced GraphSAGE with FastGCN.

Modeling temporal graphs is challenging but vital for understanding the dynamics and evolution of temporal graphs [25]. The combination of LSTM [7] and GCN aids in learning long-term and short-term dependencies as well as network structure, significantly improving the F1 score for vertex-based semi-supervised classification tasks. In the STGCN model of [26], spatial and temporal patterns are learned by adding nodes of all temporal connections to the temporal kernel and performing GCN-like convolutions on the backbone graph with static topology. A Temporal Transaction Aggregation Graph Network (TTAGN) was proposed, which enhances the performance of phishing scam detection on Ethereum by modeling the temporal relationships of historical transactions between nodes and integrating topological interactions into edge representations through edge2node [12].

The research on blockchain anomaly detection is related to dynamic Graph Neural Networks [8], which are used to handle anomalous behavior in blockchain networks. Despite some progress, many challenges remain, such as how to effectively capture the dynamic attributes of graphs, deal with new nodes, and handle large-scale, incompletely annotated data.

3 Method

In this study, we employ a series of static snapshots of Bitcoin transaction networks to define a dynamic Bitcoin transaction network. These snapshots represent the evolution of the Bitcoin transaction network along the temporal axis, denoted as $\mathbb{G}=\{\mathcal{G}^1, ..., \mathcal{G}^T\}$, where T indicates the total number of time steps. Each snapshot, G^t, is defined as $(\mathcal{V}, \mathcal{E}^t, \mathcal{A}^t, \mathcal{X}^t)$, where $\mathcal{V}$ and $\mathcal{E}^t$ respectively represent the node set $\{v_i\}_{i=1}^n$ and the edge set $\{e_{ij}\}$. Each edge $e_{ij} = (v_i, v_j)$ signifies the relationship connecting nodes v_i and v_j, $\mathcal{A}^t$ is the adjacency matrix at time step t, describing the topological structure of $\mathcal{G}^t$, and the attribute matrix $\mathcal{X}^t \in \mathbb{R}^{n\times k}$ records the k-dimensional attributes x_i of each node v_i. For simplicity, we assume all Bitcoin transaction graphs consist of n nodes; however, it should be noted that the node set and its cardinality may change over time. Within this framework, Bitcoin anomaly detection is treated as a binary classification task. Specifically, each node v_i at each time step $t = \{1, 2, \ldots, T\}$ must be classified as either "normal transaction" (label 0) or "anomalous transaction" (label 1), i.e., $\mathcal{V} \rightarrow Y \in \{0, 1\}^n$. By observing a limited number of node labels, our goal is to predict the labels of other nodes. Unless otherwise noted, throughout the process, we will use the subscript t to denote the time index, and the superscript l to denote the GAT layer index.

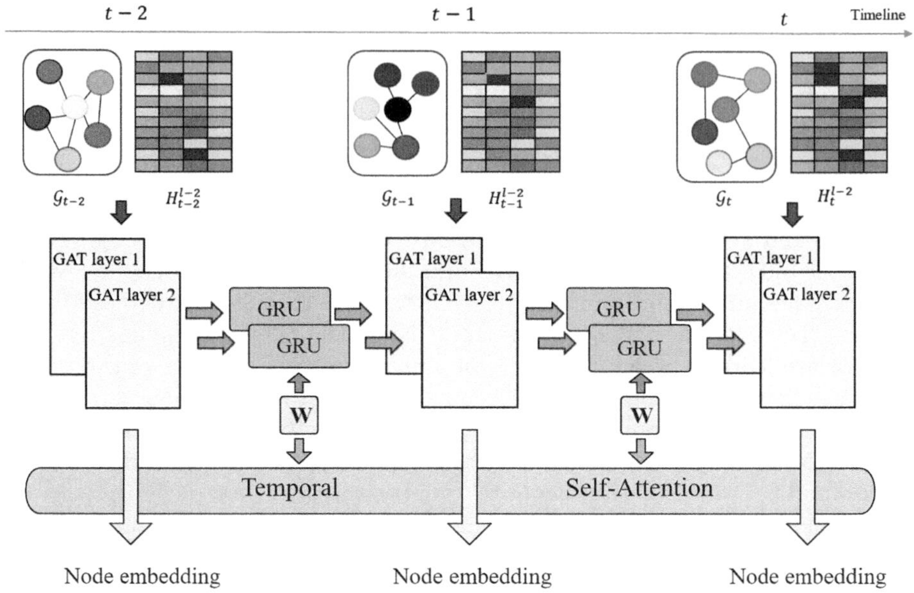

Fig. 1. The illustrative diagram of EG-SAN depicts the processing steps at each time step. First, the weights of the GAT are updated via the GRU. Next, the temporal self-attention layer evaluates the importance of these updated weights. Finally, the GAT aggregates neighborhood information to obtain the final embedding vectors.

3.1 GAT

At each time step t and for each layer l, GAT processes the features of each node v_i. The features undergo a shared, learnable linear transformation using a weight matrix $\mathbf{W}_t^l \in \mathbb{R}^{k' \times k}$, where k is the dimensionality of the input features, and k' the output features. At layer l and time step t, the features of each node v_i in the graph are represented as $H_l^t = [x_1, x_2, \ldots, x_n]^T$, with the transformation given as follows:

$$\mathbf{z}_i = \mathbf{W}_t^l \mathbf{x}_i, \tag{1}$$

$\mathbf{x}_i$ is extracted from the attribute matrix $\mathcal{X}^t$. Subsequently, the significance of node j's features to node i is determined using a single-layer feedforward neural network, parameterized by a weight vector $\mathbf{a}$, applying the LeakyReLU function:

$$e_{ij} = \text{LeakyReLU}(\mathbf{a}^\top [\mathbf{z}_i \| \mathbf{z}_j]), \tag{2}$$

where $\|$ denotes vector concatenation. To facilitate comparability of attention coefficients across different nodes, the raw attention scores are normalized using the softmax function:

$$\alpha_{ij} = \frac{\exp(e_{ij})}{\sum_{k \in \mathcal{N}_i} \exp(e_{ik})}, \tag{3}$$

where $\mathcal{N}_i$ denotes the set of neighbors of node i in the graph. Node features are updated by aggregating the transformed and weighted features of the neighbors using the normalized attention coefficients:

$$\mathbf{h}_i' = \sigma\left(\sum_{j \in \mathcal{N}_i} \alpha_{ij} \mathbf{z}_j\right) \tag{4}$$

where σ is a nonlinear activation function, such as sigmoid or ReLU. At time step t and layer $l+1$, the updated feature vectors $\mathbf{h}_i'$ of all nodes are combined into a complete feature matrix, the feature matrix reflects the output states of all nodes in that layer:

$$\mathbf{H}_t^{(l+1)} = [\mathbf{h}_1', \mathbf{h}_2', \ldots, \mathbf{h}_n']^T. \tag{5}$$

3.2 Weight Evolution

Our method employs GRU to update the weight matrices (W) in GAT, while the attention coefficients (a), dependent on real-time interactions between nodes, are not updated via GRU but are dynamically computed based on the current state of the nodes during each forward propagation.

Within the l-th layer of GAT and at time step t, we had introduced W_{t-1}^l into GRU, resulting in the update to W_t^l. Abstractly, this relationship can be expressed as follows:

$$\underbrace{\overbrace{W_t^l}^{GATweights}}_{output} = GRU(\underbrace{\overbrace{W_{t-1}^l}^{GATweights}}_{input}), \tag{6}$$

The update of the weight matrix W can be implemented using the standard GRU by extending the input state from a vector to a matrix (since the hidden state is now the GAT weight matrix). The matrix extension is straightforward: simply place the column vectors side by side to form a matrix. In other words, the same GRU is used to process each column of the GAT weight matrix. For completeness, we write out the matrix version of the GRU below. Note that all named variables (e.g., Xt and Ht) are just local variables here, do not confuse them with the mathematical notation we have used so far.

With the matrix version GRU function above, we have now fully specified the recursive architecture:

$$W_t^l = GRU\left(W_{t-1}^l\right) := MatrixBasedGRU\left(W_{t-1}^l\right) \tag{7}$$

Algorithm 1. Matrix-based Gated Recurrent Unit (Matrix-based GRU)

Input: X_t, Current input X_t is the same as the past output H_{t-1}
Output: H_t

function MatrixBasedGRU(X_t, H_{t-1})
  $Z_t = \sigma(W_z X_t + U_z H_{t-1} + B_z)$
  $R_t = \sigma(W_R X_t + U_R H_{t-1} + B_R)$
  $\widetilde{H}_t = \tanh(W_H X_t + U_H(R_t \circ H_{t-1}) + B_H)$
  $H_t = (1 - Z_t) \circ H_{t-1} + Z_t \circ \widetilde{H}_t$
  return H_t
end function

3.3 Temporal Self-attention

The temporal self-attention mechanism is employed to handle the weight matrices $\mathbf{W}_t$ that are updated at each time step. Initially, these matrices undergo an update through a recurrent layer. Subsequently, they are processed by a self-attention module, which produces an integrated output $\mathbf{W}_s$. This output encapsulates the significance of various time steps. Ultimately, these attention-modified weights are utilized in GAT to generate new feature representations for each node.

Consider an input sequence $\mathbf{W} = \{\mathbf{W}_1, \mathbf{W}_2, \ldots, \mathbf{W}_T\}$, where T is the sequence length and each $\mathbf{W}_t \in \mathbb{R}^d$ represents the input at time t. The self-attention mechanism projects $\mathbf{W}$ into query Q, key K, and value V spaces:

$$Q = \mathbf{W}W_Q, \tag{8}$$
$$K = \mathbf{W}W_K, \tag{9}$$
$$V = \mathbf{W}W_V, \tag{10}$$

with projection matrices $W_Q \in \mathbb{R}^{d \times d_q}$, $W_K \in \mathbb{R}^{d \times d_k}$, and $W_V \in \mathbb{R}^{d \times d_v}$. Attention weights are computed using scaled dot-product attention:

$$\alpha = \text{softmax}\left(\frac{QK^T}{\sqrt{d_k}}\right), \tag{11}$$

where d_k helps stabilize the gradients. The output from self-attention is:

$$\text{Attention}(Q, K, V) = \sum_{j=1}^{T} \alpha_{ij} v_j. \tag{12}$$

To enhance control over self-attention, a Gated Self-Attention mechanism introduces a gating parameter g:

$$g = \sigma(w_g), \tag{13}$$

where σ denotes the sigmoid function, and w_g is a weight vector. The final module output is:

$$\mathbf{W}_s = g \cdot \text{Attention}(Q, K, V) + (1 - g) \cdot \mathbf{W}. \tag{14}$$

3.4 Evolutionary Graph Attention Unit (EGAU)

We integrate the graph attention unit proposed in Sect. 3.1, the recurrent architecture introduced in Sect. 3.2, and the temporal self-attention layer proposed in Sect. 3.3 to form the Evolutionary Graph Attention Unit (EGAU). The functional implementation is as follows:

Algorithm 2. Evolutionary Graph Attention Unit (EGAU)

Input: A_t, H_t^l, W_{t-1}^l
Output: H_t^{l+1}, W_t^l
1: **function**$[H_t^{l+1},\ W_t^l] = \text{EGAU}(A_t, H_t^l, W_{t-1}^l)$
2: $\quad W_t^l = \text{MatrixBasedGRU}\big(W_{t-1}^l\big)$
3: $\quad W_{s\_t}^l = \text{TemporalSelfAttention}\big(W_t^l\big)$
4: $\quad H_t^{l+1} = \text{GAT}(A_t, H_t^l, W_{s\_t}^l)$
5: **end function**

The EGAU utilizes the graph attention mechanism across layers to aggregate node features, while simultaneously evolving the weight matrices over time and computing the importance of weight matrices at different time steps through a self-attention layer. By connecting these units bottom-up, we can obtain a multi-layer GAT within a single time step. Then, by unrolling these units horizontally over time, we form a grid structure, where information (H_t^l and W_t^l) flows. We refer to this overall model as the Evolving Graph Self-attention Network (EG-SAN), as shown in Fig. 1.

3.5 Cross Entropy Loss

For anomaly detection, the final layer of the GAT outputs the embedding vector for each node, and these vectors are subsequently passed to a fully connected layer or other classifier. This layer is responsible for mapping the node's feature vectors to the predicted labels. Considering the common class imbalance problem in anomaly detection datasets, we adopt a weighted cross-entropy loss function [20] to train the model. This loss function is particularly well-suited for tasks such as fraud detection, where certain classes (e.g., fraudulent activities) occur far less frequently than others. By assigning higher weights to minority classes, the weighted cross-entropy loss function enhances the model's ability to recognize these harder-to-detect classes. The weighted cross-entropy loss function is expressed as:

$$WCE = -\sum_{i=0}^{n} \alpha_i \times \rho_i \times \log(\rho_i). \tag{15}$$

Here, ρ_i is the model's predicted output probability for class i, and α_i is a pre-set weight based on the class frequency, which helps adjust the model's attention to different classes, especially those that occur less frequently.

4 Experiments

To evaluate the performance of our proposed model, we conduct extensive experiments by comparing it against seven state-of-the-art anomaly detection methods on one real-world Bitcoin transaction graph dataset and two attributed graph datasets. Moreover, we perform an ablation study to test the effectiveness of the temporal self-attention layer. All of these are aimed at answering the following questions:

- **Q1**: Does EG-SAN outperform the latest baseline methods in terms of anomaly detection performance on Bitcoin data?
- **Q2**: How is the generalization capability of the model?
- **Q3**: Does our temporal self-attention layer help in anomaly detection?
- **Q4**: How well does EG-SAN adapt to new events?

4.1 Datasets

We validate the effectiveness of our model on the largest publicly available labeled cryptocurrency transaction dataset and two widely-used real-world attributed graphs with injected anomalies. Table 1 shows the statistics of these three datasets and the details of how each dataset is divided into training, validation, and test sets based on time steps.

Elliptic [18] dataset is a publicly available collection of Bitcoin transaction data. It comprises 203,769 nodes (representing transactions) and 234,355 edges (representing transaction flows) extracted from the real Bitcoin transaction network and classified into 49 time steps. Each node has 166-dimensional features, with the first 94 dimensions representing local transaction attributes (e.g., input and output amounts, transaction fees), and the latter 72 dimensions associated with graphical features obtained by aggregating information from adjacent nodes. The data labels classify transactions as unknown, regular, or anomalous (e.g., money laundering and other illegal activities).

BlogCatalog [21] is an online social network that allows users to share blogs with the public. The network structure represents the follow-follow relationships between users, while node attributes are lists of labels describing each user.

Flickr [21] is an online image sharing network. The network structure is organized similarly to BlogCatalog, while node attributes are generated using tags that reflect users' interests.

4.2 Baselines and Experimental Setting

We evaluate the proposed method by comparing it against ten representative and state-of-the-art deep graph learning-based anomaly detection approaches, as follows:

Table 1. Dataset statistics and split details

Dataset	Statistics				Time Steps		
	# Nodes	# Edges	# Attributes	# Anomalies	Train	Val	Test
Elliptic	203,769	234,355	166	4,545	31	5	13
BlogCatalog	5,196	172,759	8,189	298	6	1	2
Flickr	7,575	241,277	12,047	445	8	2	3

- **GCN** [10] is an anomaly detection method composed of a two-layer graph convolutional network encoder and a fully-connected layer that directly assigns labels to nodes.
- **GAT** [22] employs two layers of graph attention networks to guide the information aggregation process during graph representation learning. Similar to GCN, it utilizes the learned node representations to identify anomalous or normal nodes.
- **GraphSAGE** [6] samples neighboring nodes to generate node representations and inductively identifies anomalous nodes.
- **GCN-GRU** is a single GCN model that is jointly trained with a recurrent model (LSTM) on node embeddings. We refer to this approach as GCN-GRU.
- **EvolveGCN** [17] uses an RNN to update GCN filter parameters based on the current graph snapshot across time steps.
- **GeniePath** [13] incorporates a neighbor information filtering process in GCN by exploring informative sub-graphs and paths for graph anomaly detection.
- **FdGars** [23] aims at detecting anomalies in online review networks by modeling their behavioral features and relationships from review logs.

In our experiments, we set the hyperparameters according to the descriptions in the original papers and used the original codebases provided by the developers of the existing baseline models, as well as code from an open-source library to implement anomaly detection.

Our model is developed within the PyTorch framework. The GAT model comprises two layers, with the hidden and output embedding dimensions both set to 256. We employ the Adam optimizer [9] with a learning rate of 0.001. On the Elliptic dataset, the sequence learning time window is set to 10 time steps, while on the BlogCatalog and Flickr datasets, it is set to 2 time steps. To validate the contribution of the temporal self-attention layer for anomaly detection, we conduct an ablation study on the EG-SAN-TA model without the temporal self-attention layer across all three datasets.

4.3 Evaluation Metrics

We employ five evaluation metrics-macro precision, macro recall, macro F1 scores, ROC, and AUC-to measure anomaly detection performance, effectively addressing data imbalance issues, particularly in the Bitcoin transaction dataset where anomalous transactions account for only 2%.

Table 2. Macro- Precision, Recall, and F1-score on three datasets. (best in bold)

Method	Elliptic			BlogCatalog			Flickr		
	Precision	Recall	F1	Precision	Recall	F1	Precision	Recall	F1
CCN	0.813	0.734	0.766	0.612	0.515	0.516	**0.905**	0.658	**0.723**
GAT	0.692	0.729	0.708	0.662	0.508	0.501	0.788	0.646	0.685
GraphSAGE	0.843	0.753	0.781	**0.783**	0.612	0.641	0.783	0.607	0.642
GCN-GRU	0.873	0.798	0.802	0.754	0.621	0.652	0.894	0.629	0.677
EvolveGCN	0.852	0.714	0.763	0.774	0.594	0.635	0.887	0.592	0.635
GeniePath	0.425	0.419	0.433	0.473	0.498	0.487	0.497	0.483	0.476
FdGars	0.534	0.652	0.712	0.515	0.564	0.471	0.559	0.658	0.594
EG-SAN-TA	0.953	0.813	0.857	0.768	0.621	0.651	0.836	0.654	0.678
EG-SAN	**0.964**	**0.827**	**0.882**	0.776	**0.622**	**0.666**	0.842	**0.674**	0.697

- **Macro-Precision** is the unweighted average of the ratios of true anomalies among all detected anomalies and true normal nodes among all identified normal nodes.
- **Macro-Recall** is the unweighted average of the ratio of true anomalies detected among all true anomalies and the ratio of true normal nodes detected among all true normal nodes.
- **Macro-F1 Score** is the unweighted average of the F1 scores for the two classes (anomalous and normal)
- **ROC and AUC** measure a detection model's ability to distinguish anomalous nodes from normal ones by adaptively evaluating the true positive rate and false positive rate at different thresholds.

4.4 Detection Performance and Generalization (Q1, Q2)

We use the widely adopted evaluation metrics introduced in Sect. 4.3 to assess the anomaly detection capabilities of our proposed model and the baselines.

As shown in Table 2, on the Elliptic dataset, EG-SAN achieves the highest scores across all metrics, with a macro precision of 0.964, macro recall of 0.827, and macro F1-score of 0.882, significantly outperforming the second-best model, GCN-GRU. This is because the EG-SAN model captures the dynamic properties of graphs by evolving the GAT parameters via GRUs and leverages the self-attention mechanism to dynamically adjust the weights of the GAT layers at each time step, thereby better capturing the temporal dynamics and structural features of nodes in the graph. This is particularly important when dealing with complex dynamic graphs, such as the financial transaction graphs in the Elliptic dataset, where transaction patterns change rapidly over time, and traditional graph neural network models like GCN and GAT may fail to effectively capture these dynamic changes. Although the GCN-GRU method attempts to capture the dynamic properties of graphs by combining recurrent neural networks, its performance is still inferior to EG-SAN, possibly due to its limited capability in dynamically updating graph structural information. In contrast, EG-SAN can more precisely adjust and optimize network weights through the self-attention mechanism, better adapting to the temporal evolution of graphs. The GeniePath model performs poorly in handling complex time-series data because its path discovery mechanism fails to effectively capture critical temporal information, making it difficult to identify anomalous patterns in complex dynamic graphs. FdGars is primarily designed for anomaly detection on static graph data, such as online review networks, and its performance is limited when dealing with financial transaction data that requires considering structural dynamics.

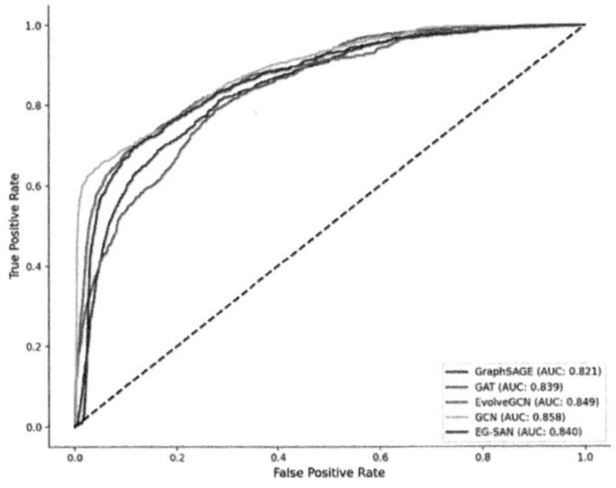

Fig. 2. ROC Curves and AUC scores of different models on Elliptic.

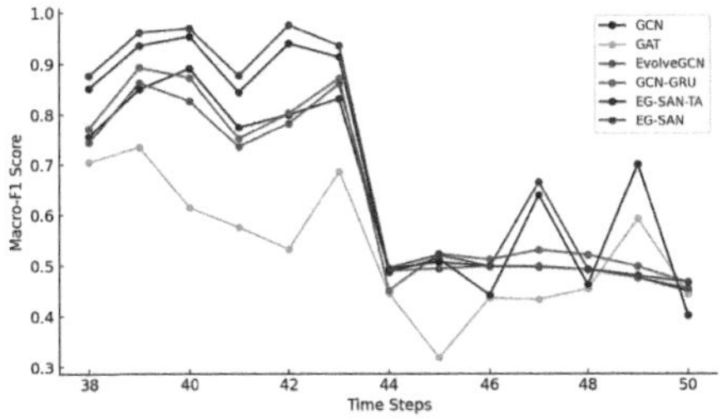

Fig. 3. Performance of anomaly detection over time.

As can be seen from Fig. 2, although the EG-SAN model performs slightly worse than GCN and EvolveGCN, it still exhibits decent predictive capability according to the ROC curve. Specifically, EG-SAN has an overall good performance, with an AUC value of 0.840, which, although lower than GCN and EvolveGCN, is significantly higher than the random guess of 0.5, indicating strong discriminative ability. When the false positive rate is low, EG-SAN's true positive rate is almost on par with GCN, suggesting that EG-SAN can also achieve a high hit rate in scenarios where a low false alarm rate is desired.

Although the BlogCatalog and Flickr datasets differ from transaction graphs, EG-SAN also demonstrates its robustness. On BlogCatalog, EG-SAN leads with an F1-score of 0.666, closely followed by GraphSAGE. For Flickr, EG-SAN not only maintains consistent precision but also exhibits the highest recall rate, reflecting its generalization ability across various domains.

4.5 Ablation Study (Q3)

To further investigate the specific impact of the temporal self-attention layer in our EG-SAN model, we conducted an ablation study comparing the performance of the full EG-SAN model with its variant EG-SAN-TA, which removes the temporal self-attention layer. The analysis results in Table 2 show that across all metrics and datasets, the complete EG-SAN model outperforms its variant. For instance, on the Elliptic dataset, after removing the temporal self-attention layer, the macro precision drops from 0.964 to 0.953, the macro recall drops from 0.827 to 0.813, and the macro F1 decreases from 0.882 to 0.857. Similar trends are observed on the BlogCatalog and Flickr datasets. The inclusion of the temporal self-attention layer significantly enhances the model's ability to handle time-series data, particularly in capturing long-term dependencies within the graph. This is because the layer can effectively discriminate and reinforce critical information across historical time steps. Meanwhile, traditional graph neural network architectures, such as GAT and GraphSAGE, typically focus solely on the spatial properties of graphs while overlooking the complexities and dynamics of the temporal dimension.

4.6 EG-SAN Robustness (Q4)

To observe the temporal effects of the model, we plotted the macro F1 scores of six methods at different time steps on the D1 dataset in Fig. 3. From step 43 onwards, the performance of all methods deteriorates, which is related to the closure of the black market. This newly occurring event causes a performance drop for all methods, with non-dynamic models being affected the most. However, our model can quickly recover after the transaction volume increases, demonstrating good adaptability. Nevertheless, even dynamic models cannot reliably perform well, as the newly occurring event has yet to be learned.

5 Conclusions

This paper introduces an innovative approach called the Evolutionary Graph Self-Attention Network (EG-SAN) aimed at detecting illicit activities in cryptocurrency transactions. Compared to existing methods, EG-SAN can more comprehensively capture the dynamic evolution and structural changes of transaction graphs. By combining self-attention mechanisms across both the structural neighborhood and temporal dynamic dimensions, EG-SAN not only captures the spatial relationships among nodes in the graph data but also tracks the evolution of node features over time. Evaluation results on the real-world Bitcoin transaction dataset Elliptic demonstrate that EG-SAN significantly outperforms state-of-the-art baseline methods in detecting illicit cryptocurrency transactions. To validate the model's versatility, we further apply it to two graph datasets from different domains - Flickr and BlogCatalog - and the experimental results consistently confirm its effectiveness and robustness, showcasing its broad application potential. Through these efforts, we hope to provide a promising solution for combating illicit activities in the cryptocurrency domain.

Acknowledgments. This paper is supported by the National Natural Science Foundation of China (61962042), and Natural Science Foundation of Inner Mongolia

(2022MS06020), and the Central Government Guides Local Science and Technology Development Fund (2022ZY0064), and the University Youth Science and Technology Talent Development Project (Innovation Group Development Plan) of Inner Mongolia A. R. of China (Grant No. NMGIRT2318), and the Fund of Supporting the Reform and Development of Local Universities (Disciplinary construction).

References

1. Agarwal, R., Barve, S., Shukla, S.K.: Detecting malicious accounts in permissionless blockchains using temporal graph properties. Appl. Netw. Sci. **6**(1), 1–30 (2021)
2. Chandola, V., Banerjee, A., Kumar, V.: Anomaly detection: a survey. ACM Comput. Surv. (CSUR) **41**(3), 1–58 (2009)
3. Chen, T., et al.: Understanding ethereum via graph analysis. ACM Trans. Internet Technol. (TOIT) **20**(2), 1–32 (2020)
4. Dou, Y., Liu, Z., Sun, L., Deng, Y., Peng, H., Yu, P.S.: Enhancing graph neural network-based fraud detectors against camouflaged fraudsters. In: Proceedings of the 29th ACM International Conference on Information and Knowledge Management, pp. 315–324 (2020)
5. Farrugia, S., Ellul, J., Azzopardi, G.: Detection of illicit accounts over the ethereum blockchain. Expert Syst. Appl. **150**, 113318 (2020)
6. Hamilton, W., Ying, Z., Leskovec, J.: Inductive representation learning on large graphs. In: Advances in Neural Information Processing Systems, vol. 30 (2017)
7. Hochreiter, S., Schmidhuber, J.: Long short-term memory. Neural Comput. **9**(8), 1735–1780 (1997)
8. Jin, M., et al.: A survey on graph neural networks for time series: forecasting, classification, imputation, and anomaly detection. arXiv preprint (2023). arXiv:2307.03759
9. Kingma, D.P., Ba, J.: Adam: a method for stochastic optimization. arXiv preprint (2014). arXiv:1412.6980
10. Kipf, T.N., Welling, M.: Semi-supervised classification with graph convolutional networks. arXiv preprint (2016). arXiv:1609.02907
11. Le Khac, N.A., Markos, S., Kechadi, M.T.: A data mining-based solution for detecting suspicious money laundering cases in an investment bank. In: 2010 Second International Conference on Advances in Databases, Knowledge, and Data Applications, pp. 235–240. IEEE (2010)
12. Li, S., Gou, G., Liu, C., Hou, C., Li, Z., Xiong, G.: TTAGN: temporal transaction aggregation graph network for ethereum phishing scams detection. In: Proceedings of the ACM Web Conference 2022, pp. 661–669 (2022)
13. Liu, Z., et al.: Geniepath: graph neural networks with adaptive receptive paths. In: Proceedings of the AAAI Conference on Artificial Intelligence, vol. 33, pp. 4424–4431 (2019)
14. Luo, B., Zhang, Z., Wang, Q., Ke, A., Lu, S., He, B.: AI-powered fraud detection in decentralized finance: a project life cycle perspective. arXiv preprint (2023). arXiv:2308.15992
15. Manessi, F., Rozza, A., Manzo, M.: Dynamic graph convolutional networks. Pattern Recogn. **97**, 107000 (2020)

16. Moore, T., Han, J., Clayton, R.: The postmodern ponzi Scheme: empirical analysis of high-yield investment programs. In: Keromytis, A.D. (ed.) FC 2012. LNCS, vol. 7397, pp. 41–56. Springer, Heidelberg (2012). https://doi.org/10.1007/978-3-642-32946-3_4
17. Pareja, A., et al.: Evolvegcn: evolving graph convolutional networks for dynamic graphs. In: Proceedings of the AAAI Conference on Artificial Intelligence, vol. 34, pp. 5363–5370 (2020)
18. Robinson, T.: The elliptic data set-working with the community to combat financial crime in cryptocurrencies
19. Sun, X., et al.: MonLAD: money laundering agents detection in transaction streams. In: Proceedings of the Fifteenth ACM International Conference on Web Search and Data Mining, pp. 976–986 (2022)
20. Taleb, I., Dssouli, R., Serhani, M.A.: Big data pre-processing: a quality framework. In: 2015 IEEE International Congress on Big Data, pp. 191–198. IEEE (2015)
21. Tang, L., Liu, H.: Relational learning via latent social dimensions. In: Proceedings of the 15th ACM SIGKDD International Conference on Knowledge Discovery and Data Mining, pp. 817–826 (2009)
22. Velickovic, P., Cucurull, G., Casanova, A., Romero, A., Lio, P., Bengio, Y.: Graph attention networks. Stat **1050**(20), 10–48550 (2017)
23. Wang, J., Wen, R., Wu, C., Huang, Y., Xiong, J.: Fdgars: fraudster detection via graph convolutional networks in online app review system. In: Companion Proceedings of the 2019 World Wide Web Conference, pp. 310–316 (2019)
24. Weber, M., et al.: Anti-money laundering in bitcoin: experimenting with graph convolutional networks for financial forensics. arXiv preprint (2019). arXiv:1908.02591
25. Xue, G., Zhong, M., Li, J., Chen, J., Zhai, C., Kong, R.: Dynamic network embedding survey. Neurocomputing **472**, 212–223 (2022)
26. Yan, S., Xiong, Y., Lin, D.: Spatial temporal graph convolutional networks for skeleton-based action recognition. In: Proceedings of the AAAI Conference on Artificial Intelligence, vol. 32 (2018)
27. Yu, A.W., et al.: Qanet: combining local convolution with global self-attention for reading comprehension. arXiv preprint (2018). arXiv:1804.09541
28. Yu, L., Jing, Q., Li, R., Cheng, Z., Xu, C.: ParGCN: abnormal transaction detection based on graph neural networks. In: 2022 IEEE 22nd International Conference on Software Quality, Reliability and Security (QRS), pp. 797–808. IEEE (2022)

Auto-TFCE: Automatic Traffic Feature Code Extraction Method and Its Application in Cyber Security

Junjiang He(✉), Jiayan Wang, Jiangchuan Chen, Wenbo Fang, Lei Zhang, and Tao Li

School of Cyber Science and Engineering, Sichuan University, Chengdu, People's Republic of China
hejunjiang@scu.edu.cn

Abstract. Traffic signature code refers to the distinctive fields within network traffic that differentiate it from other applications and facilitate application identification. Its extraction serves as the foundation for application layer security protection, user behavior analysis, intrusion detection, etc., playing an important role in network traffic analysis and network security. Traditional traffic feature code extraction methods employ pattern mining algorithms to mine frequently occurring feature code strings in data traffic, which can only extract part of the continuous feature code, there still exists the issue of discontinuous feature code extraction being missing, alongside redundancy in the extracted feature codes due to overwriting. Based on this, we propose an automatic traffic feature code extraction method called Auto-TFCE in this paper. Firstly, the similarity of application sessions is measured by Levenstein ratio, and a hierarchical clustering algorithm is used to cluster the traffic to obtain single-application traffic. Subsequently, the traffic features are mined using closed frequent pattern mining algorithm, which takes into account the offsets between discontinuous sequences and extracts the continuous and discontinuous feature codes of the application traffic to form a feature code database. Finally, the feature codes extracted by this paper's method is applied to the firewall application recognition system for experiments. The experimental results show that the accuracy of application identification is improved by 10.8% when feature codes extracted by TFCE algorithm is applied to the firewall application identification control system.

Keywords: Mixed Traffic Separation · Automatic Feature Code Extraction · Hierarchical Clustering · Firewall Application Recognition Control System

This work was supported in part by the National Key Research and Development Program of China (No. 2020YFB1805400); in part by the National Natural Science Foundation of China (No. 62032002, and No. 62101358); in part by the Sichuan Province science and technology plan key research and development project (Grant No. 2023YFG0294); in part by the key laboratory of data protection and intelligent management ministry of education (SCUSACXYD202301).

S. Goel et al. (Eds.): ICDF2C 2024, LNICST 614, pp. 39–50, 2025.
https://doi.org/10.1007/978-3-031-89360-5_3

1 Introduction

The rapid development of information technology, the Internet has penetrated into every aspect of people's lives. While bringing people a more efficient and convenient experience, it has also brought a series of network security problems. In recent years, colleges and universities and companies have suffered numerous cyberattacks, causing huge losses to schools and society. The iterative updating of attack tools and means has rendered various network monitoring and protection means ineffective, bringing great challenges to network security assurance. Likewise, non-compliance and illegal traffic in the network propagation, making the network load heavier, affecting the normal business life, a variety of malicious attack traffic is hidden in the massive data traffic is difficult to identify. How to accurately identify network traffic characteristics, according to which to achieve intrusion detection and real-time situational analysis is an important task of network defense.

With the growth of network traffic and the continuous development of traffic obfuscation and encryption methods, traffic identification techniques have evolved gradually. The existing application identification techniques mainly include port-based, flow dynamic behavior-based, and feature code-based approaches, one or more of which are usually adopted for application identification control [1].

The port-based application identification technology is suitable for programs that use the default port numbers of the Transmission Control Protocol (TCP) or the User Datagram Protocol (UDP) [2]. This identification method was once widely used because of its simple algorithmic implementation and low spatial and temporal complexity. However, it has been demonstrated in literature [3] that the current recognition rate of port mapping-based identification techniques is already less than 20%, and they are usually used as an auxiliary means for application identification. The flow dynamic behavior-based application identification technology relies on the essential features of flows such as statistical, temporal, and behavioral features for identification, and using machine learning algorithms such as support vector machines, decision trees, random forests [4–7] etc. for modeling and identification. As cyberattack and defense confrontation becomes more and more intense, methods using deep packet [8], Inception-LSTM neural network [9] and integrated learning [10] have been proposed one after another. However, this technology needs to use deep learning models for modeling, facing difficulties such as difficult sample collection, high system overhead, and high difficulty in real-time recognition, which is still to be developed in the future. The feature code-based application identification technology uses reverse engineering to analyze the traffic payload part [11], select a field that is different from other protocol fields and frequently occurs in the interaction process, namely feature code. The principle and implementation of feature code-based application recognition technology is simple, having good real-time recognition and a wide range of applications, and is the technology adopted by most of the current application recognition control systems [18, 19]. However, this method requires manual analysis to separate single application traffic from mixed network traffic and extract the feature codes on this basis. Therefore, many scholars have studied using cluster analysis methods to obtain single application traffic from mixed traffic [13, 14], and then use sequential pattern mining methods to extract feature codes from single application traffic.

In order to accurately separate the mixed traffic with less human intervention and to improve the efficiency of feature code extraction, researchers use Jaccard coefficient to measure the coding similarity and extend the ROCK algorithm, and adopt parallel adaptive Canopy-K-means algorithm, Expectation Maximization clustering algorithm, density-based heuristic clustering and other methods of cluster analysis for the separation of mixed traffic [12, 14, 15]. In order to achieve automatic extraction of traffic feature codes, researchers used pattern mining algorithms and with the help of frequent pattern mining algorithms to mine frequently occurring feature strings in the data traffic, and used algorithms such as PrefixSpan based pattern mining, FIUFP-Growth, and BIDE-Discriminative to mine the spatial and temporal features of frequent closed sequences, which achieves highly efficient pattern mining [16–19]. However, the existing hybrid traffic separation methods have the problems of non-significant differentiation of different application traffic due to inappropriate setting of similarity metrics, easy bias caused by manual setting of similarity thresholds, and low efficiency of algorithms. Correspondingly, the existing feature mining methods have problems such as incomplete mining feature code and feature redundancy.

To address the above problems, this paper proposes an automatic traffic feature code extraction model Auto-TFCE, which is used to obtain purer network traffic and extract more complete and effective features. The main contributions of this paper are as follows:

1. A network application traffic separation method based on Levenstein ratio and hierarchical clustering is proposed. In contrast to traditional Jaccard-based mixed traffic separation methods, this approach takes into account the relative positions between bytes and eliminates the need for manually setting a similarity threshold, resulting purer and more single application traffic is obtained.
2. An automatic feature code extraction method is proposed, compared with the traditional feature code extraction algorithm based on sequence pattern mining, which only targets closed sequences and incorporates the inter-sequence offset distance, obtaining a more complete recognition feature code and reducing feature redundancy.
3. Rules are generated for the feature codes extracted by Auto-TFCE algorithm, which are then validated in a firewall application identification control system, resulting in a 10.8% improvement in recognition accuracy.

The rest of this paper is organized as follows. In Sect. 2, Auto-TFCE, an automatic traffic feature code extraction method proposed in this paper, is introduced in detail. In Sect. 3, the method is applied to firewall application identification control system for experiments. We conclude the paper in Sect. 4 with some suggestions for future work.

2 Research Methods

The feature code-based application identification method has a wide range of application scenarios and is the main application identification control method at present. However, the existing methods have problems such as poor hybrid traffic separation, incomplete feature code extraction, and feature redundancy. In this paper, we propose a traffic feature code extraction model Auto-TFCE. The model consists of three parts, including data preprocessing, mixed traffic separation, and automatic extraction of traffic feature codes.

The model realizes accurate separation of mixed traffic and can extract more complete feature codes with less feature redundancy, which provides support for the development of application identification control technology. The framework of the model is shown in Fig. 1:

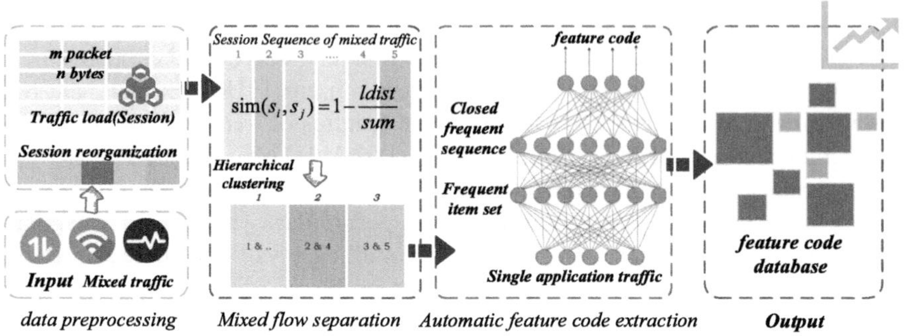

Fig. 1. Framework of the Auto-TFCE model

2.1 Data Preprocessing

The data processed by this algorithmic model is mixed traffic generated by multiple applications, which needs to be preprocessed first to reorganize the sessions of the messages in the traffic and extract the load content to form session sequences before clustering and separating them.

The traffic of the dataset is reorganized into sessions according to five-tuple, the load of each packet is obtained according to the protocol stack parsing, and the contents of the first n bytes of the first m packets in the session load are extracted. From the literature [20], it can be seen that for applications with load characterization fields, the characterization field will be at the beginning of the data stream. In the early part of the service provided by the application, it tends to send a lot of information such as negotiation and control while in the later part is the transmission of data, and there is almost no appearance of the protocol feature field. Therefore, the values of m and n are small, which can reduce the noise in the separation process and improve the efficiency of clustering and separation.

2.2 Mixed Flow Separation

After obtaining the session sequences of each traffic in the dataset to form a collection of session sequences, the collection of sequences is separated by clustering, and the traffic of the same application are clustered into one category. In order to make the similarity measure include the position of each byte in the encoding, improve protocol differentiation, and reduce misclassification, this paper chooses Levenshtein ratio to define the similarity between two sessions. Let s_i, s_j be two sessions, then the similarity formula is defined as follows:

$$sim(s_i, s_j) = 1 - \frac{ldist}{sum}, 0 \leq sim(s_i, s_j) \leq 1 \tag{1}$$

where *sum* denotes the sum of the lengths of the two strings, and *ldist* denotes the class edit distance. The class edit distance is the minimum number of edit operations describing the conversion of one string to another, which covers insertion, deletion, and replacement; the class edit distance is added once for insertion and deletion operations while twice for replacement operations. When two sessions are completely different, $\mathrm{sim}(\mathrm{s_i}, \mathrm{s_j}) = 0$, the similarity is minimized; when the two sessions are exactly the same, $sim(s_i, s_j) = 1$, the similarity is maximized.

For a dataset containing n sessions, each session is denoted by $s_k (1 \leq k \leq n)$, and the set of sequences formed after serializing all the sessions is denoted as $S = \{s_1, s_2, ..., s_n\}$. If the desired number of clusters is denoted as k, then the set of clusters obtained by clustering is $C_k = \{C_1, C_2, ..., C_k\}$. The specific process of mixed traffic separation is as follows:

1. Initialize the set of session sequences and the similarity matrix, treating each session as a clustered cluster;
2. Calculate the similarity between the two cluster classes based on the Levenstein ratio, merge the two clusters with the highest similarity, and recalculate the similarity matrix;
3. The clusters are merged bottom-up into larger and larger clusters, and the operation is performed in a loop until the algorithm ends when a given number of clusters k is reached.

2.3 Automatic Extraction of Traffic Feature Codes

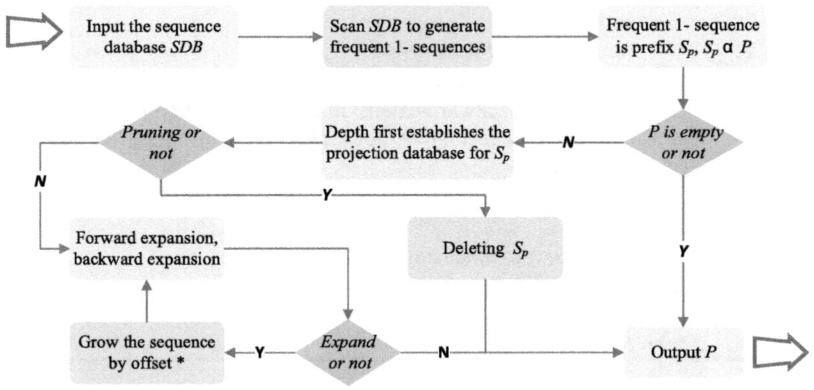

Fig. 2. Flowchart of traffic feature code extraction algorithm

Since the BIDE-Discriminative algorithm [19] grows the prefix sequences and recursively obtains the set of closed sequences based on the frequent term set, but frequent item sets tacitly approve that there is no offset between the item and the prefix sequence, so the final sequences are only continuous sequences. Aiming at the deficiency of BIDE-Discriminative algorithm that cannot extract the non-continuous feature code sequence, this paper proposes Auto-TFCE algorithm for traffic feature code extraction, which records the offset between the non-continuous sequences every time the prefix sequence is increased, realizing the double extraction of continuous and non-continuous sequences. The feature code extraction algorithm is shown in Fig. 2.

Algorithm 1: Traffic feature code extraction Algorithm

Input: *SDB* (sequence database), *min_sup* (minimum support)
Output: *FCS* (Frequent Closing Sequence)

BEGIN
$FCS = \varnothing$
F_1 = frequent 1-sequences *(SDB, min_sup)*
for each f_1 in F_1 **do**
    SDB^{f_1} = pseudo projected database (*SDB*)
end for
for each f_1 in F_1 **do**
    if (! BackScan (f_1, SDB^{f_1})) **then**
        LFI = locally frequent items (SDB^{f_1})
        $LFI_n = \{LFI_1, LFI_2, ..., LFI_n\}$ = classify (LFI)
        for each LFI_i in LFI_n **do**
            $FEI = |\{z \in LFI_i \mid z.sup = sup^{SDB}(f_1)\}|$
            if $((BEI + FEI) == 0)$ **then**
                $FCS = FCS \cup \{f_1\}$
            end if
            $offset = LFI_i.index() - f_1.last\_index()$
            for each i in LFI_i **do**
                $F_S^i = \langle f_1, wildcard(offset), i \rangle$
                $SDB^{F_S^i}$ = pseudo projected database (SDB^{f_1}, F_S^i)
            end for
            for each i in $LFIi$ **do**
                if (! BackScan (F_S^i, $SDB^{F_S^i}$)) **then**
                    BEI = backward extension check (F_S^i, $SDB^{F_S^i}$)
                    call bide recursively for (SDB^{f_1}, F_S^i, *min_sup*, *BEI*, *FCS*)
                end if
            end for
        end for
        BEI = backward extension check (f_1, SDB^{f_1})
    end if
end for
return *FCS*

The specific implementation steps of the traffic feature code extraction algorithm in this paper are as follows:

1. Scan the sequence database *SDB* and find the frequent 1-sequences, each frequent 1-sequence is considered as a prefix and all prefixes form the prefix set *P*;

2. If the prefix set P does not exist in S_p, then the program terminates, otherwise the program continues;
3. For each prefix S_p in the prefix set, a projection database is built in depth-first order. If S_p pruning is not possible, then calculate its backward expansion term, otherwise delete the prefix S_p in prefix set P;
4. Scan the pseudo projected database of prefixes to find their local frequent items or forward extensions;
5. Frequent sets are divided into subsets according to the offsets of the frequent set items to the end byte of the prefix sequence, and frequent items with the same offset are divided into a subset;
6. Grow the prefix sequence by traversing the subsets, and for each subset, add the offset value of a wildcard * after its corresponding prefix sequence to form a new prefix S_p.
7. If there are neither backward nor forward expansion terms, the output is used as a frequent closed sequence;
8. To increase S_p and its local frequent term (if it exists) to increase the prefix set P.

A pseudo-code description of the algorithm sees Algorithm 1.

3 Experimental Evaluation

In order to verify the effectiveness of this paper's method for real application controls, the feature codes extracted by using Auto-TFCE model are added to the firewall application recognition control system. Compare the application identification effect of the firewall before and after the feature codes are added.

3.1 Experimental Environment

The experiments were conducted on Windows 10 environment, the related software version is Python 3.6 and Pycharm 2018.3.2.

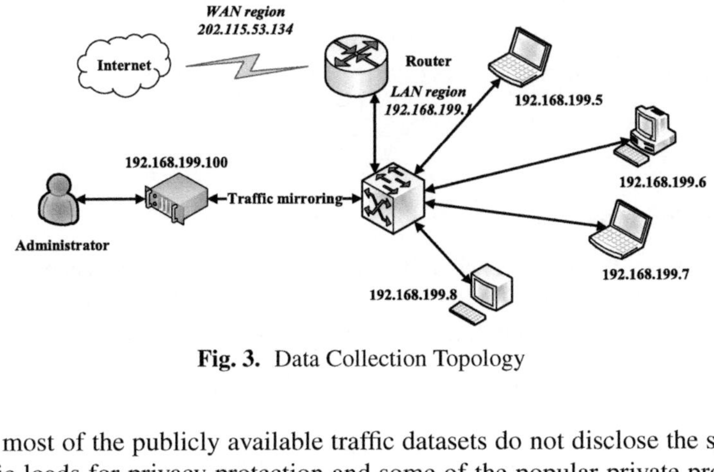

Fig. 3. Data Collection Topology

Since most of the publicly available traffic datasets do not disclose the specifics of their traffic loads for privacy protection and some of the popular private protocols are difficult to access for network traffic, the dataset in this paper consists of two parts: the public dataset and the local dataset. The public dataset comes from USTC-TFC2016 [21], HTTP, FTP, MySQL, Outlook, BitTorrent and Facetime are extracted from normal categories of traffic as part of the dataset in this paper. The local data was partially obtained from the network environment shown in Fig. 3. Applications were run on each of the five hosts from PC1-PC5, with only one application running on each host in order to capture the pure data traffic, and then the Tcpdump software was run on the packet capture server to capture the traffic, with each piece of captured traffic data labeled with the application that generated it. The web application traffic of QQ, WeChat, PPStream and NetEase cloud music was captured using this method.

The environment of Fig. 3 is also utilized to capture a portion of the data traffic, plus the SCUNET dataset as the validation dataset. The SCUNET dataset is obtained from the gateway of a university campus network for network application identification, which contains common application traffic such as file download and upload, streaming media and instant messaging, etc. The combined validation dataset contains about 3000 sessions for each application. The dataset/validation set for this experiment is shown in Table 1:

Table 1. Experimental Data Set/Validation Set

Application	Session	Packet	Percentage of traffic session
HTTP	1080/2918	57538/163241	10.0/9.8%
FTP	1202/3013	22743/54034	11.2/10.1%
MySQL	891/2871	34964/103505	8.3/9.7%
Outlook	1023/2758	30835/90783	9.5/9.3%
BitTorrent	1171/3279	538301/1423764	10.9/11.0%
QQ	1106/2965	32864/99439	10.3/10.0%
Facetime	976/2809	25875/77001	9.1/9.5%
WeChat	1074/3063	10769/33342	10.0/10.3%
PP-Stream	1189/3101	62480/181433	11.1/10.4%
NetEase-Music	1034/2940	53347/152078	9.6/9.9%

3.2 Evaluation Indicators

In order to evaluate the effectiveness of feature codes extraction in this paper for application recognition, Precision Rate, Recall Rate and Accuracy Rate are used as evaluation indexes. The formulas for their calculation are as follows:

$$Precision = \frac{TP}{TP + FP} \times 100\% \tag{2}$$

$$Recall = \frac{TP}{TP + FN} \times 100\% \tag{3}$$

$$Accuracy = \frac{TP + TN}{TP + FP + TN + FN} \times 100\% \tag{4}$$

3.3 Experimental Analysis

An experimental environment as shown in Fig. 4 is built to evaluate the experimental effect, in which PC-Replay is used to replay the collected pcap packet. The destination IP address and destination mac address of the packets in the dataset are modified to the addresses of the corresponding PC_1 to PC_n hosts according to the applications, and the corresponding application control rules are formulated in the firewall web interface to match the corresponding application traffic. Meanwhile, the packets that are not recognized by the firewall application recognition control system will be captured by PC_1.

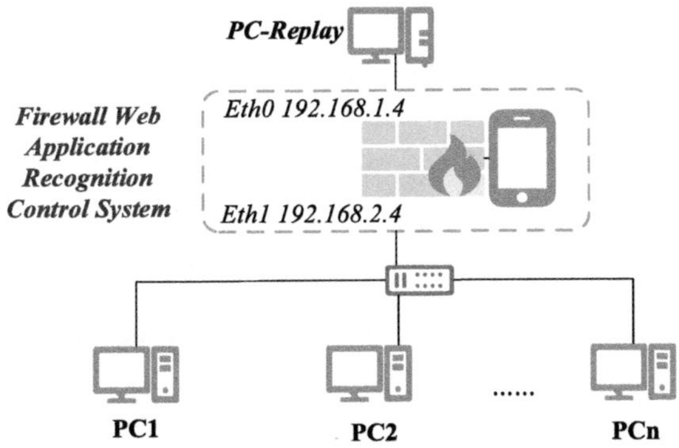

Fig. 4. Experimental Environment

Before adding feature codes to the feature library of the firewall application control identification system, there may be false alarms between different categories during traffic identification due to the possible existence of similar feature codes for various application traffic, possible conflicts in the extracted feature codes, and possible conflicts between the extracted feature codes and the existing features in the system's feature library. Therefore, conflict detection is performed before each addition of feature codes to the firewall application recognition system.

In this paper, the existing feature conflicts are categorized into two types: equal conflict and coverage conflict, equal conflict means that the sequence of feature codes of one application is equal to the sequence of feature codes of another application; coverage conflict means that the sequence of feature codes of one application is a subsequence of the feature codes of another application. If there is an equal conflict between the extracted feature code and the feature code in the feature library, it cannot be used as the recognition feature of the current application protocol. If there is an equal conflict between the extracted feature codes, neither of them can enter the library. Additionally, when a coverage conflict occurs, if both are feature codes extracted in this paper, the discontinuous feature code can be stored as the feature code of the corresponding application, otherwise, the extracted feature code cannot enter the library.

The two sets of experiments without joining this paper's feature codes and joining this paper's feature codes are successively run in the environment of Fig. 4, and the feature conflict detection is carried out when joining the feature code, and the experimental results are obtained as shown in Fig. 5, Fig. 6 and Table 2.

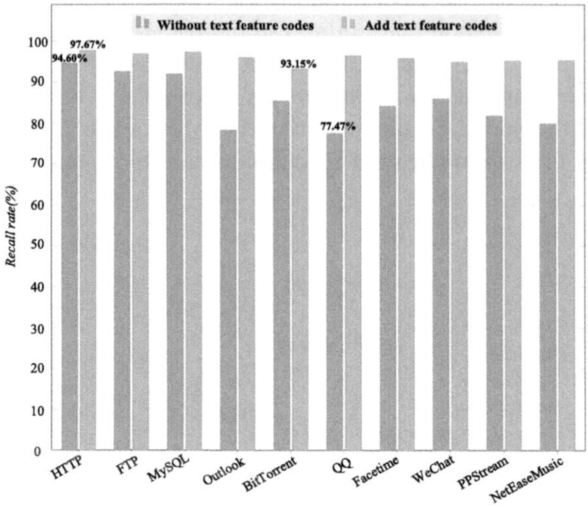

Fig. 5. Recall before and after adding feature codes of this paper

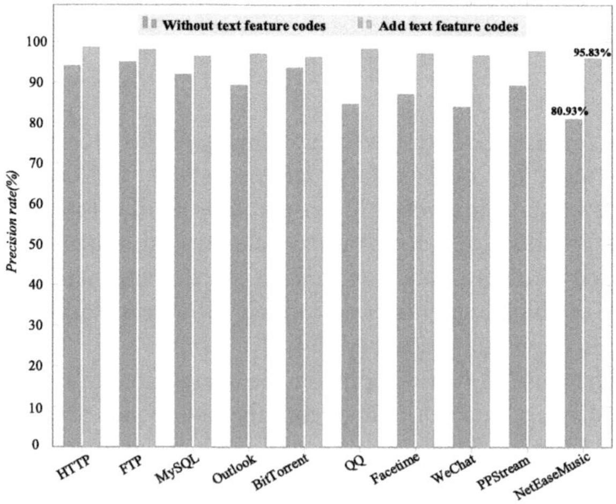

Fig. 6. Precision before and after adding feature codes of this paper

Figure 5 shows that the minimum recall for each application after adding feature codes extracted in this paper is 93.15%, which is a substantial increase in class recall for most applications compared to the class recall before adding the feature codes. Figure 6 shows that the precision rate for each application after adding feature codes extracted in this paper is above 95%, while the recognition precision rate for most applications before adding feature codes is below 90%, which shows that the feature codes extracted in this paper help to reduce the inter-class false alarms.

As can be seen from Table 2, the overall recognition accuracy increases from 85.1% to 95.9% after adding feature codes in this paper, which is an improvement of 10.8%, and a better recognition effect is obtained. Meanwhile, before adding feature codes extracted in this paper, the class recall rate of BitTorrent application is 77.47%, which is improved by 13.18% compared with the recognition of feature codes extracted by relying solely on the Auto-TFCE algorithm, due to the fact that the system itself adopts a hybrid recognition technique to recognize the encrypted traffic therein.

Table 2. Application Recognition Control System Verification Results

Evaluation index	Application scenarios	
	Without this article's feature codes	Add this article's feature codes
ACC	85.1%	95.9%

The experimental results show that applying feature codes extracted by the Auto-TFCE algorithm to the firewall application recognition control system can effectively reduce false alarms and omissions between application classes, obtain a high class recall rate, and improve the application recognition precision rate and overall recognition accuracy.

4 Conclusion

Application identification of network traffic can discover network anomalies and existing security threats in time, and realize real-time monitoring and rapid response to the network environment, playing an important role in maintaining cyberspace security. In this paper, we propose a traffic feature code extraction model Auto-TFCE, which adopts hierarchical clustering method to separate network mixed traffic, as well as carries out automatic extraction of continuous and non-continuous feature codes in pure application traffic classes. Finally, we apply the extracted feature codes to the firewall application recognition control system, which effectively improve the precision rate and the overall accuracy rate of network application recognition. In the future, we will continue to optimize the current solution to achieve automatic generation and storage of application identification rules, while conducting more experiments to verify the effectiveness of the TFCE method in mixed traffic separation and reducing feature redundancy, as well as its advancement compared to existing improved methods, and further improve the degree of automation of application identification. In addition, we will study related feature code extraction algorithms to explore more potential identification features in application protocols, and realize feature extraction and identification of application traffic without feature codes and encrypted traffic.

References

1. Yin, Y., et al.: IGRF-RFE: a hybrid feature selection method for MLP-based network intrusion detection on UNSW-NB15 dataset. J. Big data, **10**(1) (2023)
2. Dong, S.: Multi class SVM algorithm with active learning for network traffic classification. Expert Syst. Appl. **176** (2021)
3. Moore, A.W., Zuev, D.: Internet traffic classification using bayesian analysis techniques. ACM SIGMETRICS Perform. Eval. Rev. **33**(1), 50–60 (2005)
4. Dainotti, A., Pescape, A., Claffy, K.C.: Issues and future directions in traffic classification. IEEE Netw. **26**(1), 35–40 (2012)
5. Mohammadi, M., et al.: A comprehensive survey and taxonomy of the SVM-based intrusion detection systems. J. Netw. Comput. Appl. **178** (2021)
6. Arndt, D.J., Zincir-Heywood, A.N.: A comparison of three machine learning techniques for encrypted network traffic analysis. In: IEEE Symposium on Computational Intelligence for Security and Defense Applications, pp. 107–114 (2011)
7. Fosić, I., Žagar, D., Grgić, K., Križanović, V. Anomaly detection in NetFlow network traffic using supervised machine learning algorithms. J. Industr. Inf. Integr. **33** (2023)
8. Lotfollahi, M., Siavoshani, M.J., Zade, R.S.H., Saberian, M.: Deep packet: a novel approach for encrypted traffic classification using deep learning. Soft. Comput. **24**(3), 1999–2012 (2020)
9. Lu, B., Luktarhan, N., Ding, C., Zhang, W.: ICLSTM: encrypted traffic service identification based on inception-LSTM neural network. Symmetry, **13**(6) (2021)
10. Al-Haija, Q.A., Al-Badawi, A.: Attack-Aware IoT network traffic routing leveraging ensemble learning. Sensors, **22**(1) (2021)
11. Liu, H., Lang, B., Liu, M., Yan, H.: CNN and RNN based payload classification methods for attack detection. Knowl.-Based Syst. **163**, 332–341 (2019)
12. Azab, A., Khasawneh, M., Alrabaee, S., Choo, K.K.R., Sarsour, M.: Network traffic classification: techniques, datasets, and challenges. Digital Commun. Netw. (2022)
13. Misbahuddin, M., Zaidi, S.M.A.: Clustering based semi-supervised machine learning for DDoS attack classification. J. King Saud Univ. Comput. Inf. Sci. **33**(4), 436–446 (2021)
14. Xia, D., Ning, F., He, W.: Research on parallel adaptive canopy-k-means clustering algorithm for big data mining based on cloud platform. J. Grid Comput. **18**(2), 263–273 (2020)
15. Sheng, C., Yao, Y., Li, W.X., Yang, W., Liu, Y.: Unknown attack traffic classification in SCADA network using heuristic clustering technique. IEEE Trans. Netw. Serv. Manage. **20**(3), 2625–2638 (2023)
16. Thurachon, W., Kreesuradej, W.: Incremental association rule mining with a fast incremental updating frequent pattern growth algorithm. IEEE Access **9**, 55726–55741 (2021)
17. Kang, J.S., Baek, J.W., Chung, K.: PrefixSpan based pattern mining using time sliding weight from streaming data. IEEE Access **8**, 124833–124844 (2020)
18. Fradkin, D., Mörchen, F.: Mining sequential patterns for classification. Knowl. Inf. Syst. **45**(3), 731–749 (2015)
19. Jindal, R., Singh, I.: Detection of malicious transactions using frequent closed sequential pattern mining and modified particle swarm optimization clustering. In: 6th International Conference for Convergence in Technology, pp. 1–8 (2021)
20. Deri, L., Fusco, F.: Using deep packet inspection in cybertraffic analysis. In: IEEE International Conference on Cyber Security and Resilience, pp. 89–94 (2021)
21. Zhang, X., Hao, L., Gui, G., Wang, Y., Adebisi, B., Sari, H.: An automatic and efficient malware traffic classification method for secure Internet of Things. IEEE Internet Things J. **11**(5), 8448–8458 (2023)

Improved Federated Learning Model Against Poisoning Attacks by Using Iterative Blockchain Validators

Song Ding[1], Fuya Xu[1], Peiyun Zhang[1](✉), Zhangjie Fu[1], and Kezhong Lu[2]

[1] Nanjing University of Information Science and Technology, Nanjing 210044, Jiangsu, China
{20211221008,202212210042,zpy}@nuist.edu.cn

[2] Chizhou University, Chizhou 247000, Anhui, China

Abstract. Federated Learning (FL) is a distributed machine learning technology that enables multiple users to collaborate in training shared models while protecting data privacy. However, FL is susceptible to poisoning attacks, where malicious local model parameters are uploaded to disrupt the performance and correctness of global models. To resist poisoning attacks, this work proposes a new FL model based on a blockchain. Firstly, blockchain validators are iteratively obtained to generate a blockchain consensus committee to validate local model parameters uploaded by trainers. It can effectively exclude malicious nodes with the low accuracy of local model parameters, thus obtaining high-quality local model parameters quickly. Secondly, based on the obtained high-quality local model parameters, an enhanced aggregation rule is proposed. It randomly selects one from the enhanced aggregation functions in each round of FL, making it difficult for malicious nodes to attack the proposed model due to randomization. The experimental results show that the proposed method has higher accuracy than its peers in defending against both data poisoning attacks and model poisoning attacks.

Keywords: Blockchain · Poisoning attack · Committee mechanism · Iterative validators · Federated learning · Enhanced aggregation rule

1 Introduction

1.1 Background

Artificial intelligence (AI) is rapidly developing in various industries, but application environments are becoming more complex, and potential risks are also increasing. Therefore, it is crucial to improve the trustworthiness of AI. Data is the foundation of AI, and the quality of data largely determines the quality of AI. However, in traditional distributed machine learning, data has great security risks, such as leakage, tampering, and contamination. These issues may lead to serious consequences. For example, if training data is maliciously modified, even with minimal distortion in autonomous driving, it may lead to severe traffic accidents [1].

S. Goel et al. (Eds.): ICDF2C 2024, LNICST 614, pp. 51–70, 2025.
https://doi.org/10.1007/978-3-031-89360-5_4

To address these issues, a new distributed machine learning framework, i.e., Federated Learning (FL), allows multiple participants to train shared models on local devices without directly exchanging data, protecting data privacy, and reducing communication overhead, thereby improving model efficiency and generalization ability [2]. However, FL also faces security challenges, such as poisoning attacks that disrupt the performance of global models [3].

One possible solution to prevent these attacks and improve the security and trustworthiness of FL systems is to use blockchain technology [4]. Blockchain is a new distributed computing technology that can achieve decentralization, immutability, and traceability [5]. It can provide FL with a secure and trustworthy data storage environment by recording and validating the behavior and contributions of each participant and encouraging honest cooperation through incentive mechanisms. Blockchain can also be used to authenticate nodes to ensure their trustworthiness [6, 7, 8] and to maintain mutual trust among nodes by calculating trust values and publishing them [9]. However, it still faces poisoning attacks and needs to study new methods to solve this issue.

1.2 Motivations and Contributions

The traditional Federated Averaging [10] method aggregates local model parameters uploaded by all training nodes (referred to as trainers) but does not consider excluding local model parameters with low accuracy from malicious nodes. Li et al. [11] use a consensus mechanism to address this issue and maintain a good blockchain community through mutual validation among trainers. However, their method requires all trainers to participate in validation, resulting in low validation efficiency and high communication overhead. Li et al. [4] use a blockchain consensus committee method to improve the situation. Trainers vote to select validation nodes (referred to as validators) to form a blockchain consensus committee, which is responsible for validating data and local model parameters. Their method can alleviate communication overhead issues during validation, but there are still the following issues:

P1: It cannot guarantee whether the given validators face the security issue and the process of choosing validators also requires large resource costs.

To address problem P1, this work proposes a novel method by using iterative blockchain validators for the blockchain consensus committee during the continuous rounds of global models. In the first round of training, all trainers can voluntarily participate in the validation and form the initial blockchain consensus committee. Then, in each round of a global model, a specific number of validators with low model accuracy are removed from the blockchain consensus committee and improved to form a new blockchain consensus committee for validation in the next round. All trainers can participate in validation with decentralization. As a model continues to iterate, the selection of validators becomes more and more reasonable, and validation overhead also decreases.

In terms of global model aggregation, the traditional aggregation rules use the number of local samples from each trainer as aggregation weights [10], as malicious nodes can intentionally use large datasets to increase their aggregation weights, thus causing damage to models. To address this issue, some studies have proposed some aggregation rules, but there are still some shortcomings. For example, the method of Median [12] can exclude the effect of extreme local model parameters (i.e., malicious nodes intentionally generate local model parameters that are much larger or smaller than the scope of normal values). However, it only utilizes the median of the local model parameter set and does not fully use the information of other ones. In contrast, the method of TrimmedMean [12] can fully use the remaining local model parameters after discarding limited extreme ones. The method of Krum [13, 14] can detect malicious local model parameters according to the Euclidean distance in feature space because malicious nodes may upload local model parameters that are far from those uploaded by honest ones. Their method may be affected by a single malicious one. In summary, the existing methods have the following problems:

P2: Attackers may target an aggregation rule to attack a model, significantly decreasing model effectiveness.

To address problem P2, an enhanced aggregation rule is proposed, which randomly selects one aggregation function to prevent malicious nodes from targeted attacks on model aggregation. Based on the above motivations, the main contributions of this work include:

1) It proposes a novel FL model by using iterative blockchain validators. It combines FL and blockchain to resist poisoning attacks. The iteratively improved validators form a blockchain consensus committee to validate the local model parameters uploaded by trainers, thus obtaining high-quality local model parameters for global model aggregation.
2) Based on the proposed model, it designs an enhanced aggregation rule that includes three aggregation functions, i.e., one of the enhanced aggregation functions is randomly selected for model aggregation in each round of FL, making it impossible for malicious nodes to target specific ones and thus resist poisoning attacks.

The rest of this work is as follows: Sect. 2 introduces related work. Section 3 proposes the proposed model and algorithms. Section 4 gives the experimental results and analysis. Section 5 summarizes this work and proposes ideas for future work.

2 Related Work

2.1 Blockchain-Based FL

Traditional centralized FL has many risks, including single point of failure and privacy leakage. Che et al. [15] propose a serverless FL framework with a committee mechanism where committee validators communicate with each other through broadcasting. Each committee validator sends its evaluation results to others and then determines which local model parameters can be aggregated based on selection strategies. However, in this communication method, each validator needs to perform validation, which increases overhead and latency.

Distributed FL can naturally be combined with blockchain mechanisms. Blockchains can used to store data in FL with consensus mechanisms to realize communication among validators. Since blockchain mechanism is tamper-proof and transparent. Every data update will be recorded on blockchains, forming a public and unchangeable log. This means that it is difficult for attackers to tamper with data or model parameters without being discovered, because all nodes can see the complete history of each data update. At the same time, due to the decentralized characteristic of the blockchain mechanism, it does not rely on a single trusted node during the verification process, but rather ensures the authenticity and reliability of the data through the consensus of multiple nodes. Li et al. [4] propose a blockchain-based distributed FL framework, which has a blockchain consensus committee and uses blockchain to store local model parameters. Their method is based on the reputation and contribution values of the trainers. However, it needs to calculate the local model accuracy of all trainers in each round. Zhang et al. [16] use a randomly selected validator to improve the model's generalization and reduce overfitting from a machine-learning perspective. However, when malicious nodes are disguised, it is difficult to identify them. Liu et al. [17] apply a blockchain-based FL mechanism to healthcare systems, where each hospital designates a trustworthy validator to form a blockchain consensus committee. The blockchain consensus committee elected in this way is more reliable and accountable, but their model significantly weakens blockchains' decentralization, faces difficulties in selecting trustworthy validators, and is unsuitable for general distributed scenarios. Li et al. [18] divide nodes into edge and fog ones. The latter have more computing and storage capabilities than the former to form a blockchain consensus committee to validate local model parameters. However, their method cannot ensure that fog nodes are trustworthy. Liu et al. [19] define a satisfaction function to select validators, and the factors that affect satisfaction are satisfaction coefficient, benefit, and communication delay. Peng et al. [20] similarly calculate node trust values and randomly select members from nodes to form a blockchain consensus committee. The above methods [19, 20] essentially use an evaluation form to select validators, which increases the attack cost of malicious ones. However, the time and overhead of selecting validators are enormous.

2.2 Aggregation Rule in FL

The traditional aggregation rule [10, 21] does not consider the issues of malicious nodes, and the central server aggregates all local model parameters without checking them. Traditional aggregation rules assign weights to aggregate models based on the size of the local dataset. If malicious nodes appear and intentionally disrupt the aggregation of the models, resulting in a significant decrease in model accuracy, serious consequences may arise. In a distributed environment without a trusted central server, this problem is even more severe. Due to the lack of a trusted central server, it is challenging to complete the validation of local model parameters. To address this issue, some studies have proposed Byzantine aggregation rules to resist the disruption of global models by malicious nodes in FL.

Malicious nodes may pass some wrong or extreme parameters to disrupt model aggregation, while good trainers train local model parameters with close values. Therefore, Yin et al. [12, 22] propose the TrimmedMean method, which removes local model parameters from the edges and aggregates the remaining local model parameters according to the traditional mean [23] method that their method outperforms by reducing the influence of extreme local model parameters but has a very limited ability to remove malicious nodes and may still be influenced by them. To greatly remove extreme local model parameters, Yin et al. [12, 24] also propose a method called Median that takes the median of the local model parameter set as the model aggregation. Chen et al. [25]

propose a method to calculate the geometric median of the local model parameter set at high latitudes as the global model parameters by data up-dimensioning. The above two methods can reduce the impact of malicious nodes, but there is a problem with not fully utilizing the local model parameters. In addition, in some special cases, the geometric median approach may have great defects, such as double-peaked distribution. Their method makes it difficult to distinguish between honest trainers and malicious nodes when uploading local model parameters. Blanchard et al. [14, 26] propose the Krum method to compute the geometric median of the local model parameter set and select local model parameters close to the geometric median ones used for model aggregation. Their method can utilize more data than the direct median method. However, the same boosting method has a similar double-peak distribution problem, and the Euclidean distance between local model parameters may be affected by a single local model parameter, causing the abandonment of local model parameters uploaded by many honest trainers. Mhamdi et al. [27] propose the Bulyan method, which combines the advantages of the Krum and TrimmedMean methods. Firstly, Krum selects local model parameters and then uses TrimmedMean to aggregate them. However, their method is computationally expensive and requires the calculation of pairwise distances of local model parameters, which typically incurs a huge computational workload, making it challenging to implement concretely. Geometric-median [28] is greatly affected by the distribution of bimodal data, leading to the inability of the model to converge. The convergence speed of the model in Faba (Fast Aggregation algorithm against Byzantine Attacks, Faba) [29] is too slow. Cc (Centered Clipping, Cc) [30] and Scc (Self Centered Clipping, Scc) [31] can continuously update global model parameters using the difference of the parameters in each round. However, the methods have low accuracy in resisting Sign-flipping attacks.

The current studies show that existing methods have flaws in that attackers may attack the target model, significantly reducing model effectiveness. To solve the problem of high time and cost in selecting validators, this work proposes a new method to remove malicious validators and continuously develop the blockchain consensus committee to improve model accuracy with an enhanced aggregation rule, thus resisting poisoning attacks.

3 Proposed Model

FL is a distributed machine learning paradigm that enables multiple data owners to aggregate models without sharing data, thereby addressing data silos and user privacy issues. This work is mainly conducted in the context of the Internet of Things (IoT), such as the Internet of Vehicles, the Internet of Ships, as well as industrial and medical IoTs. IoT consists of various devices with storage and computational capabilities, such as smart watches, vehicles, drones, and cell phones. Humans essentially manipulate these smart devices to participate in FL, hence the manipulators are the users in FL. The proposed model mainly includes nodes of a task publisher, the blockchain consensus committee with validators, and trainers. The framework of the proposed model is shown in Fig. 1.

1) A task publisher: It is the initiating node of FL to release tasks and train parameters by sending tasks to the committee. After each round, it aggregates local model parameters to form a global model. It sends updated tasks based on the global model parameters after aggregation.
2) The blockchain consensus committee: It consists of iteratively improved blockchain validators that have two functions. The first one is to generate task blocks. The second one is to validate the local model parameters broadcasted by trainers and package the validated ones to blocks and store them in its blockchain by the blockchain consensus committee.
3) Trainers: They receive FL tasks from the blockchain consensus committee, train their local models using local data, and then send the local model parameters to the blockchain consensus committee.

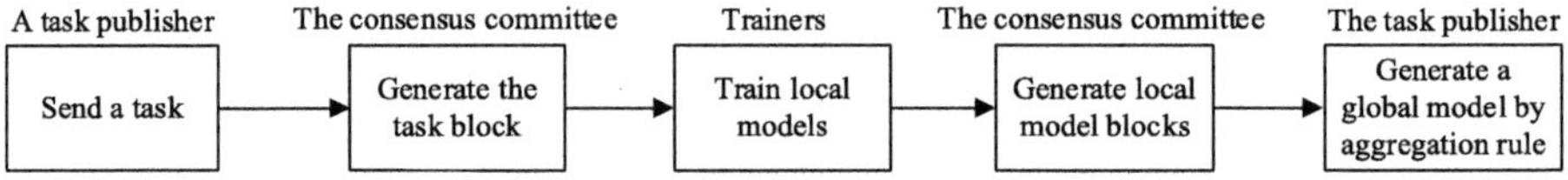

Fig. 1. The module diagram of the proposed model

3.1 Blockchain-Based Storage Structure

The proposed model requires blockchain technology to store various types of information, such as global and local model parameters and validator information. The data type of model parameters depends on the specific machine learning algorithm. Typically, model parameters are a set of values used to represent its structure and function. For example, if the logistic regression algorithm is used, the model parameters are a set of weights and biases used to calculate the prediction probabilities of samples. If a neural network algorithm is used, the model parameters are a set of matrices and vectors to represent the connections and activations between neurons, and the model weights are floating point numbers or integers. Due to the need to store tasks and local models in the proposed model, two types of blocks need to be designed: Task and local model blocks, respectively, as shown in Fig. 2.

Each block consists of a header and a body, and the block header mainly includes four fields: 1) *index*; 2) *hash*; 3) *previous_hash*; and 4) *timestamp*. When adding a new block, the blockchain can compare the parameter relationships between the new and the existing blocks to validate the legitimacy of the new block. There are differences in the body content of the two types of blocks. The body of a task block has *Global_model_parameters*, and a new block of this type is generated after each round of model aggregation, providing global model parameters for the next round. The body of the local-model block contains *Validator*, *Accuracy* (i.e., model accuracy), and *Local_model_parameters* packaged in the block.

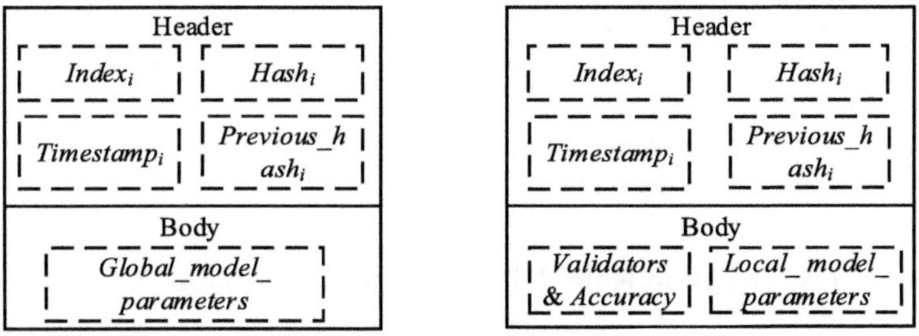

(a) Task block (b) Local model block

Fig. 2. Task and local model blocks

3.2 Iteratively Improved Blockchain Validators

This work proposes a novel method to iteratively improve validators for the blockchain consensus committee. The validator obtains the local model parameters uploaded by the trainer from the blockchain, imports their local framework, and validates them with their dataset. Each trainer has the chance to be a validator for a task in the initial stage. Because validators are rewarded for validating, they may actively participate in validation. After each round of FL, the next round of blockchain consensus committee is selected, i.e., after each round of model training and aggregation, the validators with low local model accuracy are removed from the blockchain consensus committee in the current round. The validation performance gets better and better, and the validation time decreases with the iteratively improved blockchain validators for the blockchain consensus committee. The following steps are used to obtain the iterative blockchain validators:

Step 1: After a task is published, IoT devices can participate in the training task as trainers. Let $\boldsymbol{M}$ be the set of trainers:

$$\boldsymbol{M} = \{p_1, p_2, \ldots, p_n\} \tag{1}$$

where p_n denotes the nth trainer. Trainer $c \in \boldsymbol{M}$. Let $Z = |\boldsymbol{M}|$ be the trainer count.

Step 2: In the initial stage, all trainers can be validators to form a committee. Let V_i denote the set of the ith round committee. $K_i = |\boldsymbol{V}_i|$ and $i \geq 0$. $\boldsymbol{V}_i \subset \boldsymbol{M}$. The validators in the blockchain consensus committee participate in the training and validate local model parameters sent by other trainers. The validators are denoted as $v_{ij} \in \boldsymbol{V}_i$ and $j \in \{1, 2, \ldots, K_i\}$.

Step 3: In the validation stage, the validators are ranked from the minimum to the maximum according to the reputation of their local models to obtain $\{v_{i1}, v_{i2}, \ldots, v_{iK_i}\}$ in round i. After selecting the local models from the blockchain consensus committee for validation in each round, the validators with the lower local model accuracy than Δ are selected and put into set $\boldsymbol{F}_i$, where $\boldsymbol{F}_i = \{v_{i1}, v_{i2}, \ldots, v_{ia}\}$. $\boldsymbol{F}_i \subset \boldsymbol{V}_i$ denotes the set of malicious validators in round i. v_{ia} denotes the ath one in round i.

Step 4: The malicious nodes in the set $\boldsymbol{F}_i$ are removed from $\boldsymbol{V}_i$ to obtain the blockchain consensus committee $\boldsymbol{V}_{i+1}$:

$$\boldsymbol{V}_{i+1} = \boldsymbol{V}_i - \boldsymbol{F}_i \tag{2}$$

Step 5: When $i < \Gamma\Gamma$ ($\Gamma$is the threshold for the number of rounds) or the number of validators is greater than $\sqrt{K_i}$ ($\sqrt{K_i}$ is the threshold for the number of validators, which is set to ensure the decentralization of the blockchain consensus committee and the security of the federated learning process), *i*++ and the process goes to Step 3. Otherwise, the blockchain consensus committee election ends.

3.3 Enhanced Aggregation Rule (HBlend) Against Poisoning Attacks

Based on the proposed model, this work proposes an enhanced aggregation rule, called HBlend that focuses on how to discard malicious local model parameters of malicious nodes. Based on the rule, one function is randomly selected from three aggregation ones, i.e., Improved Median (IMedian), Improved TrimmedMean (ITrimmedMean), and Improved Faba (IFaba). Let $\boldsymbol{X}$ be the set of local model parameters validated by the blockchain consensus committee:

$$\boldsymbol{X} = \{\boldsymbol{x}_1, \boldsymbol{x}_2, \ldots, \boldsymbol{x}_n\} \tag{3}$$

where $\boldsymbol{x_n}$ is the local parameter set of the *n*th trainer:

$$\boldsymbol{x}_n = \{x_{1d}, x_{2d}, \ldots, x_{nd}\} \tag{4}$$

$$\boldsymbol{L_d} = [g_{1d}, g_{2d}, \ldots, g_{nd}] \tag{5}$$

where g_{nd} is the *n*th sorted local model parameter. $\boldsymbol{L}_d$ is the sorted set of local model parameters in the *d*th dimension. It is sorted according to the accuracy of the local parameters verified by the blockchain consensus committee. Let $\boldsymbol{G}$ be the sorted set of local model parameters:

$$\boldsymbol{G} = \{\boldsymbol{L_d} | d = 1, 2, \ldots, R\} \tag{6}$$

where R is the tensor dimensionality. Since parameters in $\boldsymbol{x_n}$ are sorted, thus making it simple and fast to use.

HBlend requires generating a random number, i.e., $r \in \{0, 1, 2\}$, at each round of aggregation. In round *i*, one function is selected from *IMedian*(), *ITrimmedMean*(), and *IFaba*() according to different *r*. Let $\boldsymbol{\omega}$ be the global model parameter set:

$$\boldsymbol{\omega} = \begin{cases} IMedian() & ifr = 0 \\ ITrimmedMean() & ifr = 1 \\ IFaba() & ifr = 2 \end{cases} \tag{7}$$

IMedian() generates the median of a set of local model parameters. Let $\overline{X}_d$ be the median in $\boldsymbol{L_d}$ to be taken as the result of the global model parameter:

$$\bar{X}_d = \begin{cases} g_{\frac{n+1}{2}} & If\ n\ is\ odd \\ \frac{g_{\frac{n}{2}d} + g_{\frac{n+1}{2}d}}{2} & Otherwise \end{cases} \tag{8}$$

ITrimmedMean() converts the trimmed mean algorithm from statistics to FL and independently processes each local model parameter. Let f be the threshold of parameter count deleted from $\boldsymbol{L_d}$. The first and last $f/2$ parameters are removed from $\boldsymbol{L_d}$ to obtain the result of the global model parameter, as follows:

$$\overline{X}_d = \frac{g_{(\frac{f}{2}+1)d} + g_{(\frac{f}{2}+2)d} + \cdots + g_{(n-\frac{f}{2})d}}{n-f} \tag{9}$$

IFaba() is a function that dynamically removes malicious parameters, which has the following steps:

Step 1: Set the initial value of f as 0;

Step 2: Calculate the average value in the local model parameter list (i.e., $\boldsymbol{L_d}$) as follows:

$$\overline{g}_d = \frac{g_{1d} + g_{2d} + \cdots + g_{nd}}{n} \tag{10}$$

Step 3: Remove the local model parameter from $\boldsymbol{L_d}$, which has the largest difference from $\overline{g}_d$, as follows:

$$\begin{gathered} \boldsymbol{L_d} = \boldsymbol{L_d} - \{g_{id}\} \\ \text{s.t. } \exists i, Max_{i=1}^{n}\left(\left|g_{id} - \overline{g}_d\right|\right) \end{gathered} \tag{11}$$

If a trainer submits this local model parameter g_{id}, it is considered malicious and removed from set $\boldsymbol{M}$, and $f = f + 1$;

Step 4: If $f \geq Z/3$, the process goes to Step 2. Otherwise, it goes to Step 5, indicating that the Byzantine threshold for the number of malicious nodes tolerated has been reached;

Step 5: $\overline{g}_d$ is used as the global model parameter, as follows:

$$\overline{X}_d = \{\overline{g}_d\} \tag{12}$$

3.4 Model Analysis

The data structure of *Local_model_parameters*:

$$Local\_model\_parameters = <R, \boldsymbol{G}> \tag{13}$$

where R and $\boldsymbol{G}$ denote the number of dimensions of *Local_model_parameters* and the set of sorted local model parameters, respectively. The sequence chart of the proposed model is shown in Fig. 3.

1) Send a task: The task publisher sends a training task to the committee.
2) Generate the task block: After achieving a consensus in the blockchain, the blockchain consensus committee generates and stores a task block after training tasks. Then, the committee sends the task block to the trainers.
3) Train local models: Trainers train local models based on task block information and local data. They send local model parameters to the blockchain consensus committee after completing the training, as shown in Steps 6.1–6.*n* in Fig. 3.

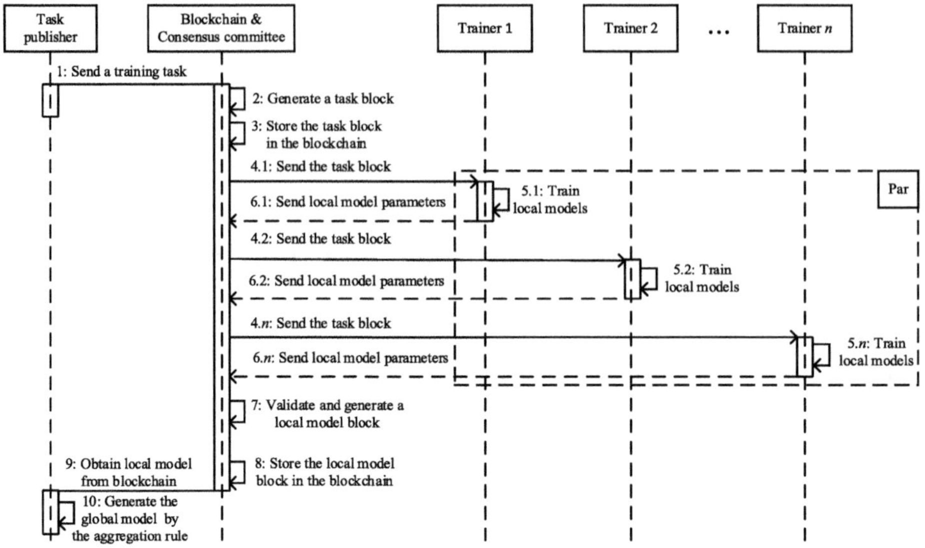

Fig. 3. The framework of the proposed model

4) Generate local model blocks: The blockchain consensus committee validates the local model parameters sent by the trainers, generates local model blocks for each trainer, and stores them in the blockchain.
5) Generate the global model by using the proposed enhanced aggregation rule: The task publisher obtains the local model parameter blocks from the blockchain and generates the global model based on them by using the rule, which is given in detail next.

4 Experiments

4.1 Experimental Settings

The experiments use an AMD Ryzen 7 CPU @ 3.7 GHz, NVIDIA GeForce GTX 1650 GPU, and Windows 10 64bit. Python 3.9 and Pytorch 1.12 are used for programing.

1) Simulation environments and dataset

This work is based on a Byzantine environment, where Z trainers are set to upload local model parameters for aggregation. The experiments evaluate the accuracy of the softmax [32] training task with a dataset using MNIST [33], which is from the National Institute of Standards and Technology and contains 60,000 training images of handwritten digits, written from 0 to 9. The training set consists of digits handwritten by 250 different people, of which 50% are high school students and 50% are Census Bureau staff.

a) Local data distribution

There are two types of local data distribution ways in FL, i.e., Independently and Identically Distributed (I.I.D.) and NON- I.I.D. [31], as follows:

I.I.D.: It implies that each local data is independently sampled from the same distribution, i.e., each has similar data characteristics and label distribution.

NON-I.I.D.: It implies that each trainer's data is sampled from a different distribution, i.e., data has a different data feature and label distribution.

b) Node distribution

There are three types of node distributions [31], as follows:

Two-Castle node distribution: It has two dimensions: The number of communication rounds, indicating the number of local model parameters exchanged between participants during an FL process and model accuracy.

Octopus node distribution: It has two dimensions: Communication overhead and model accuracy. The former indicates the amount of data to be transmitted between participants during the FL process.

Erdos-Renyi node distribution: It is a random graph model that connects each pair of nodes with probability.

The Two-Castle node distribution is influenced by communication rounds. The Octopus node distribution is affected by communication overhead. The two node distributions are chosen because the resources required for communication in FL are mainly related to communication rounds and overhead. The Erdos-Renyi node distribution can represent the node distribution of various attributes, indicating the distribution of FL under various possible node distribution methods.

2) Parameter settings and FL byzantine attacks

The specific parameter settings of the experiment are shown in Table 1. All data are evenly distributed to each trainer. This work sets the initial coefficient to 0.01 and the squared parametric regularization of the batch size is 32.

Table 1. Parameter settings

Parameter	Description	Value
Γ	The number of rounds in FL	50000
η	Learning rate	0.01
α^k	A step size of time stamp q during training	$0.9/\sqrt{q+1}$
ε	The threshold of global model accuracy	92%
Δ	The threshold of local model accuracy	80%
Z	Trainer count	100
f	The number of low local model parameters that are deleted in each round	2
α	The proportion of low local model parameters that are deleted in each round	1/3

Based on the analysis in [34–36], the formal threat models for poisoning attacks include data poisoning attacks and model poisoning attacks, as follows:

a) Data poisoning attacks

Sign-flipping [35]: It is an attack against FL data where malicious nodes randomly or purposefully modify some sample labels in a local dataset, thereby affecting the generalization ability and accuracy of the global model. This attack is undirected and aims at disrupting model accuracy.

Sample-duplicating [36]: It is an attack against FL data where malicious nodes affect a global model by copying or modifying their local data. Malicious nodes can add samples with specific labels or features to local data, leading to the global model having preferences or misjudgments for these labels or features.

b) Model poisoning attacks

Gaussian [34]: It is an attack against FL models where malicious nodes add Gaussian noise in the local model update, thus affecting the convergence and performance of the global model. It is undirected and aims to disrupt model accuracy.

Isolation [36]: It is an attack against FL models and data where malicious nodes interfere or disrupt the training process of a global model by modifying their local model or data. The purpose of this attack is to make the global model unable to correctly classify specific categories of data, thereby reducing the accuracy and generalization ability of models.

3) Compared methods

Some representative methods are selected for comparison. They are also used in other work for comparative experiments [23, 31].

No-comm [21]: It is often used as a benchmark in the absence of an attack.

Mean [31]: It is a weighted average method that sets weights according to the size of each local data and then aggregates the global model by weighting uploaded local model parameters and averaging them.

TrimmedMean [22]: It is based on the mean method by removing local model parameters at the edges. Honest trainers may train local model parameters close to each other, while malicious nodes may upload some extreme parameters to break model aggregation. After removing the edge data, it calculates the average of the remaining local model parameters as the global ones.

Median [24]: It uses the median value of the local model parameters as the aggregation of the global model. Values in the local model parameters are sorted from minimum to maximum. If there are odd values in the local model parameters, then the median is the middle value. The median is the middle value if there are odd values in the local model parameters.

Geometric-median [28]: It is a generalization of the one-dimensional median method, which solves for the geometric median of local model parameters as the global ones. The geometric median is the point with the smallest sum of Euclidean distances to all points.

Krum [26]: Inspired by a geometric median, it aggregates global models using local parameters close to the geometric median. It needs to calculate the Euclidean distance between any two local model parameters, thus increasing the calculation and communication overhead, especially when the dimension or the number of local model parameters is large.

Faba [29]: It aggregates local models by iteratively removing data from malicious nodes. Specifically, the mean of all local model parameters is first used by removing the farthest one. Then, the remaining ones are calculated as the mean value and compared again, iterating until the number of malicious local model parameters removed reaches the Byzantine tolerance threshold.

Cc [30]: It is based on local model parameter pruning and weighted averaging. That is, each trainer compares its local model parameters with those of neighboring trainers before sending them and truncates them to a reasonable range if they deviate too large. Each trainer assigns different local model parameters based on the reliability and network topology of neighboring trainers and then calculates the weighted average of all received local model parameters.

Scc [31]: It changes the aggregation rule for local model parameter pruning and weighted average in Cc to the self-centered pruning aggregation rule. Self-centered pruning means that each trainer compares its local model parameters with its historical ones before sending them and truncates them to a reasonable range if they deviate too large.

The Median method can effectively exclude malicious nodes. The TrimmedMean method can fully utilize local model parameters. The Faba method is less capable of excluding malicious nodes and using local model parameters than Median and TrimmedMean, but its combination ability is stronger. The proposed model combines and improves these three methods. Experiment results show that it can better resist attacks.

4.2 Analysis of Experimental Results

1) The global model accuracy under I.I.D. and NON-I.I.D. based on Two-Castle node distribution.

Table 2 shows that the global model accuracy, i.e., Ω (%), is obtained under I.I.D. based on Two-Castle node distribution subjected to Gaussian, Sign-flipping, Isolation, and Sample-duplicating attacks, respectively. It shows four attack scenarios, i.e., Gaussian, Sign-flipping, Isolation, and Sample-duplicating. No-comm has an accuracy of 89.66% in the absence of attacks, which is used as a reference for the accuracy of the other nine methods. The accuracy of the TrimmedMean is 91.69% without attacks, while it has higher accuracy in Gaussian, Isolation, and Sample-duplicating attacks. Median has an accuracy of 91.52% without attacks with higher accuracy in Gaussian, Isolation, and Sample-duplicating attacks, but lower accuracy in Sign-flipping attacks. Geometric-median has an accuracy of 91.67% without attacks, and higher accuracy in the presence of attacks such as Gaussian and Sample-duplicating, with some decrease in accuracy in the presence of Isolation attacks, but a significant decrease in accuracy in the presence of Gaussian and Sign-flipping attacks. Krum's accuracy is 90.89% without the attacks and does not decrease significantly in these four attacks. The accuracy of

Cc is 91.44% without attacks, and Cc also has high accuracy under Gaussian, Sign-flipping, and Sample-duplicating attacks. However, the accuracy of Cc is only 23.71% under Sign-flipping attacks, indicating that the model has been severely attacked. Scc improves Cc, but also has the same problem, i.e., Scc cannot resist the Sign-flipping attack. The proposed model has higher accuracy than its peers under all four attacks.

Table 2. Model accuracy, i.e., Ω (%), under I.I.D. based on Two-Castle node distribution

Method	No-attack	Gaussian	Sign-flipping	Isolation	Sample-duplicating
No-comm	89.66	-	-	-	-
Mean	91.41	10.27	14.88	89.66	91.50
TrimmedMean	91.69	91.48	85.19	91.30	91.35
Median	91.52	91.13	86.20	91.12	91.16
Geometric-median	91.67	91.45	86.21	89.66	91.38
Krum	90.89	90.81	89.72	89.87	90.15
Faba	91.63	91.52	91.46	91.50	91.39
Cc	91.44	91.44	23.71	91.36	91.44
Scc	91.59	91.49	23.71	91.38	91.50
The proposed	**91.81**	**91.76**	**91.76**	**91.75**	**91.78**

Table 3 shows the global model under NON-I.I.D. based on Two-Castle node distribution under Gaussian, Sign-flipping, Isolation, and Sample-duplicating attacks. NON-I.I.D. usually brings more significant challenges because it may lead to inconsistent weights, convergence difficulties, and performance degradation during model training. Therefore, NON-I.I.D. is not as accurate as I.I.D. in FL. No-comm is unable to train models under NON-I.I.D. even without attacks successfully. Both Faba and the proposed model maintain high accuracy after four attacks: Gaussian, Sign-flipping, Isolation, and Sample-duplicating, with accuracy of 91.52%, 91.45%, 91.48%, 88.34%, and 91.83%, 91.77%, 91.76%, and 89.52%, respectively, indicating that these two methods have strong robustness. The overall accuracy of TrimmedMean and Median is relatively low, especially when subjected to Isolation attacks, with the accuracy of only 57.87% and 32.74%, respectively. Cc and Scc also maintain high accuracy of 91.40% and 91.44%, as well as 91.41% and 91.50%, respectively, under Gaussian and Sample-duplicating attacks, indicating that these two methods strongly resist these two attacks. However, their accuracy is very low under Sign-flipping and Isolation attacks, especially less than 50% under Sign-flipping attacks. Krum performs poorly in all cases, with an accuracy of less than 30%, indicating poor method robustness. The Geometric-median accuracy is less than 10% under Sign-flipping and Isolation attacks, meaning that the method is susceptible to these two attacks. In general, except for the Sample-duplicating attack, the proposed model outperforms well with high accuracy in all cases under Sample-duplicating attack, thus the proposed method is generally more robust.

Table 3. Model accuracy, i.e., Ω (%), under NON-I.I.D. based on Two-Castle node distribution

Method	No-attack	Gaussian	Sign-flipping	Isolation	Sample-duplicating
No-comm	9.87	-	-	-	-
Mean	91.71	21.16	34.86	9.87	91.49
TrimmedMean	91.47	73.21	71.56	57.87	86.65
Median	77.90	73.24	73.35	32.74	80.07
Geometric-median	89.11	73.19	9.86	9.87	89.86
Krum	18.82	19.74	19.00	19.88	28.71
Faba	91.70	91.52	91.45	91.48	88.34
Cc	91.47	91.40	44.79	86.90	91.44
Scc	91.50	91.41	44.79	86.90	**91.50**
The proposed	**91.83**	**91.83**	**91.77**	**91.76**	89.52

2) The global model accuracy under I.I.D. and NON-I.I.D. based on the Octopus node distribution.

Tables 4 and 5 show the accuracy of ten methods based on the Octopus node distribution in four attack scenarios. The former shows the results under I.I.D., while the latter shows the results under NON-I.I.D.

Table 4. Model accuracy, i.e., Ω (%), under I.I.D. based on Octopus node distribution

Method	No-attack	Gaussian	Sign-flipping	Isolation	Sample-duplicating
No-comm	90.31	-	-	-	-
Mean	91.73	16.12	68.33	91.05	91.66
TrimmedMean	91.79	91.77	90.24	91.77	91.72
Median	91.60	91.51	91.23	91.60	91.38
Geometric-median	91.84	91.64	90.58	91.22	91.61
Krum	91.12	90.97	91.04	90.95	90.87
Faba	91.78	91.76	91.58	91.69	91.72
Cc	91.65	91.65	82.26	91.39	91.60
Scc	91.73	91.72	85.04	91.43	91.67
The proposed	**91.83**	**91.83**	**91.78**	**91.80**	**91.86**

In Table 4, the Mean method has a low model accuracy when attacked by Gaussian and Sign-flipping attacks. Cc and Scc cause severe damage to model accuracy when subjected to Sign-flipping attacks. The proposed model has higher accuracy than the other methods when they are not attacked or suffer from these four attacks, indicating

Table 5. Model accuracy, i.e., Ω (%), under NON-I.I.D. based on Octopus node distribution

Method	No-attack	Gaussian	Sign-flipping	Isolation	Sample-duplicating
No-comm	10.00	-	-	-	-
Mean	88.14	15.82	32.91	14.92	88.08
TrimmedMean	88.18	87.75	81.59	85.73	87.06
Median	36.23	36.56	36.34	34.52	36.56
Geometric-median	59.16	60.18	51.26	31.35	60. 48
Krum	19.82	17.61	19.73	17.61	19.75
Faba	87.90	87.89	87.89	87.86	87.45
Cc	87.89	87.84	47.59	64.66	87.91
Scc	88.11	88.53	47.39	67.95	**88.27**
The proposed	**88.55**	**88.69**	**88.70**	**88.68**	88.10

that the proposed method is superior. Table 5 shows model accuracy under NON-I.I.D based on the Octopus node distribution. Similar to Table 4, even if not attacked, the model aggregation accuracy of No-comm is very low. The performance of Geometric-media is slightly better than the Median, but the accuracy is very low. Cc and Scc perform poorly under Sign-flipping and Isolation attacks, while Faba and the proposed method have advantages in all cases, except for the Sample-duplicating attack, where the accuracy of the model aggregation is higher than that of all other methods. Therefore, overall, the proposed model is the best among them.

3) The global model accuracy under I.I.D. and NON-I.I.D. based on the Erdos-Renyi node distribution.

Tables 6 and 7 show the experimental results of the model aggregation based on the Erdos-Renyi node distribution. The impact of different attack and aggregation rules on the accuracy of the Federated learning model is shown in the case of I.I.D. and NON-II.D., respectively. From Table 6, the Mean method is susceptible to Gaussian and Sign-flipping attacks, and its accuracy is extremely low after the attacks, while the accuracy of TrimmedMean, Median, and Geometric-median decreases significantly after the Sign-flipping attacks. The accuracy of Cc and Scc significantly decreases after being attacked by Sign-flipping attacks. The rest of the methods have relatively high model accuracy, with the proposed model having the highest accuracy. In Table 7, the model accuracy of No-comm is also very low under NON-I.I.D. The Mean method has the highest model accuracy under the Sample-duplicating attack, but significantly decreases under Gaussian, Sign-flipping, and Isolation attacks. TrimmedMean, Geometric-median, Cc, and Scc have low model accuracy when subjected to Sign-flipping and Isolation attacks. Both Faba and the proposed method have high accuracy under all attacks, while the proposed method overall has higher accuracy, making it the optimal one.

Table 6. Model accuracy, i.e., Ω (%), under I.I.D. based on Erdos-Renyi node distribution.

Method	No-attack	Gaussian	Sign-flipping	Isolation	Sample-duplicating
No-comm	89.66	-	-	-	-
Mean	91.48	15.79	21.69	89.66	91.47
TrimmedMean	91.47	91.45	85.46	91.29	91.35
Median	91.23	91.45	86.52	91.21	91.24
Geometric-median	91.35	91.45	86.31	89.66	91.35
Krum	90.13	91.45	90.12	90.11	90.48
Faba	91.47	91.45	91.46	91.46	91.36
Cc	91.45	91.43	24.67	91.08	91.45
Scc	91.49	91.48	24.78	91.29	91.47
The proposed	**91.82**	**91.77**	**91.73**	**91.78**	**91.74**

Table 7. Model accuracy, i.e., Ω (%), under NON-I.I.D. based on Erdos-Renyi node distribution

Method	No-attack	Gaussian	Sign-flipping	Isolation	Sample-duplicating
No-comm	9.87	-	-	-	-
Mean	91.43	17.00	36.99	9.87	**91.40**
TrimmedMean	91.31	90.03	70.60	53.93	87.00
Median	75.61	77.11	65.80	34.38	78.15
Geometric-median	87.28	87.99	9.75	9.87	87.96
Krum	19.44	19.91	19.91	19.91	29.87
Faba	91.37	91.35	91.35	91.29	88.16
Cc	91.32	91.26	55.47	78.02	91.30
Scc	91.47	91.35	44.20	85.99	91.39
The proposed	**91.64**	**91.60**	**91.62**	**91.61**	89.39

5 Conclusions and Future Work

To solve the problem of poisoning attacks in FL, this work proposes a method that combines FL with blockchain to improve the security and efficiency of model training. Firstly, it obtains the iterative blockchain validators for the blockchain consensus committee, thus quickly validating the local models trained by trainers and obtaining high-quality local models for model aggregation. It can effectively decrease malicious nodes, iteratively improve validation results, and reduce the communication overhead of FL. Then, a new federated learning method with an enhanced aggregation rule is proposed, which includes three aggregation functions, namely improved *IMedian*(), *ITrimmedMean*(), and *IFaba*(). By randomly selecting one of them, malicious nodes cannot target trainers' local models. The experimental results show that the proposed model has high effectiveness and superiority in defending against poisoning attacks, thereby improving model accuracy.

In the future, we plan to validate and evaluate the proposed model in various application scenarios, such as medical, financial, and educational fields, and analyze the performance and adaptability of the proposed model under different data features and requirements [37, 38]. More aggregation rules can be explored to compare their advantages and disadvantages in resisting poisoning attacks and improving model accuracy and design more improvements with flexible aggregation rules. In addition, it is necessary to study other potential roles of blockchains in FL, such as incentives, data sharing, and reputation evaluation, to improve user engagement and system efficiency.

Acknowledgment. This work is supported by the National Key R&D Program of China under grant 2021YFB2700900.

References

1. Cao, D., Chang, D., Lin, Z., Liu, Z., Sun, D.: Understanding distributed poisoning attack in federated learning. In: Proceedings of 2019 IEEE 25th International Conference on Parallel and Distributed Systems (ICPADS), pp. 233–239. Tianjin (2019)
2. Tao, G., Song, G., Junxiao, W., Xueyang, T., Wenchao, X.: PromptFL: Let federated participants cooperatively learn prompts instead of models – federated learning in age of foundation model. IEEE Trans. Mob. Comput. **23**(5), 5179–5194 (2024)
3. Rubinstein, B., et al.: ANTIDOTE: Understanding and defending against poisoning of anomaly detectors. In: Proceedings of the 9th ACM SIGCOMM Conference on Internet Measurement, pp. 1–14. Chicago, Illinois, USA
4. Li, Y., Chen, Y., Liu, Y., Huang, Y., Zheng, Y., Yan, Y.: A blockchain-based decentralized federated learning framework with committee consensus. IEEE Netw. **35**(1), 234–241 (2021)
5. Bakkiam, D.D., Seong, O.H.: Healthcare applications using blockchain with a cloud-assisted decentralized privacy-preserving framework. IEEE Trans. Mob. Comput. **23**(5), 5897–5916 (2024)
6. Kim, Y., Park, Y., Bennis, Y., Kim, Y.: Blockchained on-device federated learning. IEEE Commun. Lett. **24**(6), 1279–1283 (2020)
7. Ma, C., et al.: When federated learning meets blockchain: a new distributed learning paradigm. IEEE Comput. Intell. Mag. **17**(3), 26–37 (2022)
8. Feng, C., Liu, C., Yu, K., Goudos, K., Wan, S.: Blockchain-empowered decentralized horizontal federated learning for 5G-enabled UAVs. IEEE Trans. Industr. Inf. **18**(5), 3582–3592 (2022)
9. Rehman, M.H., Dirir, A., Salah, K., Damiani, E.: TrustFed: a framework for fair and trustworthy cross-device federated learning in IIoT. IEEE Trans. Industr. Inf. **17**(12), 8485–8494 (2021)
10. Mcmahan, H., Moore, H., Ramage, H., Hampson, S., Arcas, S.: Communication-efficient learning of deep networks from decentralized data. In: Proceedings of the 20th International Conference on Artificial Intelligence and Statistics, pp. 1273–1282. Lauderdale (2017)
11. Li, Z., et al.: Byzantine resistant secure blockchained federated learning at the edge. IEEE Netw. **35**(4), 295–301 (2021)

12. Yin, D., Chen, D., Ramchandran, K., Bartlett, P.: Byzantine-robust distributed learning: Towards optimal statistical rates. In: Proceedings of the 35th International Conference on Machine Learning (ICML), pp. 5650–5659. Stockholm (2018)
13. Shayan, M., Fung, C., Yoon, C., Beschastnikh, I.: Biscotti: a blockchain system for private and secure federated learning. IEEE Trans. Parallel Distrib. Syst. **32**(7), 1513–1526 (2021)
14. Blanchard, P., El Mhamdi, P., Guerraoui, P., Stainer, P.: Machine learning with adversaries: byzantine tolerant gradient descent. In: Proceedings of the 31st International Conference on Neural Information Processing Systems (NIPS), pp. 118–128. Morehouse Lane, Red Hook, NY, United States (2017)
15. Che, C., Li, X., Chen, C., He, X., Zheng, Z.: A decentralized federated learning framework via committee mechanism with convergence guarantee. IEEE Trans. Parallel Distrib. Syst. **33**(2), 4783–4800 (2022)
16. Zhang, Z., et al.: Refiner: a reliable incentive-driven federated learning system powered by blockchain. In: Proceedings of the Very Large Data Bases, pp. 2659–2662. Copenhagen (2021)
17. Liu, Y., Yu, W., Ai, Z., Xu, G., Li, J., Zhang, Y.: A blockchain-empowered federated learning in healthcare-based cyber physical systems. IEEE Trans. Netw. Sci. Eng. **10**(5), 2685–2696 (2023)
18. Li, B., Guo, Y., Du, Q., Zhu, Z., Li, J., Zhang, Y.: P^3: privacy-preserving prediction of real-time energy demands in EV charging networks. IEEE Trans. Industr. Inf. **19**(3), 3029–3038 (2023)
19. Liu, J., Dong, H., Xue, Y.: A secure and privacy-preserved delegate-based blockchain and federated learning for 6G networks. Int. J. Commun. Syst. e5367 (2022)
20. Peng, Z., et al.: VFChain: Enabling verifiable and auditable federated learning via blockchain systems. IEEE Trans. Netw. Sci. Eng. **9**(1), 173–186 (2022)
21. Zhang, Z., Wu, L., Ma, C., Li, J., Liu, X., Zhang, Y.: LSFL: a lightweight and secure federated learning scheme for edge computing. IEEE Trans. Inf. Forensics Secur. **18**, 365–379 (2022)
22. Wang, Y., Zhai, D.H., He, Y., Xia, Y.: An adaptive robust defending algorithm against backdoor attacks in federated learning. Futur. Gener. Comput. Syst. **143**, 118–131 (2023)
23. Pillutla, K., Kakade, S.M., Harchaoui, Z.: Robust aggregation for federated learning. IEEE Trans. Signal Process. **70**, 1142–1154 (2022)
24. Zhou, H., Zheng, Y., Zhou, X., Jia, X., Yan, Z.: Toward robust hierarchical federated learning in Internet of Vehicles. IEEE Trans. Intell. Transp. Syst. **24**(5), 5600–5614 (2023)
25. Chen, Y., Su, L., Xu, J.: Distributed statistical machine learning in adversarial settings: byzantine gradient descent. In: Proceedings of the ACM on Measurement and Analysis of Computing Systems, vol. 1, no. 2, pp. 1–25 (2017)
26. Zhang, H., Zeng, K., Lin, S.: Federated graph neural network for fast anomaly detection in controller area networks. IEEE Trans. Inf. Forensics Secur. **18**, 1566–1579 (2023)
27. El Mhamdi, El M., Guerraoui, R., Rouault, S.: The hidden vulnerability of distributed learning in Byzantium. In: Proceedings of the 35th International Conference on Machine Learning, pp. 3521–3530. Andreas (2018)
28. Xia, Q., Tao, Z., Li, Q., Chen, S.: Byzantine tolerant algorithms for federated learning. IEEE Trans. Netw. Sci. Eng. **10**(6), 3172–3183 (2023)
29. Qu, Z., et al.: Partial synchronization to accelerate federated learning over relay-assisted edge networks. IEEE Trans. Mob. Comput. **21**(12), 4502–4516 (2022)
30. Peng, J., Li, W., Ling, Q.: Byzantine-robust decentralized stochastic optimization over static and time-varying networks. Signal Process. **183**, 108020 (2021)
31. Fang, C., Yang, Z., Bajwa, W.: BRIDGE: byzantine-resilient decentralized gradient descent. IEEE Trans. Signal Inf. Process. Over Netw. **8**, 610–626 (2022)

32. Grave, E., Joulin, A., Cissé, M., Grangier, D., Jégou, H.: Efficient softmax approximation for GPUs. In: Proceedings of the 34th International Conference on Machine Learning, pp. 1302–1310. Sydney (2017)
33. LeCun, Y., Bottou, L., Bengio, Y., Haffner, P.: Gradient-based learning applied to document recognition. Proc. of the IEEE **86**(11), 2278–2324 (1998)
34. Li, Y., Jiang, Y., Li, Z., Xia, S.: Backdoor learning: a survey. IEEE Trans. Neural Netw. Learn. Syst. **35**(1), 5–22 (2024)
35. Qammar, A., Ding, J., Ning, H.: Federated learning attack surface: taxonomy, cyber defences, challenges, and future directions. Artif. Intell. Rev. **55**(5), 3569–3606 (2022)
36. Liu, P., Xu, X., Wang, W.: Threats, attacks and defenses to federated learning: Issues, taxonomy and perspectives. Cybersecurity, **5**(4) (2022)
37. Hassan, S., Khan, M., Khan, M., Hassan, S., Khan, S.: Integration of blockchain and federated learning for Internet of Things: recent advances and future challenges. Comput. Secur. **108**, 102355 (2021)
38. Lu, Y., Huang, X., Dai, Y., Maharjan, S., Zhang, Y.: Blockchain and federated learning for privacy-preserved data sharing in Industrial IoT. IEEE Trans. Industr. Inf. **16**(6), 4177–4186 (2020)

ThreatResponder: Dynamic Markov-Based Defense Mechanism for Real-Time Cyber Threats

Zhiling Zhu, Tieming Chen(✉), Qijie Song, Yiheng Lu, and Yulin Zheng

School of Computer Science and Technology, Zhejiang University of Technology, Hangzhou 310014, China
{zhilingzhu,tmchen,songqijie,luyiheng,iszhengyulin}@zjut.edu.cn

Abstract. The frequency and sophistication of cyber-attacks necessitate robust defense mechanisms to protect critical infrastructure and ensure system resilience. Existing static models often fail to capture the dynamic nature of these threats, leading to ineffective defense strategies. To address this, we propose ThreatResponder, a dynamic adjustment mechanism based on instantaneous state Markov processes. ThreatResponder precisely represents attack behaviors and defense strategies by leveraging real-time data to adjust the number of concurrent attacks the system can handle. Through continuous parameter updates, ThreatResponder predicts attack occurrences and defense effectiveness, enabling adaptive responses to evolving threats. Comprehensive simulation experiments validate ThreatResponder's ability to significantly reduce system shutdown probabilities and enhance operational efficiency. The results demonstrate that ThreatResponder accurately models the complex dynamics of cyber attacks and defenses, offering a robust framework for minimizing disruptions and maintaining system integrity. ThreatResponder enhances current defense mechanisms and offers valuable insights for future research in developing more advanced and effective cybersecurity strategies.

Keywords: Cyber Security · Markov Model · Intrusion Detection

1 Introduction

In the current digital landscape, the frequency and severity of cybersecurity attacks have reached unprecedented levels, necessitating the development of comprehensive and robust defense and recovery mechanisms. Cyber threats are increasingly sophisticated and varied, ranging from distributed denial-of-service (DDoS) attacks to advanced persistent threats (APTs) that can compromise the integrity of entire networks [1,2]. The rapid evolution of these threats has made it imperative for organizations and governments to implement effective strategies to protect critical infrastructure and ensure the resilience of digital systems. The

S. Goel et al. (Eds.): ICDF2C 2024, LNICST 614, pp. 71–89, 2025.
https://doi.org/10.1007/978-3-031-89360-5_5

complexity and unpredictability of these threats require advanced modeling and predictive techniques to anticipate and mitigate potential impacts efficiently.

Despite the pressing need, a significant gap exists in precisely modeling attack behaviors. Existing methods often rely on static or overly simplified models that fail to capture the dynamic and evolving nature of cyber attacks. For example, Malik et al. [3] applied a Markov Decision Process to enhance threat modeling and analysis, while Theodosiadou et al. [4] developed a real-time threat assessment model based on hidden Markov models. Le and Hoang [5] proposed a threat computation model using a Markov Chain and the common vulnerability scoring system for cloud security, and Al-Karaki et al. [6] conducted a probabilistic analysis of security attacks in cloud environments using hidden Markov models. Kalnoor and Gowrishankar [7] designed an intrusion detection system model using hidden Markov and variational Bayesian models for IoT-based wireless sensor networks. While these works provide valuable insights, they often lack the capability to dynamically adjust to the real-time changes in the threat landscape, leading to suboptimal defense strategies that are not adaptable to evolving threats.

To address this gap, we propose a model based on instantaneous state Markov processes, named ThreatResponder, which provides a detailed and accurate representation of attack behaviors and defense strategies. The Markov process framework is particularly well-suited for this application due to its ability to model complex stochastic systems with states that change over time. By leveraging parameter estimation techniques, ThreatResponder can predict both the occurrence of attacks and the effectiveness of various defense mechanisms. This approach allows for dynamic adjustments to defense strategies based on real-time data, ensuring that systems remain resilient against a wide range of cyber threats. The use of instantaneous state Markov models offers several advantages, including the ability to handle the probabilistic nature of attack occurrences and the flexibility to update predictions as new information becomes available.

Our experimental results demonstrate that ThreatResponder accurately captures the intricate dynamics of both attacks and defenses. The model's ability to reduce system shutdown probabilities significantly enhances the overall resilience and operational efficiency of digital systems. Through rigorous simulations, we validate that our approach not only improves the precision of attack and defense predictions but also offers a robust framework for minimizing disruptions and maintaining system integrity. The instantaneous state Markov model's capacity to provide real-time, adaptive responses to evolving threats makes it a powerful tool for enhancing cybersecurity defenses in an increasingly hostile digital environment.

In summary, the main contributions of this paper are listed as follows:

- We proposed ThreatResponder, a dynamic adjustment mechanism based on instantaneous state Markov processes, which provides a detailed and accurate representation of cyber attack behaviors and defense strategies.

- We validated the effectiveness of the proposed mechanism through comprehensive simulation experiments, demonstrating its ability to reduce system shutdown probabilities and enhance overall operational efficiency.
- We open-sourced our data and analysis scripts, which can benefit future research.

Paper Organization: The rest of the paper is organized as follows. Section 2 introduces the background and terminology used in this paper. Section 3 introduces the threat model and Sec. 4 describes the design detail of ThreatResponder. Then, Sec. 5 reports the experiments driven by three research questions. Section 6 discusses the threats of validity. Finally, Sec. 7 concludes the paper.

2 Background

2.1 Markov Model

Markov Models are mathematical models used to describe systems that transition from one state to another in a stochastic (or random) manner, where the probability of transitioning to a future state depends only on the current state and not on the sequence of events that preceded it. This characteristic is known as the Markov property, which asserts a memoryless behavior in the stochastic process. The models are particularly valuable for modeling and analyzing a wide array of real-world processes that exhibit random state changes.

Markov Chain models [8] are used to study systems that exhibit random transitions from one state to another, with the future state depending only on the current state and not on the sequence of events that led to it. The general steps in employing a Markov Chain model begin with defining the states of the system, which encapsulates all possible conditions or configurations that the system can assume. Following this, one determines the transition probabilities between the states, often represented in a transition matrix P, where each entry p_{ij} denotes the probability of moving from state i to state j. These probabilities are typically derived from historical data or experimental observations. Next, the initial state distribution is established, which indicates the likelihood of the system starting in each state. This setup allows for the analysis of state transitions over time, enabling predictions about future states and their steady-state probabilities where the system's behavior becomes stable over time.

Markov Chains are particularly strong in applications where the system dynamics are inherently stochastic and where state transitions do not depend on the path taken to reach the current state [9]. These models are extensively used in areas such as finance to model credit rating transitions, in queueing theory for service systems like call centers or hospitals, and in biology for understanding genetic drift or disease progression. In the realm of computer science, they serve algorithms in randomized processes and to model user behavior in web navigation. The strength of Markov Chains lies in their simplicity and the robust theoretical framework they provide, which allows for the analysis of complex stochastic processes using relatively straightforward mathematical tools. Their ability to predict long-term behavior from short-term dynamics is invaluable, making them an essential tool in both theoretical research and practical applications across a multitude of disciplines.

Markov models have been widely applied in various aspects of cybersecurity, from intrusion detection to risk assessment and mitigation [10,11]. These models help in understanding the probabilistic behavior of attackers and the impact of different defense strategies. For example, Markov Decision Processes (MDPs) extend the basic Markov model to include decision-making capabilities, allowing security analysts to evaluate the effectiveness of different actions under uncertainty. By modeling the system's state transitions and the potential outcomes of different defense strategies, Markov models provide a powerful tool for enhancing cybersecurity resilience.

2.2 Markov Models in Cybersecurity

Markov Models are widely used in cybersecurity to model and analyze various threats and defense strategies. For instance, Malik et al. [3] applied a Markov Decision Process to enhance threat modeling and analysis. Theodosiadou et al. [4] developed a real-time threat assessment model based on hidden Markov models. Le and Hoang [5] proposed a threat computation model using a Markov Chain and the common vulnerability scoring system for cloud security. Al-Karaki et al. [6] conducted a probabilistic analysis of security attacks in cloud environments using hidden Markov models. Kalnoor and Gowrishankar [7] designed an intrusion detection system model using hidden Markov and variational Bayesian models for IoT-based wireless sensor networks.

While these works provide a foundation for understanding and mitigating cyber threats, our approach, ThreatResponder, differentiates itself by focusing on the dynamic adjustment mechanism based on instantaneous state Markov processes. This allows for real-time adaptability to evolving threats, a feature that is critical in handling sophisticated attacks such as Advanced Persistent Threats (APTs) and Distributed Denial-of-Service (DDoS) attacks.

2.3 Existing Defense Strategies

Traditional defense strategies in cybersecurity, such as firewalls, intrusion detection systems (IDS), and static configuration policies, have been foundational in network security. Firewalls control incoming and outgoing network traffic based on predetermined security rules, blocking unauthorized access while permitting legitimate communication. Despite their essential role, firewalls can be limited by their static nature, making them less effective against sophisticated and evolving attack techniques that bypass predefined rules.

Intrusion Detection Systems (IDS) monitor network traffic for suspicious activities and potential threats [12]. They can be categorized into network-based IDS (NIDS) and host-based IDS (HIDS). NIDS monitor traffic across the network, while HIDS are installed on individual devices to monitor system-level activities. IDS detect known attack patterns through signature-based detection or identify unusual behavior through anomaly-based detection. However, IDS can face challenges such as high false-positive rates and difficulty detecting new, unknown threats without updated signatures [13].

These traditional strategies often fall short when facing advanced persistent threats (APTs), which are sophisticated, targeted attacks designed to infiltrate and remain undetected within a network for extended periods [14]. APTs use a combination of techniques, including zero-day exploits and lateral movement within the network, making them difficult to detect with static defenses [15].

In response to these limitations, there is a growing emphasis on developing dynamic and adaptive defense strategies. These strategies aim to provide real-time protection by continuously monitoring and analyzing network traffic, adapting to new threats as they emerge, and proactively mitigating potential risks. Techniques such as machine learning and artificial intelligence are increasingly integrated into cybersecurity solutions to enhance their adaptability and responsiveness. These advanced techniques enable systems to learn from past incidents, identify emerging patterns, and predict potential threats, offering a more robust and resilient defense framework.

While traditional defense strategies remain essential, their limitations highlight the need for flexible, adaptive, and proactive defense mechanisms that can respond to evolving threats in real-time. This need forms the basis for exploring and developing innovative solutions, such as the dynamic adjustment mechanism proposed in this study, which leverages advanced modeling techniques and real-time data analysis to enhance system resilience and operational security.

3 Threat Model

We consider a threat model in which an attacker initiates cyber attacks on a host at a rate λ, modeled as a Poisson process [16]. This attack arrival rate represents the frequency of malicious attempts, such as Distributed Denial-of-Service (DDoS) attacks, aimed at overwhelming the system with traffic. Attackers are assumed to have the capability to launch high-frequency attacks, targeting specific vulnerabilities within the system.

When a host experiences an intrusion, it undergoes a non-stop repair process without shutting down, analogous to real-time mitigation efforts like traffic filtering and rate limiting. The duration of this repair process is uncertain and is modeled as a random variable with a probability density function $g(x)$, reflecting the variability in response times.

If the host encounters M consecutive attacks during a single non-stop repair period, it switches to a shutdown repair mode. This scenario models a coordinated Advanced Persistent Threat (APT) attack, where multiple intrusion attempts are detected within a short time frame. During shutdown repair, the host is immune to further attacks, but the operational efficiency of the system is significantly compromised. This state represents intensive offline remediation efforts, such as forensic analysis and comprehensive patching. Consecutive attacks refer to multiple successful attempts that occur within a specified time frame, which could indicate a coordinated effort to breach the system.

4 The Proposed ThreatResponder

4.1 Overview

ThreatResponder models the problem based on the instantaneous Markov process. First, the state and state transition diagram are defined, and then the differential equations under each state are extracted. After obtaining the differential equations, the Laplace transform is used to solve these equations. Finally, the known conditions are substituted to derive the shutdown probability model. To enhance accuracy and responsiveness, real-time estimates of the attack arrival rate (λ) and repair time distribution ($g(x)$) are continuously integrated, allowing ThreatResponder to dynamically adjust the maximum number of simultaneous attacks (M) the system can handle.

4.2 Definition of States and Symbols

States Definition

- **State** A_i: Indicates that an intrusion attack is currently being processed, and there are still i intrusion attacks to be processed.
- **State** I: Indicates that there is no intrusion attack and the system is operating normally.
- **State** S: Indicates that the system has been shut down for repair because the unprocessed intrusion attacks have exceeded the upper limit.

State Transition Diagram. Based on the defined states, the state transition diagram is shown as Fig. 1.

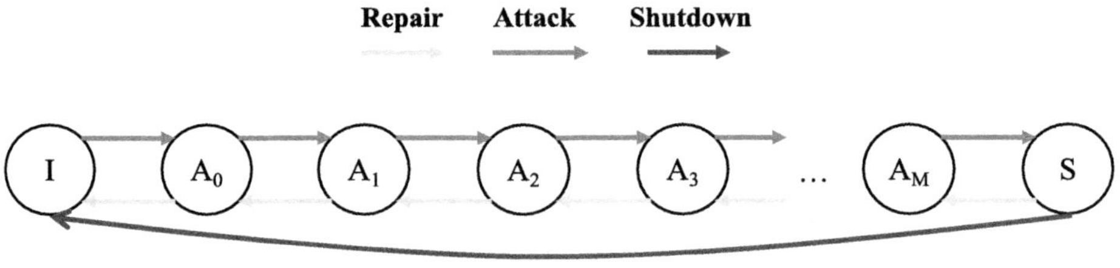

Fig. 1. The state transition diagram of ThreatResponder.

Definition of Symbols. First, we define the probability for each state:

- $P_I(t)$: The probability that the system is in the state I at time t.
- $P_j(t)$: The probability that the system is in the state A_j at time t.
- $P_S(t)$: The probability that the system is in the state S at time t.
- M: This number indicates the number of attacks that the system can allow to be repaired at the same time. If the number exceeds this, the system will enter the shutdown repair mode.

Since the instantaneous Markov process considers the state at the next instant, in order to characterize whether the intrusion attack is completed, we introduce the hazard function to characterize this probability.

The hazard function, also known as the failure rate or hazard rate, is a concept commonly used in survival analysis and reliability engineering [17]. This function describes the conditional probability of failure in a very short time interval, given that the individual has not yet failed up to a specific time. Specifically, if a random variable T, such as survival time or the operating time of a device, the hazard function $h(t)$ is defined as:

$$h(t) = \lim_{\Delta t \to 0} \frac{P(t \leq T < t + \Delta t \mid T \geq t)}{\Delta t} \tag{1}$$

which $P(t \leq T < t + \Delta t \mid T \geq t)$ represents the probability that failure occurs in the next short interval Δt, given that T has lasted at least until time t. The hazard function also relates to the survival function $S(t)$ and the probability density function $f(t)$ through the following formula:

$$h(t) = \frac{f(t)}{S(t)} \tag{2}$$

where $f(t)$ is the probability density function of the failure time, and $S(t)$ is the survival function, representing the probability of survival until at least time t. Therefore, we define the probability of completing the intrusion attack at time t as:

$$\sigma(t) = \frac{g(x)}{1 - G(x)} \tag{3}$$

which $G(t)$ represents the cumulative distribution function.

In addition, we also define the instantaneous probability of being in different states in an instant as $p_j(t,x)dx$, in which j and t represent the system at state A_j at time t. We use $X(t)$ to represent the deadline t, the processing time consumed on the current attack, which satisfies $x < X(t) < x + dx$.

4.3 Building Differential Equations

For each state of the instantaneous Markov process, we analyzed the possible situations of each state and calculated the steady-state probability and transition probability respectively.

Normal State. The system is working normally at time $t + \Delta t$, including three different situations:

- The system is operating normally at time t and has not been attacked within time Δt.
- At time t, the system is in state A_0 and is processing an attack with a cumulative duration of x. The system is repaired within time Δt and has not been attacked within time Δt.
- At time t, the system is in state S and is processing an attack with a cumulative duration of x. The system is repaired within time Δt.

Therefore, the probability that the system is in the normal working state at time t is the sum of the probabilities of the above three situations:

$$\begin{aligned} P_I(t + \Delta t) =& P_I(t) \cdot (1 - \lambda \Delta t) \\ &+ \int_0^\infty p_0(t,x)[\sigma(x) \cdot t](1 - \lambda \Delta t + \sigma(\Delta t))\, dx \\ &+ P_S(t) \cdot [\sigma(x)\Delta t] \end{aligned} \tag{4}$$

Simplifying the above equation, we get the first differential equation:

$$\frac{d}{dt}P_I(t) + \lambda P_I(t) - P_S(t)\sigma(x) = \int_0^\infty p_0(t,x)\sigma(x)\, dx \tag{5}$$

State A_0. The system is in the state A_0 at the time $t + \Delta t$ while the cumulative processing time of the current attack is $x + \Delta t$. This situation can be equivalent to that at time t, the system is in state A_0, the cumulative processing time is x, and there is no attack within time Δt, and the attack being repaired is still being repaired. Therefore, this equivalence can be expressed as:

$$p_0(t + \Delta t, x + \Delta t)dx = p_0(t,x)dx \cdot (1 - \lambda \Delta t) \cdot [1 - \sigma(x)\Delta t] \tag{6}$$

Simplifying the above equation, we get the second differential equation:

$$\frac{\partial p_0(t,x)}{\partial t} + \frac{\partial p_0(t,x)}{\partial x} + [\lambda + \sigma(x)] \cdot p_0(t,x) = 0 \tag{7}$$

State A_j. The system is in the state A_j at the time $t + \Delta t$ while the cumulative processing time of the current attack is $x + \Delta t$. This situation can be equivalent to that at time t, the system is in state A_j, the cumulative processing time is x, and there is no attack within time Δt, and the attack being repaired is still being repaired. Similar to Eq. (7), the differential equation can be obtained as:

$$\frac{\partial p_j(t,x)}{\partial t} + \frac{\partial p_j(t,x)}{\partial x} + [\lambda + \sigma(x)] \cdot p_j(t,x) = 0 \tag{8}$$

State A_0 within time Δt. In a very short time interval Δt, the system is in state A_0, and there are three situations:

- The system is in the state A_0 at the time $t + \Delta t$. The cumulative processing time of the current attack is s, which satisfies $s \leq \Delta t$.
- The system is in state A_1 at time t, and the cumulative processing time is x. The system has not been attacked within time Δt, and the attack being processed has been processed.
- At time t, the system is in state I and is attacked once within time Δt.

According to the above situation, it can be abstracted into the following equation:

$$p_0(t, t+\Delta t, s)dx = \int_0^{\infty} (1-\lambda\Delta t) \cdot [\sigma(x)\Delta t] \cdot p_1(t,x)\, dx + P_I(t) \cdot \lambda\Delta t \tag{9}$$

Simplifying the above equation, we get the fourth differential equation:

$$p_0(t, 0) = \int_0^{\infty} \sigma(x) \cdot p_1(t,x) + \lambda P_I(t) \tag{10}$$

State A_j within time Δt. The system is in the state A_j at the time $t + \Delta t$. The cumulative processing time of the current attack is s, which satisfies $s \leq \Delta t$. Also, another situation is that the system is in state A_{j+1} at time t, and the cumulative processing time is x. The system has not been attacked within time Δt, and the attack being processed has been processed. Therefore, it can be abstracted into the following equation:

$$p_j(t+\Delta t, s)dx = \int_0^{\infty} p_{j+1}(t,x) \cdot (1-\lambda\Delta t) \cdot \sigma(x)\Delta t\, dx \tag{11}$$

When Δt approaches 0, s approaches 0. Therefore, the fifth differential equation is:

$$p_j(t, 0) = \int_0^{\infty} p_{j+1}(t,x) \cdot \sigma(x)\, dx \tag{12}$$

State S. The system is in the state S at the time $t + \Delta t$. This state is that at time t, the system is in the A_M state, and the cumulative attack processing time is x. At the same time, the system is attacked once within time Δt, and the attack being processed has not been repaired. This can be represented as:

$$P_S(t+\Delta t) = \int_0^{\infty} p_M(t,x) \cdot [1 - \sigma(x)\Delta t]\, dx \tag{13}$$

When Δt approaches 0, this equation can be simplified as:

$$P_S(t) = \int_0^{\infty} p_M(t,x)dx \tag{14}$$

4.4 Solving Equations Based on Laplace Transform

The Laplace transform is a widely used integral transform in mathematics and engineering, defined by the formula [18]:

$$\mathcal{L}\{f(t)\} = F(s) = \int_0^{\infty} e^{-st} f(t)\, dt, \tag{15}$$

where $f(t)$ is a time-domain function, $t \geq 0$, and s is a complex variable $s = \sigma + i\omega$. This transform is particularly effective for analyzing linear systems and solving differential equations. It converts differential equations in the time domain into simpler algebraic equations in the s-domain:

$$\lim_{t \to \infty} f(t) = \lim_{s \to 0} sF(s) \tag{16}$$

Substituting the initial conditions, when time is 0, the system is in state I, which can be represented as:

$$P_I(0) = 1, p_j(0, x) = 0, P_S(0) = 0 \tag{17}$$

Based on Laplace transform, the above differential equations(i.e.,Equation (5), (7), (8), (10), (12), (14)) can be transformed into the following equations:

$$\begin{cases} (s+\lambda)P_I^*(s) - 1 - P_S^*(s)\sigma(x) = \int_0^{\infty} p_0^*(s,x) \cdot \sigma(x)\, dx \\ \dfrac{dp_j^*(s,x)}{dx} + [\lambda + s + \sigma(x)] \cdot p_j^*(s,x) = 0 \\ p_0^*(s,0) = \int_0^{\infty} \sigma(x) \cdot p_1^*(s,x)\, dx + \lambda P_I^*(s) \\ p_j^*(s,0) = \int_0^{\infty} \sigma(x) \cdot p_{j+1}^*(s,x)\, dx \\ P_S^*(s) = \int_0^{\infty} p_M^*(s,x)\, dx \\ P_I + \sum_{j=0}^{M} P_j + P_S = 1 \end{cases} \tag{18}$$

which $f^*(x)$ represents the Laplace transformed function of $f(x)$.

Solving the above equations, we can calculate the shutdown probability P_s, which is related to the attack rate λ, the maximum supported number of attacks M, and the processing time distribution $g(x)$. Since the attack processing time distribution $g(x)$ and attack occurrence rate λ cannot be controlled, we can adjust the shutdown probability by controlling M so that the shutdown probability is less than a certain threshold, which balances the trade-off of shutdown and repairing overhead.

4.5 Dynamic Adjustment Strategy

To maintain optimal system resilience in the face of cyber attacks, we implement a dynamic adjustment strategy based on real-time data collection and periodic distribution estimation. This process begins with the continuous monitoring and recording of attack events and repair processes. Using monitoring tools, we collect the timestamps of each attack and the start and end times of each repair. These data are securely stored for subsequent analysis.

The attack arrival rate, denoted as λ, is estimated periodically, such as daily or weekly, based on the collected data. Assuming that attack arrivals follow a Poisson process, we use maximum likelihood estimation (MLE) to calculate λ. The MLE for the arrival rate is given by

$$\hat{\lambda} = \frac{N}{T} \tag{19}$$

where N is the total number of attacks observed during the period T. For more robust estimation, Bayesian methods can be applied. By selecting a suitable prior distribution, such as the Gamma distribution, and updating it with observed data, we obtain the posterior distribution of λ. The Bayesian estimate can be taken as the mean or median of the posterior distribution.

Similarly, the repair time distribution is periodically estimated using the collected repair duration data. Kernel density estimation (KDE) is employed to estimate the probability density function $g(x)$ of repair times, providing a smoothed, continuous estimate based on observed data. Alternatively, repair times can be fitted to known probability distributions, such as exponential or normal distributions, using MLE to estimate the distribution parameters.

With updated estimates of λ and $g(x)$, we calculate the shutdown probability

$$P_{\text{shutdown}} = f(\lambda, g(x), M) \tag{20}$$

by substituting these values into the derived formula. Numerical methods or simulations are used to compute P_{shutdown} for different values of M. To ensure the system operates within an acceptable shutdown probability threshold θ, we start with $M = 1$ and incrementally increase M, calculating the corresponding shutdown probability for each value. The minimum M that ensures

$$P_{\text{shutdown}} < \theta \tag{21}$$

which is identified and applied to the system.

This dynamic adjustment strategy, involving real-time monitoring, periodic distribution estimation, and optimization of the parameter M, helps maintain system resilience by minimizing the probability of shutdowns and ensuring operational efficiency. The effectiveness of this strategy is regularly evaluated by comparing shutdown frequency and system stability metrics through real-world applications and simulations.

5 Evaluation

5.1 Research Questions

To evaluate the performance of ThreatResponder, we try to answer the following research questions (RQs):

- **RQ1: Parameter Estimation.** How accurately does the dynamic adjustment strategy estimate the attack arrival rate (λ) and repair time distribution $g(x)$?
- **RQ2: Shutdown Probability.** How effective is the dynamic adjustment strategy in minimizing the system shutdown probability?
- **RQ3: Efficiency Trade-offs.** What are the trade-offs between minimizing shutdown probability and maintaining operational efficiency?

5.2 Experiment Environments

The running environment of all experiments is Ubuntu 22.04, and the kernel version is Linux Kernel 5.15.0-91-generic. The CPU is Intel(R) Core(TM) i9-9900K @ 3.60GHz (8 cores/16 threads), the memory is 32GB, and the storage is 1TB SSD.

5.3 RQ1: Parameter Estimation

To evaluate the accuracy of the dynamic adjustment strategy in estimating the attack arrival rate (λ) and repair time distribution ($g(x)$), we designed a simulation experiment. In this experiment, we generated synthetic data with known parameters for attack arrival and repair times. The attack arrival rate λ was set to 5, meaning that, on average, five attacks occur per unit time. Attack events were modeled using a Poisson process, which is suitable for representing the random nature of attack occurrences. The repair times followed an exponential distribution with a mean of 1 unit of time, reflecting the typical scenario where shorter repair times are more likely, but longer repair times are possible.

We used Maximum Likelihood Estimation (MLE) and Bayesian Estimation to estimate the attack arrival rate λ. We employed Kernel Density Estimation (KDE) for repair time distribution and fitted an exponential distribution to the observed repair times. The KDE method provides a non-parametric way to estimate the probability density function of repair times while fitting an exponential distribution offers a parametric approach for comparison.

The results of the simulation and estimation are illustrated in the Fig. 2. The histogram of the repair times, overlaid with the KDE estimate and the exponential fit, shows how well each method approximates the true repair time distribution. The KDE method produced a smooth density function closely matching the empirical data, while the exponential fit provided a reasonable approximation but with some deviations.

For the attack arrival rate λ, the MLE estimated approximately 4.98, very close to the true value of 5, with a negligible absolute error of 0.018. The Bayesian

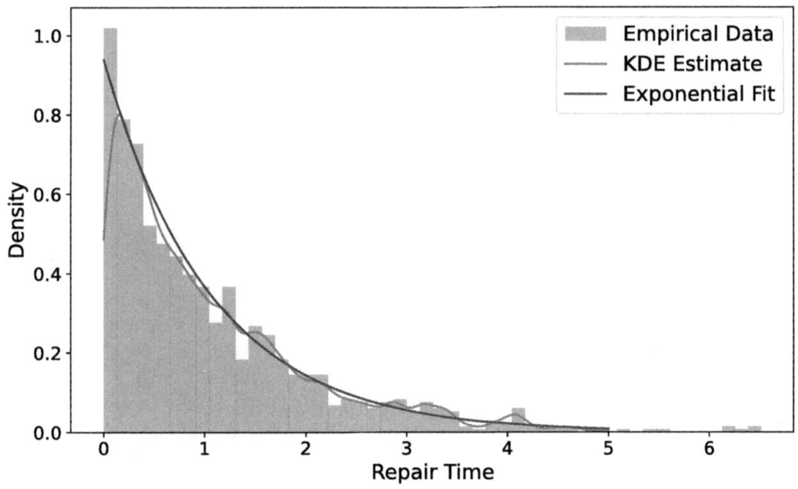

Fig. 2. The evaluation of the estimates parameters.

Estimation, using a Gamma prior, yielded an estimate of around 4.96, with a slightly higher absolute error of 0.037. These results indicate high accuracy in the estimation methods used.

For the repair time distribution, the true mean repair time was 1 unit. The estimated mean repair time using the exponential fit was approximately 1.07, resulting in an absolute error of 0.066. While the KDE provided a highly accurate estimate of the repair time distribution, the parametric exponential fit showed a minor deviation from the true mean.

Answer to RQ1: The dynamic adjustment strategy demonstrated high accuracy in estimating both the attack arrival rate and the repair time distribution in our simulation experiment. The MLE and Bayesian Estimation methods effectively approximated the true attack arrival rate with minimal error. Similarly, the KDE method provided a highly accurate estimate of the repair time distribution, closely matching the empirical data.

5.4 RQ2: Shutdown Probability

To evaluate the effectiveness of the dynamic adjustment strategy in minimizing the system shutdown probability, we designed a series of simulation experiments with varying attack arrival rates (λ). The simulations tested three different values of λ (3, 5, 7) to represent varying intensities of attack scenarios. Repair times were modeled using an exponential distribution with a mean of 1 unit of time, reflecting typical repair durations where shorter times are more likely but longer times are possible. The system enters a shutdown state if the number of simultaneous attacks exceeds M. For the dynamic strategy, M was periodically adjusted based on real-time estimates of λ and the repair time distribution $g(x)$, aiming to keep the shutdown probability below a preset threshold ($\theta = 0.05$). For comparison, a fixed value of $M = 5$ was used throughout the simulation for the static strategy.

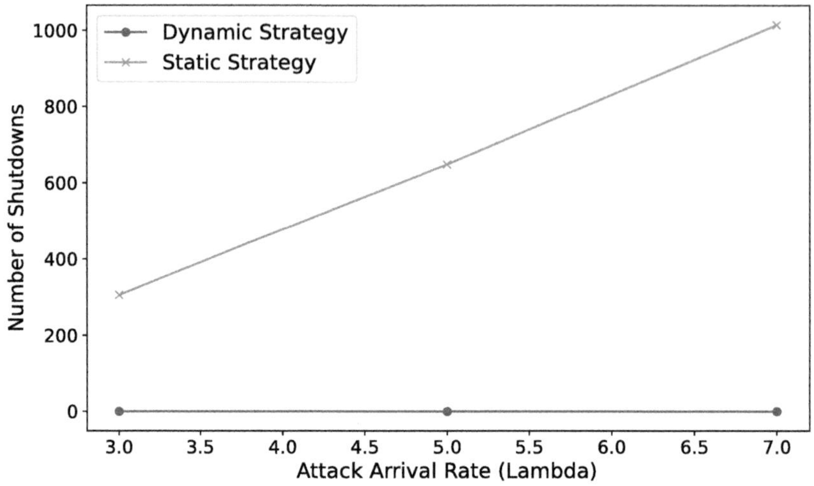

Fig. 3. The evaluation of the shutdown rate.

As shown in Fig. 3, the results of the simulations showed a stark contrast between the dynamic and static strategies across all tested values of λ. Specifically, the dynamic adjustment strategy resulted in zero shutdowns for $\lambda = 3$, 5, and 7, with the corresponding dynamically adjusted values of M being 60, 100, and 140, respectively. In contrast, the static strategy, with a fixed $M = 5$, resulted in a significant number of shutdowns: 306 for $\lambda = 3$, 649 for $\lambda = 5$, and 1015 for $\lambda = 7$. These results highlight the effectiveness of the dynamic adjustment strategy. By periodically adjusting M based on current estimates of attack arrival rates and repair time distributions, the dynamic strategy effectively minimized the probability of shutdowns, maintaining system stability even under high attack intensities. Conversely, the static strategy failed to adapt to varying conditions, leading to frequent shutdowns as the attack rate increased.

Answer to RQ2: The dynamic adjustment strategy demonstrated superior effectiveness in minimizing system shutdown probability compared to the static strategy. The dynamic strategy's ability to adaptively adjust the maximum number of simultaneous attacks (M) in response to real-time estimates of attack arrival rates and repair time distributions allowed it to maintain the shutdown probability below the preset threshold, resulting in no shutdowns during the simulation.

5.5 RQ3: Memory Consumption

To evaluate the trade-offs between minimizing shutdown probability and maintaining operational efficiency, we conducted a series of simulation experiments with varying attack arrival rates (λ) and shutdown probability thresholds (θ). The simulation parameters were defined as follows: the attack arrival rates (λ) were set to 3, 5, and 7 to represent different intensities of attack scenarios. The repair times were modeled using an exponential distribution with a mean of 1 unit of time. The system enters a shutdown state if the number of simultaneous attacks exceeds the dynamic threshold M. The dynamic threshold M was adjusted based on real-time estimates of λ and the repair time distribution $g(x)$ to maintain the shutdown probability below the preset threshold θ. The θ values were set to 0.02, 0.04, 0.06, 0.08, and 0.1. In this study, M was used to approximate system resource usage, as the number of simultaneous attacks that the system can handle directly impacts resource consumption.

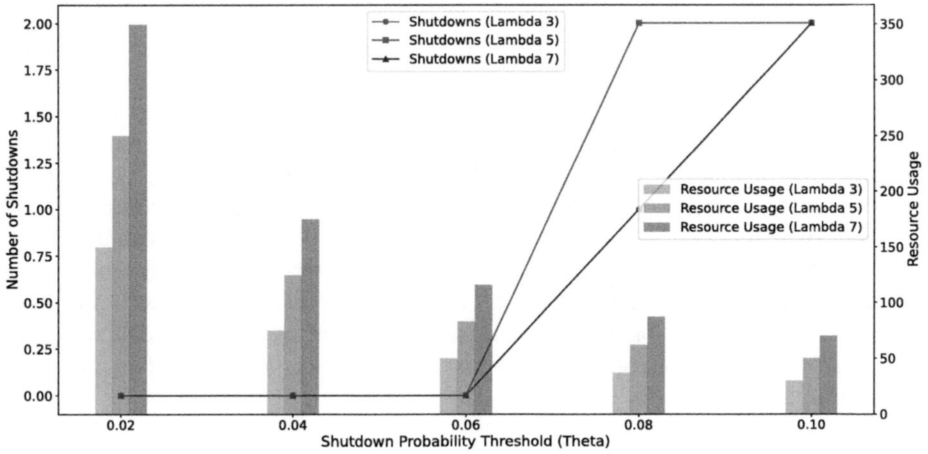

Fig. 4. The evaluation of the shutdown rate and the system overhead.

As shown in Fig. 4, the experimental results reveal the intrinsic trade-offs between system stability and resource efficiency in the context of dynamic attack management. As the shutdown probability threshold (θ) increased, the system's capacity to handle concurrent attacks (denoted by M) also increased, which in turn influenced both resource usage and the frequency of shutdowns.

For $\lambda = 3$, a lower θ (e.g., 0.02) resulted in a higher M (150), enabling the system to handle a large number of concurrent attacks without shutdowns, but at the cost of higher resource consumption. As θ increased to 0.04 and 0.06, the value of M decreased proportionally (to 75 and 50, respectively), maintaining system stability without shutdowns while reducing resource usage. However, further increasing θ to 0.08 and 0.1 reduced M to 37 and 30, respectively, which led to a higher likelihood of system shutdowns (1 and 2 shutdowns, respectively) despite lower resource usage.

Similar patterns were observed for $\lambda = 5$ and $\lambda = 7$. At lower θ values (e.g., 0.02), the system's M values were higher (250 for $\lambda = 5$ and 350 for $\lambda = 7$), allowing the system to manage high attack rates without shutdowns but with significant resource consumption. As θ increased to moderate levels (0.04 and 0.06), the M values decreased (to 125 and 83 for $\lambda = 5$, and to 175 and 116 for $\lambda = 7$), achieving a balance between resource usage and system stability. At higher θ values (0.08 and 0.1), the system's M values dropped further (to 62 and 50 for $\lambda = 5$, and to 87 and 70 for $\lambda = 7$), leading to an increase in the frequency of shutdowns, albeit with reduced resource usage.

These results indicate that the dynamic adjustment of M based on real-time estimates of λ and $g(x)$ can effectively balance the trade-offs between minimizing shutdown probability and maintaining operational efficiency. Lower θ values ensure higher system stability at the expense of greater resource consumption, while higher θ values reduce resource usage but increase the risk of system shutdowns.

Answer to RQ3: The experimental findings demonstrate a clear trade-off between minimizing system shutdown probability and maintaining operational efficiency. As the shutdown probability threshold (θ) increases, the system can handle more concurrent attacks, leading to lower resource usage but higher risk of shutdowns. At lower values of θ (e.g., 0.02 and 0.04), the system remains stable with no shutdowns, albeit at the cost of higher resource usage. Conversely, higher θ values (e.g., 0.08 and 0.1) allow for reduced resource consumption but increase the likelihood of shutdowns, especially at higher attack arrival rates. This study highlights the necessity for dynamic adjustment strategies that balance system resilience and operational efficiency by carefully selecting appropriate θ values based on specific system demands and attack intensities.

6 Threats of Validity

6.1 Internal Validity

The primary concern for internal validity in our study is the accuracy and reliability of the simulation model. The assumptions, such as the exponential distribution of repair times and the Poisson process for attack arrivals, might not fully capture the complexity of real-world scenarios. These simplifications can introduce biases that affect the internal consistency of the results. To mitigate this threat, we used historical data from actual cybersecurity incidents to estimate parameters, ensuring that our model is grounded in real-world observations.

Another potential threat is the precision of the real-time estimates of attack rates and repair time distributions. Any inaccuracies or delays in these estimations could lead to suboptimal adjustments, thereby impacting the overall performance of the mechanism. To address this, we employed both Maximum Likelihood Estimation (MLE) and Bayesian methods to enhance the robustness of our parameter estimates. Additionally, we conducted sensitivity analyses to understand how variations in parameter estimates affect the outcomes.

Moreover, the effectiveness of the dynamic adjustment mechanism heavily relies on the timely and accurate detection of ongoing attacks. Our model assumes that attacks are detected and responded to in real-time, which may not always be feasible in practice due to detection latency or evasion techniques used by attackers. We suggest further research into integrating advanced detection mechanisms, such as machine learning-based anomaly detection, to improve the detection accuracy and timeliness.

6.2 External Validity

The external validity of our study concerns the generalizability of the results to real-world systems. Our simulation experiments were conducted in a controlled environment with specific parameters and assumptions, which may not fully represent the diversity and complexity of actual cyber environments. Different systems might exhibit varied responses to the same adjustment mechanism due to differences in architecture, resource availability, and operational constraints.

To address these concerns, we validated the dynamic adjustment mechanism using historical data from diverse real-world cybersecurity incidents. However, the applicability of our findings across different types of systems, such as cloud services, IoT devices, and enterprise networks, remains an open question. Future work should focus on validating ThreatResponder in various real-world environments and under different attack scenarios to ensure its robustness and adaptability across different contexts.

Additionally, our model does not currently account for potential evasion mechanisms that attackers might employ to avoid detection and mitigation efforts. For instance, advanced persistent threats (APTs) often use stealthy techniques to remain undetected for extended periods. Integrating methods to counter such evasion strategies, including behavioral analysis and deception technologies, could further enhance the robustness of our approach.

7 Conclusion

This paper introduces ThreatResponder, a dynamic adjustment mechanism based on instantaneous state Markov processes, to address the growing challenge of cyber attacks. Unlike static models, ThreatResponder offers a precise and adaptive representation of the interactions between attack behaviors and defense strategies. By leveraging real-time data, ThreatResponder dynamically adjusts the system's capacity to handle concurrent attacks, significantly reducing shutdown probabilities and enhancing operational efficiency. Comprehensive simulations validate the effectiveness of ThreatResponder across various attack scenarios, demonstrating its robustness and adaptability. The model's ability to provide real-time, adaptive responses to evolving threats makes it a valuable tool for enhancing cybersecurity defenses and underscores the need for flexible and robust strategies in protecting digital infrastructure. Our findings highlight ThreatResponder's potential to improve existing defense mechanisms and encourage further research through the provided open-sourced data and analysis scripts.

Acknowledgements. This work is supported by the following projects: National Natural Science Foundation of China under Grant No. 62002324, U22B2028, and U1936215. Science and Technology Projects of Zhejiang Province - High-Level Talents Special Support Program under Grant No. 2020R52011.

References

1. Osanaiye, O., Choo, K., Dlodlo, M.: Distributed denial of service (DDoS) resilience in cloud: review and conceptual cloud DDoS mitigation framework. J. Netw. Comput. Appl. **67**, 147–165 (2016)
2. Alshamrani, A., Myneni, S., Chowdhary, A., et al.: A survey on advanced persistent threats: Techniques, solutions, challenges, and research opportunities. IEEE Commun. Surv. Tutorials **21**(2), 1851–1877 (2019)
3. Malik, S.U., Anjum, A., Moqurrab, S.A., Srivastava, G.: Towards enhanced threat modelling and analysis using a markov decision process. Comput. Commun. **1**(194), 282–91 (2022)
4. Theodosiadou, O., Chatzakou, D., Tsikrika, T., Vrochidis, S., Kompatsiaris, I.: Real-time threat assessment based on hidden Markov models. Risk Anal. **43**(10), 2069–81 (2023)
5. Le, N.T., Hoang, D.B.: A threat computation model using a markov chain and common vulnerability scoring system and its application to cloud security. J. Telecommun. Digit. Econ. **7**(1), 37–56 (2019)
6. Al-Karaki, J.N., Gawanmeh, A., Almalkawi, I.T., Alfandi, O.: Probabilistic analysis of security attacks in cloud environment using hidden Markov models. Trans. Emerg. Telecommun. Technol. **33**(4), e3915 (2022)
7. Kalnoor, G., Gowrishankar, S.: A model for intrusion detection system using hidden markov and variational bayesian model for IoT based wireless sensor network. Int. J. Inf. Technol. **14**(4), 2021–33 (2022)
8. Norris, J.R.: Markov chains. Cambridge University Press (1998)
9. Ching, W.K., Ng, M.K.: Markov chains. Models, Algorithms and Applications, 650 (2006)
10. Ahmadian Ramaki, A., Rasoolzadegan, A., Javan, J.A.: A systematic review on intrusion detection based on the hidden markov model. Stat. Anal. Data Min. ASA Data Sci. J. **11**(3), 111–134 (2018)
11. Hu, J., Yu, X., Qiu, D., et al.: A simple and efficient hidden Markov model scheme for host-based anomaly intrusion detection. IEEE Netw. **23**(1), 42–47 (2009)
12. Liao, H.J., Lin, C., Lin, Y.C., et al.: Intrusion detection system: a comprehensive review. J. Netw. Comput. Appl. **36**(1), 16–24 (2013)
13. Biermann, E., Cloete, E., Venter, L.M.: A comparison of intrusion detection systems. Comput. Secur. **20**(8), 676–683 (2001)
14. Zhu, T., Yu, J., Xiong, C., et al.: Aptshield: a stable, efficient and real-time apt detection system for linux hosts. IEEE Trans. Dependable Secure Comput. (2023)

15. Zhu, T., Wang, J., Ruan, L., et al.: General, efficient, and real-time data compaction strategy for APT forensic analysis. IEEE Trans. Inf. Forensics Secur. **16**, 3312–3325 (2021)
16. Kingman, J.F.C.: Poisson processes. Clarendon Press (1992)
17. Anderson, J.A., Senthilselvan, A.: Smooth estimates for the hazard function. J. R. Stat. Soc. Ser. B Stat Methodol. **42**(3), 322–327 (1980)
18. Spiegel, M.R.: Laplace transforms. McGraw-Hill, New York (1965)

Social Media Threat Intelligence: A Framework for Collecting and Categorizing Threat-Related Data

Victor Obojo[1], Haula Galadima[1], and Richard Ikuesan[2(✉)]

[1] Cyber Threat Intelligence Division, CyberDome Nigeria, No. 3 Bobo Close, Maitama, Abuja 900271, Nigeria
{obojo.v,galadima.h}@cyberdome.net

[2] Department of Computing and Applied Technology, College of Technological Innovation, Zayed University, Abu Dhabi, UAE
richard.ikuesan@zu.ac.ae

Abstract. The exponential growth of social media, now encompassing approximately five billion users globally, has transformed these platforms into critical sources of information, mirroring diverse societal interactions. However, this vast data repository also introduces significant threats, including terrorism, online fraud, and the spread of disinformation, underscoring the need for robust monitoring and categorization mechanisms. This study presents an innovative framework designed to systematically collect and categorize social media data using weighted keywords tailored to various threat categories. By leveraging semi-automated data collection and keyword weighting techniques, this framework enhances threat detection accuracy and integrates diverse data collection methods such as APIs, bots, and scraping tools. Preliminary results demonstrate the framework's efficacy in identifying and categorizing threat-related content, highlighting its potential to significantly advance threat intelligence capabilities. This groundbreaking approach promises to revolutionize social media threat intelligence, equipping organizations with the tools to anticipate emerging threats and bolster national security.

Keywords: Social media intelligence · Cyber threat intelligence · Kaviel Model · Threat Intelligence Analysis · Social Media data

1 Introduction

Social networks have experienced exponential growth in recent years, fundamentally transforming how information is distributed, utilized, and influenced. Platforms such as Facebook, Twitter, WhatsApp, TikTok, and Telegram have become integral to the daily lives of people, revolutionizing the dissemination of news, trends, and social movements globally. This rapid evolution has normalized information sharing, connecting, and communicating on an unprecedented

S. Goel et al. (Eds.): ICDF2C 2024, LNICST 614, pp. 90–109, 2025.
https://doi.org/10.1007/978-3-031-89360-5_6

scale over the internet [1]. However, these advancements bring significant challenges and threats. The extensive reach and real-time nature of social media have created fertile ground for risks including misinformation, disinformation, cybercrime, defamation, and terrorism [2].

The immense volume, velocity, and variety of data generated by social media platforms present formidable challenges for intelligence analysts seeking to identify, track, and mitigate these threats [3]. Every minute, millions of posts, tweets, images, and videos are uploaded, creating a complex and vast environment that traditional intelligence-gathering methods struggle to keep pace with. Keyword-based searches and manual analyses are often insufficient to uncover and manage sophisticated threat actors and emerging trends. The varying nature of social media data further complicates these efforts, as information can spread across different platforms and geographic boundaries in seconds. Additionally, the rise of echo chambers and filter bubbles complicates the distinction between factual information and fake content [4]. Algorithms designed to personalize user experiences inadvertently reinforce biases, making recognising and assessing diverse information perspectives difficult. This environment allows false narratives to thrive, adding complexity for intelligence analysts. Addressing these challenges necessitates an adaptable framework for social media threat intelligence. Such a framework must support efficient data collection and processing while enabling accurate categorization and prioritisation of threats. By integrating natural language processing (NLP) methods with advanced machine learning algorithms, this study develops a system capable of identifying and monitoring evolving threats effectively [5]. This system should analyze large volumes of data in real time, providing intelligence analysts with the tools needed for quick and informed decision-making.

The evolving landscape of cyber threats on social media platforms highlights the necessity for comprehensive threat intelligence solutions. For instance, the detection and mitigation of disinformation campaigns require sophisticated tools that can identify coordinated inauthentic behaviour across multiple platforms. Similarly, the tracking of cybercriminal activities, such as phishing and fraud, demands real-time analysis and rapid response mechanisms to prevent financial losses and protect user data [6]. Moreover, countering terrorism-related content involves not only identifying extremist narratives but also understanding the underlying networks that propagate such content [7]. Previous studies have explored various approaches to social media threat intelligence, including sentiment analysis, network analysis, and anomaly detection [8]. While these studies have provided valuable insights into specific threat categories or platforms, these studies often lack broad applicability. Moreover, the evaluation of these methods is frequently hindered by the absence of comprehensive datasets and standardized evaluation criteria. There is an urgent need for a system that can be universally applied across social media platforms and threat types to enhance the effectiveness of threat detection, increasing accuracy, precision, and recall. This study aims to bridge these gaps by developing a framework applicable across social media platforms and capable of categorizing threats into specific contexts. The framework employs weighted keyword selection, NLP techniques, and human validation to improve the accuracy and precision of threat detection. This study will also evaluate the framework's effectiveness in supporting informed decision-making by intelligence analysts. The ultimate goal is to create a system that enhances the identification and tracking of threats on social media, enabling proactive measures to mitigate potential risks [1].

By addressing the multifaceted challenges presented by the dynamic social media environment, this research seeks to contribute to the broader field of cybersecurity. The proposed framework aims to offer a scalable and adaptable solution that improves current threat intelligence practices and anticipates future threats, safeguarding public discourse and enhancing national security. The remainder of this manuscript is structured as follows: Sect. 2 provides an overview of existing research and methodologies in social media threat intelligence, highlighting the strengths and limitations of current approaches. Section 3 details the proposed framework, including the data collection methods, keyword selection and weighting scheme, and the machine learning models used for categorization. Section 4 presents the results of the experiments, including the performance metrics for each threat category and a comparative analysis with other models. Section 5 interprets the results, compares them with existing literature, and discusses the implications of the findings for threat intelligence practices. Finally, Sect. 6 summarizes the key findings of the research, discusses the limitations of the study, and outlines directions for future research.

2 Literature Review

Over the years, social media platforms have become essential mediums for global communication and information sharing. This presents both unprecedented opportunities and formidable challenges in threat intelligence [2]. This literature review delves into existing research and methodologies relevant to social media threat intelligence, focusing on approaches to data collection, keyword analysis, threat categorization frameworks, and the ethical considerations inherent in leveraging social media data for security purposes (Fig. 1).

2.1 Data Collection Methods

Effective data collection is crucial for social media threat intelligence. Traditional manual monitoring is precise but not scalable [6]. Automated techniques, such as APIs and web scraping, are now preferred. APIs provide real-time, structured data but face limitations such as rate limits and data availability [8,9]. Web scraping allows for flexible data extraction, including unstructured information, but raises issues related to data quality, legality, and ethics [9].

2.2 Keyword Analysis and Threat Identification

Keyword analysis is essential for identifying threats. Simple keyword searches can produce irrelevant results, making advanced techniques necessary. Natural Language Processing (NLP) and machine learning enhance threat detection

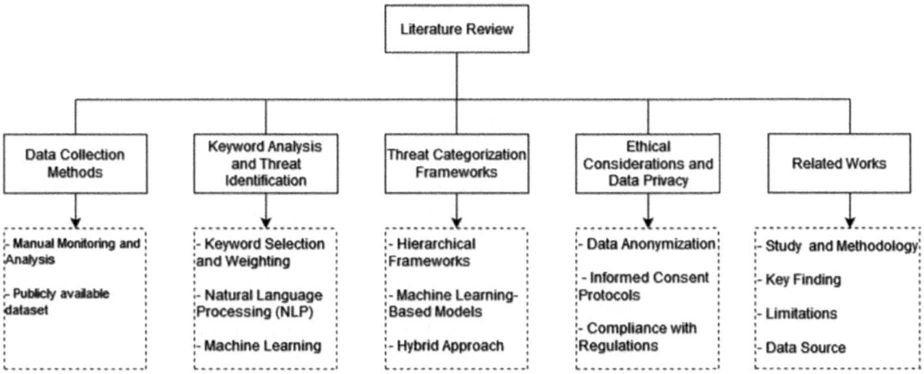

Fig. 1. Synopsis of the Literature Review

by analyzing context and identifying patterns in language [2,10,11]. Effective systems rely on meticulous keyword selection and weighting to discern subtle nuances indicative of threats such as terrorism and cyber fraud [12].

2.3 Threat Categorization Frameworks

Categorizing and prioritizing threats is vital for efficient threat intelligence. Hierarchical taxonomies classify threats based on predefined criteria, facilitating resource allocation [10]. Machine learning models, trained on historical data, adapt to new patterns and autonomously categorize threats [2]. A hybrid approach combining hierarchical structures and machine learning can enhance categorization accuracy.

2.4 Ethical Considerations and Data Privacy

Ethical considerations are paramount in social media threat intelligence, particularly concerning data privacy and user consent [5]. Researchers must comply with complex regulatory landscapes and ethical guidelines for data collection, storage, and analysis [12]. Measures such as data anonymization and informed consent protocols are essential to maintain public trust [13]. The proposed framework integrates stringent ethical standards to protect user privacy while leveraging social media data for threat intelligence.

2.5 Related Works

The body of existing research on social media threat intelligence is extensive, encompassing various methodologies and approaches. Table 1 summarizes key studies in this field, highlighting crucial contributions and methodologies. Suffice it to highlight that these studies have reported low accuracies and the lack of a multifaceted approach towards threat intelligence. The methodology for the proposed solution to address these limitations is presented in the next section.

Table 1. Summary of Key Studies in Social Media Threat Intelligence

Study	Methodology	Key Findings	Limitations	Data Source
The study focuses on using OSINT and national security in combating terrorism [14]	Social media data analyzed for intelligence gathering and surveillance.	OSINT and Big Data analytics aid in identifying terrorist networks and radicalization activities	The study does not offer specific solutions or recommendations to address these technical challenges to data storage/sharing and effectively analyse large volumes of data.	Social media data collected for OSINT through user-generated content.
The study focuses on the role of Twitter (X) in gathering threat intelligence. It aims to assess IoC reliability and bot involvement in disseminating threats [1]	RoIoC evaluates IoC reliability and Twitter's threat information distribution speed. Machine Learning classifies Twitter accounts as automated or human-operated	Twitter provides timely threat warnings against novel cyber-attacks. 48.67% of IoCs reported on Twitter are malicious. Twitter reports 36.7% of CVEs earlier than NVD.	Limited to just Twitter data, not comprehensive cyber threat intelligence.	Twitter API was used for data collection.
Identifies gaps in existing cyber threat intelligence ontologies. Proposes a multi-layered cyber threat intelligence ontology for development. [15]	OpenIOC schema describes technical characteristics to identify known threats.	Cyber security lacks comprehensive threat intelligence ontology. Evaluation reveals shortcomings in existing cyber threat intelligence ontologies.	Lack of standardised ontology covering the complete threat intelligence spectrum and the absence of OWL constraints in evaluated ontologies hinder reasoning capabilities.	Extract data using TAPIO tool for semantic graph creation.
The study focuses on extracting cyber threat intelligence from social media. It includes case studies on Twitter and Reddit for CTI extraction. [6]	Extract CTI from social media using trustworthy accounts and data sources. Employ social network data as secondary intelligence sources. Develop trustability metrics for reputable accounts on Twitter and Reddit.	Proposing a trustability metric for reputable accounts in cyber security.	Trustability metric is not authoritative and requires further research. Publicly available measures used for trust index computation.	Data collected from Reddit using Python script with PRAW integration and publicly available Twitter dataset
The study focuses on monitoring social media activities during crises [16]	Twitter data was collected using a web crawler with specific keywords. The analysis includes geolocation and sentiment analysis of real-time tweets.	Social media analysis aids crisis management by providing real-time insights. SOCMINT combines OSINT and Web mining to enhance national security.	Social media complexity hinders intelligence analysts in crises. Data mining techniques lack in determining the value of models.	Web crawler used to collect tweets with geographic coordinates.

3 Methodology

The methodology employs a systematic approach to develop and implement the framework for collecting and categorizing threat-related data from social media platforms. This comprehensive methodology encompasses the general operation of the framework, which includes an overview of the framework and four critical phases: data collection, keyword selection, weighting scheme development, and the categorization process.

3.1 Framework Overview

The proposed Social Media-based Threat Intelligence Framework is designed to collect, preprocess, analyze, and report on threat-related data from social media platforms. This framework aims to enhance the ability of organizations to detect and respond to emerging threats by leveraging real-time data from various social media sources. The framework is structured into multiple phases, each comprising specific tasks handled by dedicated micro-services. These phases ensure comprehensive data processing, contextual threat analysis, and the generation of standardized outputs for compatibility with various security systems.

To develop the core components of the proposed framework, a systematic approach to data collection and data analysis is required. The proposed framework outlines ten components that work together to extract valuable insights from social media chatter and identify potential threats, as shown in Table 2.

Table 2. Table showing the Key Components of the Framework

Component	Description
Initial Data Collection	This phase involves gathering raw data from social media platforms using both manual and automated methods.
Filtering and Preprocessing	The collected data is cleaned and standardised to ensure consistency and relevance.
Keyword-based Extraction	Posts with predefined threat keywords are identified and prioritized based on weighted significance.
Contextual Analysis	Analyze the context of the keywords to determine the potential threat level and categorize the posts.
Redundancy Removal	Eliminating duplicate and similar posts to reduce noise.
False Alarm Handling	Manages and verifies false positives to ensure accuracy.
Data Reduction	Filters out irrelevant content to focus on high-priority threats.
Threat Context Identification	Detects nuanced threat indicators using advanced analysis techniques.
Threat Keyword Update	Regularly updates keywords and weights to adapt to evolving threats.
Standardized Output	Generates standardized threat reports compatible with various security systems.

The framework handles each phase independently, allowing for modularity, scalability, and efficient processing. It provides a robust solution for social media-based threat intelligence (Fig. 2).

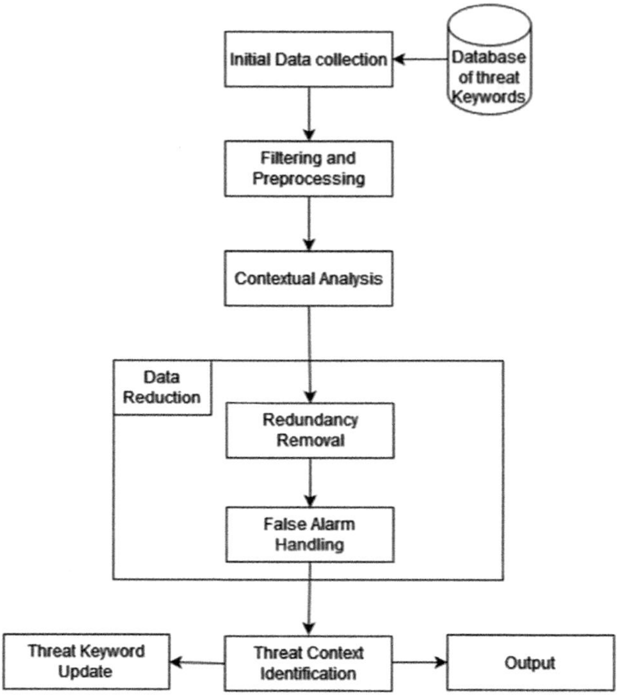

Fig. 2. Proposed Social Media-based Threat Intelligence Framework

3.2 Operational Framework

The operational framework outlines the approach used to collect, process, and categorize threat-related data from social media platforms. This framework integrates multiple phases, from data collection to categorization, ensuring a structured and efficient method for threat intelligence gathering. The key components of the operational framework are described in Fig. 3:

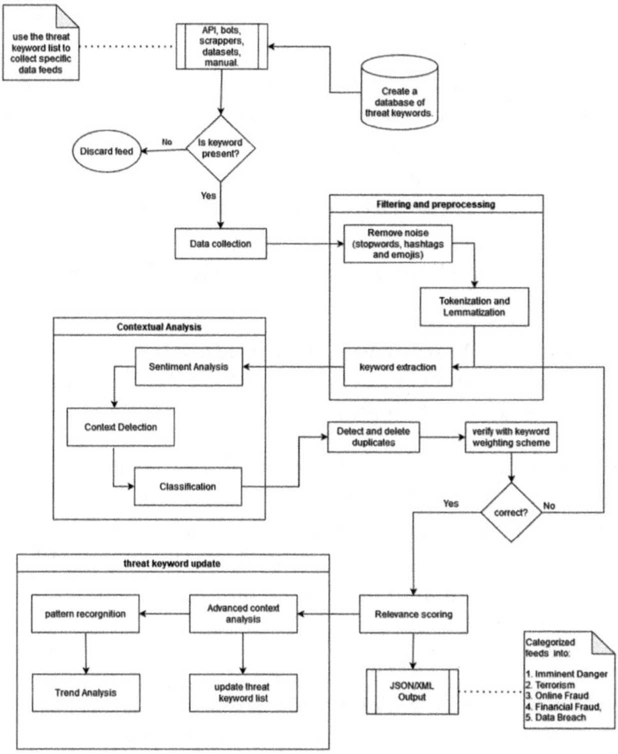

Fig. 3. Operational Framework

3.3 Data Collection

The data collection phase is a fundamental component of the proposed framework in 2. This phase involves the systematic gathering of social media posts that potentially contain indicators of various threat categories. It relies on manual methods and available online datasets to ensure comprehensive and high-quality data collection.

3.3.1 Selection of Social Media Platforms The framework targets major social media platforms such as X (formerly Twitter), Facebook, and Telegram due to their significant user bases and the availability of real-time information. These platforms are selected based on their relevance to threat intelligence and their potential to provide diverse data reflecting various threat indicators.

3.3.2 Manual Data Collection Manual data collection involves a meticulous examination of social media platforms to identify relevant posts. This process includes:

1. **Keyword Search:** Utilizing predefined keywords, hashtags, and phrases indicative of potential threats. These keywords are regularly reviewed and updated to reflect emerging threats and evolving language usage.
2. **Content Analysis:** Scrutinizing posts for context and relevance. This step ensures that the collected data is not only relevant but also provides a nuanced understanding of the potential threats.
3. **Recording and Documentation:** Extracting and recording relevant posts for further analysis. This manual approach allows for the careful capture of context-specific data that might have been missed by automated methods.

3.3.3 Utilization of Available Online Datasets In addition to manual collection, the framework incorporates available online datasets relevant to social media threat intelligence. This includes:

1. **Public Datasets:** Leveraging publicly available datasets that have been compiled by researchers, organizations, and institutions. These datasets provide a valuable resource for historical data and broader context.
2. **Open Data Initiatives:** Incorporating data from open data initiatives and platforms that share threat-related information. These sources are vetted to ensure reliability and relevance.

3.3.4 Data Preprocessing The collected data undergoes a preprocessing phase to ensure consistency and relevance. This includes:

1. **Data Cleaning:** Removing duplicates, irrelevant content, and noise from the dataset. This step ensures that the data is clean and ready for further analysis.
2. **Standardization:** Standardizing the data format to ensure compatibility with the subsequent analysis phases. This involves normalizing text formats, handling missing values, and ensuring uniform data structures.

3.3.5 Integration of Data Sources Combining data from both manual collection methods and available online datasets provides a comprehensive dataset for analysis. The integration process includes:

1. **Data Merging:** Merging datasets from different sources to create a unified dataset. This step ensures that the data is comprehensive and includes various perspectives.
2. **Quality Assurance:** Implementing quality checks to verify the accuracy and reliability of the data. This involves cross-referencing data points and validating sources.

To maintain the relevance and accuracy of the framework, the data collection process is continuous. Regular updates to keywords, continuous monitoring of social media platforms, and periodic reviews of the data collection methods ensure that the framework adapts to new threats and changing environments.

3.4 Keyword Selection and Weighting Scheme

The Keyword Selection and Weighting Scheme section elucidates the methodology employed to identify and prioritize keywords for detecting threat-related content on social media platforms. This section encompasses the selection criteria for keywords, the development of a weighting scheme to assign importance to each keyword, and considerations for application in categorizing threat data.

1. **Selection of Keywords:** The initial step in the keyword selection process involves identifying potential threat categories and associated indicators present in social media content. Keywords are selected based on relevance, specificity, and frequency in indicating threats such as imminent danger, terrorism, online fraud, financial fraud, and data breaches. This selection process draws from domain knowledge, previous research, and analysis of historical threat incidents.
2. **Criteria for Keyword Selection:** Keywords are chosen based on specific criteria designed to maximize effectiveness in identifying threat-related content:
   - **Relevance:** Keywords must directly relate to the identified threat categories and indicators.
   - **Specificity:** Keywords should be precise enough to capture relevant posts without generating excessive noise.
   - **Frequency:** Keywords should appear frequently enough in social media posts to ensure sufficient data for analysis.
3. **Development of Weighting Scheme:** Once selected, keywords are assigned weights that reflect their importance in identifying and categorizing threats. The weighting scheme prioritises keywords based on their significance in each threat category. Factors influencing keyword weighting may include:
   - **Severity of Threat:** Keywords associated with high-impact threats receive higher weights.
   - **Contextual Analysis:** Keywords are assessed based on their context within social media posts and their potential to indicate imminent or ongoing threats.
4. **Weighted Keywords:** The following table provides an illustrative example of weighted keywords assigned to different threat categories (Table 3):

3.5 Model Selection Criteria and Categorization Process

This study selected and fine-tuned the "RoBERTa-base" model to effectively classify potential threat data on social media, creating the KIV model to categorize data into five contexts. RoBERTa-Base was chosen for its superior performance on various datasets. It incorporates several architectural improvements over the original BERT model, including dynamic masking, which exposes the model to a variety of masking patterns, leading to more robust learning. Additionally, RoBERTa is trained on larger datasets and benefits from extended

Table 3. Example of Weighted Keywords for Threat Categorization

Category	Keywords	Weight
Imminent Danger	bomb threat, active shooter, emergency alert	High[a]
Terrorism	terrorist attack, bomb blast, bandit, kidnap	High
Online Fraud	phishing scams, cyber scams, ransomware, fake website	Medium
Financial Fraud	banking fraud, credit card fraud, money laundering	Medium
Data Breach	data breach, personal data exposed, cybersecurity incident	Medium

[a] In cases where a feed has keywords from various categories, the higher weight is priority

training periods, enhancing its ability to capture a wider range of linguistic patterns and nuances.

The suitability of RoBERTa-Base for this task lies in its ability to comprehend context, identify subtle cues, and differentiate between similar categories, making it ideal for categorizing threat-related texts. Its sophisticated training regimen enables it to accurately process complex sentence structures and semantic details, crucial for effective threat detection. Furthermore, RoBERTa-Base's availability in the Hugging Face model repository facilitates easy integration and offers extensive documentation for fine-tuning, allowing for efficient adaptation to the specific needs of the framework. This makes it a robust and adaptable choice for addressing the challenges of social media threat intelligence.

Once collected, social media posts undergo a rigorous categorization process aimed at identifying and classifying the data into predefined threat categories. This process leverages the KIV model, designed to analyze each post based on the presence and significance of weighted keywords associated with specific threat categories. The selected keywords and respective weights play a vital role in this categorization process. During data analysis, posts containing these keywords are identified and categorized into relevant threat categories based on the highest-weighted keyword detected within the content. This ensures that the most pertinent threats are accurately identified and prioritized for further analysis and intervention.

3.6 Evaluation Metrics

In assessing the performance of the framework, several evaluation metrics are leveraged, in tandem with existing studies on the exploration of machine learning algorithms [17–19]. These metrics, which include accuracy, AUC, precision, recall, and F1-score, provide a quantitative basis for evaluating the effectiveness and efficiency of the framework in identifying and categorizing threats from social media data. Precision measures the proportion of true positive threat detection among all detected threats. It is calculated as:

$$\text{Precision} = \frac{TP}{TP + FP} \quad (1)$$

where TPTP is the number of true positives, and FPFP is the number of false positives. High precision indicates that the framework produces fewer false alarms. Recall, on the other hand, also known as sensitivity, measures the proportion of true positive detections among all actual threats. It is calculated as:

$$\text{Recall} = \frac{TP}{TP + FN} \tag{2}$$

where TPTP is the number of true positives, and FNFN is the number of false negatives. High recall indicates that the framework is effective in detecting most actual threats. The F1-Score is the harmonic mean of precision and recall, providing a single metric to evaluate the balance between the two metrics. It is calculated as:

$$\text{F1-Score} = 2 \cdot \frac{\text{Precision} \cdot \text{Recall}}{\text{Precision} + \text{Recall}} \tag{3}$$

A high F1-Score indicates that the framework maintains a good balance between precision and recall. For accuracy measures, the proportion of correctly identified posts (both true positives and true negatives) among all posts evaluated is computed. It is calculated as:

$$\text{Accuracy} = \frac{TP + TN}{TP + TN + FP + FN} \tag{4}$$

where TNTN is the number of true negatives. High accuracy indicates that the framework correctly identifies both threat-related and non-threat-related posts.

3.7 Implementation and Adaptability

The implementation of the framework is designed to be straightforward and adaptable to various environments. The framework can be deployed on cloud platforms to leverage scalable resources for handling large volumes of social media data. The modular design allows for easy integration with existing security infrastructure and other threat intelligence systems. Adaptability is achieved through the framework's ability to update threat keywords regularly and adjust to new threat patterns and terminologies. Additionally, the framework's components can be fine-tuned or replaced to address specific requirements or to integrate new technologies. This flexibility ensures the framework remains effective and relevant in dynamic threat landscapes.

4 Results

The results section presents an analysis of the framework's performance in identifying and categorizing threat-related content from social media. Utilizing a dataset collected through manual and automated methods, the framework's effectiveness was evaluated based on key performance metrics: accuracy, precision, recall, and F1 score. This section details the experimental setup, data preprocessing steps, and the application of the keyword weighting scheme and machine learning model for categorization. Additionally, this study discusses the quantitative outcomes of the evaluation metrics, providing insights into the strengths and limitations of the proposed framework. Through this analysis, the study aims to demonstrate the practical utility of the framework in enhancing threat detection and response capabilities on social media platforms.

4.1 Data Summary

The dataset used for this study was obtained from a combination of publicly available sources, including Kaggle, X (formerly known as Twitter), and Telegram, focusing on posts related to threats. The dataset comprised 2,500 social media posts, categorized into five threat types: Imminent Danger, Terrorism, Online Fraud, Financial Fraud, and Data Breach. Figure 4 shows the distribution of social media posts across different threat categories. This pie chart helps visualize the proportion of each threat type within the dataset.

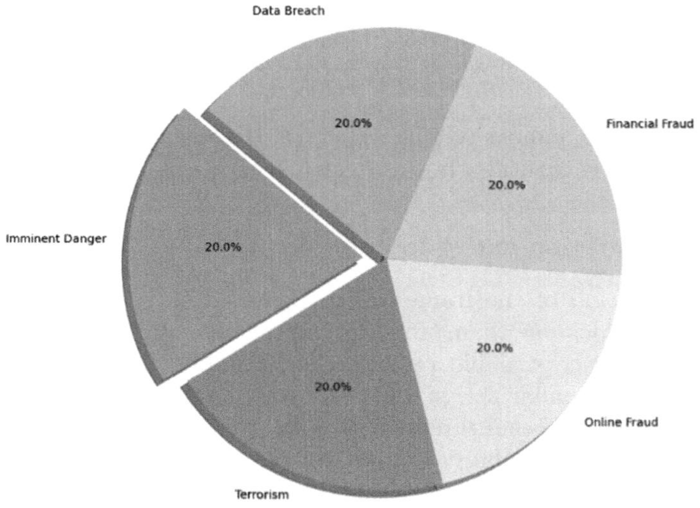

Fig. 4. Distribution of Social Media Posts Across Threat Categories

4.2 Categorization Process

Using the proposed keyword selection and weighting scheme, each post was analyzed to determine its relevance to the predefined threat categories. The categorization process involved:

- Identifying the presence of predefined keywords in each post.

- Applying the weighted scoring mechanism to determine the significance of each keyword.
- Categorizing each post based on the highest-weighted keyword.

To evaluate the performance of the categorization model, this study calculated the Area Under the Curve (AUC) of the Receiver Operating Characteristic (ROC) curve for each of the categories. The ROC curve provides a graphical representation of the model's ability to distinguish between different threat categories (Fig. 5).

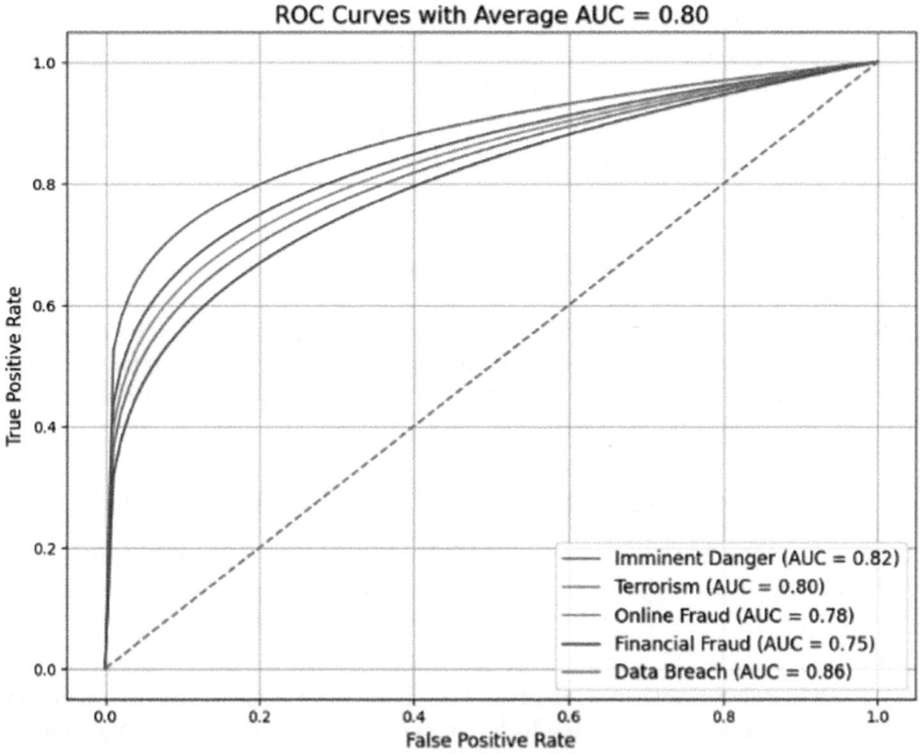

Fig. 5. ROC Curve for the Categorization Model.

4.3 Performance Metrics

To evaluate the effectiveness of the framework, this study calculates the accuracy, precision, recall, and F1 score for each threat category. The metrics are defined as follows:

Accuracy: The proportion of correctly categorized posts out of the total posts.

Precision: The proportion of true positive results in the identified threat category.

Recall: The proportion of actual threat-related posts that were correctly identified.

F1 Score: The harmonic mean of precision and recall (Table 4).

Table 4. Category-Specific Performance Metrics

Threat Category	Accuracy	Precision	Recall	F1 Score
Imminent Danger	88.2%	87.0%	89.4%	88.2%
Terrorism	86.7%	85.5%	87.8%	86.6%
Online Fraud	83.5%	82.1%	84.9%	83.5%
Financial Fraud	84.8%	83.3%	86.2%	84.7%
Data Breach	85.1%	83.7%	86.5%	85.1%

In summary, the framework's performance metrics-85.6% accuracy, 84.3% precision, 86.1% recall, and an 85.2% F1 score-demonstrate its high effectiveness in identifying and categorizing threat-related content on social media. These results highlight the framework's potential to significantly enhance threat detection and response capabilities, providing a reliable tool for organizations to monitor and mitigate threats in real-time.

4.4 Comparative Analysis of Threat Detection Frameworks

To further evaluate the performance of the framework, this study compared it with Logistic Regression and Naive Bayes models. The comparison focused on the same performance metrics: accuracy, precision, recall, and F1 score.

4.4.1 Model Selection Criteria The models selected for comparison were chosen based on prevalence and efficiency in text classification tasks, particularly in the context of social media threat detection:

Logistic Regression: A widely used linear model known for its simplicity, interpretability, and efficiency in binary and multi-class classification problems.

Naive Bayes: A probabilistic classifier based on Bayes' theorem, which is commonly used for text classification due to its speed and effectiveness with large datasets.

The comparative results are presented in Table 5.

The proposed framework demonstrates superior overall performance across all metrics compared to Logistic Regression and Naive Bayes, highlighting its effectiveness in accurately identifying and categorizing threat-related content on social media. While the other models are competitive, the models fall short in

Table 5. Comparative Performance Metrics of Threat Detection Frameworks

Metrics	KIV	Logistic Regression	Naive Bayes
Accuracy	85.6%	82.3%	81.5%
Precision	84.3%	82.0%	80.8%
Recall	86.1%	83.5%	82.7%
F1 Score	85.2%	82.7%	81.7%

accuracy, precision, recall, and F1 score. This analysis shows the reliability and robustness of the framework, acknowledging that other models can be useful but may not match the performance of its approach.

Our framework's superior performance can be attributed to its advanced feature extraction and classification techniques. The higher accuracy and recall suggest that this model is more effective in correctly identifying true threat-related posts, reducing the likelihood of missing critical threats. The balanced precision and recall also indicate that the model minimizes false positives, ensuring that non-threat posts are less likely to be incorrectly classified as threats.

Logistic Regression and Naive Bayes, while simpler and faster, fall short in performance due to limitations in capturing complex patterns in text data. Logistic Regression, being a linear model, may not fully capture the nuances in threat-related content, leading to lower accuracy and F1 scores. Naive Bayes, though efficient, makes strong independence assumptions between features, which can result in lower precision and recall.

Therefore, this framework's advanced capabilities provide a more reliable and robust solution for social media threat detection, making it a valuable tool for organizations aiming to monitor and mitigate threats in real-time.

4.5 Key Observations

The evaluation of the social media threat detection framework yielded several key findings, highlighting its strengths in identifying and classifying potential threats. These include:

1. High Accuracy and F1 Scores: The overall accuracy of 85.6% and F1 score of 85.2% indicate that the framework performs well in categorizing social media posts into the relevant threat categories.
2. Comparative Performance: Compared to Logistic Regression and Naive Bayes, the proposed framework consistently outperforms these lighter models across all metrics, showcasing its superior accuracy, precision, recall, and F1 score.
3. Category Performance: The Imminent Danger category achieved the highest performance metrics, with an F1 score of 88.2%, suggesting that the framework is particularly effective in identifying posts related to immediate threats.
4. Balanced Precision and Recall: All categories exhibited a good balance between precision and recall, with values consistently above 80%, highlighting

the framework's robustness in both identifying relevant posts and minimizing false positives.

5 Discussion

The results demonstrate that the proposed framework for collecting and categorizing threat-related data from social media is effective, with an overall accuracy of 85.6% and an F1 score of 85.2%. These metrics suggest that the framework can reliably categorize posts into the predefined threat categories with a high degree of precision and recall. The proposed framework demonstrates significant effectiveness in collecting and categorizing threat-related data from social media, achieving an overall accuracy of 85.6% and an F1 score of 85.2%. These metrics indicate a high level of reliability in categorizing posts into predefined threat categories with notable precision and recall. The Imminent Danger category, with an F1 score of 88.2%, shows the framework's particular strength in identifying immediate threats, which is crucial for timely intervention. The consistent performance across other categories such as Terrorism (F1 score of 86.6%), Online Fraud (83.5%), Financial Fraud (84.7%), and Data Breach (85.1%) further emphasizes the robustness and versatility of the framework.

5.1 Comparison with Existing Literature

The framework's performance metrics are competitive with those reported in existing studies on social media threat intelligence. The study focusing on OSINT and national security in combating terrorism highlights the importance of social media data for intelligence gathering and surveillance, but it does not offer specific solutions for technical challenges to data storage and analysis [14]. Similarly, the study on the role of Twitter (X) in gathering threat intelligence reports timely threat warnings, but it is limited to Twitter data and does not provide comprehensive cyber threat intelligence [1]. Our framework addresses these issues by employing a weighted keyword selection and categorization process that enhances precision and recall, achieving a more balanced performance across diverse threat categories. The study identifying gaps in existing cyber threat intelligence ontologies proposes a multi-layered ontology for development, but it lacks a standardized ontology covering the complete threat intelligence spectrum [15]. Our framework, on the other hand, offers a more comprehensive approach by encompassing various social media sources and threat categories. Additionally, the study focusing on extracting cyber threat intelligence from social media, including case studies on Twitter and Reddit, proposes a trustability metric for reputable accounts but acknowledges the need for further research on the metrics authority [15]. Our framework's broader scope and emphasis on real-time data processing provide a more robust solution. Notable trends from analysing this study indicate that categories like Imminent Danger and Terrorism had more correctly identified posts. This trend mirrors the current global emphasis on these threats and suggests that the proposed framework is well-tuned to detect such high-priority issues effectively. The balanced performance across various threat categories demonstrates the framework's versatility, making it a valuable tool for comprehensive threat monitoring.

5.2 Implications

The high effectiveness of the proposed framework implies substantial potential for enhancing threat detection and response capabilities. Organizations can leverage this framework to monitor social media in real-time, thereby improving situational awareness and response strategies. The modular and scalable design of the framework ensures that it can be adapted to evolving threats, maintaining its relevance and utility over time. While the framework shows high effectiveness, certain limitations must be acknowledged. The reliance on predefined keywords may lead to challenges in identifying novel or evolving threats that do not fit established patterns. Future research could focus on integrating adaptive learning mechanisms that can update the keyword database in real-time based on emerging threat trends. Additionally, expanding the framework to incorporate multimedia content analysis (e.g., images and videos) could further enhance its threat detection capabilities. In addition, future research should focus on addressing current limitations, such as the need for more extensive datasets and standardized evaluation criteria. Continuous refinement of the NLP models and machine learning algorithms is essential to keep pace with the rapidly changing landscape of social media. Expanding the framework's applicability to emerging social media platforms and integrating more sophisticated analytical tools will further strengthen its efficacy. By fostering collaboration between researchers, practitioners, and industry stakeholders, the framework can be continuously improved to meet the evolving demands of social media threat intelligence.

6 Conclusion

This study presents a novel framework for collecting and categorizing threat-related data from social media, achieving high-performance metrics across multiple threat categories. The framework demonstrated an overall accuracy of 85.6% and an F1 score of 85.2%, with particularly high effectiveness in identifying Imminent Danger and Terrorism posts. The weighted keyword selection and categorization process effectively balanced precision and recall, addressing common challenges in the existing literature and underscoring the framework's potential to enhance social media threat intelligence by providing a reliable and robust method for detecting and categorizing various cybersecurity threats. This research introduces a comprehensive and effective method for social media threat intelligence, which has practical implications for improving detection and response strategies. The proposed framework leverages advanced data collection, natural language processing (NLP), and machine learning techniques to identify and categorize threats with high accuracy and precision. By integrating various data collection methods such as APIs, bots, and scraping tools, the framework ensures robust data acquisition and preprocessing while maintaining the integrity and privacy of the collected data. The initial results demonstrate the framework's effectiveness in identifying and categorizing threat-related content, showcasing its potential to significantly advance current threat intelligence practices. In conclusion, this study significantly contributes to the field, providing a scalable and adaptable solution that enhances the detection process of threat intelligence within the social media sphere. As organizations increasingly rely on social media for threat intelligence, the proposed framework offers a robust approach to safeguarding public discourse and enhancing national security.

References

1. Arikkat, D.R., et al.: Can twitter be used to acquire reliable alerts against novel cyber attacks? (2023)
2. Sufi, F.: A new social media-driven cyber threat intelligence. Electronics **12**(5), 1242 (2023)
3. Huang, S.-Y., Ban, T.: Monitoring social media for vulnerability-threat prediction and topic analysis, 1771–1776 (2020)
4. Alevizopoulou, S., Koloveas, P., Tryfonopoulos, C., Raftopoulou, P.: Social media monitoring for IOT cyber-threats, 436–441 (2021)
5. King, T.C., Aggarwal, N., Taddeo, M., Floridi, L.: Artificial intelligence crime: an interdisciplinary analysis of foreseeable threats and solutions. Sci. Eng. Ethics **26**, 89–120 (2020)
6. Jakstaite, D., Ricardo, M.: Extracting cyber threat intelligence from social media with case studies in twitter and reddit. Soc. Netw. **25**(24), 17
7. Ateş, A.: Current challenges and trends in intelligence. Güvenlik Bilimleri Dergisi **9**(1), 177–204 (2020)
8. Mansour, S.: Social media analysis of user's responses to terrorism using sentiment analysis and text mining. Procedia Comput. Sci. **140**, 95–103 (2018)
9. AlAjlan, S.A., Saudagar, A.: Machine learning approach for threat detection on social media posts containing Arabic text. Evol. Intel. **14**(2), 811–822 (2021)
10. Sari, A.: Context-aware intelligent systems for fog computing environments for cyber-threat intelligence. In: Fog Computing: Concepts, Frameworks and Technologies, pp. 205–225 (2018)
11. Lee, K.-C., Hsieh, C.-H., Wei, L.-J., Mao, C.-H., Dai, J.-H., Kuang, Y.-T.: Sec-buzzer: cyber security emerging topic mining with open threat intelligence retrieval and timeline event annotation. Soft. Comput. **21**, 2883–2896 (2017)
12. Guo, Y., et al.: A framework for threat intelligence extraction and fusion. Comput. Secur. **132**, 103371 (2023)
13. Zhang, H., Shen, G., Guo, C., Cui, Y., Jiang, C.: Ex-action: automatically extracting threat actions from cyber threat intelligence report based on multimodal learning. Secur. Commun. Netw. **2021**(1), 5586335 (2021)
14. Staniforth, A.: Open source intelligence and the protection of national security. In: Open Source Intelligence Investigation: From Strategy to Implementation, pp. 11–19. Springer (2017)
15. Mavroeidis, V., Bromander, S.: Cyber threat intelligence model: an evaluation of taxonomies, sharing standards, and ontologies within cyber threat intelligence. In: 2017 European Intelligence and Security Informatics Conference (EISIC), pp. 91–98 . IEEE (2017)

16. Iftene, A.: The significance of online monitoring activities for the social media intelligence (SOCMINT). In: Conference on Mathematical Foundations of Informatics, pp. 230–240 (2018)
17. Adeyemi, I.R., Razak, S.A., Salleh, M., Venter, H.S.: Observing consistency in online communication patterns for user re-identification. PLoS ONE **11**(12), 0166930 (2016)
18. Adeyemi, I.R., Abd Razak, S., Salleh, M.: Understanding online behavior: exploring the probability of online personality trait using supervised machine-learning approach. Front. ICT **3**, 8 (2016)
19. Ikuesan, A.R., Razak, S.A., Venter, H.S., Salleh, M.: Polychronicity tendency-based online behavioral signature. Int. J. Mach. Learn. Cybern. **10**, 2103–2118 (2019)

A Comprehensive Survey on Basic Safety Message Attacks and Their Detection

Ahmed Mohamed and Mengjun Xie(✉)

University of Tennessee at Chattanooga, Chattanooga, TN 37403, USA
wff394@mocs.utc.edu, mengjun-xie@utc.edu

Abstract. Vehicular Ad-hoc Networks (VANETs) are a crucial component of Cooperative Intelligent Transportation Systems (C-ITS), enabling vehicles to communicate and share vital information to enhance road safety and efficiency. Basic Safety Messages (BSMs), periodically broadcast by vehicles to provide real-time kinematic data, form the foundation of numerous safety applications within VANETs. Ensuring the security of BSMs is paramount, as malicious entities can exploit vulnerabilities to launch attacks that could have catastrophic consequences. In this study, we provide a comprehensive analysis of BSM attacks and detection mechanisms in VANETs. We begin by outlining the system model, security requirements, and attacker models relevant to BSMs. Then, we categorize and describe a range of attacks, from simple position falsification to more sophisticated and evasive techniques, such as the SixPack attack. We also classify existing attack detection methods into machine learning-based, deep learning-based, plausibility and consistency-based, and software-defined networking (SDN)-based mechanisms, analyzing their effectiveness and limitations. Additionally, we highlight the challenges in securing BSMs, such as the trade-off between model accuracy and real-time performance. Future research directions are also discussed. This survey paper serves as a foundational step towards building safe, secure, and reliable cooperative intelligent transportation systems and their associated applications.

Keywords: VANET Security · Basic Safety Message · BSM Attack · Misbehavior Detection · Position Falsification · Plausibility Check

1 Introduction

The number of fatalities from accidents in the U.S. in 2022 is 42,795 according to the U.S. Department of Transportation [1]. A high percentage of those accidents could have been avoided if the drivers had been alerted before the accidents [2]. A Vehicular Ad-hoc Network (VANET) is a network of vehicles and other roadside

This work was supported in part by the National Science Foundation (awards 1663105 and 2234910).

S. Goel et al. (Eds.): ICDF2C 2024, LNICST 614, pp. 110–130, 2025.
https://doi.org/10.1007/978-3-031-89360-5_7

units (RSUs) in which nodes communicate with one another in different communication modes such as V2V (Vehicle to Vehicle), V2I (Vehicle to Infrastructure), and I2I (Infrastructure to Infrastructure) [3]. One of the most important types of information transmitted over a VANET is basic safety message (BSM). BSMs are messages broadcasted ten times per second by every vehicle to other nodes in the network [4]. The primary purpose of BSM is to increase road safety by exchanging critical information with other vehicles and infrastructure elements. Many safety applications over VANET rely on BSM. The Vehicle Safety Communications Applications project led by the U.S. and car manufacturers has proposed a number of safety applications that utilizes BSMs to enhance vehicular safety including Emergency Electronic Brake Light (EEBL), Forward Collision Warning (FCW), and Intersection Movement Assist (IMA) [5].

A basic safety message (BSM) has two parts. Part one contains the kinematic information (e.g., position, speed, acceleration, heading, etc.) and must be included in every BSM. Part two contains optional information that could be transmitted as a response to an event as auxiliary information such as path history, path prediction, and other information about vehicle components [4,6]. BSMs are not encrypted as a critical requirement in BSM applications is low latency. BSMs are typically signed to ensure their authenticity and integrity. A malicious entity, however, may send erroneous BSMs to gain personal benefits or cause damages on the road. To detect such erroneous or malicious messages, numerous misbehavior detection systems (MDSes) have been designed to improve the security of BSM.

Clearly, the security of BSM is vital to VANETs and cooperative intelligent transport systems (C-ITSes), Unfortunately, a comprehensive analysis of BSM attacks and detection methods remains unseen even though there are many survey papers on VANET security. In this survey study, we focus on BSM attacks and analysis of BSM misbehavior detection systems. To achieve a comprehensive study, we first searched related papers in Google, Google Scholar, and IEEE Xplore using the following keywords: Basic Safety Messages, VANETs security, VANET attacks, misbehavior in VANETs, misbehavior detection systems, and other related keywords. Then, we read through abstracts of the papers to determine whether a searched paper is relevant to this study or not. The references on examined papers were also checked to incorporate possible material for this study. After careful examination and filtering, a total of 36 papers that are directly relevant to BSM attacks and misbehavior detection were selected and then thoroughly analyzed in this study.

The rest of this paper is organized as follows: We provide a brief overview of related work in Sect. 2. We then present the system model of VANETs, security requirements, and BSM attacker model in Sect. 3. We categorize and briefly describe various attacks targeting BSM in Sect. 4 and then present classification and analysis of BSM misbehavior detection methods in Sect. 5. After that, we discuss challenges and future research directions in BSM security in Sect. 6. Finally, we conclude this paper in Sect. 7.

2 Related Work

Numerous articles that survey the security of VANET and V2X, e.g., [7–13], have been published. However, almost all of them only provide a high level overview or summary in terms of BSM security. This study specifically focuses on BSM security and surveys recent advancements in BSM related simulation frameworks, attacks, and defenses.

Recent years have witnessed substantial research efforts on the security of BSMs, especially the generation of datasets and simulation tools. To our best knowledge, the VeReMi dataset [14] is the first open-source BSM dataset with simulated BSM traces and attacks [13]. The original VeReMi dataset contains five simple position falsification attacks and was used by many researchers to implement defenses and compare results. The Framework for Misbehavior Detection (F2MD) [15] is another important work on BSM security. F2MD allows for easier implementation of misbehavior detection systems and adds a global authority scheme to facilitate the implementation of node-based misbehavior detection. F2MD was used to create an improved and extended version of VeReMi with additional attacks. VASP [16] is a more recent framework for BSM attack creation that includes many attacks from VeReMi. Both F2MD and VASP were built as a submodule of the open source network simulation framework VEINS to facilitate the development of new attacks.

Besides popular VeReMi and F2MD, new BSM datasets and attacks have also been generated for BSM security research. Pollicino *et al.* created a novel evasive attack that appears to be difficult to detect by pretending to brake and slow down and then accelerating again [17]. Wang *et al.* used the NGSIM dataset, a detailed vehicle trajectory data collected by the federal highway administration, as well as PeMS, a dataset containing vehicle mileage, travel time, and performance information collected from real traffic. However, it is not clear how misbehavior in the two datasets was defined. Many researchers (e.g., [18–21]) also used the VEINS framework to create their own attacks. For example, Trabelsi *et al.* created three simple position forging attacks [18]; Boualouache *et al.* developed a constant offset attack and a Sybil ghost vehicles attack [20]; Kamel *et al.* proposed a trust-based scheme to defend against Sybil attacks and implemented a fake alert attack [21]. Using the MATLAB VANET 5G communication toolboxes with the SUMO [22], Nguyen *et al.* created three attacks, a data falsification attack, a Sybil attack, and a collusion attack in which multiple vehicles collude to report false data. Grover *et al.* used NCTuns-5.0 [23] to implement various misbehavior attacks including identity spoofing, position forging, replay and detention attacks [24]. Iqbal *et al.* [25] used the Eclipse MOSAIC framework to simulate two attacks, a data replay attack and a bogus information attack. Eclipse MOSAIC, previously known as V2X Simulation Runtime Infrastructure (VSimRTI), is a relatively new open-source simulation framework. It is similar to VEINS. It supports multiple simulators including SUMO and PHABMACS for traffic simulation, NS3, OMNET++, and SNS for communication simulation, and Eclipse MOSAIC Application for application simulation [26].

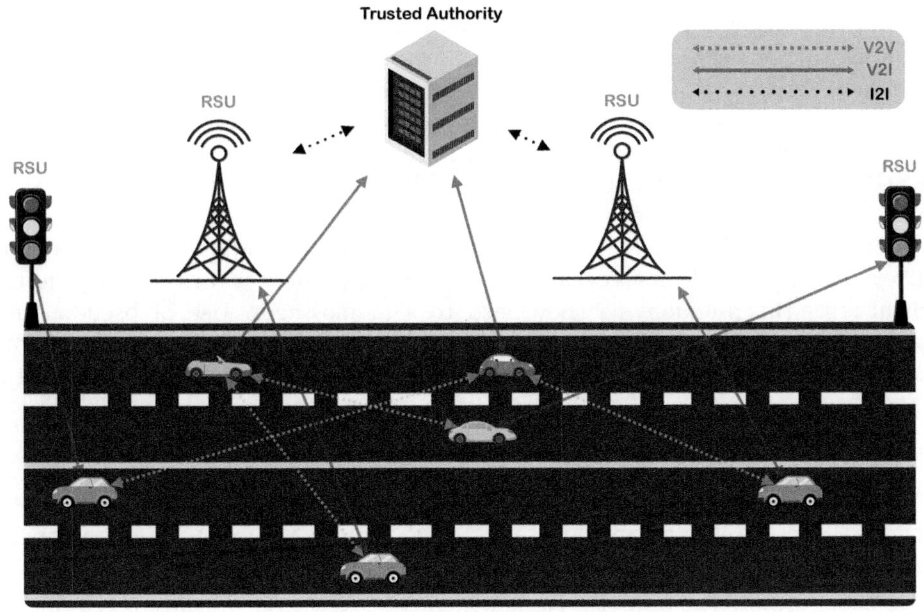

Fig. 1. VANET System Model

3 System Models

3.1 VANET System Model

The VANET is the cornerstone of a cooperative intelligent transport system (C-ITS). In a VANET, vehicles and roadside units exchange messages and data. The VANET system model encompasses a unique architecture designed to create a seamless communication experience and interactions among moving vehicles, road side unites, and trusted authorities. One essential characteristic of VANETs is the direct communication between vehicles through onboard units (OBUs) in vehicles. A VANET system model is illustrated in Fig. 1.

OBUs are small processing units with networking capabilities, which can implement the proper communication protocol for dedicated short range communications (DSRC). The IEEE 802.11p tailored for VANET is the protocol used for this purpose. A specific frequency from the 5.9GHZ domain is reserved for V2V and V2I direct communication. Seven channels (channels 172, 174, 176, 178, 180, 182, 184) are available for DSRC over this range. Channel 172 is the one used for basic safety messages [11]. The wireless access for vehicular environments protocol is also utilized to establish the communication in V2V and V2I modes. It has a communication range of 1000 m and data transfer speeds up to 27 Mbps [9].

Roadside units (RSUs) are fixed location elements in a VANET. They are a critical component of VANET infrastructure and they play an important role in ensuring safety and extending the communication range. RSUs offer various services to the network ranging from safety application to Internet and infotainment services. RSUs are not limited by size or power constraints that OBUs have, which allows for greater computational power and enhanced security. They can also be used to share traffic and hazardous information with nearby vehicles. RSUs may interact with each other in the I2I mode to share critical information and extend the network size.

Trusted Authorities (TA) are another important component of VANETs. They are responsible for registering vehicles into the network and providing them with the pseudonyms they need to sign messages. Use of pseudonyms preserves the privacy of network nodes since only a TA can link a pseudonym to a true identity. TAs can also revoke certificates from vehicles in a trust-based misbehavior detection system when misbehavior is detected.

3.2 VANET Security Challenges

The dynamic nature of VANET nodes and their high speed and short connection duration make securing VANETs difficult. Rapidly growing number of vehicles also poses a challenge on network management. As not all vehicles are equipped with the necessary components for connecting to a VANET, connected vehicles in a VANET will need to handle non-connected vehicles. Last but not the least, the nature of transportation and driving makes safety and reliability critically important as any misbehavior might lead to catastrophic results. All of these challenges must be considered while developing VANET security solutions [27].

3.3 VANET Security Requirements and Relationship with BSMs

Based on the VANET security requirements introduced in previous studies [8, 11, 28], the following security requirements are considered in this work and their relationship with BSM security is presented in this section.

Authentication. Authentication is the first line of defense in a VANET. User authentication refers to the process of ensuring each user's authentic identity through the usage of certificate or other means (e.g., biometrics). Only verified users are able to use the network, and recipients of messages are assured that these messages are from a legitimate source. In the context of BSM, user authentication is achieved by the Certificate Authority that issues digital certificates (pseudonyms) to each vehicle. Message authentication is the process of verifying messages are from legitimate sources and no tampering has occurred.

Integrity. This requirement ensures that data shared in a VANET can be verified and any tampering can be detected. BSM integrity is highly important as it is easy to forge or tamper with BSMs. It often achieved through the use of misbehavior detection system (MDS) to classify messages as genuine or malicious.

Confidentiality. This requirement assures that messages should only be disclosed to authorized users. It prevents malicious and non-authorized users from gaining access to messages, which is usually achieved using encryption. This requirement in general is not a big concern for BSM. Quick message sharing is more important and the high encryption overhead is not tolerable.

Availability. This requirement refers to the need for the system to be always available for authorized users to use. It is a critical requirement in safety-related applications such as BSM sharing. Preventing and mitigating denial-of-service (DOS) attacks is key to high availability.

Authorization. Only legitimate nodes are allowed to use the network. It is a general VANET requirement that should be implemented at the network level. BSM message sharing should only be allowed among the vehicles and RSUs that have been authorized by the network.

Privacy. Real identities of vehicles in a VANET should be preserved for privacy. This can be done by issuing different digital identities (pseudonyms) to a vehicle. Vehicles will change their digital identity used in BSM periodically according to the change policy.

Non-repudiation. A malicious entity must not be able to deny its messages after sending them, which is a crucial requirement in safety applications. For BSMs, this requirement is usually enforced by the TA by linking a vehicle's real identity to its pseudonyms.

3.4 BSM Attacker Model

Regarding the attacker model, some of previous works define it based on attacks, e.g., [16,22,29,30]. Within the scope of VANET, it is more often to define the attacker model based on activity level, location with respect to the network, purpose of attack, scope and distribution of controlled entities, and ability to control certificates and messages [8,11,12,15,16,18], which our study is also based on. The breakdown of our BSM attacker mode is as follows:

Active Attacker vs. Passive Attacker. An active attacker is an attacker who is able to actively tamper with BSM content, while a passive attacker only eavesdrops BSM information. BSM attackers usually are active attackers.

Internal Attacker vs. External Attacker. An internal attacker is within the network and communication range and is able to sign messages and participate in the communication, while an external attacker does not have access to either the network or a pseudonym. Attackers in existing BSM studies are all internal since external attackers are very limited in their capabilities due to the certification requirement and constant change of pseudonyms.

Rational Attacker vs. Malicious Attacker. Attackers can be rational seeking to gain personal benefits from attacks. They can also be malicious with objective of causing harm on the road. Both rational attackers and malicious attackers exist in BSM attacks.

BSM Data and Certificate Access. Attackers may tamper with BSMs or use them to launch denial-of-service attacks. They may also generate crafted BSMs with their pseudonyms to launch various Sybil attacks.

Local Attack vs. Distributed Attack. This criterion is concerned with whether an attacker can only attack the local node, or is able to attack multiple nodes in different locations in the network. In the context of BSM, most of attacks have not taken it into consideration. Currently, an attacker is able to launch several attacks using different pseudonyms.

Faulty Entities vs. Malicious Entities. The difference between malicious entities and faulty entities has been mentioned in the literature. Faulty nodes usually refer to those nodes that produce incorrect or inaccurate data due to faults in sensors without malicious intent [12]. Misbehavior Detection Systems (MDSes) should be able to catch this type of misbehavior in a similar manner to catching malicious misbehavior.

4 Attacks on Basic Safety Message

Numerous BSM attacks have been discovered or developed over the years. As the format and usage of BSM are simple, many attacks have focused on falsifying BSM content. While some kinematic information falsifications might be considered as malfunctioning, in this study, all misbehavior is regarded as malicious since kinematic information falsification still constitutes a misbehavior that needs to be detected by misbehavior detection systems. Another class of attacks exploits the multiple identities (pseudonyms) issued to vehicles for privacy protection. These pseudonyms are maliciously used by attackers to create ghost vehicles on the road, disrupting the network. Such attacks are known as Sybil attacks and have various forms.

Since the introduction of VeReMi, researchers had extensively used the five attacks in VeReMi to develop misbehavior detection systems. This motivated the authors of VeReMi to create a newer version with 20 attacks [31]. More recently, Ansari *et al.* developed a new BSM attack simulation framework named VASP [16]. Similar to F2MD, VASP was built as a submodule of VEINS, but it focuses on attack creation and does not include misbehavior detection systems. They used VASP to create 68 attacks, most of which are variations of BSM content falsification. Notably, Ansari *et al.* also introduced attacks against BSM applications EEBL and IMA. Compared to most of BSM attacks, a more sophisticated position attack named SixPack was introduced by Pollicino *et al.* in which a forged stop is followed by continuous normal behavior [17]. In the rest of this section, we will first briefly describe the attacks introduced by the VeReMi extension dataset [31] and then summarize the attacks introduced by VASP and SixPack, respectively.

4.1 Attacks in VeReMi Extension Dataset

The 20 attacks introduced by the VeReMi extension dataset are as follows:

Constant Position Attack: The attacker sends a fixed position in every BSM message. This attack is classified as a malfunction in the dataset and can be easily detected by observing the position information in two consecutive BSMs.

Constant Position Offset Attack: The attacker adds a constant offset to its position in every message. It is classified as a malfunction and can be easily detected by plausibility checks.

Random Position Attack: The attacker sends a random position instead of its actual position in every BSM. It is classified as a malfunction and is also easy to catch over multiple consecutive messages.

Random Position Offset Attack: The attacker adds a random offset to every BSM. This attack is classified as a malfunction and is fairly simple to catch with plausibility checks.

Constant Speed Attack: The attacker sends a fixed speed value in every BSM. This attack is classified as a malfunction in the dataset and can be easily detected by observing the speed information in two consecutive BSMs.

Constant Speed Offset Attack: The attacker adds a constant offset to its speed in every BSM. It is classified as a malfunction and can be easily detected by plausibility checks.

Random Speed Attack: The attacker sends a random speed value in every BSM. It is classified as a malfunction and can be easily detected by observing the speed information over multiple consecutive BSMs.

Random Speed Offset Attacks: The attacker adds a random offset to its speed in every BSM. It is classified as a malfunction and can be easily detected by plausibility checks.

Stale Messages Attack: Legitimate messages are sent with a delay.

Disruptive Attack: The attacker stores messages from its neighboring vehicles and then sends them again later. These messages intend to overwhelm the system.

Data Replay Attack: It is similar to Disruptive Attack. However, in this attack, the attacker keeps replaying the messages of a specific target for a period of time, which makes it appear to be one vehicle following another vehicle.

Eventual Stop Attack: The attacker behaves normally for a while and then suddenly forges stopping by sending a fixed location to disrupt the flow of the system.

Congestion Sybil Attack: The attacker uses all of its pseudonyms to pretend to be multiple vehicles on the road all at once by sending different position information in every message and maintaining the correct frequency for every created vehicle.

Denial Of Service (DOS) Attack: The attacker sends messages with a much higher frequency to overload and disrupt the network for legitimate usage.

Denial Of Service (DOS) Random Attack: It is similar to normal DOS attacks. The difference is that the attacker puts random values instead of real ones in its BSM fields.

Denial Of Service (DOS) Disruptive Attack: In this form of DOS attack, the attacker keeps replaying messages from different vehicles in the network at a high frequency.

Denial Of Service (DOS) Random Sybil Attack: In this variation of DOS attack, the attacker combines it with the Sybil attack by using all of the attacker's pseudonyms and sending a large number of messages with random values at a much higher frequency.

Denial Of Service (DOS) Disruptive Sybil Attack: This attack is similar to the DOS random Sybil attack. The difference is that instead of using random values in BSM, the attacker uses values previously by other nodes in the network.

Data Replay Sybil Attack: The attacker targets several nodes in the network and replays their messages with a certain delay at a consistent frequency while signing each message with a different pseudonym.

MA (Misbehavior Authority) Stress Attack: This VeReMi attack is not implemented in the literature. In the architecture implemented in F2MD, a node that detects misbehavior can choose to report that misbehavior to a global authority named the misbehavior authority. This attack aims to stress the misbehavior authority by issuing a large number of fake reports.

4.2 Attacks from VASP

A total of 68 attacks can be implemented using VASP [16]. The complete list of those attacks can be found on VASP's GitHub page [32]. Most of the attacks are created by changing certain values in BSM, e.g., by setting the new value to either a high, low, constant, or random value. Some of them are similar to the attacks in VeReMi such as the sudden appearance attack. Some attacks in VASP are more sophisticated such as the braking from communication range attack. For that attack, the attacker first selects a specific target; Based on its position, the attacker estimates the target nodes communication range. Then, the attacker creates a ghost vehicle at the edge of the estimated communication range of the target. After that, the attacker will reduce the distance between the ghost vehicle and the target node over subsequent BSMs. An important type of attacks introduced by VASP is those attacks that target specific BSM applications such as EEBL and IMA, which are not available in previous datasets or simulation tools.

4.3 SixPack Attack

Created by Pollicino *et al.* [17], the SixPack attack is one of the first sophisticated attacks on VANETs that were developed after VeReMi falsification attacks. It was created with the purpose of defeating state-of-the-art MDSes. This attack targets the EEBL application. The rationale behind the attack is to cause a reaction by vehicles on the road by pretending to stop suddenly and then forging quick acceleration in the following BSMs to return to the original location of the vehicle.

5 Detection of BSM Attacks

Misbehavior detection techniques for VANET and V2X can be classified in different manners. However, their underlying classification criteria are similar. Sedar *et al.* took a general classification approach and categorized the defenses mechanisms into proactive measures and reactive measures [8]. The proactive measures are further classified into cryptography based, physical layer security based, and privacy preservation based, while the reactive measures are classified into signature based, anomaly based, and context based. The reactive classification, especially the anomaly and context based, is consistent with the classification of misbehavior detection systems found in the literature [7,10,11,13]. BSM misbehavior detection systems work at a lower level in the defense mechanisms taxonomy. They mainly rely on reactive anomaly based mechanisms. While most of the misbehavior detection systems in the literature are data centric, node centric architectures were also designed that work as an extra layer of defense in addition to the data centric model.

In this study, we have examined the BSM misbehavior detection systems in the literature and classified them based on their underlying methods. The classification of BSM misbehavior detection systems is shown in Fig. 2. In the rest of this section, we will analyze machine learning based, deep learning based, plausibility based, and SDN based misbehavior detection systems, respectively.

5.1 Machine Learning Based Misbehavior Detection Systems

Numerous methods have been proposed to leverage machine learning (ML) techniques for BSM misbehavior detection. These approaches train various classic machine learning models, such as Support Vector Machines (SVM), K-Nearest Neighbors (KNN), Random Forests (RF), Decision Tree (DT), Nave Bayes (NB), and Ensemble methods, on datasets such as VeReMi to learn patterns that distinguish normal behavior from malicious behavior. Key advantages of machine learning based methods include their ability to learn complex patterns from data, adapt to new attack types, and achieve high detection accuracy. However, they also face challenges such as computational resource constraints on vehicular systems, sensitivity to noisy or incomplete data, and the need for continuous retraining as new attacks emerge.

So *et al.* employed KNN and SVM models and leveraged location and mobility plausibility to assess BSMs [33]. Their features include predicting future movement and checking consistency between displacement and reported velocities. Sharma and Liu conducted a study [30] similar to [33], but they incorporated other ML models including SVM, KNN, NB, RF, Ensemble Boosting, and

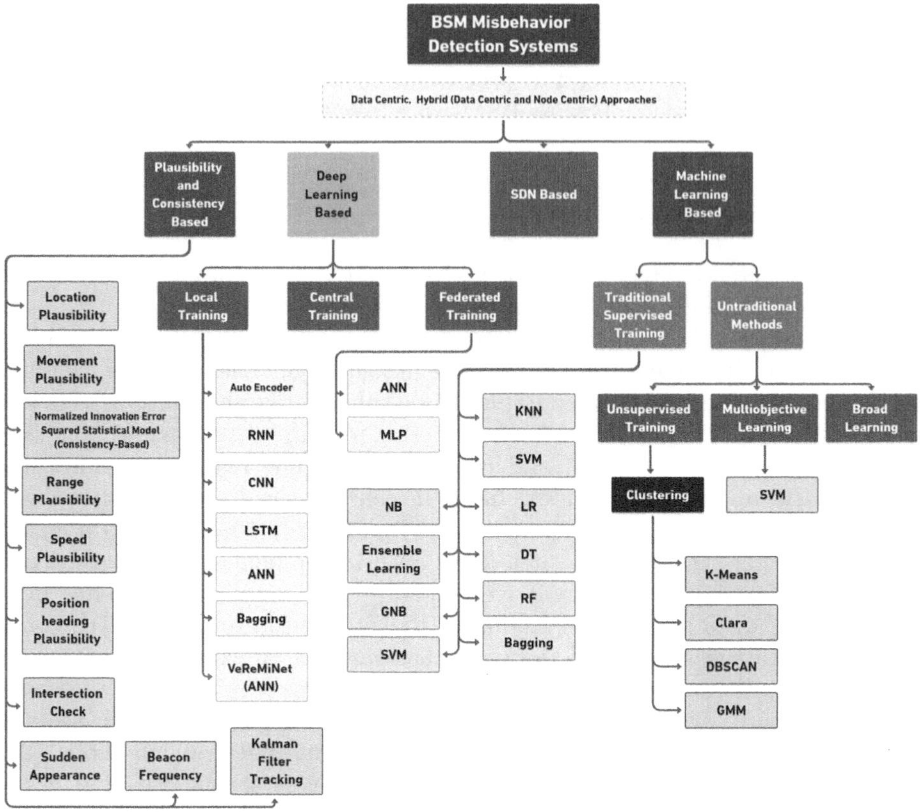

Fig. 2. Classification of BSM Misbehavior Detection Systems

Ensemble Voting. They also used movement and location plausibility as features and performed a comparative analysis. Their results show that overall ensemble learning algorithms (boosting and voting) perform the best, with AUC values around 0.85 for detecting all attack types. Adding plausibility checks improves the precision by approximately 5% and recall by 2% for the majority of attacks. Their results align with the findings of [34], which was published a year later.

Gyawali and Qian introduced a cooperative scheme for misbehavior detection [19]. They implemented several ML models (LR, KNN, DT, RF, and Bagging and tested them against a fake alert attack and a position falsification attack from VeReMi. For the fake alert attack, the cooperative scheme uses information from surrounding vehicles such as vehicle density, speed, and flow. For the position falsification attack, the scheme uses common features such as changes in speed, position, receiving distance, and received signal strength indicator (RSSI). Their scheme also uses trust based approaches. When a vehicle detects an attack, it will broadcast a warning message to neighboring vehicles to add the attack vehicle into a blacklist.

Ercan *et al.* applied new features to KNN and RF models [35]. They combined angle of arrival (AoA) and estimated distance with existing features such as RSSI, position, and distance between sender and receiver. Their results show that the proposed approach with new features can outperform existing methods or achieve comparable performance. However, they only used the constant offset attack from the VeReMi dataset for testing.

Hawlader *et al.* employed variations in position between subsequent messages as features to evaluate six ML models (SVM, DT, RF, KNN, NB, LR) [29]. The models did not perform well with multi-class classification using the VeReMi dataset. However, the decision tree (DT) algorithm can achieve 100% accuracy using a simulated version of VeReMi dataset.

Dutra *et al.* [36] used signal strength and displacement compliance (similar to [33]) as their features. Their main contribution, however, is that they used sliding windows of varying lengths (2, 3, 8, 13, 18, and 23 BSMs) for decision making. Four traditional machine learning models (KNN, DT, RF, and Multi-layer Perceptron (MLP)), and a deep learning model (LSTM) were employed for evaluation. They also included the inference time which appears to be a good evaluation criterion in the context of high-speed vehicular networks. The evaluation results suggest that the decision tree (DT) algorithm achieve the best cost benefit ratio, with an average F1 score of 0.878, a training time of 47.62 s, and an inference time of 0.09 s. Later, the same research team conducted a similar study but with five predictors [37]. They implemented a federated learning scheme instead of local training. In their architecture, vehicles train MLP models locally and share the weights with the server that runs a federated averaging algorithm.

Wang *et al.* applied a Broad Learning System (BLS) approach with incremental learning to vehicle misbehavior detection [38]. Their system architecture consists of four modules: data collection and sharing module, feature extraction module, detection model establishment and decision module, and model update module. Evaluated with VeReMi, PeMS, and NGSIM datasets, their model achieves F1 scores of 0.914, 0.968, and 0.955 over the three datasets, respectively, with fast training and inference times.

Huang *et al.* introduced multi-objective learning in misbehavior detection [39]. Their model aims to maximize recall (detecting malicious messages) and specificity (identifying normal messages correctly). A multi-objective immune algorithm is adopted to generate a set of Pareto-optimal SVM models during training, which are then combined using an evidential reasoning based strategy during testing. The detection is performed locally on individual vehicles, only using features extracted from a single BSM. When evaluated against five position falsification attacks from the VeReMi dataset, the proposed model outperforms the original VeReMi work [14] as well as the work by Sharma and Liu [30] in terms of precision and recall for most attack types.

Sharma and Jaekel proposed to perform misbehavior detection at roadside units (RSUs) instead of onboard units (OBUs) to leverage RSU's computational power and connectivity [40]. Similarly to [36,37], their approach uses data from two consecutive BSMs. When a new BSM is received, the RSU retrieves the last received BSM from the same sender and combines the information from both messages. The authors evaluated their method with several ML algorithms including KNN, RF, DT, and NB. The proposed approach outperforms existing techniques across different attack types in terms of precision and recall, with significant improvement observed for the constant offset attack. However, the study does not consider the processing capabilities of OBUs and RSUs or the ability to have shared RSU databases in real-world scenarios.

Hsu *et al.* proposed to conduct model training at RSUs but perform misbehavior detection at OBUs [41]. When a vehicle enters the service zones of RSUs, it will download or update the pre-trained detection model from the nearest RSU. Their proposed detection method consists of a convolutional neural network (CNN) model and a long short-term memory (LSTM) model for position reconstruction, and an SVM binary classifier for misbehavior detection using 11 features, including reconstruction error and features derived from plausibility checks. A key contribution of their work is incorporating acceleration information in the reconstruction model inputs. Their method can achieve an average F1 score of 0.9611 across 19 misbehavior types and outperform other algorithms in comparison.

Ilango *et al.* introduced a two-layer system called NPFADS that uses both ML and DL techniques [42]. The proposed NPFADS system has two modules: an RF-based MDS and a novel attack detection module (NADM). The architecture is based on a 5G-enabled VANET, with fog nodes located in the Access and Mobility Management Function (AMF) of the 5G core network. The RF-based MDS, installed in each vehicle's OBU and fog nodes, is responsible for detecting known position falsification attacks. The NADM, only installed in fog nodes, consists of an autoencoder and an RF model and is used to discover novel position falsification attacks and extract samples to retrain the MDS. The system also incorporates trust based features by maintaining a database of misbehaving vehicles. The evaluation shows that NPFADS is able to learn and detect novel position falsification attacks while maintaining high detection performance for known attacks.

Slama *et al.* evaluated various ML and DL techniques including binary classification, multi-class classification for three classes using the Classic Learning Approach for Multi-class Classification (C-LAMC), and a novel Guided Learning Approach for Multi-class Classification (G-LAMC) [43]. The G-LAMC addresses learning from imbalanced data by grouping similar misbehavior into one class. The study used the VeReMi extension dataset and employed a variety of classifiers including RF, KNN, NB, LR, DT, MLP, ANN, CNN, and LSTM. Feature selection methods, including recursive feature elimination (RFE) and analysis of variance (ANOVA), were used to improve performance. The evaluation results show that the binary classification performs better than the multi-class classification for specific misbehavior classes, with G-LAMC outperforming C-LAMC. Additionally, RF classifiers are more efficient than DL classifiers in classifying misbehavior, and RFE performs better than other feature selection methods.

El Attar *et al.* applied unsupervised learning techniques to detect DOS attacks in VANETs [44]. Four clustering algorithms, i.e., K-Means, CLARA, DBSCAN, and Gaussian Mixture Model (GMM), were evaluated for detecting three types of DOS attacks (Normal, Random, and Disruptive) from the VeReMi extension dataset. The proposed system collects attack and benign traffic at RSUs and sends it to central/distributed servers for analysis using the clustering algorithms. The GMM algorithm is able to achieve the best performance with an F1 score of around 95% for all DOS attack categories. However, the computational complexity of certain algorithms, such as GMM, can be prohibitively high for real-time detection in large-scale vehicular networks.

5.2 Deep Learning Based Misbehavior Detection Systems

Recent studies have increasingly explored deep learning (DL) for detecting misbehavior in vehicular networks. DL-based approaches typically involve training deep models, such as convolutional neural networks (CNNs), recurrent neural networks (RNNs), or autoencoders on datasets that contain both normal and malicious BSM data. The models learn to extract high-level features and patterns that can distinguish legitimate from falsified messages.

A major advantage of deep learning is its ability to automatically learn rich representations from raw data, capturing complex non-linear relationships that are difficult to discover manually. However, deep models are often data-hungry and computationally expensive. Lack of interpretability is another challenge to deep models. Furthermore, deploying DL models on resource-constrained vehicular systems also poses challenges. Nonetheless, deep learning shows promise in enhancing detection accuracy, especially for sophisticated attacks.

Many studies that employ both deep learning and machine learning techniques have been discussed in Sect. 5.1. In this section, we focus on those studies that exclusively employ deep learning techniques.

In 2019, Kamel *et al.* proposed a Misbehavior Authority (MA) system for detecting Sybil attacks [45], targeting four types of Sybil attacks from the VeReMi extension dataset. This work expands the F2MD framework, with the MA system taking misbehavior reports (MBRs) as input and predicting the attack type. The system operates in three phases: 1) General Misbehavior Type Detection that uses autoencoders and RNNs to detect misbehavior related to a single pseudonym, 2) Pseudonym Linkage that links pseudonyms of the same vehicle using a Linkage Authority or machine learning, and 3) Sybil Type Detection that applies RNNs on the linked pseudonyms. The detection accuracy for Sybil attacks can achieve 94.97% by using the Linkage Authority and 88.83% by using the machine learning linkage approach.

Uprety *et al.* proposed a privacy-preserving federated learning approach for misbehavior detection [46]. Acting as local nodes, vehicles receive an initial artificial neural network (ANN) model from a central authority. The vehicles train the model locally on their own BSM data and then send back the updated models to the central authority, which will average them to create a globally improved model for attack detection. Evaluated on the five attacks from the original VeReMi dataset, the proposed federated approach can achieve higher overall attack detection accuracy compared to a centrally trained model, although the centralized model has slightly higher recall.

Saudagar and Ranawat proposed an amalgamated model for misbehavior detection [47]. Their architecture conducts central training at RSUs instead of OBUs, with RSUs maintaining a shared database about all nodes to enable a trust-based scheme. The proposed deep learning model also uses a teaching-learning-based marine predator algorithm for feature selection to identify the best attributes to improve accuracy and reduce complexity. Evaluated on the five original VeReMi attacks, the proposed model outperforms previous works in detecting the random offset and eventual stop attacks, while showing similar performance for the other three attacks.

Around the same time, Lochbihler *et al.* proposed a two-model deep learning based MDS [48]. Model 1 uses sequence-to-sequence prediction (LSTM and Transformer) to learn expected normal vehicle behavior by taking ten BSMs as input and predicting the next BSM. Model 2 employs a CNN and an XGBoost for classifying vehicles as non-attacking or attacking based on features such as vehicle position, speed, nearby vehicle data, and predictions from Model 1. The CNN and XGBoost models are trained on all attack types to detect unknown attacks. The evaluation results show that Model 1 can achieve an RMSE of 0.078/0.065 for position and 0.15/0.105 for speed prediction. For Model 2, the CNN model can achieve an accuracy of 0.72 and a precision of 0.81, while the XGBoost model can achieve an accuracy of 0.73 and a precision of 0.73.

5.3 Plausibility and Consistency Based Misbehavior Detection Systems

Plausibility and consistency based checks, which are short predefined series of checks performed on received BSMs, have also been employed in the literature. These checks use information either from a single BSM or across several consecutive BSMs to verify consistency among the checks. As they can be performed rapidly, these checks are suitable for the applications such as VANET security that require fast decisions. Although these checks are often combined with machine learning techniques and used as features for training, as mentioned in Sect. 5.1, they were also used as a major detection method in previous studies.

In 2019, Kamel *et al.* proposed the CaTch model, a confidence range tolerant misbehavior detection method [21]. The authors employed two attacks, a Constant Offset attack and a Sybil attack, to test their model using VEINS and F2MD. Their misbehavior detection method performs multiple plausibility and consistency checks, similar to the checks used in F2MD, while also considering the confidence level of kinematic information. The authors compared the CaTch detector with a legacy detector using two detection applications: a simple threshold-based application and an advanced ML-based application. A set of metrics were employed including precision, recall, F1 score, accuracy, Bookmaker Informedness, and Matthews Correlation Coefficient. Their evaluation results show that both detection approaches can achieve 79–84% F1 scores. However, more attack types need to be evaluated and further research is needed to optimize the CaTch model.

In 2020, Nguyen *et al.* [22] proposed a consistency based approach to enhancing misbehavior detection in 5G vehicle-to-vehicle communications against single data falsification, Sybil, and collusion attacks. Their method uses physical layer information from 5G multi-array beamforming antennas and an unscented Kalman filter to predict vehicle trajectories. A normalized innovation error squared (NIES) statistical model was used to detect inconsistencies between estimated and reported positions from BSMs and classify vehicles as normal or abnormal. Their simulation results suggest the proposed method can achieve over 0.97 accuracy in detecting abnormal reports, with an average response time of 2.266 ms. However, the system needs to be evaluated against a broader range of attacks to assess its robustness.

5.4 SDN Based Misbehavior Detection Systems

The motivation behind applying Software-Defined Networking (SDN) to VANET misbehavior detection systems lies in addressing the inherent challenges and limitations of traditional VANETs. Due to dynamic topologies, high mobility, and intermittent links, it is challenging to deploy effective security solutions in VANETs. SDN's programmability and centralized control features offer an attractive solution to these challenges. By incorporating SDN into VANETs, the network can be made adaptive and context-aware, enabling dynamic adjustment to security parameters and detection mechanisms based on real-time network conditions, such as vehicle density, attack types, and network traffic patterns. Additionally, The SDN's global view of network allows for efficient monitoring and management of network activities, facilitating implementation of misbehavior detection systems that can accurately identify and mitigate various forms of internal attacks in VANETs.

Sultana *et al.* [49] proposed a novel SDN-based framework for misbehavior detection. They used the five original attacks from the VeReMi dataset and leveraged the F2MD framework. Their architecture combines SDN and VANETs. The network is divided into clusters with RSUs acting as SDN controllers (RSCs) for the clusters and a global SDN controller (GSC) at the Trusted Authority. The Local detection involves data-centric checks by vehicles and node-centric ML detection by RSCs, which generate reports for the global detection by the GSC. The framework aims to adapt detection based on the context such as vehicle density. The evaluation of using KNN on the VeReMi dataset shows high precision (0.92–0.95) and recall (0.79–0.99) for the constant location attack.

Around the same time, Boualouache *et al.* [20] proposed an adaptive SDN-based MDS that adjusts security parameters based on the context such as mobility and attacker presence. It has a hierarchical SDN control structure with local, regional, and global controllers. Key aspects include context-aware parameter adaptation, secure clustering and watchdog selection, a trust model combining direct and indirect trust, and Sybil attack resistance. Their results show that the proposed SDN-based MDS can achieve higher detection rates and lower false positives than a static MDS. Although those SDN-based detection systems leverage SDN's programmability for context-aware misbehavior detection in VANETs, they also have to address challenges in realizing their architectures and quantifying overheads in real systems, e.g., overheads incurred by frequent inter-controller communications.

6 Challenges and Future Directions

Securing BSMs against attacks in VANETs remains a significant challenge, with numerous open research questions. While many machine learning and deep learning techniques offer promising enhancements for anomaly detection and attack classification, a comprehensive exploration of the trade-offs between computational complexity and model accuracy is still largely lacking. This trade-off is critical for resource-constrained vehicular systems, where computational complexity, such as that found in Gaussian mixture models, may be prohibitively high for real-time detection in large-scale vehicular networks. Additionally, these algorithms can be sensitive to hyperparameter selection, impacting both accuracy and speed. Further investigation is also needed into the number of BSMs and their feature selection for accurate prediction and classification.

Despite significant efforts to improve attack detection accuracy, there remains noticeable room for enhancement. Detection accuracy can be adversely affected by sophisticated Sybil attacks that mimic normal behavior, false positives from malfunctioning sensors or faulty vehicles, and scenarios with low vehicle density or sparse misbehavior reports. Currently, some proposed deep learning models fail to detect specific anomalies and attacks, such as offset-based anomalies, eventual stop, and grid Sybil attacks, where the behavior closely resembles normal vehicle behavior. The reliance of deep learning approaches on learning position sequence representations of normal vehicles can be exploited by attackers replicating those sequences to evade detection.

Many proposed detection methods assume the availability of accurate and reliable data from neighboring vehicles and infrastructure, which may not always be the case in real-world scenarios. Nearby vehicles can be malicious or compromised, and sensor errors, malfunctions, or noise in input data can degrade the performance of MDS. These challenges underscore the need for robust data preprocessing and filtering techniques.

While training at RSUs has been proposed, it remains unclear whether these methods can scale effectively for large geographic areas. Furthermore, public simulated datasets that are often used in federated learning approaches may not fully capture the real-world non-ID and unbalanced data properties required for effective training. Another significant challenge is the lack of support for shared RSU databases and the undefined training times and processing capabilities of OBUs and RSUs in simulation frameworks and literature. These limitations hinder accurate evaluation and reproducibility of proposed methods. Further research in these areas is essential for advancing BSM security.

A critical future research direction is the improvement of existing simulation frameworks and development of new simulation frameworks so that they can better represent real-world implementations and constraints. These frameworks should support the implementation of BSM-consuming applications such as Emergency Electronic Brake Lights (EEBL), Intersection Movement Assist (IMA), cooperative driving, and platooning. As these applications become more prevalent, their security and resilience against adversarial activities will become increasingly important. Many existing studies do not adequately address the issues of false positives (legitimate vehicles flagged as malicious) and false negatives (malicious vehicles flagged as legitimate) in detection. Incorporating BSM-consuming applications into simulation platforms would allow for systematic study of the consequences of misclassification and stimulate research on adversarial attacks and evasion techniques designed to bypass MDS, an area that has not been well explored.

The development of new BSM attacks is also critical. Existing attack types in publicly available tools likely do not cover all possible BSM attacks in VANETs. While tools like VeReMi and its extension, as well as more recent VASP, provide numerous attacks for research, more sophisticated attacks that incorporate realistic path modeling, traffic conditions, and the specificities of simulation maps are needed to reflect real-world situations and advance BSM security research. Additionally, the orchestration of multiple simultaneous attacks of different types remains underexplored. New attacks, such as Sixpack, are important for testing the generalizability and applicability of proposed methods.

Reproducibility and comparability of BSM attack detection methods also require more attention and research efforts. Many existing studies either lack technical details such as simulation parameters or fail to compare with state-of-the-art methods. It is also not uncommon for features used in training to be unmentioned, and for the computational complexity and resource requirements of proposed models–particularly for real-time deployment on OBUs–to be overlooked or insufficiently investigated. The lack of key information for replicating or comparing BSM attack detection methods hampers validation and, consequently, the advancement of research in this area.

Finally, digital certificates play a critical role in BSM security. However, research on revoking the certificates of misbehaving vehicles and preventing them from rejoining the network appears to be lagging.

7 Conclusion

Securing basic safety messages (BSMs) is crucial for ensuring the reliable and safe operation of VANETs and their associated safety applications. In this paper, we have provided a comprehensive overview of the current state of research in this field, emphasizing the critical role BSMs play in enabling safety-critical applications within VANETs, as well as the potentially catastrophic consequences of successful attacks on these messages. We categorized and analyzed a variety of attacks targeting BSMs, ranging from simple position falsification to more sophisticated and evasive strategies, such as the SixPack attack. Furthermore, we classified different BSM attack and misbehavior detection mechanisms, including machine learning-based, deep learning-based, plausibility and consistency-based, and software-defined networking-based techniques. While these methods have shown promising results in detecting various BSM attacks, significant challenges and open research questions remain. We discussed the ongoing challenges and potential research directions in BSM security, highlighting areas where further investigation is needed to advance the field.

References

1. NHTSA. Early estimate of motor vehicle traffic fatalities in 2022. https://crashstats.nhtsa.dot.gov/Api/Public/ViewPublication/813428
2. Roy, A., Chakraborty, J.: Communication based accident avoidance and congestion control mechanism in VANETs. In: 2015 International Symposium on Advanced Computing and Communication (ISACC), pp. 320–327 (2015)
3. Offor, P.: Vehicle ad hoc network (VANET): safety benefits and security challenges. SSRN Electron. J. **12** (2012)
4. Kenney, J.B.: Dedicated short-range communications (DSRC) standards in the united states. Proc. IEEE **99**(7), 1162–1182 (2011)
5. NHTSA. Vehicle safety communications applications (VSC-A), First annual report. https://www.nhtsa.gov/sites/nhtsa.gov/files/811073.pdf
6. University of Michigan transportation research institute. Safety pilot model deployment: Rx basic safety messages (2022)
7. Sangwan, A., Sangwan, A., Singh, R.P.: A classification of misbehavior detection schemes for VANETs: a survey. Wireless Pers. Commun. **129**(1), 285–322 (2023)
8. Sedar, R., Kalalas, C., Vázquez-Gallego, F., Alonso, L., Alonso-Zarate, J.: A comprehensive survey of v2x cybersecurity mechanisms and future research paths. IEEE Open J. Commun. Soc. **4**, 325–391 (2023)
9. Dong, S., Su, H., Xia, Y., Zhu, F., Hu, X., Wang, B.: A comprehensive survey on authentication and attack detection schemes that threaten it in vehicular ad-hoc networks. IEEE Trans. Intell. Transp. Syst. **24**(12), 13573–13602 (2023)
10. Khan, U., Agrawal, S., Silakari, S.: A detailed survey on misbehavior node detection techniques in vehicular ad hoc networks. In Mandal, J.K., Satapathy, S.C., Sanyal, M.K., Sarkar, P.P., Mukhopadhyay, A., (eds.) Information Systems Design and Intelligent Applications, pp. 11–19. Springer, New Delhi (2015)
11. Yuan, Z., Xu, X., Wang, Y., Wang, P.: Comprehensive review on misbehavior detection for vehicular ad hoc networks. J. Adv. Transp. **2022**, 4725805 (2022)
12. Van der Heijden, R.W., Dietzel, S., Leinmüller, T., Kargl, F.: Survey on misbehavior detection in cooperative intelligent transportation systems. IEEE Commun. Surv. Tutorials **21**(1), 779–811 (2019)
13. Slama, O., Alaya, B., Zidi, S., Tarhouni, M.: Comparative study of misbehavior detection system for classifying misbehaviors on VANET. In: 2022 8th International Conference on Control, Decision and Information Technologies (CoDIT), vol. 1, pp. 243–248 (2022)
14. Van der Heijden, R.W., Lukaseder, T., Kargl, F.: VeReMi: a dataset for comparable evaluation of misbehavior detection in VANETs. In Beyah, R., Chang, B., Li, Y., Zhu, S., (eds.) Security and Privacy in Communication Networks, pp. 318–337. Springer, Cham (2018)
15. Kamel, J., Ansari, M.R., Petit, J., Kaiser, A., Jemaa, I.B., Urien, P.: Simulation framework for misbehavior detection in vehicular networks. IEEE Trans. Veh. Technol. **69**(6), 6631–6643 (2020)
16. Ansari, M.R., Petit, J., Monteuuis, J.P., Chen, C.: Vasp: V2x application spoofing platform. In: Proceedings Inaugural International Symposium on Vehicle Security & Privacy, ndss-symposium (2023)
17. Pollicino, F., Stabili, D., Bella, G., Marchetti, M.: Sixpack: abusing abs to avoid misbehavior detection in VANETs. In: 2021 IEEE 93rd Vehicular Technology Conference, pp. 1–6 (2021)

18. Trabelsi, Z., Shah, S.S., Hayawi, K.: Multi-BSM: an anomaly detection and position falsification attack mitigation approach in connected vehicles. Electronics **11**(20), 3282 (2022)
19. Gyawali, S., Qian, Y.: Misbehavior detection using machine learning in vehicular communication networks. In: ICC 2019 - 2019 IEEE International Conference on Communications (ICC), pp. 1–6 (2019)
20. Boualouache, A., Soua, R., Engel, T.: SDN-based misbehavior detection system for vehicular networks. In: 2020 IEEE 91st Vehicular Technology Conference (VTC2020-Spring), pp. 1–5 (2020)
21. Kamel, J., Kaiser, A., ben Jemaa, I., Cincilla, P., Urien, P.: CaTch: a confidence range tolerant misbehavior detection approach. In: 2019 IEEE Wireless Communications and Networking Conference (WCNC), pp. 1–8 (2019)
22. Nguyen, V.-L., Lin, P.-C., Hwang, R.-H.: Enhancing misbehavior detection in 5G vehicle-to-vehicle communications. IEEE Trans. Veh. Technol. **69**(9), 9417–9430 (2020)
23. Wang, S.Y., Lin, C.C.: NCTUns 5.0: a network simulator for IEEE 802.11(p) and 1609 wireless vehicular network researches. In: 2008 IEEE 68th Vehicular Technology Conference, pp. 1–2 (2008)
24. Grover, J., Laxmi, V., Gaur, M.S.: Misbehavior detection based on ensemble learning in VANET. In: Thilagam, P.S., Pais, A.R., Chandrasekaran, K., Balakrishnan, N. (eds.) Advanced Computing, Networking and Security, pp. 602–611. Springer, Heidelberg (2012)
25. Iqbal, S., Ball, P., Kamarudin, M.H., Bradley, A.: Simulating malicious attacks on VANETs for connected and autonomous vehicle cybersecurity: a machine learning dataset (2022)
26. Weber, J.S., Neves, M., Ferreto, T.: VANET simulators: an updated review. J. Braz. Comput. Soc. **27**(1), 1–31 (2021). https://doi.org/10.1186/s13173-021-00113-x
27. Phull, N., Singh, P.: A review on security issues in VANETs. In: 2019 6th International Conference on Computing for Sustainable Global Development (INDIACom), pp. 1084–1088 (2019)
28. Stundefinedpień, K., Poniszewska-Marańda, A.: Security solution methods in the vehicular ad-hoc networks. In: MoMM2019, pp. 127–135. Association for Computing Machinery, New York (2020)
29. Hawlader, F., Boualouache, A., Faye, S., Engel,T.: Intelligent misbehavior detection system for detecting false position attacks in vehicular networks. In: 2021 IEEE International Conference on Communications Workshops (ICC Workshops), pp. 1–6 (2021)
30. Sharma, P., Liu, H.: A machine-learning-based data-centric misbehavior detection model for internet of vehicles. IEEE Internet Things J. **8**(6), 4991–4999 (2021)
31. Kamel, J., Wolf, M., Van Der Hei, R.W., Kaiser, A., Urien, P., Kargl, F.: Veremi extension: a dataset for comparable evaluation of misbehavior detection in VANETS. In: ICC 2020 - 2020 IEEE International Conference on Communications (ICC), pp. 1–6 (2020)
32. Github. https://github.com/quic/vasp
33. So, S., Sharma, P., Petit, J.: Integrating plausibility checks and machine learning for misbehavior detection in VANET. In: 2018 17th IEEE International Conference on Machine Learning and Applications (ICMLA), pp. 564–571 (2018)
34. Sultana, J., Grover, J., Tripathi, M.: Exploiting machine learning and deep learning models for misbehavior detection in VANET. Int. J. Comput. Appl. **44**(11), 1024–1038 (2022)

35. Ercan, S., Ayaida, M., Messai, N.: New features for position falsification detection in VANETs using machine learning. In: ICC 2021 - IEEE International Conference on Communications, pp. 1–6 (2021)
36. Dutra, F., Bonfim, K., Siqueira, C., Pereira, L.A., Santos, A., Meneguette, R.I.: Dismiss-BSM: an architecture for detecting position spoofing in basic safety messages. In: GLOBECOM 2022 - 2022 IEEE Global Communications Conference, pp. 3381–3386 (2022)
37. Bonfim, K.A., Dutra, F.D.S., Siqueira, C.E.T., Meneguette, R.I., Dos Santos, A.L., Júnior, L.A.P.: Federated learning-based architecture for detecting position spoofing in basic safety messages. In: 2023 IEEE 97th Vehicular Technology Conference (VTC2023-Spring), pp. 1–5 (2023)
38. Wang, X., Zhu, Y., Han, S., Yang, L., Haixia, G., Wang, F.-Y.: Fast and progressive misbehavior detection in internet of vehicles based on broad learning and incremental learning systems. IEEE Internet Things J. **9**(6), 4788–4798 (2022)
39. Huang, J., Lv, J., Zhou, Z., Gyawali, S., Qian, Y.: A multi-objective model for misbehavior detection in IOV. In: GLOBECOM 2022 - 2022 IEEE Global Communications Conference, pp. 4395–4400 (2022)
40. Sharma, A., Jaekel, A.: Machine learning based misbehaviour detection in VANET using consecutive BSM approach. IEEE Open J. Veh. Technol. **3**, 1–14 (2022)
41. Hsu, H.Y., Cheng, N.H., Tsai, C.W.: A deep learning-based integrated algorithm for misbehavior detection system in VANETS. In: Proceedings of the 2021 ACM International Conference on Intelligent Computing and Its Emerging Applications, ACM ICEA 2021, pp. 53–58. Association for Computing Machinery, New York (2022)
42. Ilango, H.S., Ma, M., Su, R.: A misbehavior detection system to detect novel position falsification attacks in the internet of vehicles. Eng. Appl. Artif. Intell. **116**, 105380 (2022)
43. Slama, O., Alaya, B., Zidi, S.: Towards misbehavior intelligent detection using guided machine learning in vehicular ad-hoc networks (VANET). Inteligencia Artif. **25**, 138–154 (2022)
44. El Attar, A., Fadlallah, A., Chbib, F., Khatoun, R.: Unsupervised learning algorithms for denial of service detection in vehicular networks. In: 2022 International Conference on Electrical, Computer, Communications and Mechatronics Engineering (ICECCME), pp. 1–7 (2022)
45. Kamel, J., Haidar, F., Jemaa, I.B., Kaiser, A., Lonc, B., Urien, P.: A misbehavior authority system for sybil attack detection in cits. In: 2019 IEEE 10th Annual Ubiquitous Computing, Electronics & Mobile Communication Conference (UEMCON), pp. 1117–1123 (2019)
46. Uprety, A., Rawat, D.B., Li, J.: Privacy preserving misbehavior detection in IOV using federated machine learning. In: 2021 IEEE 18th Annual Consumer Communications & Networking Conference (CCNC), pp. 1–6 (2021)
47. Saudagar, S., Ranawat, R.: An amalgamated novel ids model for misbehaviour detection using vereminet. Comput. Stan. Interfaces **88**, 103783 (2023)
48. Lochbihler, A., Husseinat, A., Ma, M., Abuibaid, M., Huang, J.S., Zhu, B.: Misbehaviour detection of 5G-connected vehicles using deep learning. In: 2023 IEEE 20th International Conference on Mobile Ad Hoc and Smart Systems (MASS), pp. 646–651. IEEE Computer Society, Los Alamitos (2023)
49. Sultana, R., Grover, J., Tripathi, M.: A novel framework for misbehavior detection in SDN-based VANET. In: 2020 IEEE International Conference on Advanced Networks and Telecommunications Systems (ANTS), pp. 1–6 (2020)

BGETC: An Encrypted Traffic Classification Method Based on BERT and GRU

Xiaotong Yang[1,2], Nurbol Luktarhan[1,2(✉)], Yihe Mei[1,3], Yi Meng[1,2], and Guodong Zhao[1,3]

[1] Xinjiang University, Urumqi 830000, Xinjiang Uygur Autonomous Region, People's Republic of China
nurbol@xju.edu.cn

[2] School of Computer Science and Technology, Xinjiang University, Urumqi 830046, China
{107552204103,107552204052}@stu.xju.edu.cn

[3] School of Software, Xinjiang University, Urumqi 830091, China
{107552204789,107552204851}@stu.xju.edu.cn

Abstract. With the continuous development of network encryption technologies, classifying encrypted traffic has become a focal point of recent research. Accurately classifying encrypted traffic remains challenging, yet it is crucial for enhancing network security and management. Existing methods that rely on pre-trained models often overlook the temporal characteristics of traffic data. We propose a model based on BERT and Recurrent Neural Networks for Encrypted Traffic Classification (BGETC) to address this issue. Our model operates in two phases: The first phase employs a BERT-based pre-training module designed to learn generic traffic representations from large-scale unlabelled encrypted traffic datasets. The second phase involves fine-tuning, where temporal features are incorporated at the output layer of the BERT model using Recurrent Neural Networks. Combining comprehensive features from the BERT model and temporal features significantly enhances performance, exceeding state-of-the-art baselines in several encrypted traffic classification tasks. Our method notably increases the F1 score to 99.39% for ISCX-VPN-App (packet) and 99.40% for USTC-TFC (flow), thereby markedly improving encrypted traffic classification performance.

Keywords: Encrypted Traffic Classification · BERT · Recurrent Neural Network

1 Introduction

Encrypted traffic classification is a technology that identifies specific applications or services by monitoring and analyzing network traffic. With the rapid growth of internet traffic, the security of network connections has become particularly

S. Goel et al. (Eds.): ICDF2C 2024, LNICST 614, pp. 131–145, 2025.
https://doi.org/10.1007/978-3-031-89360-5_8

important. Data encryption technologies, such as Secure Socket Layer/Transport Layer Security (SSL/TLS) [1], are widely used to protect network connections. Although these encryption technologies ensure user security and privacy, they pose significant challenges and obstacles to classifying encrypted traffic.

Over the past few years, many methods have been proposed to improve the performance of encrypted traffic classification [2]. Early research utilized the method of building fingerprints, using the remaining plaintext in encrypted traffic (such as certificates) to create fingerprints for classification. These methods do not apply to emerging encryption technologies (e.g. TLS 1.3). Some studies have used statistical methods based on machine learning algorithms designed for classification [3, 4]. Traditional machine learning methods largely depend on manually designed feature sets, and the quality of these feature sets directly affects classification performance, significantly reducing accuracy in encrypted traffic classification problems. Compared to machine learning algorithms, deep learning algorithms can automatically extract features. This characteristic gives deep learning models an advantage in handling complex data, reducing the burden of data preprocessing and improving model training efficiency. As a result, they have been widely applied in fields such as computer vision and speech recognition in recent years. However, these methods highly depend on the quantity and distribution of labelled training data, which can easily lead to model bias and difficulty adapting to new encryption methods. In recent years, pre-training models have made significant breakthroughs in natural language processing, computer vision, and other fields [5]. Pre-training methods use a large amount of unlabelled data to learn unbiased data representations. These data can easily be transferred to downstream tasks through fine-tuning with limited labelled data. The latest work has proposed a new pre-training model for encrypted traffic classification [6], achieving advanced performance on several encrypted traffic datasets. However, this method uses BERT [5] for pre-training and fine-tuning but ignores the temporal features in traffic. While this method has achieved advanced results in encrypted traffic, there is still room for improvement.

In this paper, we propose an encrypted traffic classification method based on BERT and Recurrent Neural Networks (BGETC), combining the BERT model and Gated Recurrent Unit (GRU) networks, and explain the effectiveness of BGETC from multiple research perspectives:

1. What is the impact of GRU layers on the BGETC model? We will explore how the number of GRU layers affects the performance of the BGETC model. 2. How effective is BGETC in classifying encrypted traffic? We will evaluate the performance of the BGETC model on different datasets for encrypted traffic classification and compare it with existing methods to verify its effectiveness. 3. How do the scale of the BERT model and GRU modules affect classification? We will use BERT-base and BERT-Large for pre-training to explore how the scale of BERT affects the model's classification performance.

By addressing these three questions, we aim to further understand the advantages, shortcomings, and applicability of the BGETC method and provide valuable ideas for the research and practice of encrypted traffic classification. In BGETC, we use the ET-BERT [6] pre-training network to perform self-supervised learning on large-scale unlabelled encrypted traffic, extracting packet-level generic information flow representations. Then, BGETC fine-tunes using small batches of labelled data to extract traffic feature vectors and combines these with GRU to capture temporal features. These two parts of features are connected to form the final feature representation. The main contributions of this paper are:

1. We use BERT-base and BERT-Large for pre-training, obtaining the weights of two different pre-training models. 2. We propose an encrypted traffic classification method based on BERT and Recurrent Neural Networks, which better represents traffic features. 3. Our method achieves advanced performance in four encrypted traffic classification tasks, including VPN encrypted application classification, VPN encrypted service classification, encrypted malware classification, and TLS1.3 encrypted application classification tasks. Among these, our method significantly surpasses existing research results in VPN encrypted service classification and encrypted malware classification with a performance advantage of 97.53% (↑0.2%) and 99.40% (↑0.1%), respectively.

2 Related Work

2.1 Encrypted Traffic Classification

Encrypted traffic classification aims to identify the sources of traffic captured by specialized software, thereby analyzing which applications or services the encrypted network traffic belongs to. This work is of significant importance for network management, security monitoring, and performance optimization. In this section, we summarize the main methods of network traffic classification. Based on the technologies used, methods can be broadly divided into fingerprint construction, statistical methods, and deep learning models, as shown in Table 1.

Table 1. Work related to the classification of encrypted traffic

Type	Method
Fingerprint construction	FlowPrint [7]
Statistical methods	AppScanner [8], BIND [9]
Deep learning models	FS-Net [10], DF [11], Deep-packet [12], TSCRNN [13], TFE-GNN [14]
Pre-training models	PERT [15], NetGPT [16], ET-BERT [6]

Fingerprint Construction: FlowPrint [7] is an automated fingerprint construction method for encrypted traffic analysis. It does not rely on deep inspection of packet contents. Instead, identifies applications and services by analyzing traffic patterns and network flow characteristics such as packet size, time intervals, and duration of flows. FlowPrint generates fingerprints based on the characteristics of flows and identifies specific applications or services by clustering similar flows. However, this method depends on specific encryption protocols and has issues with model timeliness.

Statistical Methods: This approach classifies encrypted traffic by analyzing the statistical characteristics of network traffic, making it independent of encryption methods. AppScanner [8] uses unique statistical characteristics displayed by each application in network traffic to train a random forest classifier, while BIND [9] focuses on behavioural characteristics, such as access patterns and traffic timing. However, with the increasing complexity of a vast array of applications and websites, it is challenging to design universal models that require massive traffic data, and our model does not rely on manually designed features.

Deep Learning Models: The widespread adoption of deep learning has significantly impacted the field of encrypted traffic classification. Supervised deep learning methods have achieved good results in encrypted traffic classification. FS-Net [10] uses Recurrent Neural Networks (RNN) to automatically extract features from sequences of raw packet sizes in encrypted traffic. DF [11] uses Convolutional Neural Networks (CNN) for encrypted traffic classification. Deep-packet [12] and TSCRNN [13] automatically extract features and classify traffic using raw packet payloads, forming a framework for traffic classification. TFE-GNN [14] uses Graph Neural Networks to classify traffic. However, these methods require a large amount of labelled data, which our method does not need.

2.2 Pre-training Models

The basic principles and processes of pre-training models in Natural Language Processing (NLP) include two main stages: pre-training and fine-tuning. This method learns a general representation of language through a large amount of unlabelled data, which is then adjusted with a small amount of labelled data specific to the task. Especially since the advent of the BERT (Bidirectional Encoder Representations from Transformers) model, NLP has entered the era of Transformer-based architectures [5]. By capturing deep bidirectional contextual relationships with a bidirectional Transformer encoder, BERT achieves outstanding performance in a range of downstream tasks such as question answering, text classification, and named entity recognition through fine-tuning. RoBERTa [17] and ALBERT [18], based on BERT, further enhance model performance through different training techniques and network structures. mBERT [19] supports multilingual processing, enabling knowledge transfer between various languages. DistilBERT [20] reduces the computational demands of the model through knowledge distillation techniques, allowing it to operate on edge devices. Pre-training models have also demonstrated broad adaptability and strong performance in areas like computer vision and audio processing.

Although encrypted traffic lacks explicit semantics in packet payloads, Sengupta et al. [21] use the syntactic structure of communication protocols, sentence dependency of packets, and specific types of traffic packet sizes and timing patterns to differentiate applications, suggesting that encrypted traffic has natural language properties. PERT [15] was the first to apply pre-training models in encrypted traffic classification, achieving a 93.23% F1 score on the ISCX-VPN-Service dataset [22]. However, the model was not designed with specific encrypted traffic pre-training tasks, limiting its generalization ability. NetGPT [16] provides a pre-training model for traffic understanding and generation tasks. In contrast, the ET-BERT [6] model was designed with two types of pre-training tasks, achieving state-of-the-art performance in five encrypted traffic classification tasks.

3 BGETC

3.1 Model Architecture

In recent years, the combination of BERT with Recurrent Neural Networks has achieved good performance in the Natural Language Processing (NLP) domain, such as in sentiment analysis [23], punctuation restoration [24], and text similarity detection [25]. Inspired by these works, we propose the BERT and Gated Recurrent Unit based Encrypted Traffic Classification (BGETC) model. The architecture of this model is illustrated in Fig. 1 (see Fig. 1). Our approach consists of two main stages: a pre-training phase, where the BERT model uses a large amount of unlabeled data to learn a general representation of encrypted traffic, and a fine-tuning stage, where the model is fine-tuned with a small number of labelled packets or traffic data using BERT and Recurrent Neural Networks to classify encrypted traffic.

In the pre-training phase, we primarily draw from the existing ET-BERT [6], which forms a general encrypted traffic pre-training model by studying large-scale unlabeled encrypted traffic data. This model introduces three components: 1. The Datagram2Token method, which transforms encrypted traffic into token units preserved for pre-training. 2. Two pre-training tasks, the masked BURST [6] model and homologous BURST prediction, to learn context datagram representations. 3. Two fine-tuning strategies tailored to different traffic classification scenarios, divided into packet-level and flow-level.

In the fine-tuning part, the outputs of BERT are pooled to obtain the hidden state corresponding to the [CLS] token of BERT's last layer and the subsequent parts after [CLS]. The [CLS] token itself has no semantics but, after attention mechanisms, provides a weighted average of all words, offering a better representation of sentence semantics than other tokens. Further processing through a GRU network on the subsequent parts after [CLS] produces new outputs and hidden states, capturing temporal features. These hidden states from [CLS] and the outputs processed through the GRU network are combined. Finally, a fully connected layer is used to classify and predict the category of encrypted traffic.

In contrast to previous studies [24], our fine-tuning strategy differs in that it directly utilizes the hidden states corresponding to the last layer [CLS] token and subsequent parts for downstream tasks, whereas the study used a CNN module to extract features from the outputs of the BERT embedding layer and then concatenated these with features obtained from a fully trained BERT module.

Our main network architecture consists of multiple layers of bidirectional transformer blocks [26]. Each block comprises multi-head attention layers, which capture the implicit relationships between encoded traffic units in datagrams. In this work, we use both BERT-base and BERT-large configurations. BERT-base consists of 12 transformer blocks, each with 12 attention heads and dimensions of 768 for each input token, with a total of 512 input tokens; BERT-large consists of 16 transformer blocks, each with 24 attention heads and dimensions of 1024 for each input token, also totalling 512 tokens.

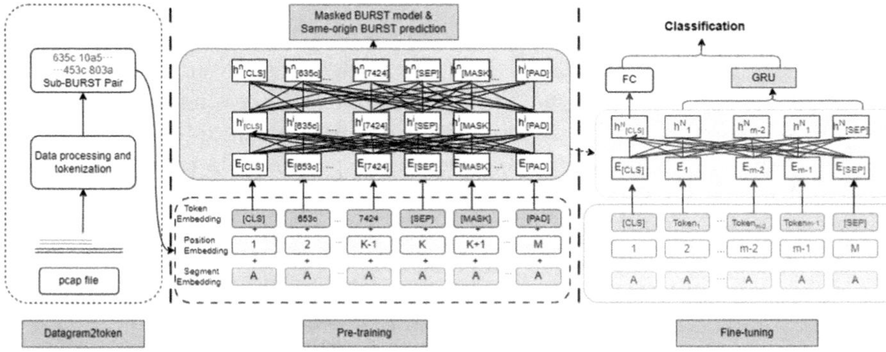

Fig. 1. Overview of BGETC Framework.

3.2 Fine-tuning BGETC

Fine-tuning serves the downstream classification tasks well for the following reasons: (1) The pre-training model can be trained under various traffic category environments, offering better generalizability. It can be applied to any category of traffic representation. (2) Fine-tuning leverages the rich knowledge learned from many unlabeled traffic data during pre-training, achieving good performance with only a small amount of labelled encrypted traffic data. (3) The [CLS] token output from the pre-training model, having been processed by the attention mechanism to obtain a weighted average of all words, provides a better representation of sentence semantics, which can be directly used for classification. We use the negative log-likelihood as the loss function, defining it as:

$$L(y, \hat{y}) = -\log(\hat{y}[y]) \tag{1}$$

y is the index of the true category of the sample, and $\hat{y}$ is the probability distribution of the model outputs.

As the fine-tuning architecture is largely similar to pre-training, we input specific task packets or network traffic representations into the pre-training BGETC model and fine-tune all parameters in an end-to-end model. The hidden states corresponding to the [CLS] output and those processed through the GRU network are combined in the output layer. We adopt two fine-tuning strategies based on the size of the fine-tuning data: using packet-level inputs, i.e., BGETC(packet), to verify if BGETC is suitable for more granular traffic data, and using BGETC(flow), for a fair and objective comparison of BGETC with other input methods in traffic methods.

4 Experiments

In this section, we will address the three research questions mentioned in the introduction to comprehensively evaluate and analyze the performance and effectiveness of our method in anomaly detection tasks. These research questions include:

Question 1: Does the number of GRU layers have a large image of the BGETC model?

Question 2: How effective is BGETC in classifying encrypted traffic?

Question 3: Do the scale of the BERT model and the GRU module significantly impact classification?

We will conduct experiments following the order of these research questions, providing detailed experimental designs, method explanations, and result analyses. For question three, we will design an ablation study to validate and demonstrate the effectiveness of our method in handling different encrypted scenarios.

4.1 Experimental Setup

4.1.1 Datasets and Downstream Tasks Pre-training Dataset: In this work, we used the 30 GB of unlabeled traffic data publicly available from ET-BERT [6] for pre-training. This dataset consists of two parts: (1) 15 GB of traffic from public datasets [22,27]; (2) approximately 15 GB of traffic passively collected by the authors under the China Science and Technology Network (CSTNET). Additionally, this dataset includes a wide variety of network protocols. Fine-tuning Dataset: To assess the effectiveness and generalizability of BGETC, we conducted experiments on three datasets across four encrypted traffic classification tasks. The tasks and corresponding datasets are shown in Table 2.

Task 1: VPN Encrypted Traffic Classification (VETC) involves classifying traffic that uses Virtual Private Networks (VPNs) for network communication. We chose the ISCX-VPN [22] dataset, provided by the Canadian Institute for Cybersecurity, used for researching and evaluating VPN and non-VPN network traffic. VPNs make detection challenging by circumventing censorship and accessing

Table 2. Statistical information on datasets.

Task	Dataset	#Flow	#Packet	#Label
VETC	ISCX-VPN-Service [22]	3,694	60,000	12
	ISCX-VPN-App [22]	2,329	77,163	17
EACT-1.3	CSTNET-TLS 1.3 [6]	46,372	581,709	120
EMC	USTC-TFC [28]	9,853	97,115	20

geographically restricted services. We conducted service and application identification tasks on this dataset, with 12 service categories and 17 application categories, as shown in the Table 3.

Task 2: TLS1.3 Encrypted Application Classification (EACT-1.3) aims to classify encrypted traffic on the new encryption protocol TLS1.3. This dataset was collected by Lin [6] and others on the China Science and Technology Network and includes 120 applications, making it a TLS1.3 dataset.

Task 3: Encrypted Malware Classification (EMC) consists of a dataset of encrypted traffic made up of malware and benign applications collected by researchers at CTU University in a natural network environment [28]. The dataset includes ten categories of malicious traffic and ten categories of benign traffic.

Ethical Considerations. The datasets used in this study were collected from public network traffic and adhered strictly to privacy and data protection regulations. The use of this dataset is purely for academic research and involves no commercial interests.

Table 3. ISCX-VPN dataset composition

Traffic type	Categories
Service	Chat, Email, File_Transfer, P2P, Streaming, VoIP, VPN-Chat
	VPN-Email, VPN-FT, VPN-P2P, VPN-Streaming, VPN-VoIP
Application	AIM_Chat, Email, Facebook, Gmail, Hangout, ICQ, Netflix
	SCP, Skype, Spotify, Tor, Torrent, Vimeo, VoipBuster, VPN-Ftps, VPN-Sftp, Youtube

4.1.2 Data Preprocessing We performed preprocessing on the data. We removed some packets, such as Address Resolution Protocol (ARP) and Dynamic Host Configuration Protocol (DHCP), because they are unrelated to the specific content of transmitted traffic. To avoid interference from strong identifying information (like IP and port) that packet headers might possess

[12,22]. We utilize the Datagram2Token module proposed by ET-BERT [6]. First, we extract continuous packets between the client and server in a session stream, referred to as BURST to represent partial complete information of the session. Then, the information in BURST is converted into token embeddings through a bi-gram model. BURST is split into two parts, and the BURST representation is converted into tokens for pre-training. Finally, the token embedding, position embedding, and segmentation embedding of each token are concatenated as the input representation for pre-training. we used the same dataset samples for fine-tuning as ET-BERT [6]. To reduce bias caused by data imbalance, we randomly select up to 500 flows and 5000 packets from each category in all datasets. Each dataset is divided into training, validation, and test sets in a ratio of 8:1:1. The processed data are shown in the Table 4.

Table 4. Preprocessed data format.

Label	Hexadecimal sequence
8	021a 1ac5 c501 0100 0000 0002 021a 1ac5 c502 0200 0000 0008 0800 0045 4500 0000 003f 3f4f 4fe0 e040 4000 0020 2006 0688 888d 8d01 0102 0243 43d3 d301 0101 013c 3c76 760c 0cea ea48 48c2 c25d 5d16 16fb fb13 13d5 d557 5743 4314 1480 8018 181c 1c48 48a6 a6cc cc00 0000 0001 0101 0108 080a 0a0f 0f44 44f2 f2c3 c3fd fde5 e564
11	021a 1ac5 c501 0100 0000 0002 021a 1ac5 c502 0200 0000 0008 0800 0045 4500 0005 05b1 b1ed ed75 7540 4000 0020 2006 06af af5e 5e01 0102 026d 6d5d 5d01 0101 0149 4913 1301 01bb bbde de17 17f7 f732 32c5 c5d9 d97a 7a38 38f1 f19c 9c80 8018 185a 5a80 8069 69ee ee00 0000 0001 0101 0108 080a 0a1e 1eb5 b53d 3d55 550d 0d3e 3e2b
0	021a 1ac5 c502 0200 0000 0002 021a 1ac5 c501 0100 0000 0008 0800 0045 4500 0000 0091 9183 83b1 b140 4000 0020 2006 0691 914b 4b01 0101 0167 67ee ee01 0102 02db db79 7974 743d 3d01 01bb bb33 334f 4fae aea7 a747 475d 5d51 5153 5380 8018 189e 9e60 60c0 c016 1600 0000 0001 0101 0108 080a 0a11 11f5 f5ae aecd cd23 2325 255b
...	...

4.1.3 Evaluation Metrics and Implementation Details We evaluated and compared our model's performance using four typical metrics: Accuracy (AC), Precision (PR), Recall (RC), and F1 Score (F1) [7,14]. We also used macro-averaging [29] to calculate each category's average AC, PR, RC, and F1 to avoid biases caused by the imbalance of multiple categories. All experiments were conducted using Python 3.8, Pytorch 1.11.0, and UER [30] on the Ubuntu 20.04 operating system with NVIDIA RTX3090 GPUs. In pre-training, the batch size is 32, and the total steps are 500,000. We set the learning rate to 2×10^{-5}, and the ratio of warm-up is 0.1. We fine-tuned with the AdamW optimizer for ten epochs, where the learning rate was set to 2×10^{-5}. The batch size was 32, and the dropout rate was 0.5.

The model parameters are as follows: In the BERT layer, we set the maximum input length to 128 tokens and the token embedding dimension to 768. In the GRU layer, we set the number of hidden neurons to 128 and the number of layers to 2.

4.2 Question 1: Does the Number of GRU Layers Have a Large Image of the BGETC Model?

Figure 2 (see Fig. 2) shows the impact of varying the number of GRU layers on our model's performance. Increasing the number of GRU layers in the neural network can enhance the model's complexity and learning capability. A single-layer GRU typically captures only simple time series features, whereas multiple layers can learn the temporal hierarchy of data more deeply, thus more effectively handling complex time dependencies. However, adding more layers can also increase the training difficulty and time [31]. Moreover, too many layers might lead to overfitting. Therefore, choosing the appropriate number of layers is crucial for balancing model performance and computational efficiency to achieve higher accuracy. The selection of GRU layers depends on the specific dataset and task. We conducted experiments using the USTC-TFC(flow) dataset. The experiments showed that with two layers, the model achieved the highest accuracy of 99.39% in classifying encrypted malicious traffic. Based on this analysis, we will set the number of GRU layers to two in our subsequent work.

4.3 Question 2: How Effective Is BGETC in Classifying Encrypted Traffic?

We compared BGETC with 12 of the most advanced (SOTA) methods in encrypted traffic classification, including (1) fingerprint construction methods: FlowPrint [7] and k-fingerprinting (K-fp) [32]; (2) statistical feature methods: AppScanner [8] , CUMUL [33], BIND [9]; (3) deep learning methods: DeepFingerprinting (DF) [11], GraphDApp [34], FS-Net [10], TSCRNN [13], Deeppacket [12]; (4) pre-training methods: PERT [15], NetGPT [16], ET-BERT [6]. The experimental results are shown in Table 5.

VETC. BGETC surpassed the existing state-of-the-art model ET-BERT on ISCX-VPN-Service(flow) and ISCX-VPN-App(packet) datasets, achieving 0.2% and 0.02% improvement respectively, and matched ET-BERT on the ISCX-VPN-Service(packet). Both datasets have issues with data imbalance. Our model, along with ET-BERT and Deeppacket, mitigated the impact of data imbalance by learning the correlations between datagrams.

EACT-1.3. As shown in Table 5, on the CSTNET-TLs 1.3 (packet), our method performed best across all four evaluation metrics and surpassed all baseline models. BGETC achieved the highest accuracy, precision, recall, and F1 scores of

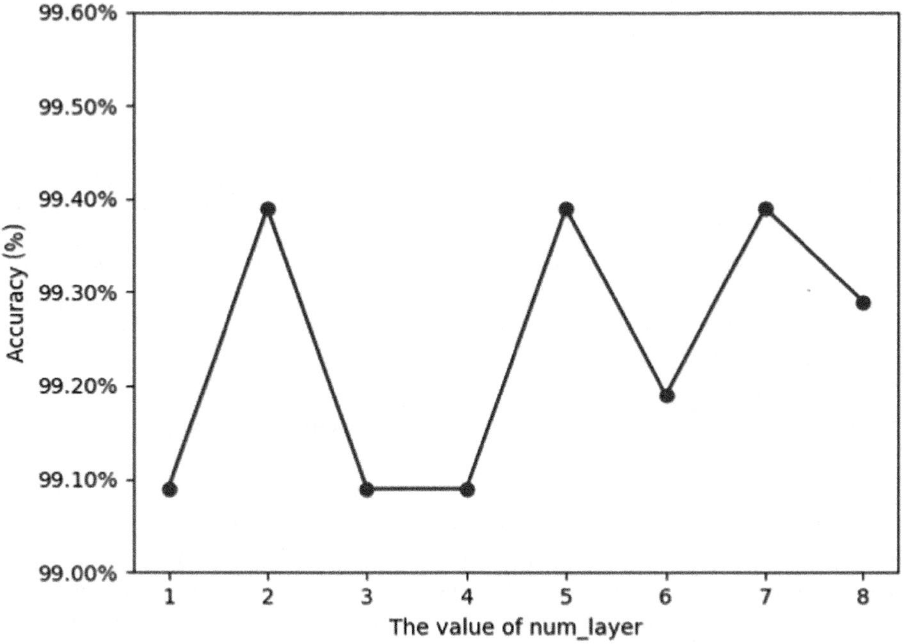

Fig. 2. Effect of different layers.

96.81%, 96.86%, 96.87%, and 96.85%, respectively. TLS 1.3 posed new challenges for FlowPrint and Deeppacket, demonstrating that BGETC could better learn the implicit patterns in datagrams and use these patterns for classification.

EMC. As seen in Table 5, in the USTC-TFC(flow) task, our method achieved the best performance in terms of accuracy, precision, recall, and F1 score, which were 99.39%, 99.40%, 99.43%, and 99.40%, respectively. BGETC achieved a 0.1% improvement over the existing state-of-the-art model ET-BERT on USTC-TFC(flow).

4.4 Question 3: Do the Scale of the BERT Model and the GRU Module Significantly Impact Classification?

For Question 3, we will design an ablation study to validate and explore the contribution of the GRU module to the widely compared ISCX-VPN-App(packet) and investigate the impact of the scale of the BERT model. In Fig. 3 (see Fig. 3), 'default' represents using BERT-base for pre-training (as mentioned in Sect. 3.1) and including GRU; 'BERT-base' represents using BERT-base for pre-training with GRU removed during the fine-tuning phase; 'BERT-large' represents using BERT-large for pre-training with GRU removed during the fine-tuning phase; 'BERT-large+GRU' represents using BERT-large for pre-training and including GRU during the fine-tuning phase. This experiment shows that a

Table 5. Comparison Results on ISCX-VPN-Service, ISCX-VPN-App, CSTNET-TLS 1.3 and USTC-TFC datasets.

Dataset	ISCX-VPN-Service				ISCX-VPN-App				CSTNET-TLS 1.3 datasets				USTC-TFC			
Method	AC	PR	RC	F1	AC	PR	RC	F1	AC	PR	RC	F1	AC	PR	RC	F1
AppScanner [8]	0.7182	0.7339	0.7225	0.7197	0.6266	0.4864	0.5198	0.4935	0.6662	0.6246	0.6327	0.6201	0.8954	0.8984	0.8968	0.8892
CUMUL [33]	0.5610	0.5883	0.5676	0.5668	0.5365	0.4129	0.4535	0.4236	0.5391	0.4942	0.5060	0.4904	0.5675	0.6171	0.5738	0.5513
BIND [9]	0.7534	0.7583	0.7488	0.7420	0.6767	0.5152	0.5153	0.4965	0.7964	0.7605	0.7650	0.7560	0.8457	0.8681	0.8382	0.8396
K-fp [32]	0.6430	0.6492	0.6417	0.6395	0.6070	0.5478	0.5430	0.5303	0.4036	0.3969	0.4044	0.3902	——	——	——	——
FlowPrint [7]	0.7962	0.8042	0.7812	0.7820	0.8767	0.6697	0.6651	0.6531	0.1261	0.1354	0.1272	0.1116	0.8146	0.6434	0.7002	0.6573
DF [11]	0.7154	0.7192	0.7104	0.7102	0.6116	0.5706	0.4752	0.4799	0.7936	0.7721	0.7573	0.7602	0.7787	0.7883	0.7819	0.7593
FS-Net [10]	0.7205	0.7502	0.7238	0.7131	0.6647	0.4819	0.4848	0.4737	0.8639	0.8404	0.8349	0.8322	0.8846	0.8846	0.8920	0.8840
GraphDApp [34]	0.5977	0.6045	0.6220	0.6036	0.6328	0.5900	0.5472	0.5558	0.7034	0.6464	0.6510	0.6440	0.8789	0.8226	0.8260	0.8234
TSCRNN [13]	——	0.9270	0.9260	0.9260	——	——	——	——	——	——	——	——	——	0.9870	0.9860	0.9870
Deeppacket [12]	0.9329	0.9377	0.9306	0.9321	0.9758	0.9785	0.9745	0.9765	0.8019	0.4315	0.2689	0.4022	0.9640	0.9650	0.9631	0.9641
PERT [15]	0.9352	0.9400	0.9349	0.9368	0.8229	0.7092	0.7173	0.6992	0.8915	0.8846	0.8719	0.8741	0.9909	0.99ch811	0.9910	0.9911
NetGPT [16]	——	——	——	——	——	——	——	——	——	——	——	——	0.9563	——	——	0.9555
ET-BERT(flow) [6]	0.9729	0.9756	0.9731	0.9733	0.8519	0.7508	0.7294	0.7306	0.9510	0.9460	0.9419	0.9426	0.9929	0.9930	0.9930	0.9930
ET-BERT(packet) [6]	0.9890	0.9891	0.9890	0.9890	0.9962	0.9936	0.9938	0.9937	0.9675	0.9675	0.9675	0.9678	0.9915	0.9915	0.9916	0.9916
BGETC(flow)	**0.9756**	**0.9739**	**0.9772**	**0.9753**	0.8391	**0.7943**	**0.7895**	**0.7860**	——	——	——	——	**0.9939**	**0.9940**	**0.9943**	**0.9940**
BGETC(packet)	0.9890	0.9890	0.9891	0.9890	**0.9966**	**0.9948**	0.9931	**0.9939**	**0.9681**	**0.9686**	**0.9687**	**0.9685**	0.9906	0.9908	0.9908	0.9908

larger BERT model does not yield better results under the same scale as a pre-training dataset. Comparatively, the BERT-base performed better; removing the GRU module also significantly decreased model performance, highlighting our method's critical role and affirming our approach's indispensable contributions.

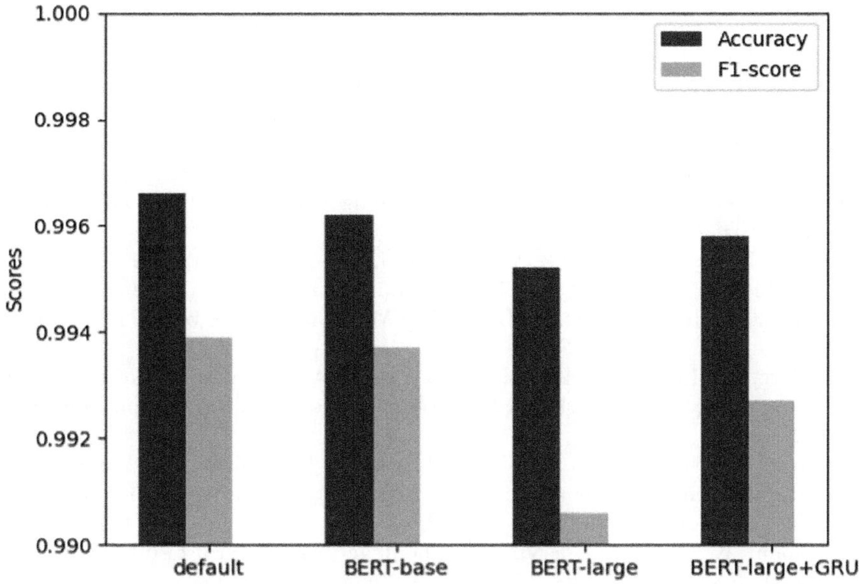

Fig. 3. The effect of BERT model size and GRU module on classification effectiveness.

5 Conclusion

In this paper, we presented a BERT and GRU-based BGETC model designed to enhance the performance of encrypted traffic classification. This model is capable of pretraining on large-scale unlabeled data to learn deep packet-level traffic representations, then fine-tunes on a small amount of labeled encrypted traffic data to accurately classify encrypted traffic across multiple scenarios. Experimental results demonstrate that our model achieved outstanding results on three public datasets, thoroughly evaluating the generalizability and robustness of BGETC. The model excelled in three encrypted traffic classification tasks: VPN encrypted traffic classification, TLS1.3 encrypted application classification, and encrypted malware classification, achieving F1 improvements of 0.2%, 0.07%, and 0.1%, respectively. Accuracy rates reached 97.53%, 96.81%, and 99.39%. Although our method has shown exceptional performance, it still has certain limitations. In the future, we hope to explore the potential for lightweight versions of the BGETC model and its ability to predict new categories of samples .

References

1. Shen, M., et al.: Machine learning-powered encrypted network traffic analysis: a comprehensive survey. IEEE Commun. Surv. Tutorials **25**(1), 791–824 (2023)
2. Shafiq, M., Tian, Z., Bashir, A.K., Jolfaei, A., Yu, X.: Data mining and machine learning methods for sustainable smart cities traffic classification: a survey. Sustain. Cities Soc. **60**, 102177 (2020)

3. Sikos, L.F.: Packet analysis for network forensics: a comprehensive survey. Forensic Sci. Int. Digit. Invest. **32**, 200892 (2020)
4. Speiser, J.L., Miller, M.E., Tooze, J., Ip, E.: A comparison of random forest variable selection methods for classification prediction modeling. Expert Syst. Appl. **134**, 93–101 (2019)
5. Devlin, J., Chang, M.W., Lee, K., Toutanova, K.: BERT: pre-training of deep bidirectional transformers for language understanding. arXiv preprint arXiv:1810.04805 (2018)
6. Lin, X., Xiong, G., Gou, G., Li, Z., Shi, J., Jing, Yu.: ET-BERT: a contextualized datagram representation with pre-training transformers for encrypted traffic classification. In: Proceedings of the ACM Web Conference, vol. 2022, pp. 633–642 (2022)
7. Van Ede, T.: Flowprint: semi-supervised mobile-app fingerprinting on encrypted network traffic. In: Network and Distributed System Security Symposium (NDSS), vol. 27 (2020)
8. Taylor, V.F., Spolaor, R., Conti, M., Martinovic, I.: Robust smartphone app identification via encrypted network traffic analysis. IEEE Trans. Inf. Forensics Secur. **13**(1), 63–78 (2017)
9. Al-Naami, K.: Adaptive encrypted traffic fingerprinting with bi-directional dependence. In: Proceedings of the 32nd Annual Conference on Computer Security Applications, pp. 177–188 (2016)
10. Liu, C., He, L., Xiong, G., Cao, Z., Li, Z.: Fs-net: a flow sequence network for encrypted traffic classification. In: IEEE INFOCOM 2019-IEEE Conference On Computer Communications, pp. 1171–1179. IEEE (2019)
11. Sirinam, P., Imani, M., Juarez, M., Wright, M. Deep fingerprinting: undermining website fingerprinting defenses with deep learning. In: Proceedings of the 2018 ACM SIGSAC Conference on Computer and Communications Security, pp. 1928–1943 (2018)
12. Lotfollahi, M., Jafari Siavoshani, M., Shirali Hossein Zade, R., Saberian, M.: Deep packet: a novel approach for encrypted traffic classification using deep learning. Soft Comput. **24**(3) 1999–2012 (2020)
13. Lin, K., Xiaolong, X., Gao, H.: TSCRNN: a novel classification scheme of encrypted traffic based on flow spatiotemporal features for efficient management of IIOT. Comput. Netw. **190**, 107974 (2021)
14. Zhang, H., et al.: TFE-GNN: a temporal fusion encoder using graph neural networks for fine-grained encrypted traffic classification. In: Proceedings of the ACM Web Conference, vol. 2023, pp. 2066–2075 (2023)
15. He, H.Y., Yang, Z.G., Chen, X.N. PERT: payload encoding representation from transformer for encrypted traffic classification. In: 2020 ITU Kaleidoscope: Industry-Driven Digital Transformation (ITU K), pp. 1–8. IEEE (2020)
16. Meng, X., Lin, C., Wang, Y., Zhang, Y.: Netgpt: generative pretrained transformer for network traffic. arXiv preprint arXiv:2304.09513 (2023)
17. Liu, Y., et al.: Roberta: a robustly optimized BERT pretraining approach. arXiv preprint arXiv:1907.11692 (2019)
18. Lan, Z., Chen, M., Goodman, S., Gimpel, K., Sharma, P., Soricut, R.: Albert: a lite BERT for self-supervised learning of language representations. arXiv preprint arXiv:1909.11942 (2019)
19. Gonen, H., Ravfogel, S., Elazar, Y., Goldberg, Y.: It's not greek to mBERT: inducing word-level translations from multilingual BERT. arXiv preprint arXiv:2010.08275 (2020)

20. Sanh, V., Debut, L., Chaumond, J., Wolf, T.: Distilbert, a distilled version of BERT: smaller, faster, cheaper and lighter. arXiv preprint arXiv:1910.01108 (2019)
21. Sengupta, S., Ganguly, N., De, P., Chakraborty, S.: Exploiting diversity in android TLS implementations for mobile app traffic classification. In: The World Wide Web Conference, pp. 1657–1668 (2019)
22. Draper-Gil, G., Lashkari, A.H., Mamun, M.S.I., Ghorbani, A.A.: Characterization of encrypted and VPN traffic using time-related. In: Proceedings of the 2nd International Conference on Information Systems Security and Privacy (ICISSP), pp. 407–414 (2016)
23. Gupta, B., Prakasam, P., Velmurugan, T.: Integrated BERT embeddings, BiLSTM-BiGRU and 1-D CNN model for binary sentiment classification analysis of movie reviews. Multimedia Tools Appl. **81**(23), 33067–33086 (2022)
24. Zhang, Z., Liu, J., Chi, L., Chen, X.: Word-level BERT-CNN-RNN model for Chinese punctuation restoration. In: 2020 IEEE 6th International Conference on Computer and Communications (ICCC), pp. 1629–1633. IEEE (2020)
25. Viji, D., Revathy, S.: A hybrid approach of weighted fine-tuned BERT extraction with deep Siamese Bi-LSTM model for semantic text similarity identification. Multimedia Tools and Appl. **81**(5), 6131–6157 (2022)
26. Vaswani, A., et al.: Attention is all you need. In: Advances in Neural Information Processing Systems, vol. 30 (2017)
27. Sharafaldin, I., Lashkari, A.H., Ghorbani, A.A., et al.: Toward generating a new intrusion detection dataset and intrusion traffic characterization. ICISSp **1**, 108–116 (2018)
28. Wang, W., Zhu, M., Zeng, X., Ye, X., Sheng, Y.: Malware traffic classification using convolutional neural network for representation learning. In: 2017 International Conference on Information Networking (ICOIN), pp. 712–717. IEEE (2017)
29. Liu, C., Wang, W., Wang, M., Lv, F., Konan, M.: An efficient instance selection algorithm to reconstruct training set for support vector machine. Knowl.-Based Syst. **116**, 58–73 (2017)
30. Zhao, Z., et al.: Uer: an open-source toolkit for pre-training models. arXiv preprint arXiv:1909.05658 (2019)
31. He, K., Sun, J.: Convolutional neural networks at constrained time cost. In: Proceedings of the IEEE Conference on Computer Vision and Pattern Recognition, pp. 5353–5360 (2015)
32. Hayes, J., Danezis, G.: k-fingerprinting: a robust scalable website fingerprinting technique. In: 25th USENIX Security Symposium (USENIX Security 16), pp. 1187–1203 (2016)
33. Panchenko, A., et al.: Website fingerprinting at internet scale. In: NDSS (2016)
34. Shen, M., Zhang, J., Zhu, L., Ke, X., Xiaojiang, D.: Accurate decentralized application identification via encrypted traffic analysis using graph neural networks. IEEE Trans. Inf. Forensics Secur. **16**, 2367–2380 (2021)

AnGSL: Graph-Based Android Malware Detection Method

Guodong Zhao[1,2], Nurbol Luktarhan[1,3(✉)], Yihe Mei[1,2], Yi Meng[1,3], and Xiaotong Yang[1,3]

[1] Xinjiang University, Xinjiang Uygur Autonomous Region, Urumqi 830000, People's Republic of China
{107552204851,107552204789,107552204052,107552204103}@stu.xju.edu.cn
[2] School of Software, Xinjiang University, Urumqi 830091, China
[3] College of Information Science and Engineering, Xinjiang University, Urumqi 830046, China
nurbol@xju.edu.cn

Abstract. In the era of widespread use of smartphones, researchers have been exploring new detection methods to cope with the threat of constantly upgrading Android malware. With the emergence of graphical neural networks, people's interest in using this technology to detect Android malware has surged. However, external connections between Android malware are often overlooked, and the graph structure is filled with redundant information. To address these challenges, this article introduces AnGSL, a graph based method designed specifically for Android malware detection. This method first uses the MTF-IDF algorithm to extract feature entities, and then calculates the Euclidean distance between the feature vectors of two Android applications to determine whether there are edges between them. Subsequently, two subgraphs were constructed using the K-nearest neighbor and diffusion matrix algorithms, and optimized and merged to obtain the final graph structure. Finally, by minimizing the cross entropy loss between the subgraph and the optimized graph, a contrastive learning method is used to train the model. Experimental evaluations conducted on publicly available Android datasets showed a detection accuracy of 98.24%. Research has shown that compared with previous model methods, the method proposed in this paper has a certain degree of performance improvement, indicating that graph based Android malware detection has broad potential and prospects in the research field.

Keywords: Android Malware detection · Graph structure learning · Graph neural networks · Contrastive Learning

1 Introduction

With the widespread use of the Android operating system and the flourishing development of the mobile application market, smartphones have become an

S. Goel et al. (Eds.): ICDF2C 2024, LNICST 614, pp. 146–161, 2025.
https://doi.org/10.1007/978-3-031-89360-5_9

indispensable part of people's daily lives. However, the increase in the number of malware software has followed suit. According to the "2023 National Mobile Application Security Observation Report," as of December 31, 2023, 3.51 million Android applications nationwide underwent risk detection through mobile application security platforms. Approximately 2.39 million applications had high-risk vulnerabilities, accounting for 76.89% of the total applications. Therefore, there is an urgent need for a large number of reliable Android malware detection tools to monitor and respond to this trend effectively.

Due to the increasing threat posed by Android malware to people's daily smartphone use, many researchers have proposed various methods for identifying Android malware. Traditional Android application analysis methods typically involve analyzing static features through reverse engineering or dynamic analysis through multi-level detection. Among these methods, with the emergence and development of graph neural networks, graphs have also been widely applied in the field of Android malware detection [8]. Many researchers use function call graphs for Android malware detection.

However, when using graphs for Android malware detection, Most papers only consider the internal relationships of Android applications, while ignoring the external connections between Android applications. That is to say, previous research mostly focused on a single Android malware and did not comprehensively consider all Android malware; Moreover, the graphs contain numerous complex structures, hindering the extraction of hidd en information within them and requiring complex preprocessing to streamline the graph structures [20]. These factors pose significant challenges to the application of graphs in the field of Android malware detection.

Based on the aforementioned issues, this paper proposes AnGSL, a new framework for Android malware detection. It leverages graph structure learning and graph neural networks to explore rich but hidden semantic information between different apps and adaptively optimize the graph structure. Specifically, we extract three types of Android entities, including permissions, APIs, and opcodes, from the decompiled APK (Android application package) and convert them into feature vectors for the corresponding APK. We treat each APK as a node in the graph, calculate the Euclidean distance between feature vectors of two APKs to approximate the closeness between them, and use this closeness as the basis for the existence of edge structures. Subsequently, we utilize KNN and diffusion matrix algorithms to construct two subgraphs and refine them through the integration of channel attention mechanisms to achieve the optimized graph structure. Finally, employing the method of contrastive learning, the cross entropy loss between the two subgraphs and the optimized graph is minimized, leading to the training of the model. This graph only contains application nodes and serves as the target during the malware detection process. In summary, the contributions of this paper are as follows:

- This paper utilizes the MTF-IDF algorithm to filter features. It also adopts the Android combination features AOP, which comprises APIs, opcodes, and

permissions. This feature combination enhances the information of entity features, thereby improving detection efficiency and accuracy.
- This paper introduces the model of AnGSL, which acquires semantic information between two APKs by calculating the Euclidean distance. This information is then used to construct an APK graph. Additionally, graph structure learning is employed to optimize the graph structure and mining hidden semantic information between APKs. Finally, contrastive learning is utilized to train the model.
- This paper evaluates using 2,100 benign samples and 2,500 malware samples, achieving an accuracy of 98.24%, with the False Positive Rate (FPR) maintained at a low level. It validates the effectiveness of AnGSL for detecting Android malware.

2 Related Work

In the ongoing battle against malicious software creators, Android researchers have devised numerous innovative and efficient detection methods. In this section, we will introduce the static analysis methods and dynamic analysis methods previously proposed by researchers. Graph-based methods have become very popular in the field of Android malware detection, with the rise and application of graph neural networks in various fields.

2.1 Static Analysis Methods

The static analysis mainly involves using decompilation tools to extract and filter features from files within APKs and conducting feature extraction of malware programs in a non-running state. Drebin [2] proposed the use of permissions to construct datasets and utilized the SVM algorithm for classifying malware. Yuan et al. [22] utilized opcodes combined with deep learning for malware classification. Zou et al. [24] proposed an Android malware detection method based on API proximity analysis. However, static analysis may fail due to simple code obfuscation, for example, Fan et al. [4] found in their research that signature-based methods perform well in identifying known malicious software. However, they are susceptible to bytecode-level transformation attacks.

2.2 Dynamic Analysis Methods

Unlike static analysis methods, dynamic analysis involves observing the runtime behavior of Android applications, including system calls, network activities, and access behaviors. DroidSpan [3] defines 52 dynamic features based on the sensitive access distribution derived from dynamic call traces and investigates the sustainability of features and models. Mohamme et al. [1] capture stateful features generated during app runtime on real phones as inputs for machine learning models and combine dynamic and static features to form hybrid features, achieving good results. Additionally, the combination of dynamic and static features allows researchers to analyze malware behaviors further. CoDroid [23] is a hybrid approach that uses a combination of dynamic system calls and static opcodes. However, dynamic analysis heavily relies on support from operating system versions and real Android devices/virtual machines, requiring data collection at runtime, which poses challenges such as complexity, time consumption, and low efficiency.

2.3 Graph-Based Methods

With the rapid development and application of graph neural networks, the focus of static analysis has gradually shifted towards extracting semantic features from graphs [14]. P. Feng et al. [7] utilize function call graphs and transform their nodes into vector representations through GCN models for embedding and detection. Yang et al. [21] optimize call graphs to extract more powerful API context information, accurately representing the behavior of each application. Hassen et al. [11] use scalable function call graphs for Android malware classification.

Graph-based malware detection is also a primary focus of this paper. However, when using graphs for Android malware detection, it's necessary to consider the relationships between APKs and simplify the graph structure to extract more hidden semantic information from the graph, aiming to achieve better detection effectiveness.

3 Methodology

This section will elaborate on the AnGSL model proposed in this paper. The architecture of the model, as shown in Fig. 1, mainly consists of the following two components: 1) Feature Extractor. 2) Graph Structure Optimizer.

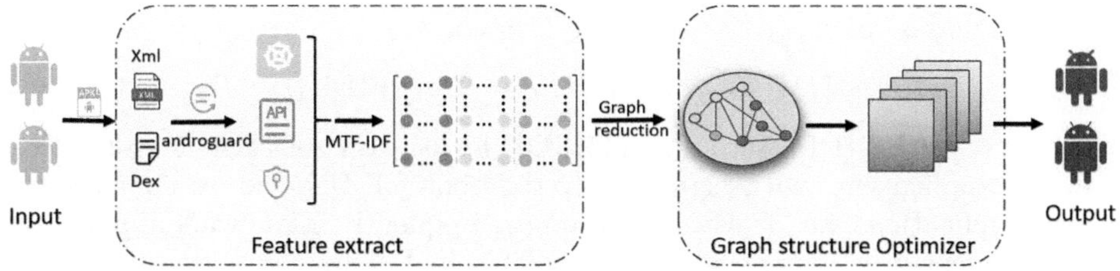

Fig. 1. Model Architecture Diagram

3.1 Feature Extractor

Android applications need to be packaged and released as APK files on the Android system. In order to analyze the original Android files more accurately, this paper uses the Androguard tool to reverse engineer APK files, extracting three types of entities: APIs, opcodes, and permissions. After extracting these feature entities inspired by the TF-IDF algorithm [13], this paper proposes the MTF-IDF algorithm to compute the MTF-IDF value of each feature. This value is used as a criterion for selecting features within each entity, forming the feature set of each entity. Finally, the Concat operation is used to combine them into the AOP feature set.

TF-IDF in the field of Android malware application detection can be used to measure the importance of features within Android entities. So, what features are essential? If a certain feature of an application in the dataset appears multiple times in the current application but relatively infrequently in other applications, then that feature is important.

TF represents the frequency of occurrence of an Android feature within an Android application, and it is calculated as shown in formula 1:

$$\mathrm{TF}\left(t_{i,j}, a_i\right) = \frac{c\left(t_{i,j}\right)}{\sum_{j=1}^{n} c\left(t_{i,j}\right)} \tag{1}$$

where $c\left(t_{i,j}\right)$ is the number of times feature $t_{i,j}$ appears in the feature set of application a_i and $\sum_{j=1}^{n} c\left(t_{i,j}\right)$ is the total number of occurrences of n features in application a_i IDF represents the frequency of occurrence of an Android feature across all Android applications, and its value is calculated as shown in formula 2:

$$\mathrm{IDF}\left(t_{i,j}, A\right) = \begin{cases} \log \frac{|A|}{|\{t_{i,j} \in a_i \mid a_i \in A\}|} & , |\{t_{i,j} \in a_i \mid a_i \in A\}| > 0 \\ \log |A| & , |\{t_{i,j} \in a_i \mid a_i \in A\}| = 0 \end{cases} \tag{2}$$

where $|A|$ is the total number of applications in the dataset and $|\{t_{i,j} \in a_i \mid a_i \in A\}|$ is the number of applications in dataset A that contain the feature $t_{i,j}$. The TF-IDF value is the product of TF and IDF. If a feature has a low frequency across the entire application dataset but a high frequency within a particular application, then this feature will have a higher TF-IDF value. The TF-IDF value is calculated as shown in formula 3:

$$TF - IDF\left(t_{i,j}, a_i, D\right) = TF\left(t_{i,j}, a_i\right) * \mathrm{IDF}\left(t_{i,j}, D\right) \tag{3}$$

Unlike the TF-IDF method, MTF-IDF focuses on selecting features from malware applications with significantly different TF-IDF values compared to benign applications, i.e., features that appear frequently in malware applications but infrequently in benign applications. This highlights the entity features in malware applications, which is beneficial for feature learning and application classification. Therefore, the MTF-IDF value for feature t is calculated as shown in formula 4:

$$MTF - IDF\left(t, A_b, A_m\right) = \overline{TF - IDF_m}\left(t, A_m\right) - \overline{TF - IDF_b}\left(t, A_b\right) \tag{4}$$

where $\overline{TF - IDF_m}\left(t, A_m\right)$ is the average TF-IDF value of feature t in the benign application dataset, and $\overline{TF - IDF_b}\left(t, A_b\right)$ is the average TF-IDF value of feature t in the malware dataset. The partial permission features obtained through the above formula are shown in Table 1 as follows:

Table 1. Top 10 Permission List.

PERMISSION
RECEIVE_BOOT_COMPLETED
WRITE_SETTINGS
CALL_PHONE
REBOOT
BROADCAST_STICKY
ACCESS_SUPERUSER
ACCESS_DOWNLOAD_MANAGER
WRITE
ACCESS_CORSE_LOCATION
ACCESS_CELL_ID

After obtaining the corresponding feature set, we consider APK to be a node in the graph. We use the number of identical entities between APKs to determine the tightness of the relationship between two applications and use this closeness as the basis for determining the existence of edge structures, as shown in the Fig. 2.

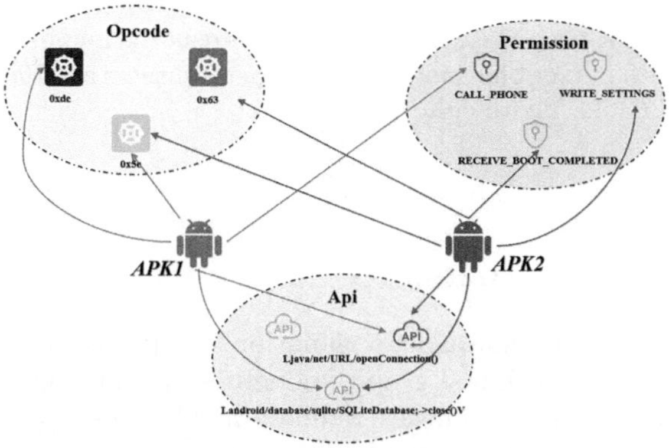

Fig. 2. Demonstration of Closeness between APKs

The more identical feature entities exist between two APKs, the stronger the closeness, and the higher the likelihood of the existence of an edge. Specifically, we construct the obtained feature entities into an n by 1*D matrix, namely the feature matrix, and approximate the closeness between two APKs by calculating the Euclidean distance between each pair of matrices. Given a threshold value, T, if the Euclidean distance is greater than the threshold T, it indicates weaker closeness between two APKs, implying the absence of an edge; conversely, if it is less than T, it signifies stronger closeness, indicating the presence of an edge. This approach is used to construct the graph structure, resulting in the most primitive Android graph. We randomly selected 30 APKs from the dataset to visualize their Euclidean distances, as shown in Fig. 3. Deeper shades of blue indicate stronger closeness, while deeper shades of red indicate weaker closeness.

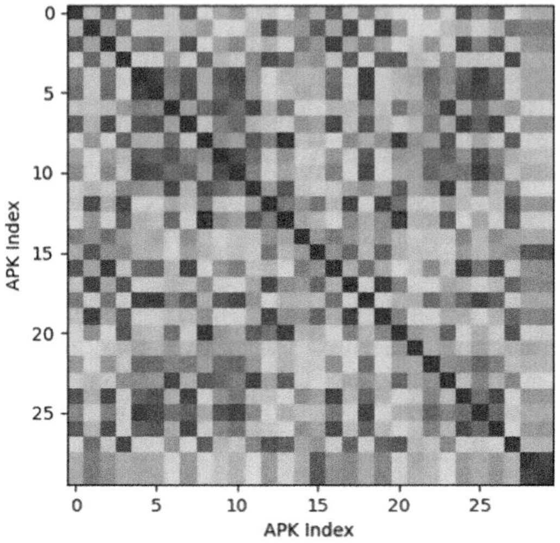

Fig. 3. Graph of APK Closeness, APK Index represents the numbering of 30 randomly selected APKs, with darker blue indicating stronger tightness and darker red indicating weaker tightness. (Color figure online)

3.2 Graph Structure Optimizer

This section provides a thorough explanation of optimizing graph structures, as shown in Fig. 3. The original graph undergoes optimization through a graph structure optimizer, which removes redundant edges and adds essential ones. This results in the final refined graph structure.

First, KNN and diffusion matrix algorithms are used as two basic perspectives to learn the original graph structure of Android, obtaining two different views. These two views contain different semantic information from the original Android graph. We design and employ an optimizer to optimize the two views. Given two different graphs, G_1 and G_2, for graph $G_1(V_1, X)$, we first obtain the embedding matrix Z^1:

$$Z^1 = \sigma(\text{GraphSAGE}(V_1, X)) \tag{5}$$

where σ is the non-linear activation function, with the embedding matrix Z^1, the probability P of the existence of an edge between every two nodes in V_1 can be recalculated. For the target node m, we connect its embedding Z_m^1 with the embedding Z_n^1 of another node n. Then, after passing through an MLP layer and normalizing the weights of node m, we obtain the probability P_{mn}^1 of the existence of an edge between node m and node n. Thus, we construct a probability matrix P^1, as shown in the Fig. 4(a).

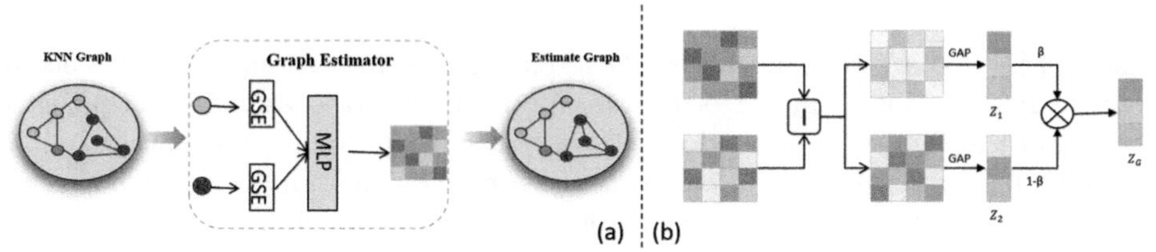

Fig. 4. Graph Structure Learner, (a) View Optimizer, (b) Interaction Graph Construction

Similarly, the optimized subgraph V_e^2 can also be obtained. For the optimized views V_e^1 and V_e^2, we use GraphSAGE-based encoders to generate a node embedding matrix E for each graph. Then, we define $\mathrm{M}_{ij} = \cos\left(E_i^1, E_j^2\right)$ as the interaction mapping M, modeling the interaction between nodes in V_e^1 and V_e^2, and constructing an interaction graph. Here, $\cos(\cdot, \cdot)$ represents cosine similarity. Next, we calculate the interaction graph of embedding matrix E_1 as $\widetilde{E_1} = M \cdot E_2$ and the interaction graph of embedding matrix E_2 as $\widetilde{E_2} = \mathbf{M^T} \cdot E_1$, as shown in the Fig. 4(b). Thus, we obtain the final node embedding matrices that capture the interaction between nodes in G_1 and G_2, respectively. Finally, we fuse E_1 and $\widetilde{E_1}$ to generate the final node embedding matrix H_1 for G_1, i.e., $H_1 = E_1 + W * \widetilde{E_1}$, where W is a self-learned parameter. Similarly, we can generate the final node embedding matrix H_2 for G_2. Lastly, we use Global Average Pooling (GAP) as the graph readout function to obtain global graph information in each channel, generating graph-level embeddings Z_1 and Z_2 for each graph G_1 and G_2, respectively. After obtaining the embeddings for both graphs, we set a self-learned parameter β and used the channel attention mechanism to fuse the two embedding vectors, obtaining the fused vector Z_G.

$$Z_G = \beta \cdot Z_1 + (1 - \beta) \cdot Z_2 \tag{6}$$

Subsequently, we optimize our model using contrastive learning. First, we train the model classifier parameters with the guidance of labels Y_L. The parameters can be optimized by evaluating the cross-entropy loss $\mathcal{L}_{cls}$ on the labels Y_L. Then, we optimize the parameters of the mutual information (MI) estimator to approach the true MI value. We aim to minimize the MI value between the two embedding vectors. In the process of reviewing the literature, we found that

InfoNCE [5,12,18] has been proven to be a lower bound on the true MI. By minimizing the InfoNCE loss, we can approximate the true MI. Therefore, we compute the InfoNCE loss function to calculate the loss between the embedding vectors $\mathcal{L}(Z_G, Z_1)$and $\mathcal{L}(Z_G, Z_2)$, and optimize the MI estimator with the following objective:

$$\mathcal{L}_{MI} = \mathcal{L}(Z_G, Z_1) + \mathcal{L}(Z_G, Z_2) \tag{7}$$

By minimizing Eq. 8, we approximate the minimized MI. Finally, we determine the following loss:

$$\mathcal{L}_{\text{total}} = \mathcal{L}_{cls} - \eta \mathcal{L}_{MI} \tag{8}$$

where η is a balancing parameter. Through this optimization, we retain useful feature information while filtering out interference noise as much as possible to obtain the final view embedding. Due to the large number of datasets, it is not possible to visualize all of them. Therefore, we randomly selected 30 APKs from the dataset to compare and display the graph structure before and after optimization, as shown in Fig. 5. In Fig. 5, blue nodes represent benign software, and yellow nodes represent malicious software; By comparing before and after, it can be clearly seen that the graph structure has been optimized, redundant edge structures have been removed, and the simplest graph structure has been obtained, reducing the complexity of learning.

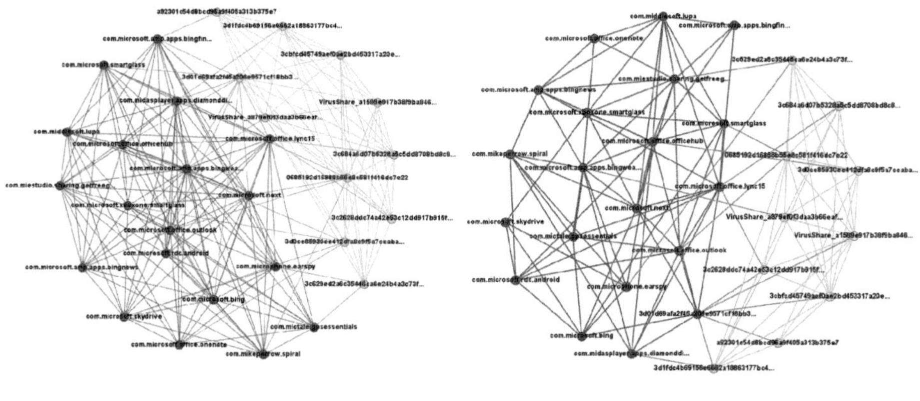

Fig. 5. Comparison of Graph Structure Optimization. Comparison of changes before and after graph structure optimization for 30 randomly selected APKs from the dataset.

Finally, we utilize the trained classification model for the detection of Android malware, resulting in the final classification results.

4 Experimentation and Evaluation

4.1 Experimental Software and Environment

This study is conducted using the PyTorch 1.10 environment as the foundation for our overall experiments. Androguard is utilized to decompile APK files and extract the required entity features. We employ PYG to construct the GraphSAGE model used in our experiments. The environment is established on a Windows 10 system with 8GB of RAM for analysis and extraction.

4.2 Dataset

Our benign software dataset consists of 4000 randomly selected APKs from the Google dataset, and a total of 3500 malicious software from Drebin [2], CICAndMal2015 [15], and VirusShare. However, due to some APKs being unable to decompile, we used Android to perform data filtering on the APK files. Finally, 3557 benign software and 3181 malicious software were selected to form the final dataset, which was divided into training, testing, and validation sets in a 6:2:2 ratio.

4.3 Experimental Procedure and Results

Several factors may influence the experimental results during this study's experimentation process. Firstly, we explore why the combination feature primarily relies on APIs, with opcodes and permissions as secondary. Based on this, we conducted separate experiments on APIs, permissions, opcodes, and combination features to verify the effectiveness of the combination features. The experimental results are shown in Fig. 6.

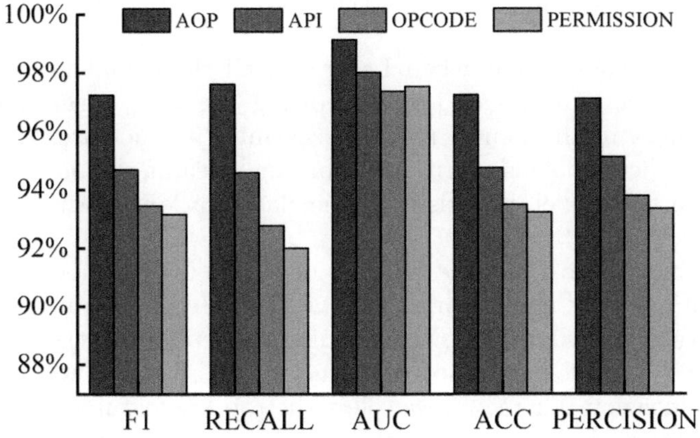

Fig. 6. Experiment Results of Entity Feature Selection

From Fig. 6, it is clear that compared to using individual features such as API, permissions, and opcodes, the performance of malware detection is better with combined features. Combined features provide more prosperous and more comprehensive behavioral feature information, offering more practical entity feature evidence for Android malware identification. Therefore, this paper selects Android combined features as the key parameters for experiments and uses them to construct the original graph structure. Additionally, the selection of the number of layers in the graph convolutional neural network (GCN) is also one of the critical factors affecting the model's performance in this paper. In this paper, the GCN participates in the optimization of the graph structure and the classification detection task. According to previous research literature [10], we tested one, two, three, and four layers of GCNs, as shown in Fig. 7.

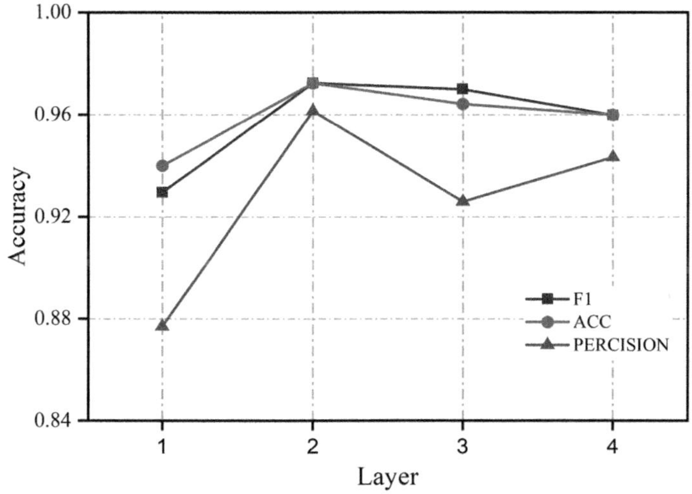

Fig. 7. Experimental Results of Different GraphSAGE Model Layers

The results indicate that when Layer = 2, all three evaluation metrics are higher than other numbers of layers, showing the best performance. As the number of layers in the neural network continues to increase, the depth and parameters of the model also increase accordingly, leading to an increased training burden on the model. Surprisingly, the classification detection performance decreases.

In addition, due to the large number of entity features (API, permissions, opcodes) obtained by decompiling the APK file (each feature class contains multiple features, as shown in Table 1), directly generating the feature matrix will affect the computational speed of the model, prolong the running time, and reduce efficiency. Therefore, we select the top k% features from the decompiled three features for verification, while minimizing the number of each type of feature while accelerating efficiency. We validate k = 10, 20, and 30 respectively, as shown in Table 2:

Table 2. Experimental Results

Layers	K	ACC	Precision	F1	AUC
1	10	0.9539	0.9315	0.9482	0.9839
	20	0.9300	0.8771	0.9296	0.9736
	30	0.9614	0.9593	0.9631	0.9879
2	10	0.9837	0.9589	0.9774	0.9901
	20	0.9824	0.9615	0.9724	0.9913
	30	0.9783	0.9519	0.9651	0.9865
3	10	0.9593	0.9689	0.9657	0.9897
	20	0.9642	0.9259	0.9699	0.9908
	30	0.9719	0.9820	0.9716	0.9962
4	10	0.9572	0.9615	0.9638	0.9910
	20	0.9600	0.9433	0.9599	0.9822
	30	0.9726	0.9517	0.9728	0.9894

From Table 2, we can observe that when the model has a lower number of layers, it relies more heavily on the quantity of features. As the number of features increases, the model's performance gradually improves. With an increase in the number of model layers, the model acquires stronger learning capabilities, reducing its reliance on the quantity of features. However, as the number of model layers continues to increase, the learned features may become redundant, leading to a decrease in the model's performance. Through various experiments, it was found that the overall best performance was achieved when Layer = 2 and K = 20, with an accuracy of 98.24% and an AUC of 99.13%. Our training process was set with Epoch = 400, as shown in the graph, where the loss function curve and accuracy curve converge completely at Epoch = 400 (Fig. 8).

This paper also compared with existing malware detection methods. The model algorithms used cover from traditional machine learning to the latest GCN models. Table 3 compares our method with existing methods. Our method shows better results and higher performance in Android malware detection.

4.4 Robustness Experiments

We conducted model robustness experiments by adding or removing edges from the original graph structure to simulate real-world data variations. Adding edges made the graph structure more complex, reflecting the diversity and richness of the data, while removing edges introduced data omissions or noise.

As shown in the Table 4, we observed that the model remained stable after edge adjustments, demonstrating good robustness. This suggests that the model can adapt to different graph structure changes and maintain reliability when facing diverse and changing data. Such experiments not only help validate the model's performance under various conditions but also improve our understand-

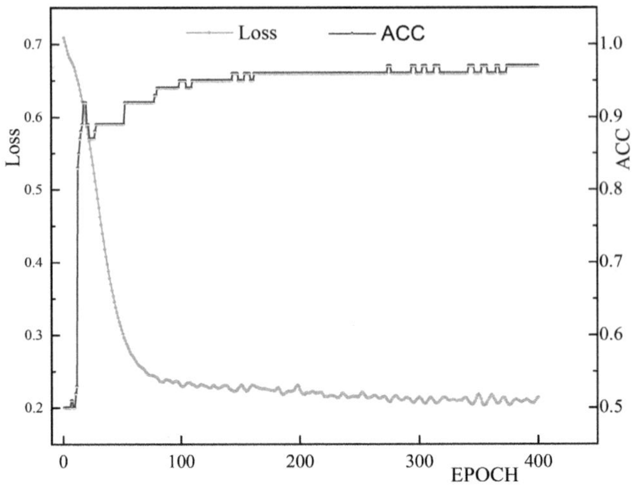

Fig. 8. Loss and accuracy curves.

Table 3. Comparison between Our Method and Existing Methods.

	F1	ACC	AUC	Recall	Precision
Derbin [2]	0.9431	0.9651	0.9765	0.9581	0.9542
MaMaDroid [17]	0.8489	0.9681	0.9599	0.9612	0.8909
DAPASA [6]	0.9422	0.9432	0.9578	0.9567	0.9356
DroidSim [19]	0.8930	0.9336	0.9141	0.9531	0.9124
AMDroid [9]	**0.9729**	0.9749	0.9748	0.9711	0.9787
McLaughlin [16]	0.9408	0.9265	0.9381	0.9138	0.9695
SeGDroid [14]	0.9665	**0.9837**	**0.9846**	**0.9896**	**0.9787**
Ours	**0.9724**	**0.9824**	**0.9913**	**0.9761**	**0.9811**

Table 4. Results of Robustness experiments

Del/Add	Rate	Count	ACC	F1	AUC
Del	5%	2840	0.9762	0.9700	0.9876
	10%	5679	0.9600	0.9658	0.9888
	15%	8518	0.9700	0.9800	0.9847
Add	5%	14196	0.9769	0.9742	0.9876
	10%	28393	0.9800	0.9710	0.9892
	15%	42589	0.9691	0.9648	0.9847

ing of the model's ability to handle graph data, thereby enhancing its credibility and utility in practical applications.

4.5 Ablation Experiments

To validate the effectiveness of each component in the model, we conducted ablation experiments. In these experiments, we systematically removed each component of the model and observed and recorded the changes in model performance. The Table 5 shows each ablation experiment group's accuracy, F1 score, and AUC.

Table 5. Results of Ablation experiments

	ACC	F1	AUC
AnGSL	**0.9824**	**0.9724**	**0.9913**
w/o KNN	0.9585	0.9683	0.9467
w/o DIFF	0.9508	0.9467	0.9881
w/o ID	0.9611	0.9658	0.9852
w/o MI	0.9605	0.9625	0.9754

From the data in the table, it can be observed that removing any component from the dual-channel structure, interaction graph, or MI estimator leads to a varying degree of performance degradation. When using a single channel to extract feature information, the ability to extract features from the original graph structure is weakened, resulting in a decrease in the detection performance of the model, thus verifying the effectiveness of the dual-channel structure. Removing the interaction graph and directly using the optimized two graph structures for fusion will reduce the ability of the two graphs to interact with each other, affecting the weight distribution during graph fusion and thus affecting the fusion effect. Comparing the three embedding vectors using the InfoNCE loss function can better adjust the model. Therefore, the use of the InfoNCE loss function is necessary. In summary, the results of the ablation experiments indicate that each component plays a crucial role in the model.

5 Conclusion and Future Work

This article introduces a novel Android malware detection method, AnGSL, that aims to establish external connections between APKs through graphs, automatically optimize graph structures, and extract hidden semantic information for more precise recognition and detection. Initially, the MTF-IDF algorithm is employed to select Android feature entities that are prevalent in malicious software datasets and absent in benign software datasets. The Euclidean distance between two APK feature vectors is calculated to approximate the closeness between the two APKs, which is used as a basis for determining whether there are edges between the two APKs, and the original graph structure is constructed. Subsequently, we utilize KNN and diffusion matrix algorithms to construct two subgraphs and refine them through the integration of channel attention mechanisms to achieve the optimized graph structure. Finally, employing the method of contrastive learning, the cross entropy loss between the two subgraphs and the optimized graph is minimized, leading to the training of the model. Experimental results and data demonstrate that our model method outperforms previous machine learning and current models based on static features and function call graphs, showing a certain degree of improvement in performance.

This article primarily focuses on constructing graph structures using three static feature entities: API, permissions, and opcodes, while neglecting the consideration and utilization of dynamic features. Additionally, due to the diverse entity categories in Android, a single homogeneous graph may only partially capture the complex relationships within. Therefore, in the next step, we will consider using dynamic features and heterogeneous graphs for Android malware detection to encompass more intricate relationships, such as node types and edge types. In conclusion, there is ample research space in the field of graph-based malware detection.

References

1. Alzaylaee, M.K., Yerima, S.Y., Sezer, S.: DL-droid: deep learning based android malware detection using real devices. Comput. Secur. **89**, 101663 (2020)
2. Arp, D., Spreitzenbarth, M., Hubner, M., Gascon, H., Rieck, K., Siemens, C.: Drebin: effective and explainable detection of android malware in your pocket. In: NDSS, vol. 14, pp. 23–26 (2014)
3. Cai, H.: Assessing and improving malware detection sustainability through app evolution studies. ACM Trans. Softw. Eng. Methodol. (TOSEM) **29**(2), 1–28 (2020)
4. Cen, L., Gates, C.S., Si, L., Li, N.: A probabilistic discriminative model for android malware detection with decompiled source code. IEEE Trans. Dependable Secure Comput. **12**(4), 400–412 (2014)
5. Chen, T., Kornblith, S., Norouzi, M., Hinton, G.: A simple framework for contrastive learning of visual representations. In: International Conference on Machine Learning, pp. 1597–1607. PMLR (2020)
6. Fan, M., Liu, J., Wang, W., Li, H., Tian, Z., Liu, T.: Dapasa: detecting android piggybacked apps through sensitive subgraph analysis. IEEE Trans. Inf. Forensics Secur. **12**(8), 1772–1785 (2017)
7. Feng, P., Ma, J., Li, T., Ma, X., Xi, N., Lu, D.: Android malware detection via graph representation learning. Mob. Inf. Syst. **2021**, 1–14 (2021)
8. Gao, H., Cheng, S., Zhang, W.: Gdroid: android malware detection and classification with graph convolutional network. Comput. Secur. **106**, 102264 (2021)
9. Ge, X., Pan, Y., Fan, Y., Fang, C.: Amdroid: android malware detection using function call graphs. In: 2019 IEEE 19th International Conference on Software Quality, Reliability and Security Companion (QRS-C), pp. 71–77. IEEE (2019)
10. Hamilton, W., Ying, Z., Leskovec, J.: Inductive representation learning on large graphs. In: Advances in Neural Information Processing Systems, vol. 30 (2017)
11. Hassen, M., Chan, P.K.: Scalable function call graph-based malware classification. In: Proceedings of the Seventh ACM on Conference on Data and Application Security and Privacy, pp. 239–248 (2017)

12. He, K., Fan, H., Wu, Y., Xie, S., Girshick, R.: Momentum contrast for unsupervised visual representation learning. In: Proceedings of the IEEE/CVF Conference on Computer Vision and Pattern Recognition, pp. 9729–9738 (2020)
13. Jianwen, P., Zhihua, Z., Gaoyi, L., Zhanqi, C.: Android malware detection based on feature selection. J. Comput. Eng. Appl. **59**(21) (2023)
14. Liu, Z., Wang, R., Japkowicz, N., Gomes, H.M., Peng, B., Zhang, W.: Segdroid: an android malware detection method based on sensitive function call graph learning. Expert Syst. Appl. **235**, 121125 (2024)
15. Mahdavifar, S., Kadir, A.F.A., Fatemi, R., Alhadidi, D., Ghorbani, A.A.: Dynamic android malware category classification using semi-supervised deep learning. In: 2020 IEEE International Conference on Dependable, Autonomic and Secure Computing, International Conference on Pervasive Intelligence and Computing, International Conference on Cloud and Big Data Computing, International Conference on Cyber Science and Technology Congress (DASC/PiCom/CBDCom/CyberSciTech), pp. 515–522. IEEE (2020)
16. McLaughlin, N., et al.: Deep android malware detection. In: Proceedings of the Seventh ACM on Conference on Data and Application Security and Privacy, pp. 301–308 (2017)
17. Onwuzurike, L., Mariconti, E., Andriotis, P., Cristofaro, E.D., Ross, G., Stringhini, G.: Mamadroid: detecting android malware by building Markov chains of behavioral models (extended version). ACM Trans. Priv. Secur. (TOPS) **22**(2), 1–34 (2019)
18. Oord, A.V.D., Li, Y., Vinyals, O.: Representation learning with contrastive predictive coding. arXiv preprint arXiv:1807.03748 (2018)
19. Sun, X., Zhongyang, Y., Xin, Z., Mao, B., Xie, L.: Detecting code reuse in android applications using component-based control flow graph. In: Cuppens-Boulahia, N., Cuppens, F., Jajodia, S., Abou El Kalam, A., Sans, T. (eds.) SEC 2014. IAICT, vol. 428, pp. 142–155. Springer, Heidelberg (2014). https://doi.org/10.1007/978-3-642-55415-5_12
20. Wu, H., Luktarhan, N., Tian, G., Song, Y.: An android malware detection approach to enhance node feature differences in a function call graph based on GCNs. Sensors **23**(10), 4729 (2023)
21. Yang, H., Wang, Y., Zhang, L., Cheng, X., Hu, Z.: A novel android malware detection method with API semantics extraction. Comput. Secur. **137**, 103651 (2024)
22. Yuan, B., Wang, J., Liu, D., Guo, W., Wu, P., Bao, X.: Byte-level malware classification based on Markov images and deep learning. Comput. Secur. **92**, 101740 (2020)
23. Zhang, N., Xue, J., Ma, Y., Zhang, R., Liang, T., Tan, Y.A.: Hybrid sequence-based android malware detection using natural language processing. Int. J. Intell. Syst. **36**(10), 5770–5784 (2021)
24. Zou, D., et al.: Intdroid: android malware detection based on API intimacy analysis. ACM Trans. Softw. Eng. Methodol. (TOSEM) **30**(3), 1–32 (2021)

Attention-Guided Contrastive Masked Autoencoders for Self-supervised Cross-Modal Biometric Matching

Haichuan Zhang[1,4], Jiaxiang Wang[2(✉)], Hanqin Shi[3], Zhenda Yu[1,4], and Yin Lin[4]

[1] Anhui Provincial Key Laboratory of Multimodal Cognitive Computation, The Information Materials and Intelligent Sensing Laboratory of Anhui Province, School of Artificial Intelligence, Anhui University, Hefei 230601, China
{wa22201018,wa22201140}@stu.ahu.edu.cn

[2] School of Computer Science and Technology, Anhui University, Hefei 230601, China
Netizenwjx@foxmail.com

[3] Xuzhou Institute of Technology, Xuzhou 221018, China
shihanqin0726@sina.com

[4] iFLYTEK AI Research Institute, Hefei 230088, China
yinlin@iflytek.com

Abstract. Cross-modal biometric matching is a significant research area in artificial intelligence and information forensics, focusing on establishing correlation between human acoustic and facial features. However, the variation of viewpoints in different scenes can lead to incomplete representations of specific voice and face images, which cannot be used to learn local critical features in the samples in an insightful way. To address these issues, we developed the Attention-Guided Contrast Masking Autoencoder Framework (ACMAE). This framework enhances cross-modal biometric performance through contrastive learning and masked data reconstruction. First, we introduce an attention-based data reconstruction method to improve feature discrimination. Second, we design multi-view contrastive learning to reduce viewpoint differences and enhance the robustness of the representations. Finally, experiments on benchmark datasets demonstrate that the ACMAE method achieves state-of-the-art performance and proves its effectiveness.

Keywords: Multi-modal information forensics · Cross-modal Biometric Matching · Masked Image Modeling · Contrastive Learning

1 Introduction

Research in neuroscience and psychology has demonstrated a connection between a person's facial images and voice features [1,2]. When provided with a facial image and voice samples, machine learning can identify which voice samples correspond to the same person as the facial image, and vice versa. This task is

S. Goel et al. (Eds.): ICDF2C 2024, LNICST 614, pp. 162–173, 2025.
https://doi.org/10.1007/978-3-031-89360-5_10

known as cross-modal biometric matching [3]. Recently, this field has garnered significant attention, aiming to leverage neural networks to learn the connection between facial and vocal features. Additionally, cross-modal biometric matching is a critical area of artificial intelligence and information forensics, essential for developing multimodal digital forensics systems [4, 5].

Cross-modal biometric matching focuses on recognizing associated identities across modalities by embedding features from different modalities into a common space to evaluate their similarity. To address this goal, Nagrani *et al.* [3] proposed SVHF-Net, an innovative approach for Cross-modal biometric matching using deep learning. However, due to modal heterogeneity, significant differences in the embedding of cross-modal features in the feature space may lead to ambiguity in the matching relationship. To address this issue, Zheng *et al.* [6] proposed the AML method, which combines adversarial learning and metric learning to jointly supervise the matching of acoustic and facial features. Adversarial methods have been widely adopted to mitigate modal heterogeneity effectively. However, reducing modal heterogeneity alone is insufficient for achieving accurate Cross-modal biometric matching, especially0 since local subtle features are still inadequately mined. Therefore, Wang *et al.* [7] proposed the multi-attribute-guided interaction-enhanced network (ACIENet), which utilizes multiple attributes to explore the connection between different key local fine-grained features. As a multi-labeled supervised approach, ACIENet achieves better matching performance, but its reliance on extensive labeling requires substantial manpower and resources.

This makes it difficult to perform effective feature mining for new unlabeled data, limiting the model's generalization ability. Researchers have begun to explore unsupervised cross-modal biometric feature-matching methods. Nagrani *et al.* [8] proposed the Pins method, which achieves audio-face matching without labeling and introduces audio-face verification and retrieval tasks. Chen *et al.* [9] proposed the Self-lifting method, which improves matching performance by alternating clustering and metric learning. Chen *et al.* [10] also proposed the EFT method, which uses a weight-sharing converter to integrate expert knowledge. First, existing methods fail to effectively overcome the modal differences between acoustic and facial image features by directly restricting sample distances through metric learning. Second, these methods do not sufficiently emphasize key features in both acoustic and facial images, affecting the accuracy of cross-modal matching. Therefore, we propose the attention-guided contrast masked autoencoder (ACMAE), which combines attention MAE [11] and contrastive learning to efficiently achieve Cross-modal biometric matching from unsupervised acoustic and facial data. Specifically, we first introduce a bootstrapping attention strategy to guide the masking operation. This strategy masks and reconstructs key parts of face images and acoustic spectrograms, prompting the network to learn more localized features for cross-modal matching. Then, cross-modal contrastive learning is performed on the acoustic and facial image features to optimize the reduction of differences between the two modalities and achieve alignment. Additionally, we conduct multi-view contrastive learning between the representation of the complete sample and the masked representation. In summary, our contributions can be summarized as follows:

- We propose an attention-guided masking strategy that efficiently learns local detail features for cross-modal biometric matching by reconstructing key parts.
- We propose two-stage contrastive learning that effectively reduces both view variability and modality variability.
- Experiments conducted on a public dataset demonstrate that our method outperforms previous approaches, highlighting its effectiveness.

2 Related Work

2.1 Cross-Modal Biometric Matching

The goal of cross-modal matching is to establish correlations between two modalities using neural networks for matching vocal and facial features. Nagrani *et al.* [3] pioneered SVHF-Net, defining the task of cross-biometric information matching. SVHF-Net utilizes independent audio and visual encoders to extract voice and facial image features, which are then combined and used in a classification task to complete the matching. Wang *et al.* [12] proposed a method to construct difficult samples by mining triples and learning embedded features of sound and facial images using bidirectional ranking, identity, and centroid constraints. Zheng *et al.* [13] introduced variant adversarial learning to guide metric learning through public attributes and enhance the discriminative power of embedded features through private attribute embedding. Wang *et al.* [14] proposed a dual enhancement mechanism with concatenated adversarial networks to reinforce salient and subtle features in parallel. Another method by Wang *et al.* [7], ACIENet, facilitates the interaction of different modal features through global alignment and employs attribute-driven networks to capture relevant subtle features, improving attribute-level recognition accuracy. However, all these methods assume a supervised environment, while real-world data is often unsupervised. Nagrani *et al.* [8] proposed the Pins method, assuming that audio and face images in the same video originate from the same person, employing self-supervised and coarse learning for training. Similarly, Chen *et al.* [9] proposed Self-Lifting, which first extracts voice and facial features using a preliminary model, generates pseudo-labels through clustering, guides metric learning, and ultimately refines the model. However, voice and face images in a video do not always correspond exactly. Zhu *et al.* [15] developed a cross-modal prototype comparison method, effectively reducing misclassification by evaluating the similarity between samples and prototypes. Chen *et al.* [10] proposed the EFT model, which integrates an existing unimodal professional model to optimize feature representation and employs an NCE loss function to guide training. Although these methods have established a link between sound and facial images, the interaction between different modal features has not been fully explored. Therefore, we propose ACMAE, which employs contrastive learning and masking reconstruction techniques to reduce inter-modal variability.

2.2 Masked Autoencoders

Given the excellent performance of masked language modeling in natural language processing [16], several studies have attempted to apply it to computer vision and speech signal processing. He *et al.* [11] proposed the Masked Auto-Encoder (MAE), which uses a transformer [17] to process variable-length data by masking out 75% of the image regions and encoding the remainder. A decoder then reconstructs the image, optimizing the embedding representation. Huang *et al.* [18] proposed the AudioMAE method, which first converts audio sequences into spectrograms to obtain a stable audio representation. It then applies an image-like masking to the spectrograms and uses the MAE for encoding and reconstruction. Gong *et al.* [19] proposed the Audio-Visual Masked Auto-Encoder (AVMAE), which combines audio spectrograms and visual images for joint encoding, optimizing audio representation with visual information and enhancing the correlation between different modalities through mask reconstruction and contrastive learning of audio-visual features. Therefore, in ACMAE, we apply an attention mechanism to strengthen the reconstruction of local features, improving the matching effect of cross-modal biometrics.

3 Method

See Fig. 1.

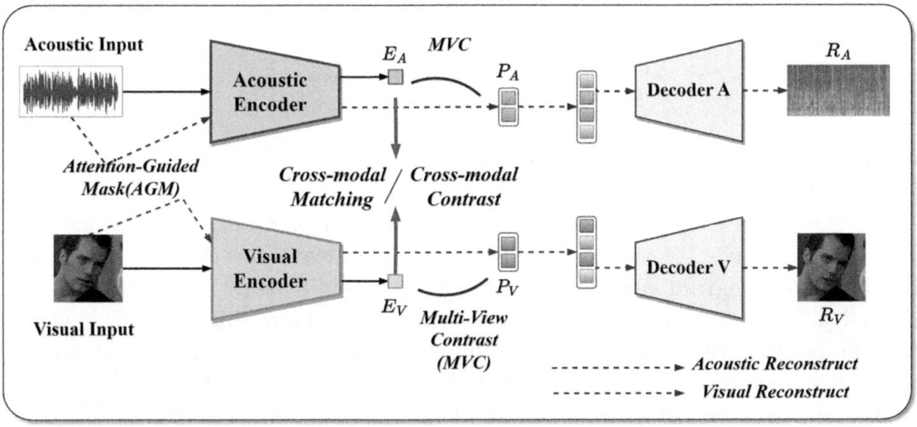

Fig. 1. Overview of our proposed ACMAE method. The dashed line represents the process of sample mask reconstruction. Contrastive learning is performed in the training phase, and cross-modal matching is only performed in the testing phase.

3.1 Unsupervised Cross-Modal Biometric Matching

We adopt the network structure of Nagrani *et al.* [8] as a baseline, with the key difference being that both our acoustic and visual encoders are based on Vision

Transformers. Following the setup of Nagrani *et al.* [8], we utilize SyncNet [20] to extract the speaker's facial dynamics and speech trajectory, thereby reducing the presence of voiceless faces and video clips with multiple faces in the dataset. We define a face image in the same video as the corresponding speech as a positive sample and any other pairing as a negative sample. In the direct pairing process, we first convert the original speech into audio spectrograms, then feed the audio spectrograms and face images into acoustic and visual encoders, which consist of Vision Transformers [21]. We denote the acoustic and visual embeddings as E_A and E_V, respectively. The network performance is then optimized by calculating the contrast loss $\mathcal{L}_{contrast}$.

3.2 Attention-Guided Masked Modeling

Inspired by earlier research on local feature learning [22,23], our goal is to model key regions of the samples in greater detail. To achieve this, we employ an Attention-Guided Masking (AGM) strategy to more accurately capture localized subtle features of acoustic and visual images. In vision transformers, we can use the $[cls]$ token for classification, it serves as the representation of an entire image. We follow a similar setting with A-CLIP [24]. For spectrograms or images processed by the visual transformer, the $[cls]$ token conveys the main acoustic or visual information. Calculating the attention weights of the $[cls]$ token with other tokens can reveal their relevance to the overall sample information. The relevance r_i of the $i-$th token can be calculated using the following equation:

$$r_i = \frac{1}{l \cdot h} \sum_{j=1}^{l} \sum_{k=1}^{h} Softmax\left(\frac{Q_{jk} \cdot K_{jk}^{i}}{\sqrt{c}}\right), \tag{1}$$

where l represents the number of network layers, h represents the number of attention heads, Q is a query vector derived from the $[cls]$ tokens, while K is a key vector generated from the token located at the i-th position, and c denotes the number of channels. Tokens with higher weights indicate that their corresponding image or spectrogram regions are more critical for feature representation. We applied a 75% masking rate to the less critical regions based on the weight r_i. This bootstrapping process helps filter out and retain regions that contain essential information, which are then fed into the encoder (Fig. 2).

To improve the robustness of sound and image representations, we reconstruct the encoded features. The decoder and encoder are designed with an asymmetric structure consisting of 6 layers. For sound processing, the remaining sound tokens after the masking operation are fed into the sound encoder. The resulting sound token vector P_A is then fed into the decoder for reconstruction, yielding R_A. To evaluate the effectiveness of the acoustic reconstruction, we compute the loss $\mathcal{L}_{recon}^{acoustic}$:

$$\mathcal{L}_{recon}^{acoustic} = \frac{1}{N} \sum_{i=1}^{N} \left(P_{A_i}^{original} - P_{A_i}^{predict}\right)^2, \tag{2}$$

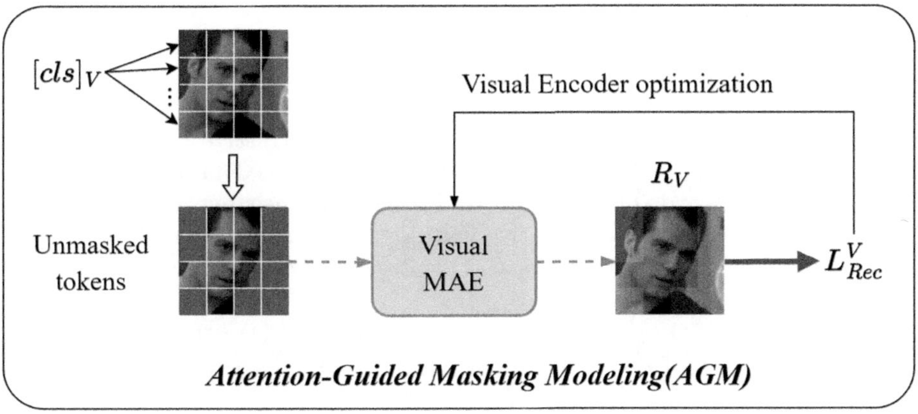

Fig. 2. Overview of the attention-guided masking. Take visual modality as an example.

where $P^{original}$represents the original patch that is masked, while $P^{predict}$ is the patch reconstructed after decoding, and N denotes the batch size. Similarly, we use a visual codec to reconstruct visual samples and compute the reconstruction loss using $\mathcal{L}_{recon}^{visual}$:

$$\mathcal{L}_{recon}^{visual} = \frac{1}{N}\sum_{i=1}^{N}\left(P_{V_i}^{original} - P_{V_i}^{predict}\right)^2, \tag{3}$$

where the total reconstruction loss is $\mathcal{L}_{recon} = \mathcal{L}_{recon}^{acoustic} + \mathcal{L}_{recon}^{visual}$. With the help of the attention-guided masking strategy, we can efficiently obtain stable acoustic representations and image representations rich in key local features (Fig. 3).

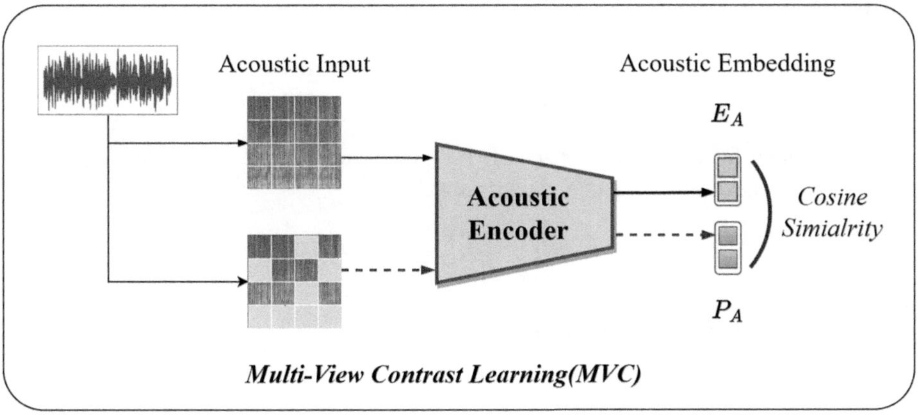

Fig. 3. An overview of multi-view contrastive learning. Take acoustic modality as an example.

3.3 Cross-Modal and Multi-view Contrast

To effectively reduce inter-modal differences and enhance the robustness of feature representations, we implement a two-stage contrastive learning process: cross-modal contrastive learning and multi-view contrastive learning (MVC), performed concurrently. In this process, we map the masked audio-coded features P_A and face image-coded features P_V to dimensions consistent with E_A and E_V, respectively, and perform contrastive learning. For the same batch of samples, we use the NCE-type contrast loss $\mathcal{L}_{contrast}$, computed as follows:

$$\mathcal{L}_{contrast}\left\langle \cdot,\cdot \right\rangle = -\frac{1}{N}\sum_{i=1}^{N}\log\left[\frac{\exp\left(sim\left\langle i,i\right\rangle/\tau\right)}{\sum_{k\neq i}\exp\left(sim\left\langle i,k\right\rangle/\tau\right)+\exp\left(sim\left\langle i,i\right\rangle/\tau\right)}\right], \tag{4}$$

where $sim\left\langle \cdot,\cdot \right\rangle$ denotes the cosine similarity between the sound embedding and the visual embedding, N is the batch size, and $\tau$is the temperature hyperparameter set to 0.05. The positive samples are defined as the sound and face in the same video clip. For voice-to-face scenarios, the contrast loss is calculated as: $\mathcal{L}_{contrast}\left\langle E_V, E_A\right\rangle$. In face-to-voice scenarios, the contrast loss is then computed as $\mathcal{L}_{contrast}\left\langle E_A, E_V\right\rangle$.

Considering the potential for sound clips and facial images to be cropped or incomplete, we undertake multi-view comparison learning within each modality. For the acoustic modality, we use masking operations as a data enhancement tool, treating the original sound and the masked sound as different views. Based on their feature representations E_A and P_A, we compute the acoustic multi-view contrast loss $\mathcal{L}_{contrast}\left\langle E_A, P_A\right\rangle$, where the positive samples are different views of the same sample and the negative samples are from different video clips. Similarly, we compute the facial multi-view contrast loss $\mathcal{L}_{contrast}\left\langle E_V, P_V\right\rangle$. Combining the acoustic and facial multi-view contrast losses yields the total multi-view contrast loss:

$$\begin{aligned}\mathcal{L}_{multiview} &= \mathcal{L}_{multiview}^{acoustic} + \mathcal{L}_{multiview}^{visual},\\ &= \mathcal{L}_{contrast}\left\langle E_A, P_A\right\rangle + \mathcal{L}_{contrast}\left\langle E_V, P_V\right\rangle,\end{aligned} \tag{5}$$

where our loss function comprises three components: the MAE reconstruction loss, the contrast loss, and the multi-view loss.

$$\mathcal{L}_{total} = \mathcal{L}_{recon} + \mathcal{L}_{contrast} + \mathcal{L}_{multiview}. \tag{6}$$

4 Experiments and Results

4.1 Dataset

VGGFace and VoxCeleb. VGGFace [25] comprises a face recognition dataset with 2,622 identities. VoxCeleb [26] is sourced from YouTube, encompassing 1,251 speakers across various scenarios, commonly utilized as benchmarks for cross-modal biometric matching. Following previous methodologies, we utilize the preprocessed version of the speech-face dataset provided by Pins [8], featuring 1,225 identities, 153,000 audio segments from VoxCeleb, and 1.2 million face frames from VGGFace. The dataset is partitioned into training, validation, and testing sets following established rules, as detailed in Table 1.

Table 1. The overview of Voxceleb [26] dataset.

Item	Train	Test	Val	Total
Facial Images	905,530	170,330	108,951	1,184,811
Audio Clips	113,322	21,850	14,182	149,354
IDs	924	189	112	1,225

4.2 Implementation Details and Experimental Results

We resized the face images and spectrograms to 224×224 pixels and set the patch size to 28 × 28 pixels, respectively. The model employs 6 attention heads in its architecture. The MAE encoder comprises 8 layers, while the decoder consists of 6 layers. For consistency with other cross-modal biometric methods and to ensure fair comparisons, we conducted voice-face (V2F) matching, face-voice (F2V) matching, and voice-face verification tasks. The number of candidate samples for the V2F matching task was increased from two to ten. The experiments were conducted using the PyTorch framework on GeForce RTX 4080 GPUs. From 100 rounds of training, we selected the best-performing result as the outcome. We utilized dynamic learning rate adjustment by reducing the learning rate by a factor of 0.1 every 10 epochs, starting from epochs 30, with an initial learning rate of 0.001.

Table 2. The qualitative results of verification and matching tasks on Voxceleb [26]. Binary denotes the 1:2 matching while multi-way denotes the $1 : k(k = 10)$ matching. '×' indicates 'not capable'. Underlined are suboptimal methods.

Methods	Venue	Verification (AUC)	Binary (ACC)		Multi-way (ACC)	
			V-F	F-V	V-F	F-V
Pins [8]	ECCV2018	78.5	80.8	81.1	31.2	31.5
CID [27]	CVPR 2021	78.2	78.3	77.6	×	×
β-VAE [28]	TMM 2021	<u>84.1</u>	82.9	<u>83.5</u>	37.9	38.0
CMPC [15]	IJCAI2022	82.6	82.2	81.5	×	×
FOP [29]	ICASSP2022	83.5	<u>83.5</u>	83.2	<u>38.5</u>	<u>38.1</u>
SBNet [30]	ICASSP2023	82.5	82.4	82.4	37.1	37.4
ACMAE	Ours	**84.9**	**86.2**	**86.6**	**41.0**	**41.6**

We evaluated the effectiveness of ACMA through comparative experiments using accuracy (ACC) for matching tasks and Area Under Curve (AUC) for verification tasks. We compared ACMA against several state-of-the-art methods, including Pins [8], CID [27], CMPC [15], β-VAE [28], FOP [29], and SBNet [30]. Pins [8] and CID [27] represent the initial research in cross-modal biometric matching, employing joint embedding techniques for matching. CMPC [15] proposed prototype comparison learning to enhance intra-class consistency. β-VAE [28] proposed a decoupled representation learning method to mitigate modal correlations and leverage latent identity traits for aligning information across modalities. FOP [29] utilized embedded orthogonality constraints to enhance clustering performance. SBNet [30] employed a single-branch network to encode multimodal features and reduce inter-modal heterogeneity.

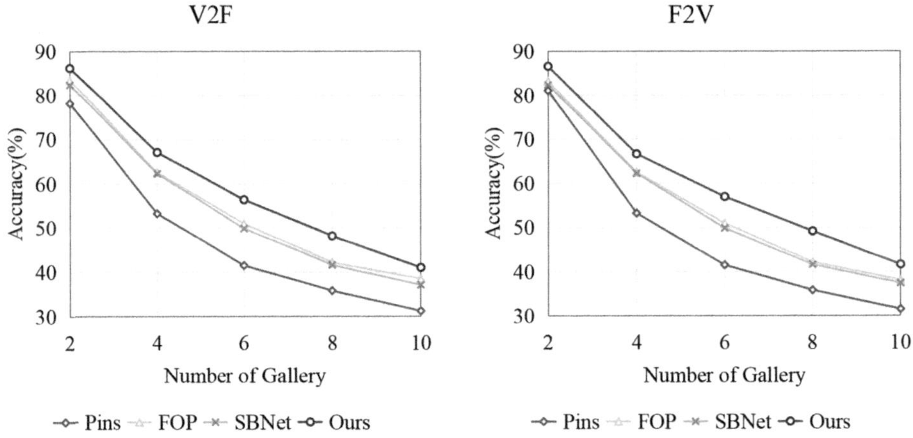

Fig. 4. Performance visualization of increasing the number of candidate scenes from 2 to 10 on the Matching task.

Table 2 summarizes the experimental results for the matching and validation tasks. ACMAE's accuracy on the matching task is significantly higher than that of the other compared methods. Specifically, ACMAE outperforms the suboptimal methods by 2.7%, 3.1%, 2.5%, and 3.5% in the binary and multiplexed scenarios, respectively. Additionally, we extended the experiment by gradually increasing the number of candidate scenarios from two to ten, with the relevant results shown in Fig. 4. These data demonstrate the superior performance of ACMAE.

4.3 Ablation Study

We conducted an ablation study to analyze the roles of each component of the model in detail. The baseline model combines MAE for encoding and cross-modal contrastive learning for alignment. To further examine the effects of these components, we introduced the Attention-Guided Masking (AGM) strategy and Multi-View contrastive learning (MVC). Figure 5 displays three sets of images: the original images, the attention maps after employing AGM, and the attention maps from the standard MAE. The data in Table 3 indicate that the network successfully captured more key features after adding AGM. In both the verification task and the binary matching task, the addition of the AGM and MVC modules significantly improved performance.

Table 3. The qualitative results of ablation study on matching and verification tasks. Matching denotes the Binary scenario while matching.

Methods	Matching (ACC)		Verification (AUC)
	V-F	F-V	
Baseline	82.2	82.7	81.9
Baseline + AGM	84.8	<u>85.2</u>	84.1
Baseline + MVC	<u>85.0</u>	84.3	<u>84.4</u>
Baseline + AGM + MVC(ours)	**86.2**	**86.6**	**84.9**

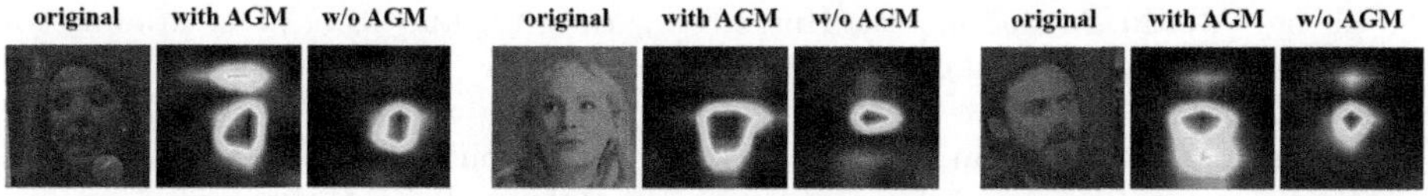

Fig. 5. Attention visualization. Each set of images from left to right is an original image, attention visualization with AGM, and without AGM.

5 Conclusion

In this paper, we introduce the ACMAE model, designed to improve Cross-modal biometric matching. First, we employ the Fourier transform to convert the sound signal into a spectral image comparable to the face image. Next, an attention-guided masking strategy filters important features in both the spectrogram and the face image. Additionally, we develop a two-stage contrastive learning scheme, comprising cross-modal contrast and multi-view contrast, to reduce heterogeneity among different modalities and enhance the robustness of the representations. The effectiveness of the ACMAE model is confirmed by testing it on the VGGFace [25] and VoxCeleb [26] datasets. Furthermore, the model can be applied to other acoustic and visual cross-modal data processing tasks.

Acknowledgments. This paper was partially supported by the National Natural Science Foundation of China (Youth Foundation Program, 62102344).

Declaration of Competing Interest. No author associated with this paper has disclosed any potential or pertinent conflicts that may be perceived to have impending conflict with this work.

References

1. Belin, P., Bestelmeyer, P., Latinus, M., Watson, R.: Understanding voice perception. Br. J. Psychol. **102**(4), 711–725 (2011)
2. Smith, H., Dunn, A.K., Baguley, T., Stacey, P.C.: Matching novel face and voice identity using static and dynamic facial images. Atten. Percept. Psychophys. **78**(3), 868–879 (2016). https://doi.org/10.3758/s13414-015-1045-8
3. Nagrani, A., Albanie, S., Zisserman, A.: Seeing voices and hearing faces: cross-modal biometric matching. In: Proceedings of the IEEE/CVF Conference on Computer Vision and Pattern Recognition, pp. 8427–8436 (2018)
4. Feng, C., Chen, Z., Owens, A.: Self-supervised video forensics by audio-visual anomaly detection. In: Proceedings of the IEEE/CVF Conference on Computer Vision and Pattern Recognition, pp. 10491–10503 (2023)
5. Oorloff, T., et al.: AVFF: audio-visual feature fusion for video deepfake detection. In: Proceedings of the IEEE/CVF Conference on Computer Vision and Pattern Recognition, pp. 27102–27112 (2024)
6. Zheng, A., Hu, M., Jiang, B., Huang, Y., Yan, Y., Luo, B.: Adversarial-metric learning for audio-visual cross-modal matching. IEEE Trans. Multimedia **24**, 338–351 (2021)
7. Wang, J., Zheng, A., Yan, Y., He, R., Tang, J.: Attribute-guided cross-modal interaction and enhancement for audio-visual matching. IEEE Trans. Inf. Forensics Secur. (2024)
8. Nagrani, A., Albanie, S., Zisserman, A.: Learnable pins: cross-modal embeddings for person identity. In: Proceedings of the European Conference on Computer Vision, pp. 71–88 (2018)
9. Chen, G., Zhang, D., Liu, T., Du, X.: Self-lifting: a novel framework for unsupervised voice-face association learning. In: Proceedings of the 2022 International Conference on Multimedia Retrieval, pp. 527–535 (2022)
10. Chen, G., Zhang, D., Liu, T., Du, X.: EFT: expert fusion transformer for voice-face association learning. In: 2023 IEEE International Conference on Multimedia and Expo (ICME), pp. 2603–2608 (2023)
11. He, K., Chen, X., Xie, S., Li, Y., Dollár, P., Girshick, R.: Masked autoencoders are scalable vision learners. In: Proceedings of the IEEE/CVF Conference on Computer Vision and Pattern Recognition, pp. 16000–16009 (2022)
12. Wang, R., Liu, X., Cheung, Y.M., Cheng, K., Wang, N., Fan, W.: Learning discriminative joint embeddings for efficient face and voice association. In: Proceedings of the 43rd International ACM SIGIR Conference on Research and Development in Information Retrieval, pp. 1881–1884 (2020)
13. Zheng, A., Yuan, F., Zhang, H., Wang, J., Tang, C., Li, C.: Public-private attributes-based variational adversarial network for audio-visual cross-modal matching. IEEE Trans. Circ. Syst. Video Technol. (2024)

14. Wang, J., Li, C., Zheng, A., Tang, J., Luo, B.: Looking and hearing into details: dual-enhanced siamese adversarial network for audio-visual matching. IEEE Trans. Multimedia **25**, 7505–7516 (2022)
15. Zhu, B., et al.: Unsupervised voice-face representation learning by cross-modal prototype contrast. arXiv preprint arXiv:2204.14057 (2022)
16. Devlin, J., Chang, M.W., Lee, K., Toutanova, K.: Bert: pre-training of deep bidirectional transformers for language understanding. arXiv preprint arXiv:1810.04805 (2018)
17. Vaswani, A., et al.: Attention is all you need. In: Advances in Neural Information Processing Systems, vol. 30 (2017)
18. Po-Yao Huang, H.X., et al.: Masked autoencoders that listen. Adv. Neural. Inf. Process. Syst. **35**, 28708–28720 (2022)
19. Gong, Y., et al.: Contrastive audio-visual masked autoencoder. arXiv preprint arXiv:2210.07839 (2022)
20. Chung, J.S., Zisserman, A.: Out of time: automated lip sync in the wild. In: Chen, C.-S., Lu, J., Ma, K.-K. (eds.) ACCV 2016. LNCS, vol. 10117, pp. 251–263. Springer, Cham (2017). https://doi.org/10.1007/978-3-319-54427-4_19
21. Dosovitskiy, A., et al.: An image is worth 16x16 words: transformers for image recognition at scale. arXiv preprint arXiv:2010.11929 (2020)
22. Cao, J., Guo, Y., Wu, Q., Shen, C., Huang, J., Tan, M.: Adversarial learning with local coordinate coding. In: International Conference on Machine Learning, pp. 707–715. PMLR (2018)
23. Cao, J., Guo, Y., Qingyao, W., Shen, C., Huang, J., Tan, M.: Improving generative adversarial networks with local coordinate coding. IEEE Trans. Pattern Anal. Mach. Intell. **44**(1), 211–227 (2020)
24. Yang, Y., et al.: Attentive mask clip. In: Proceedings of the IEEE/CVF International Conference on Computer Vision, pp. 2771–2781 (2023)
25. Parkhi, O.M., Vedaldi, A., Zisserman, A.: Deep face recognition. In: Proceedings of the British Machine Vision Conference, pp. 41.1–41.12 (2015)
26. Nagrani, A., Chung, J.S., Zisserman, A.: Voxceleb: a large-scale speaker identification dataset. arXiv preprint arXiv:1706.08612 (2017)
27. Morgado, P., Vasconcelos, N., Misra, I.: Audio-visual instance discrimination with cross-modal agreement. In: Proceedings of the IEEE/CVF Conference on Computer Vision and Pattern Recognition, pp. 12475–12486 (2021)
28. Ning, H., Zheng, X., Xiaoqiang, L., Yuan, Y.: Disentangled representation learning for cross-modal biometric matching. IEEE Trans. Multimedia **24**, 1763–1774 (2021)
29. Saeed, M.S., Khan, M.H., Nawaz, S., Yousaf, M.H., Del Bue, A.: Fusion and orthogonal projection for improved face-voice association. In: ICASSP 2022-2022 IEEE International Conference on Acoustics, Speech and Signal Processing (ICASSP), pp. 7057–7061. IEEE (2022)
30. Saeed, M.S., et al.: Single-branch network for multimodal training. In: ICASSP 2023-2023 IEEE International Conference on Acoustics, Speech and Signal Processing (ICASSP), pp. 1–5. IEEE (2023)

MSP: A Zero-Latency Lightweight Website Fingerprinting Defense for Tor Network

Tianbo Lu[1,2](✉), Xiaohan Tao[1,2], Yanfang Li[1,2], and Jiaze Shang[1,2]

[1] School of Computer Science (National Pilot Software Engineering School), Beijing University of Posts and Telecommunications, Beijing, China
{lutb,2434756958,studyli,sjz}@bupt.edu.cn

[2] Key Laboratory of Trustworthy Distributed Computing and Service (MoE), Beijing University of Posts and Telecommunications, Beijing, China

Abstract. Tor is a widely used low-latency anonymous communication network that hides the IP addresses and communication content of both parties when users are engaged in network activities. Nevertheless, attackers using Website Fingerprinting (WF) attacks can infer the real purpose of websites visited by users through eavesdropping on encrypted network traffic between Tor users and web servers, posting a threat to user privacy and security. Classical WF defense models perform poorly against the latest deep learning-based WF attack models. Furthermore, these models suffer from unreasonable assumptions and high performance overhead. In this paper, we propose a novel zero-latency lightweight WF defense model Multiple Sample Padding (MSP). The model combines multiple traffic sequence features to pad real traffic and defend against deep learning-based website fingerprinting attacks. In addition, we explore the feasibility of changing webpage loading states to interfere with website fingerprint attack models. The experimental results show that MSP can reduce the accuracy of the attack model by 71%, as well as lower the latency overhead by 27%. Changing the webpage loading status based on MSP can reduce the accuracy of the attack model by 90% with a bandwidth overhead of 164%, compared to the strongest WF defense model, while reducing the latency overhead by 78%.

Keywords: Tor · Privacy · Website Fingerprinting · Traffic Padding

1 Introduction

Tor is currently the most popular low-latency anonymous network, with millions of people online every day [6]. It protects users' privacy by hiding their location and online activities such as visiting websites, sending messages, and following posts through a three-hop route randomly selected by the client, as well as a network of onion routes. Although privacy-enhancing technologies such as Tor and HTTPS proxies can hide the content of communication and network layer information, network traffic features such as packet size, direction, and interpacket

S. Goel et al. (Eds.): ICDF2C 2024, LNICST 614, pp. 174–191, 2025.
https://doi.org/10.1007/978-3-031-89360-5_11

timing cannot be concealed. The class of attacks in which an attacker can construct unique website fingerprints to identify encrypted website traffic by modeling the characteristics of the encrypted traffic and undermine Tor's anonymity is known as Website Fingerprinting (WF) attack. With the application of machine learning, the construction of WF has been integrated into the process of training classifiers. In recent years, some researchers have been utilizing deep learning to directly classify the raw features of encrypted traffic [3,8,17,21]. Although the current state-of-the-art WF defense defends against WF attacks through high bandwidth consumption, it is really ineffective in the face of deep learning-based WF attacks.

Researchers have come up with many defenses. Typically, these defenses obfuscate encrypted traffic by buffering packets, adding virtual packets, or combining traffic from two sites into a single super sequence. The main problems with the currently prominent defense schemes are as follows:

1) Based on unreasonable assumptions. Some defense schemes assume that the defenders have prior knowledge of the loading patterns of each webpage, allowing them to design sending patterns according to the characteristics of each webpage. However, in real web environments, where most websites are frequently updated, it is difficult to know all the sending sequences in advance. Additionally, maintaining and distributing the loading data of websites would impose a significant operational burden on Tor.
2) Inability to balance defense effectiveness and overhead. Classical WF defense models such as WTF-PAD [10] and W-T [25], while not incurring significant overhead, perform poorly against deep learning-based WF attacks. On the other hand, the latest WF defense, such as Surakav [7], introduces latency overhead, which comprises user experience.

To address the aforementioned issues, we propose a new defense model called Multiple Sample Padding (MSP). It involves adding traffic features from other websites into the current website traffic to conceal its true traffic patterns and interfere with the attacker's classifier. In addition to that, building upon MSP, we explore the deception of the attacker's defense model by sending virtual packets to simulate page loading states after the actual sequence of transmission is complete. Experimental results demonstrate that MSP can reduce the accuracy rate of the Deep Fingerprinting (DF) [20] attack by 71% with a bandwidth overhead of 69%. Compared with the current advanced lightweight defense model Surakav, MSP reduces latency overhead by 27%. Changing the webpage loading status based on MSP can reduce the accuracy of DF attack by 90% with a bandwidth overhead of 164%. Compared to the strongest existing model, Tamaraw [4], changing the webpage loading status based on MSP reduces latency overhead by 78%.

In this paper, we make the following contributions:

- We propose a WF defense model MSP called multiple sample padding. The model is a zero-delay lightweight defense that performs packet padding by utilizing multiple sequences of spurious traffic, corrupting the original traffic patterns of the website.

- Building upon MSP, we explore the feasibility of altering webpage loading states to disrupt WF attack models by sending virtual packets to simulate page loading states after the actual sequence of transmission is complete.
- It is shown experimentally that MSP and changing the webpage loading status based on MSP can significantly reduce the success rate of adversaries in identifying users access to websites. Furthermore, these effects are stable across different datasets.

This paper is organized as follows. We introduce related work in Sect. 2 and describe the threat model of this paper in Sect. 3. We present the design of MSP and padding based on MSP in Sect. 4 and evaluate the defense model proposed in Sect. 5. Finally, the work of this paper is summarized in Sect. 6.

2 Related Work

2.1 WF Attacks

In an end-to-end system, a user's network activity is encapsulated in a single connection, and a passive attacker cannot directly access plaintext information, such as the Server Name Indicator (SNI) in a TLS handshake packet and information such as the website the user is accessing. However, WF (Website Fingerprinting) attacks can leverage traffic information to infer the user's browsing history. In previous studies, researchers have proposed a variety of WF attack models, among which the accuracy of early manual feature selection and traditional machine learning classifiers can reach more than 90%. In recent years, many researchers have used deep neural networks (DNN) to construct WF attack models, which further improves classification accuracy. Additionally, these models no longer require manual feature selection and fine-tuning. The defense model proposed in this paper aims to counter DNN-based WF attacks, therefore, the non-DNN attack models based on handcrafted features are out of the scope of this paper. The following are a few typical attack models:

SDAE [1]: Abe and Goto propose the Stacked Denoising Auto Encoder (SDAE) against WF attacks. Although it does not exceed the state-of-the-art in WF attack research at that time, it eliminates the need for manual feature selection and achieves 88% accuracy with only a small dataset. More importantly, they first introduce the use of +1 and -1 to denote outgoing and incoming packets, which has been broadly adopted in research on both WF attacks and defenses.

AWF [18]: Rimmer et al. implement the AWF (Adaptive Website Fingerprinting) attack using deep neural networks. The authors find that among three typical deep learning models, namely SDAE, CNN and LSTM, CNN outperforms others for WF attacks on Tor. In addition, they observe that the accuracy of WF attacks based on deep learning models is positively correlated with the amount of training data. After training on 2,500 traffic sequences for each website, AWF achieves an accuracy of over 96% in a closed-world scenario.

DF [20]: Inspired by the identification of streaming media encryption techniques, Sirinam et al. propose the Deep Fingerprinting (DF) attack. They use a more complex variant of CNN than AWF, which has more convolutional layers for feature extraction and fully connected layers for classification, achieving over 98% accuracy in a closed-world scenario. In addition, Sirinam et al. test the effectiveness of attacks against WTF-PAD [10] and Walkie Talkie [25], the two optimal WF defense models at that time. In closed world, DF has an accuracy rate of over 90% against WTF-PAD and over 49% against Walkie Talkie, effectively undermining traditional defense models.

2.2 WF Defenses

In order to counter WF attacks, researchers have proposed a number of WF defense models. These models employ techniques such as injecting virtual packets or delaying the transmission time of packets to obfuscate the data transmission patterns of websites, thereby reducing the identification accuracy of attack models [11,16]. For example, WTF-PAD uses interval sampling techniques to extract time information from the collected dataset. When no real packets are sent within a specified time interval, WTF-PAD sends virtual packets to hide the communication timing and defend against WF attacks. And the Walkie Talkie is a lightweight WF defense scheme. It is based on half-duplex communication and obscures the temporal characteristics by sending packets at constant time intervals. Meanwhile, in order to conceal the traffic sequence information of the real page, it simulates the connection of dummy pages and compares the burst sizes of the two traffic sequences. It sends the larger bursts each time, blending the two burst patterns together to accomplish traffic shaping. Although WTF-PAD and Walkie Talkie demonstrate robustness against WF attacks based on traditional machine learning, such as Pa-SVM [13], DL-SVM [23] and VNG++ [5], their performance is poor against WF attacks based on deep learning. DF [20] attacks have 91% and 49% accuracy against WTF-PAD and Walkie Talkie, respectively [2]. To address the issue of inadequate performance of traditional WF defense models, Tao Wang et al. propose a new defense Surakav [7], which uses WGAN to generate fake traffic sequence by buffering real packets and padding virtual packets, thereby transforming the real traffic sequence into a fake one to mask the characteristics of the real traffic. Despite the overall effectiveness of Surakav, it introduces latency overhead that can negatively impact the user experience of Tor. FRONT [6] is a no-latency, low-bandwidth overhead defense achieving its efficiency by targeting the early part of a website trace. Prior ML-based attacks showed that features produced from the beginning of the trace were highly weighted by the classifiers, and this motivates FRONT's design. FRONT works by inserting fake packets with timestamps drawn from two Rayleigh probability distributions dynamically generated for each trace.

3 Threat Model

As an anonymous communication system, the goal of Tor is to protect users' privacy by concealing their identities and browsing history. However, an attacker can analyze the user's traffic sequences through WF attacks to undermine the anonymity of Tor. Previous studies have shown that in some cases, attackers can identify the websites accessed by Tor users through WF attacks.

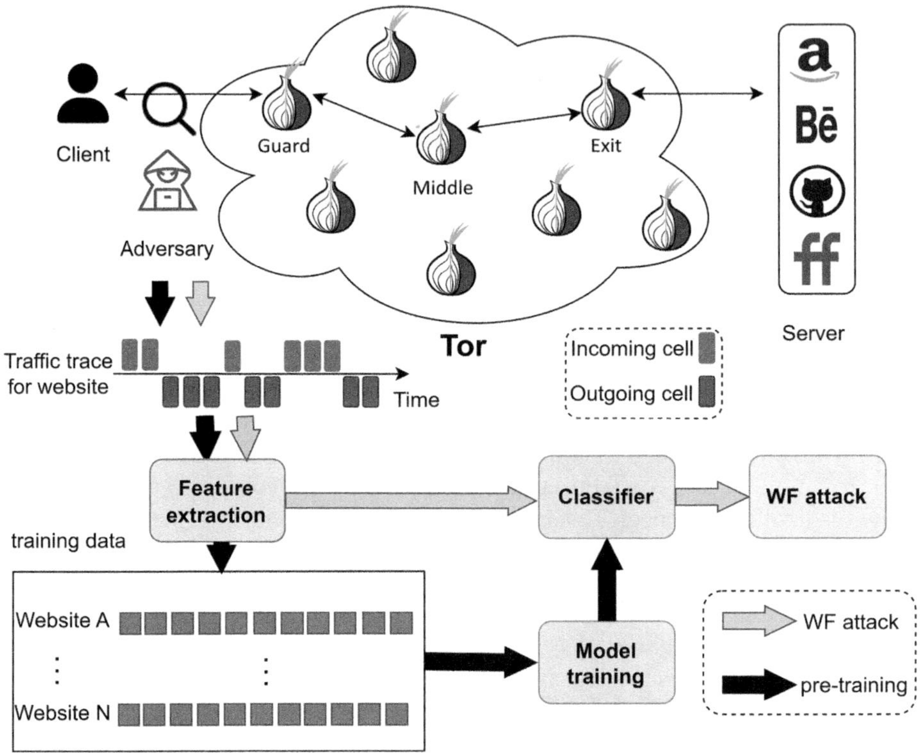

Fig. 1. WF attack process

Figure 1 illustrates the entire process of a WF attack. The attacker captures packet information from Tor, including the direction sequence, timestamps and other details. From these traffic sequences, the attacker extracts unique features for each website, such as packet size, edit distance, total transmission time, and burst counts of incoming and outgoing traffic. Subsequently, the attacker pre-trains the classifier with these features to enable the classifier to recognize the corresponding website based on the extracted features. During the actual attack, the attacker collects data information from Tor users and extracts user features, and then utilizes the trained classifier to identify the websites that the users might be visiting. The WF attack conducted by the attacker in this paper is a local passive attack. This means that the attacker can only access the data between Tor users and the entry nodes which is also called as the Guard node. The attackers cannot modify, delay, discard or decrypt the packets, they can only record the packets. It is important to note that as long as the attacker has access to the TLS connection between the user and the entry node, he can easily obtain the IP address of the user. Therefore, our defense is deployed between the client and the Guard node.

In previous study, Juarez et al. [9] assumed that the attacker could parse all the traffic generated by users accessing the Internet and could isolate it from other traffic. This includes traffic generated by browsers accessing websites other than Tor, as well as non-HTTP traffic on the Tor browser. However, this assumption only holds when the user accesses the website through the entry node controlled by the attacker. Due to the design for TLS connection multiplexing in Tor, it becomes challenging for the attacker to decipher the data obtained by eavesdropping on the connection between the client and the entry node. Tao Wang et al. developed techniques to parse multiplexed TLS traffic [24], enabling researchers to extract all the traffic generated by monitored users visiting websites from complex data streams. This provides technical support for the assumption made by Juarez et al.

Therefore, the threat assumptions in this paper are as follows:

- The attacker knows the identity of the user and only launches WF attacks.
- The attacker has already completed traffic resolution or does not require that.
- The attacker has a sufficient number of samples to pre-train the websites visited by users.

4 Design of Zero-Latency WF Defense

Since packets are the fundamental unit of network communication, delaying the original packets or adding virtual packets in the communication traffic can alter the traffic pattern of the website. At present, various WF defense schemes proposed by researchers can be simply summarized as delaying real packets or adding virtual packets. However, this is not an optimal choice because the delay of real packets will increase the loading time of webpages which negatively impacts the user experience of browsing websites. In this case, selecting a suitable traffic padding algorithm is crucial for WF defense. Currently existing traffic padding strategies are either based on unreasonable assumptions mentioned in Sect. 1 or fail to balance defense effectiveness and overhead while potentially introducing latency overhead.

4.1 Multiple Sample Padding

To address this situation, this paper proposes a novel traffic padding algorithm called MSP (Multiple Sample Padding), which compares multiple traffic sequences with real traffic and collectively determines the number of packets to

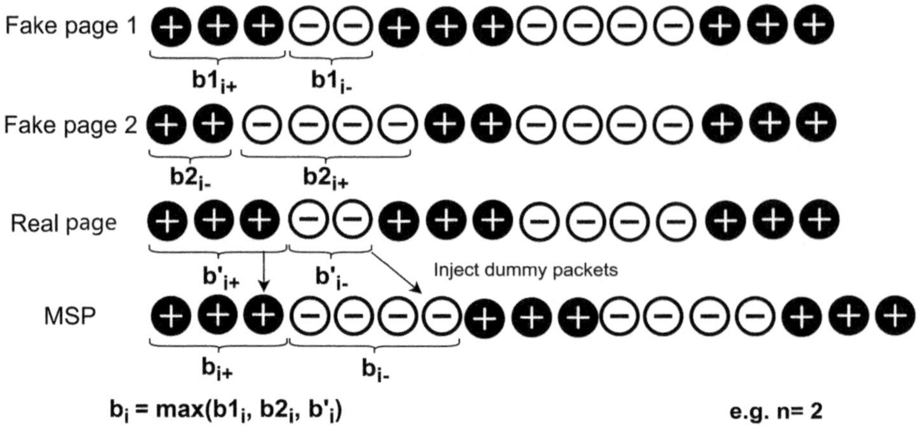

Fig. 2. Example of MSP process

be sent each time. It operates on bursts, comparing the burst sizes of multiple traffic sequences with that of real traffic, and selects the largest burst as the number of packets to be sent in the current transmission. If the final size exceeds the burst size of the real traffic, virtual packets are added after real packets until all real traffic is sent. It should be noted that in order to reduce bandwidth overhead, if the length of all reference samples is shorter than the actual traffic, MSP will not re-select traffic sequences for padding. When the length of the real sequence is shorter than some of the traffic sequences, padding will only continue until the real sequence is fully sent, and no further padding will be applied.

Since MSP simply adds padding packets to the end of real traffic, it does not introduce any latency overhead. Furthermore, MSP adjusts the burst size of the real traffic using multiple traffic sequences, which allows it to conceal the characteristics of the real traffic within the features of other traffic, preventing recognition by WF attack models. By employing a burst-based padding strategy and maintaining the flexibility to avoid standardizing the traffic patterns of all websites, it is possible to reduce defense overhead without requiring prior knowledge of the websites' traffic sequences. Algorithm 1 demonstrates the pseudocode for the MSP process.

Figure 2 shows a padding example of MSP. In the figure, n denotes the number of samples, which corresponds to the number of burst sequences. Each small circle represents a data packet, with '+' and '−' indicating the direction of traffic flow: '+' signifies incoming traffic, while '−' represents outgoing traffic. It is an example that $n = 2$, and it is assumed that there is a real sequence trace and two burst sequences *trace*0 and *trace*1, as shown in Eq. 1, Eq. 2 and Eq. 3:

$$trace = (x_1, \cdots, x_n) = (+3, -2, +3, -4, +3) \tag{1}$$

$$trace0 = (x0_1, \cdots, x0_n) = (+3, -2, +3, -4, +3) \tag{2}$$

$$trace1 = (x1_1, \cdots, x1_n) = (+2, -4, +2, -4, +3) \tag{3}$$

Algorithm 1. Multi-sample padding algorithm MSP

Input: Sample number n, generator G, web burst sequence trace
Output: Padded traffic sequence trace_padding

for generating number i in n: **do**
  z = random (0, 1, latent_dim) ▷ Generate random noise vector z
  c = random (0, number of websites in data set - 1) ▷ Generate random labels
  trace_i = G (z |c) ▷ Generate traffic trace
end for
for i in range(len(trace)): **do**
  ▷ Fill until the actual traffic is sent
  ▷ Compare the burst of original traffic with the burst of multiple samples
  ▷ Determine the final number of shipments
  trace_padding[i]=max($|trace[i]|$, $|trace\_0[i]|$, $\cdots$, $|trace\_n-1[i]|$) * sign(trace[i])
end for
return trace_padding

The sequence trace_padding adjusted based on MSP is:

$$trace\_padding = (x_1^*, \cdots, x_n^*) = (+3, -4, +3, -4, +3) \tag{4}$$

4.2 Changing the Webpage Loading Status Based on MSP

Due to the uncertainty of the actual sequence length, the length of the generated traffic sequence may be longer than that of the actual sequence. In MSP, to reduce bandwidth consumption, the model stops padding virtual packets after the page is fully loaded. However, it is found in our experiment that after page loading is completed, sending virtual packets to simulate the communication between client and server can also achieve good defense effect. Therefore, changing the webpage loading status based on MSP, which is different from MSP in that after the end of the real traffic sequence transmission, it will still send the longest traffic sequence according to the comparison scheme of MSP until the end. Since the fact that the traffic sequence is composed of burst sequences, there is a lack of time information. In order to ensure that the padded virtual packets can be correctly sent, we use the time sampling method proposed by Jiajun Gong et al. [6] to determine the packet transmission time. The scheme first learns the time interval between two outgoing bursts, and then estimates the time distribution through Kernel Density Estimation (KDE). When the page is fully loaded, changing the webpage loading status based on MSP samples the time interval from it and continues to send virtual packets.

Figure 3 illustrates an example of changing the webpage loading status based on MSP. In the figure, $n = 2$ is taken as an example, it assumes a real sequence *trace* and two burst sequences *trace*0 and *trace*1, as shown in Eq. 5, Eq. 6, Eq. 7 and Eq. 8:

$$trace = (x_1, \cdots, x_n) = (+3, -2, +3) \tag{5}$$

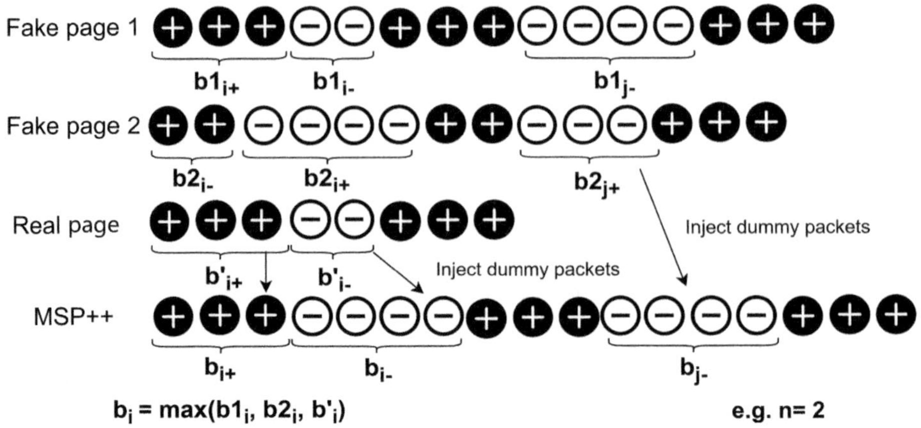

Fig. 3. Example of changing the webpage loading status based on MSP

$$trace0 = (x0_1, \cdots, x0_n) = (+3, -2, +3, -4, +3) \tag{6}$$

$$trace1 = (x1_1, \cdots, x1_n) = (+2, -4, +2, -3, +3) \tag{7}$$

It can be seen that the maximum length of *trace*, *trace*0, and *trace*1 is 5, so even if the length of trace is 3, padding will continue in MSP until the burst of the longest traffic sequence is used up. The adjusted sequence *trace_padding* based on MSP is:

$$trace\_padding = (x_1^*, \cdots, x_n^*) = (+3, -4, +3, -4, +3) \tag{8}$$

Algorithm 2 presents the pseudocode for the padding process of changing the webpage loading status based on MSP.

5 Defense Evaluation

5.1 Defense Performance

This section evaluates the performance of MSP on a dataset collected by Sirinam et al. [20] in 2018 referred to as Dataset1 in the subsequent sections of the paper, which contains 95 websites with 800 sequences of traffic each. The original dataset is perturbed using MSP and the defense model is tested using DF, and we calculate bandwidth consumption. Figure 4 shows the trends of the defense effectiveness and bandwidth consumption of MSP with the number of traffic sequences n.

As the value of n increases, it means that the number of traffic sequences compared to MSP increases, and the modifications made to the burst sequences of original traffic increase. This ensures that the perturbed sequences are able to defend against the traffic analysis attacks of the attacker. It can be seen from Fig. 4 that with the gradual increase of n, the accuracy of DF against MSP

Algorithm 2. Changing the webpage loading status based on MSP

Input: Sample number n, generator G, web burst sequence trace
Output: Padded traffic sequence trace_padding

```
for generating number i in n do
    z = random (0, 1, latent_dim)                    ▷ Generate random noise vector z
    c = random (0, number of websites in data set - 1)  ▷ Generate random labels
    trace_i = G (z | c)                              ▷ Generate traffic trace
end for
for i in range(len(trace)): do
    trace_padding[i] = max(|trace[i]|, |trace_0[i]|, ···,|trace_n − 1[i]|)*sign(trace[i])
end for
if len(trace) < len(trace_ i) then
    length = max(len(trace_i))
    for j in range(len(trace), length): do
        trace_padding [j] = max (|trace_0[i]| ,..., |trace_n − 1[i]| ) * sign(trace[i])
    end for
end if
return trace_padding
```

decreases and the defense effectiveness improves while the bandwidth consumption implemented by MSP increases. When n increases from 1 to 5, the accuracy of DF attack against MSP decreases from 53.47% to 19.64%. However, the bandwidth overhead is more sensitive to the change of n, gradually increasing from 28.76% to 97.06%. We can observe that when $n \geq 3$, MSP shows strong defense capabilities. Nevertheless, as n increases, the growth rate of MSP's defense effectiveness gradually decreases, whereas the growth rate of bandwidth overhead remains unchanged. Especially after n reaches 4, adding reference sequences cannot significantly enhance MSP's defensive capability anymore.

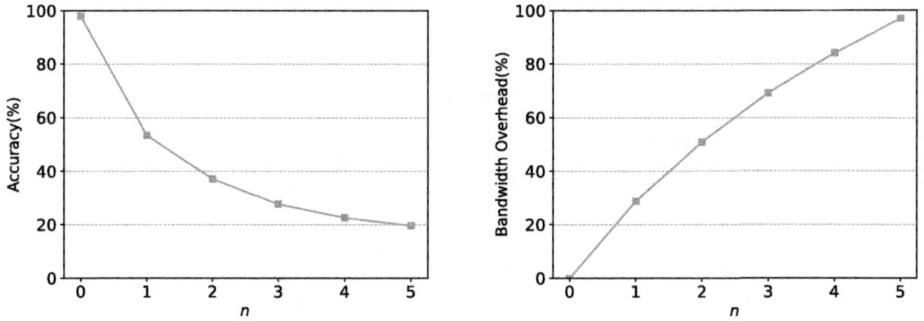

(a) Defense effectiveness (b) Bandwidth overhead

Fig. 4. Defense effectiveness and bandwidth overhead of MSP with different numbers of traffic sequences

As mentioned in Sect. 4, if the length of the selected traffic sequence is longer than the real traffic sequence, MSP will directly discard the reference sequence after the real traffic has been sent, and stop sending virtual packets. For the comparison of effects, changing the webpage loading status based on MSP is designed to send the reference sequence completely. Figure 5 demonstrates the comparison of defense effectiveness and bandwidth consumption of changing the webpage loading status based on MSP and MSP against DF attacks as the number of reference sequences n increases. It is obvious from Fig. 5 that the ability of changing the webpage loading status based on MSP to resist WF attacks is better than MSP regardless of n. When the number of fake samples is set to 2, the defense effectiveness of changing the webpage loading status based on MSP surpasses MSP with 5 fake sequences as reference. This proves that by sending false packets to simulate the communication between client and server after webpage loading is complete, Tor's ability to resist WF attacks can be effectively improved.

However, although changing the webpage loading status based on MSP has better performance, it also brings enormous bandwidth consumption. From the comparison of bandwidth consumption graph, we can observe that the bandwidth overhead caused by using one dummy sample for padding based on MSP is already similar to that of using three dummy samples for MSP. Moreover, when n is set to 2 in changing the webpage loading status based on MSP, the bandwidth consumption exceeds that of MSP with n set to 5. In addition, similar to MSP, as the number of reference false sequences required increases, the speed at which changing the webpage loading status based on MSP enhances its defensive effectiveness gradually slows down, and its defensive effectiveness will not increase infinitely with n. When $n \geq 4$, although the accuracy of DF recognition has dropped to below 6%, its bandwidth consumption has exceeded 200%. Therefore, for users who use padding based on MSP, it is not recommended that they adjust n to 3 or above.

Table 1. Comparison results of different defense models

Defense	Consumption(%)		Accuracy(%)
	Bandwidth	Delay	DF
Defenceless	-	-	98
WTF-PAD	64	0	91
W-T	31	34	49
Tamaraw	163	78	6
FRONT	48	0	81.8
Surakav	67	27	29
MSP	69	0	27
Changing the webpage loading status based on MSP	164	0	8

Based on the experimental results described above, the number of MSP and padding based on MSP reference websites are set to 3 in this paper. Table 1 illustrates the comparison results between the defense scheme proposed in this paper and the other four classical WF defense schemes. It can be seen from the table that DF [9] has an identification accuracy of up to 98% for the undefended original traffic. Therefore, when Tor is not deployed with any defense, WF attacks can pose a threat to user's anonymity. However, although the overall latency of WTF-PAD and W-T is not high, DF attacks reach a recognition accuracy of 91% and 49%, respectively, which is not good for their defensive effectiveness. The effects of MSP and Surakav are similar, both reducing DF accuracy from 98% on the original traffic to around 27%, but while the bandwidth consumption is similar, Surakav still has a delay consumption of 27%, while MSP has no delay consumption. As a result, MSP has a better effect than Surakav. The Tamaraw's situation is similar to Surakav's. Although FRONT is also a zero-delay WF defense model and the bandwidth is only 48%, DF accuracy can achieve 81.8%. Compared with changing the webpage loading status based on MSP, Tamaraw still has an additional delay consumption of 78% under similar bandwidth consumption and defense effects.

According to the analysis of the experiments described above, the defense scheme proposed in this paper, MSP, has similar performance and bandwidth consumption in resisting DF attacks as Surakav, but reduces the delay consumption by 27% of the bandwidth consumption and achieves zero latency. Both MSP and FRONT are zero-latency, while MSP has a higher bandwidth than FRONT, DF accuracy drops from 81.8% to 27%. Although the defensive effect of MSP is slightly inferior to that of Tamaraw, it reduces the bandwidth consumption by 94% and 78% of the latency consumption, while the defensive effect of padding based on MSP is similar to that of Tamaraw and reduces the bandwidth consumption by 78%. Therefore, MSP and changing the webpage loading status based on MSP perform best among many defense models.

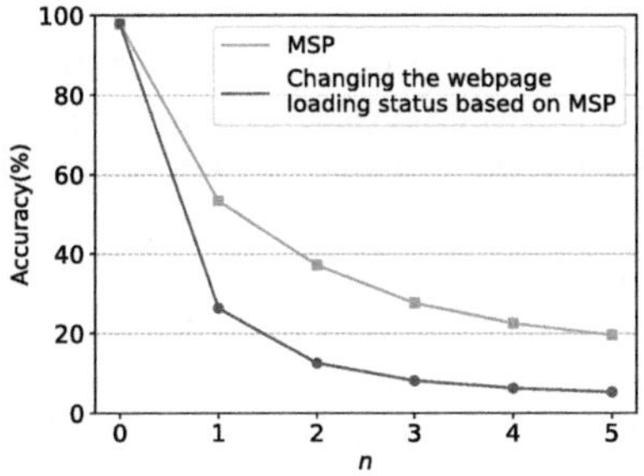

(a) Defense effectiveness

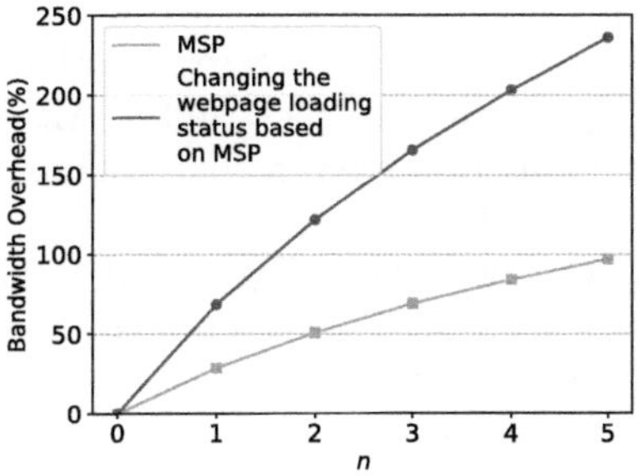

(b) Bandwidth overhead

Fig. 5. Comparison for defense effectiveness and bandwidth overhead of changing the webpage loading status based on MSP and MSP models under different parameters

Table 2. Defense performance and bandwidth consumption of MSP and changing the webpage loading status based on MSP with different parameters

Defense		Accuracy(%)		Bandwidth Assumption(%)	
		MSP	Changing the webpage loading status based on MSP	MSP	Changing the webpage loading status based on MSP
n	0	93.56	96.82	0	0
	1	44.67	26.56	27.33	73.73
	2	34.11	12.78	48.47	132.68
	3	27.33	9.11	63.53	181.92
	4	23	5.44	77.69	224.19
	5	20.22	4.56	91.45	262.07

5.2 Practicality Analysis

In order to verify the generalizability of MSP and padding based on MSP and the stability of experimental results, in addition to the dataset of Sirinam et al. [20] referred to as Dataset1 in the subsequent sections of the paper, which is the largest dataset about website fingerprint to date and has been widely adopted by many papers, including [7]. The dataset collected by Tao Wang et al. [22] referred to as Dataset2 in the subsequent sections of the paperwas also used in this paper. It includes 100 websites, each of which collected 90 traffic sequences. Table 2 shows the comparison between the accuracy of DF attacking MSP and padding based on MSP, and the bandwidth consumption with the number of selected traffic sequences under Dataset2. As can be seen from the table, MSP and changing the webpage loading status based on MSP still exhibit good defensive performance under the new dataset. When $n = 3$, the bandwidth consumption of changing the webpage loading status based on MSP is increases slightly, but the overall effect is still better than Tamaraw [4]. In order to better demonstrate the different performances of MSP and changing the webpage loading status based on MSP in the two datasets, Fig. 6 and Fig. 7 show the comparison between their defense performance and bandwidth consumption in different datasets.

As can be seen in Fig. 6 and 7, MSP and altering the webpage loading status based on MSP also perform well on the new data set. In terms of accuracy, the overall accuracy of the two datasets is similar, indicating that their defensive effects are very stable. The difference in the datasets has little influence on the performance of the two models. However, there are some differences in bandwidth consumption between the two models under different datasets. Although the increase in bandwidth consumption with n is consistent across all datasets, MSP performs better on Dataset2 than on Dataset1, regardless of n. On the other hand, altering the webpage loading status based on MSP has lower bandwidth consumption on Dataset1 than on Dataset2. By analyzing the dif-

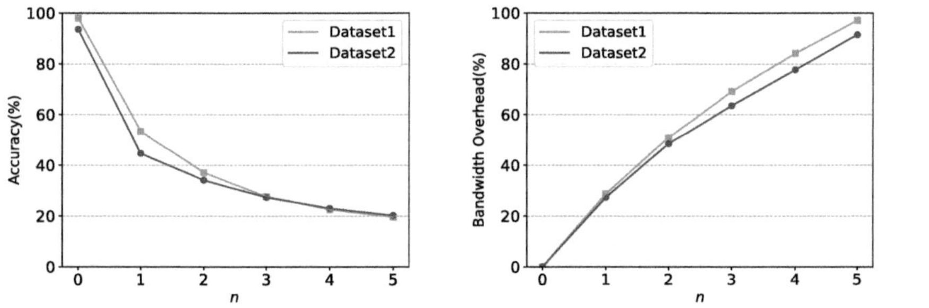

(a) Defense performance on different datasets (b) Bandwidth overhead on different datasets

Fig. 6. Defense performance and bandwidth overhead of MSP on different datasets

ferences between the two datasets, this paper speculates that it is the length difference of traffic sequences that leads to this phenomenon. The length of traffic sequences in Dataset2 is shorter than that in Dataset1, so there are relatively fewer comparisons between real traffic and reference traffic in MSP, resulting in less padding. In altering the webpage loading status based on MSP, the stopping condition for padding no longer depends solely on real traffic. When short traffic sequences are assigned long reference sequences, it will cause large bandwidth consumption, and as n increases, this situation will become more likely.

As shown in the Fig. 5b, compared with MSP, bandwidth consumption of altering the webpage loading status based on MSP is more sensitive to changes in datasets and n. In real environments, it is difficult to determine the length of traffic sequences, so an overall more stable MSP model would be more suitable for actual use. Because of the limitations of the padding pattern, altering the webpage loading status based on MSP may produce larger bandwidth consumption in actual environments. Therefore, although altering the webpage loading status based on MSP shows better defensive performance, it is not recommended to deploy it in actual environments for Tor users' experience. Nevertheless, it provides a new defensive approach against WF attacks.

5.3 Information Leakage Analysis

In this paper, WeFDE [12] is used to extract 3039 features from the original dataset without defense and the dataset with MSP defense. The information leakage of corresponding features is analyzed, as shown in Fig. 8. It can be seen that the data without defense leaks more information, especially in the six features with the highest information leakage, which are packet count, Ngram [12], Interval-II [19], Interval-III [15], packet per second, and CUMUL [14], where the maximum information leakage is close to 4 bits. The defused data set showed lower information leakage across all 3,039 features, especially in packet counting and CUMUL features, with an average decrease of 1.62 bits. In addition, the burst feature of the defended dataset has almost zero information leakage. Since

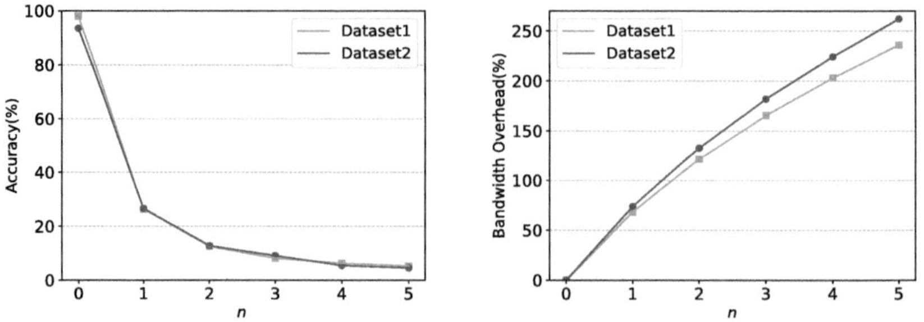

(a) Defense performance on different datasets (b) Bandwidth overhead on different datasets

Fig. 7. Defense performance and bandwidth overhead of padding based on MSP on different datasets

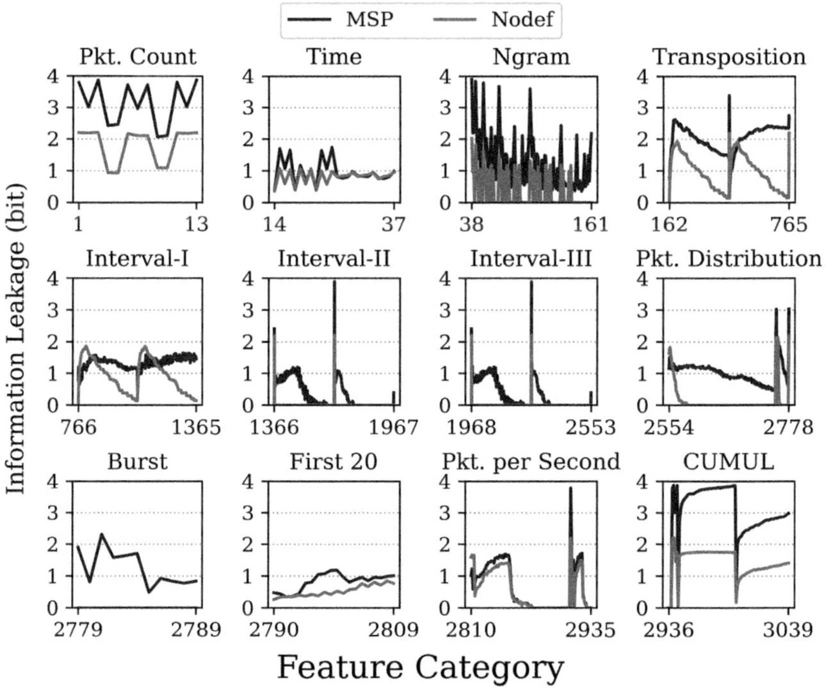

Fig. 8. Information leakage of the original dataset and the dataset defended by MSP

MSP does not delay packets, the characteristics of time and packets per second information leakage remain relatively consistent, yet the maximum extent of such leakage has been significantly diminished.

This paper plots the empirical cumulative distribution function (ECDF) diagrams of information leakage for 3039 features of the original dataset and the defended dataset, as shown in Fig. 9. It can be seen that the maximum infor-

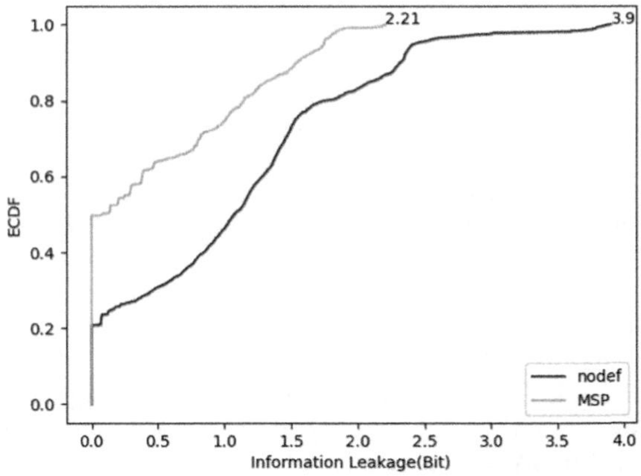

Fig. 9. ECDF diagram of information leakage of the original dataset and the dataset defended by MSP

mation leakage of the undefended dataset is as high as 3.9 bits. However, after implementing defense, the maximum information leakage decreases to 2.21 bits, which is about 76% less than that of the undefended dataset. On the other hand, the curve of MSP rises faster than that of the undefended dataset, indicating that MSP can reduce information leakage in raw traffic. In conclusion, MSP is effective in defending against deep learning-based WF attack models and protecting the privacy and security of Tor users.

6 Conclusion

In this paper, we introduce a novel Website Fingerprinting (WF) defense scheme called MSP to defend against deep learning-based attacks. The MSP fills the real traffic with the features from multiple traffic sequences to hide its features and implement WF defense. In addition, we design changing the webpage loading status based on MSP and explore the impact of adding virtual packets after webpage loading on defense performance. Experimental results show that compared with Surakav, MSP reduces 27% latency overhead. Compared to Tamaraw, changing the webpage loading status based on MSP reduces the 78% latency overhead with a bandwidth overhead of 164%, which indicates that the defense model proposed in this paper can reduce a large amount of defense overhead. Finally, we evaluate and analyze MSP and changing the webpage loading status based on MSP using two publicly available datasets. The results show that both schemes perform stably under different datasets and have strong practicability.

Acknowledgment. This work is supported by the National Natural Science Foundation of China (No. 62162060) and the National Key Research and Development Program of China (No. 2023YFB3105902). We thank the anonymous reviewers for their constructive feedback.

References

1. Abe, K., Goto, S.: Fingerprinting attack on tor anonymity using deep learning. In: Proceedings of the 2016 Asia-Pacific Advanced Network, pp. 15–20 (2016)
2. Abusnaina, A., Jang, R., Khormali, A., Nyang, D., Mohaisen, D.: DFD: adversarial learning-based approach to defend against website fingerprinting. In: Proceedings of the IEEE International Conference on Computer Communications (CCS), pp. 2459–2468. IEEE (2020)
3. Bhat, S., Lu, D., Kwon, A., Devadas, S.: Var-CNN: a data-efficient website fingerprinting attack based on deep learning. Priv. Enhancing Technol. **2019**(4), 292–310 (2019)
4. Cai, X., Nithyanand, R., Wang, T., Johnson, R., Goldberg, I.: A systematic approach to developing and evaluating website fingerprinting defenses. In: Proceedings of the ACM SIGSAC Conference on Computer and Communications Security (CCS), pp. 227–238 (2014)
5. Dyer, K.P., Coull, S.E., Ristenpart, T., Shrimpton, T.: Peek-a-boo, i still see you: why efficient traffic analysis countermeasures fail. In: Proceedings of the IEEE Symposium on Security and Privacy (S&P), pp. 332–346. IEEE (2012)
6. Gong, J., Wang, T.: Zero-delay lightweight defenses against website fingerprinting. In: Proceedings of the 2020 USENIX Conference on Security Symposium (USENIX Security), pp. 717–734 (2020)
7. Gong, J., Zhang, W., Zhang, C., Wang, T.: Surakav: generating realistic traces for a strong website fingerprinting defense. In: Proceedings of the 2022 IEEE Symposium on Security and Privacy (S&P), pp. 1558–1573. IEEE (2022)
8. Henri, S., Garcia-Aviles, G., Serrano, P., Banchs, A., Thiran, P.: Protecting against website fingerprinting with multihoming. Priv. Enhancing Technol. **2020**(2), 89–110 (2020)
9. Juarez, M., Afroz, S., Acar, G., Diaz, C., Greenstadt, R.: A critical evaluation of website fingerprinting attacks. In: Proceedings of the ACM SIGSAC Conference on Computer and Communications Security (CCS), pp. 263–274 (2014)
10. Juarez, M., Imani, M., Perry, M., Diaz, C., Wright, M.: Toward an efficient website fingerprinting defense. In: Askoxylakis, I., Ioannidis, S., Katsikas, S., Meadows, C. (eds.) ESORICS 2016. LNCS, vol. 9878, pp. 27–46. Springer, Cham (2016). https://doi.org/10.1007/978-3-319-45744-4_2
11. Karunanayake, I., Ahmed, N., Malaney, R., Islam, R., Jha, S.K.: De-anonymisation attacks on tor: a survey. IEEE Commun. Surv. Tutor. **2023**(4), 2324–2350 (2021)
12. Li, S., Guo, H., Hopper, N.: Measuring information leakage in website fingerprinting attacks and defenses. In: Proceedings of the ACM SIGSAC Conference on Computer and Communications Security (CCS), pp. 1977–1992 (2018)
13. Nasr, M., Bahramali, A., Houmansadr, A.: Defeating DNN-based traffic analysis systems in real-time with blind adversarial perturbations. In: Proceedings of the USENIX Security Symposium (USENIX Security), pp. 2705–2722 (2021)
14. Panchenko, A., et al.: Website fingerprinting at internet scale. In: Proceedings of the Network and Distributed System Security Symposium (2016)
15. Panchenko, A., Niessen, L., Zinnen, A., Engel, T.: Website fingerprinting in onion routing based anonymization networks. In: Proceedings of the Annual ACM Workshop on Privacy in the Electronic Society, pp. 103–114 (2011)
16. Papadogiannaki, E., Ioannidis, S.: A survey on encrypted network traffic analysis applications, techniques, and countermeasures. ACM Comput. Surv. (CSUR) **54**(6), 1–35 (2021)

17. Rimmer, V., Preuveneers, D., Juarez, M., Van Goethem, T., Joosen, W.: Automated feature extraction for website fingerprinting through deep learning (2017)
18. Rimmer, V., Preuveneers, D., Juarez, M., Van Goethem, T., Joosen, W.: Automated website fingerprinting through deep learning. arXiv preprint arXiv:1708.06376 (2017)
19. Shi, Y., Matsuura, K.: Fingerprinting attack on the tor anonymity system. In: Qing, S., Mitchell, C.J., Wang, G. (eds.) ICICS 2009. LNCS, vol. 5927, pp. 425–438. Springer, Heidelberg (2009). https://doi.org/10.1007/978-3-642-11145-7_33
20. Sirinam, P., Imani, M., Juarez, M., Wright, M.: Deep fingerprinting: undermining website fingerprinting defenses with deep learning. In: Proceedings of the 2018 ACM SIGSAC Conference on Computer and Communications Security (CCS), pp. 1928–1943 (2018)
21. Sirinam, P., Mathews, N., Rahman, M.S., Wright, M.: Triplet fingerprinting: more practical and portable website fingerprinting with n-shot learning. In: Proceedings of the 2019 ACM SIGSAC Conference on Computer and Communications Security (CCS), pp. 1131–1148 (2019)
22. Wang, T., Cai, X., Nithyanand, R., Johnson, R., Goldberg, I.: Effective attacks and provable defenses for website fingerprinting. In: Proceedings of the 2014 USENIX Security Symposium (USENIX Security), pp. 143–157 (2014)
23. Wang, T., Goldberg, I.: Improved website fingerprinting on tor. In: Proceedings of the ACM Workshop on Workshop on Privacy in the Electronic Society, pp. 201–212 (2013)
24. Wang, T., Goldberg, I.: On realistically attacking tor with website fingerprinting. Priv. Enhancing Technol. **2016**(4), 21–36 (2016)
25. Wang, T., Goldberg, I., et al.: Walkie-talkie: an efficient defense against passive website fingerprinting attacks. In: Proceedings of the USENIX Security Symposium (USENIX Security), pp. 1375–1390 (2017)

An IP Anti-geolocation Method Based on Constructed Landmarks

Enshang Lu[1], Shichang Ding[2(✉)], Chunfang Yang[1], Daofu Gong[1], Ruixiang Li[2], Kaijie Zhu[2,3], and Xiangyang Luo[1]

[1] Information Engineering University, Henan 450000, China
[2] Henan Key Laboratory of Cyberspace Situation Awareness, Henan 450000, China
scdingwork@outlook.com
[3] Zhongguancun Laboratory, Beijing 100194, China

Abstract. The IP geolocation based on network measurement can obtain the geographical location of target IP devices in a user independent manner, bringing significant convenience to location-based network services (LBS). However, illegal locators may also utilize this technology to steal the precise geographical location of target network devices, posing a significant security risk to the target devices. To prevent the disclosure of the geographical location information of target network devices and protect their privacy, this paper proposes an IP anti-geolocation method based on the deployment of constructed web landmarks. By arranging constructed web landmarks, this method can induce errors in the key localization data of illegal locators, achieving the effect of anti-geolocation. In an experiment targeting 156 landmarks in Shanghai, China, with a positional deviation of 20 km for the constructed web landmarks, this method can increase the mean value of the target localization error by a maximum to 31.4 km and increase the median error by 31.8 km.

Keywords: IP Anti-Geolocation · IP Geolocation · Landmark

1 Introduction

IP geolocation is a technique that determines the precise geographical location of an internet device through its IP address [1, 2]. IP geolocation technology holds significant value for numerous LBS (Location-Based Services) businesses, such as personalized advertising services, local news push notifications, network performance optimization, and network crime tracing [1–6]. Depending on the geolocation methods, IP geolocation technology can be broadly classified into three categories: IP geolocation based on databases, IP geolocation based on data mining, and IP geolocation based on network measurements [7]. Among these, IP geolocation based on network measurements, which can provide street-level geographical locations of network devices independently of users, has received considerable attention in recent years [1–3]. Measurement-based IP geolocation can geolocate a target IP after the probing host obtains the measurement data (e.g., delay) to the target IP and landmarks. Landmarks are IP addresses with known locations [4, 5].

S. Goel et al. (Eds.): ICDF2C 2024, LNICST 614, pp. 192–206, 2025.
https://doi.org/10.1007/978-3-031-89360-5_12

Currently, the academic community is primarily concerned with enhancing the accuracy of measurement-based IP geolocation techniques [1–10]. However, an important issue that has been overlooked is the potential misuse of fine-grained, user-independent IP geolocation technologies by cyber attackers. With the increasing accuracy of measurement-based IP geolocation techniques, especially those based on network measurements, these techniques have the possibility to be abused by cyber attackers and cause the leakage of the precise geographical locations of network devices and users. Moreover, it may cause the phishing behavior and spread of network viruses, posing significant threats to network security and user privacy [11]. This paper will discuss how to resist high-precision IP geolocation techniques based on network measurements, referred to herein as IP anti-geolocation. IP anti-geolocation techniques are methods that counter measurement-based IP geolocation techniques, which can increase the geolocation error based on network measurements or even cause them to fail.

Existing IP anti-geolocation methods can be broadly classified into two categories: one is hiding the true IP address, such as through the use of VPNs; the other is misleading localization techniques by modifying the response delay of the target IP. For example, as mentioned in the work of Abdou A. R. et al. in [11], uses VPNs to hide IP addresses, causing significant interference to IP geolocation; as pointed out by Abdou A. R. et al. in [12], involves increasing or decreasing the packet response delay of the protected IP, which can maximally increase the target localization error from hundreds of kilometers to 15,000 km. These methods can effectively counter city-level or country-level IP geolocation based on network measurements, causing significant deviations in the country, province, or city-level locations obtained by cyber attackers.

However, the aforementioned methods are difficult to apply in some other scenarios. Firstly, many enterprises, even individuals, need to use their real IP addresses for external communication and service provision, and the use of VPNs can significantly affect normal work efficiency, such as in large industrial enterprises. Secondly, regarding the second method mentioned above, due to the advancement of IP geolocation databases, for some critical network devices (such as government official website servers, large enterprise network servers, etc.), users can often directly query their coarse-grained geographical location information (such as national-level and provincial-level geographical location information) through the database, with an accuracy rate of over 90% [13]. Therefore, attackers can have a high degree of certainty in determining the approximate national and provincial geographical location of the target IP. If the delay is modified to cause a significant deviation, it is likely to be detected by attackers and even attract greater attention.

In fact, with the improvement of database accuracy, many enterprises are more concerned about not only concealing their national or even city-level locations, but more importantly, preventing the disclosure of the precise geographical locations of their critical network devices. In this context, our primary objective is to prevent network attackers from obtaining fine-grained locations through IP geolocation based on network measurements, and to expand the error of street-level IP geolocation techniques from the hundred-meter or kilometer level to city-level range of tens of kilometers. However, existing techniques based on delay modification are primarily targeted at national-level and provincial-level IP geolocation techniques, and due to differences in geolocation principles, they cannot be used to counter street-level IP geolocation techniques. This is the main focus of this paper.

To address this issue, this paper proposes an IP anti-geolocation method based on constructed landmarks to counter street-level IP geolocation based on network measurements. Firstly, this method introduces a constructed landmark generation strategy to make the constructed landmarks highly credible and participate in the attacker's geolocation process. Then, the deployment locations of the constructed landmarks are determined to successfully interfere with the attacker's geolocation accuracy. Finally, through actual deployment and simulation experiments, the anti-geolocation effect of this method is verified, which can increase the mean error of mainstream IP geolocation algorithms based on network measurements to 31.4 km and the median error to 31.8 km.

2 Related Work

2.1 IP Geolocation

IP geolocation technology refers to the technique of determining the geographical location of network entity devices corresponding to specific IP addresses [1]. Since the introduction of this concept, various IP geolocation methods have emerged in the academic community, differing in geolocating techniques and precision. Categorized by geolocating methods, IP geolocation technology can be primarily divided into three categories: database query-based IP geolocation, data mining-based IP geolocation, and network measurement-based IP geolocation.

Database query-based geolocation methods have gained widespread application due to their lack of extensive measurements, rapid geolocating speed, and low computational overhead. Currently, various IP geolocation databases are available on the internet for public queries, such as QQWry [29], skyhook [40], Geobytes [41], DB-IP [42], Whois [45], IPcn [46], IP138 [47], Maxmind [48], Quova [49], and IP2location [50]. However, most of these databases do not publicly disclose their construction processes. After conducting in-depth research on publicly available IP geolocation databases, studies [13–15] found that the query results at the national-level granularity are generally reliable, but the reliability of city-level geolocating accuracy is difficult to guarantee, and it is even more challenging to provide higher precision geolocating results. Moreover, the coverage of these databases is mostly concentrated in a few countries.

Data mining-based geolocation methods aim to extract and analyze the relationship between geographical locations and IP addresses from data sources such as websites, mobile applications, host domain names, and login logs that contain IP addresses and geographical location information. Typical geolocation methods include Structon [16], Checkin-Geo [17], GQL (Geolocation using Query Logs) [18], DRoP (DNS-based Router Positioning) [19], R-DNS [20], and HLOC [21]. The Structon algorithm initially utilizes web crawlers to capture homepage information from institutions on the internet, extracting information such as telephone area codes and contact addresses that can express geographical locations. Then, it converts URLs into IP addresses through domain name queries, thereby associating IP addresses with geographical locations. Finally, it iteratively derives IP addresses based on address blocks to expand the range of IP addresses that can be geolocated. The accuracy of this method depends on the accuracy of the mapping relationship between the extracted homepage location information and IP addresses, which is easily influenced by factors such as server hosting. Data mining-based geolocation methods generally do not require extensive path and delay measurements for a large number of IP addresses, resulting in lower measurement costs. However, these methods often rely on large amounts of data and often require collaboration with large internet companies for implementation.

Network measurement-based geolocating methods primarily rely on probing the target host and landmark hosts using detection hosts, acquiring and analyzing detection data, and deriving location inferences. These methods can be further categorized into fine-grained-landmark based IP geolocating and network-topology based IP geolocating.

Fine-grained-landmark based IP geolocating involves analyzing delay data between the target hosts, landmark hosts, and detection hosts. By determining the relationship model between delay and distance, the location of the target is predicted. Typical fine-grained-landmark based IP geolocating algorithms include IPvSeeYou [5], RIPGeo [10], LBG [22], CBG [23], Posit [24], GeoWeight [25], Spotter [26], Octant [27], and SLG [28]. Taking the SLG algorithm as an example, it has reduced the geolocating error of traditional methods by tens of times, making it one of the most remarkable algorithms in recent years. Researchers Wang et al. proposed a three-tier system to gradually improve positioning accuracy. The article posits that entities typically host their websites locally and provide geographical location information of the entity in the form of a postal address on the website. This allows for the acquisition of a large number of fine-grained landmarks, which in turn yield equally precise positioning results. With the aid of the three-tier system, SLG conducts thorough and meticulous landmark mining near the target IP, obtaining a plethora of web landmarks. Subsequently, it measures the relative delay between the target and the landmarks. The landmark with the lowest relative delay to the target is identified, and its geographical location is used as the geolocating result for the target IP.

Network-topology based IP geolocating algorithm enhance IP geolocating accuracy by analyzing network topology information based on acquired network measurement data. These algorithms suggest that in modern network environments, the information contained in network measurement data is insufficient, and relying solely on delay information for target IP geolocation estimation can lead to significant errors. Based on this idea, researchers consider introducing topological information among the target IP, landmarks, and detection sources. By analyzing network topology information such as the node connection relationships of the network where the target IP resides, they aim to aid in improving locating accuracy or direct locating. Typical algorithms include GNN-Geo [1], TrustGeo [2], IP2vec [7], GeoPing [30], TBG [31], and Router-Geo [32]. Taking the GeoPing algorithm as an example, it first performs network measurements on landmark IPs to obtain network measurement data and then constructs a delay matrix. The vectors that constitute the matrix describe the connection and delay relationships between landmarks, detection sources, and intermediate routers. Based on this, multiple detection sources are used to perform network measurements on the target IP, and a similar delay matrix is obtained using the aforementioned method. The vectors that make up this matrix represent the connection and delay relationships between the target and different detection sources, intermediate routers. Finally, by calculating the similarity between the target vector and the landmark vectors, the algorithm strives to find the landmark that is "most similar" to the target and ultimately uses its location as the IP geolocating result.

2.2 IP Anti-geolocation

Due to the increasing awareness of users' self-privacy protection, the security issue of location privacy has attracted widespread attention. However, existing researchers typically focus only on client-based location privacy protection issues [33–37], with less mention of location security issues independent of the client [38]. Among the studies on location security issues independent of the client, there are techniques for protecting the geographical location privacy of mobile devices [33, 35, 36, 39], as well as IP anti-geolocation. Currently, there is limited research on IP anti-geolocation.

Phillipa Gill et al. from the University of Toronto, in their paper [43], developed and evaluated two anti-geolocation methods based on latency and topology awareness. The first method increases the geolocating error by altering the respective delays of each landmark. Experiments showed that over 50% of targets in North America had geolocating errors ranging from 1,379 to 4,000 km, while outside North America, the geolocating errors exceeded 5,000 km. The second method assumes that the anti-locator can detect probe traffic from geolocation systems and employs techniques such as creating nodes, links, and delays in the network to counter geolocation. Tests revealed that for 50% of North American targets, this method increased geolocating errors to over 680 km, and for 50% of European targets, errors increased by over 929 km.

Abdou A. R. et al. from Carleton University proposed five evasion strategies for geolocation, targeting techniques based on latency and topology awareness. The authors argue that these strategies can circumvent both latency-based and topology-aware techniques, not only hiding the target's actual location but also shifting the geolocation result to a specific fake location. In papers [11, 12], Abdou A. R. et al. introduced an anti-latency-based IP geolocation strategy that can introduce significant errors into geolocating results or even accurately control the fabricated location. Experiments showed that this strategy could increase geolocating errors to 15,000 km and, in some cases, control the fake location to within 100 km of the desired geographical location.

In [44], Abdou A. R. examined the validation of Internet client geolocation. Firstly, the paper demonstrates how latency-based geolocation techniques can easily evade IP geolocating by increasing or decreasing latency. Then, the authors discuss three strategies that enable the anti-locator to control the geolocating results of latency-based IP geolocation by manipulating delays. In [11], Abdou A. R. summarized common anti-geolocation methods for network devices, such as IP hiding techniques through VPNs and anonymizers, and provided a technical overview of client presence verification (CPV) and server location verification (SLV), discussing the reliability of both techniques in real-time validation of client and server geographical locations.

Based on the aforementioned research, we have found that current IP geolocation based on network measurement have achieved high localization accuracy and precision. To prevent network attackers from estimating the locations of high-value network devices through this method, researchers have conducted studies on IP anti-geolocation.

IP anti-geolocation are methods that counter measurement-based IP geolocation techniques, which can increase the IP geolocation error based on network measurement or even cause localization failure. Existing anti-geolocation techniques primarily focus on confusing the national-level geographical locations of network devices, thus causing illegal network locators to misjudge the national-level locations of protected devices. However, for protected targets with known approximate geographical locations (such as a power system control host located in a specific region or an enterprise server that can be queried through an IP geolocation database), after applying national-level or provincial-level geographical location confusion, it is extremely easy for locators to identify errors in the geolocation results, and this method may fail when attackers perform street-level IP geolocation. Therefore, this paper conducts research on street-level IP anti-geolocation methods to counter street-level IP geolocation, resulting in street-level errors in the localization results.

3 Methodology

To counter fine-grained-landmark based street-level IP geolocation algorithms, this paper proposes an IP anti-geolocation method based on the deployment of constructed web landmarks. To better introduce the method proposed in this paper, this chapter will first elaborate on the definition of constructed landmarks and their generation and deployment methods, and then explain the working principle and process of this method.

3.1 Constructed Web Landmarks

Network landmarks, referred to as "landmarks," are the foundation and crucial elements of IP geolocation techniques based on network measurements. One of the current mainstream methods for acquiring landmarks is through web pages. This web-based landmark acquisition method primarily utilizes web crawlers and other techniques to extract information such as geographical locations, postal codes, domain names, and IP addresses from web pages. By associating IP addresses, web domain names, and geographical locations, it constructs a mapping relationship between IP addresses and geographical locations, enabling the acquisition of landmarks. To ensure the accuracy of this mapping relationship, reliability assessment methods such as path measurement and reverse domain name lookup are often employed to eliminate inaccurate or erroneous mapping entries, ultimately resulting in accurate <IP address, geographical location> mapping relationships.

Landmarks acquired through web pages are commonly known as web landmarks. The constructed landmarks mentioned in this method are abbreviations for constructed web landmarks. Unlike web landmarks, constructed web landmarks are web pages deployed by device owners to protect their devices from being illegally localized by unauthorized locators. The role of constructed web landmarks is to disguise themselves as normal web pages, waiting to be acquired by unauthorized locators through web-based landmark acquisition methods to participate in geolocation, and then utilize their unique characteristics to interfere with the geolocation process. To successfully interfere with illegal geolocation attempts, constructed web landmarks typically possess the following characteristics:

- Compliance with Web Landmark Characteristics: Constructed web landmarks should comply with the basic characteristics of web landmarks, including possessing a public IP, accessible web pages, and physical location information contained in web pages (explicitly labeled in forms such as "company address").
- Incorrect Nominal Location Information: To mislead unauthorized locators, the nominal physical location information of constructed web landmarks should differ from the actual geographical location of their servers.
- Easy Acquisition: To ensure that constructed web landmarks have a higher probability of participating in the geolocation process and achieving interference with unauthorized geolocation activities, they should be easily accessible through conventional web landmark mining methods (such as the Structon algorithm). This means they should conform to the requirements of conventional web landmark mining methods for target web pages.
- High Credibility: After being obtained by unauthorized locators through landmark mining, constructed web landmarks should be able to pass conventional landmark verification methods, making them credible landmarks that can participate in and interfere with IP geolocation.
- Good Controllability: As web pages deployed on specific servers, the launch time, quantity, response characteristics, and other aspects of constructed web landmarks should be dynamically adjustable based on actual needs and network environments.

In summary, constructed web landmarks, as web pages that conform to the characteristics of web landmarks, are characterized by their ease of acquisition through web landmark mining methods, high credibility, and good controllability, which facilitates their management.

3.2 Principle

The IP anti-geolocation method based on the deployment of constructed landmarks primarily targets the street-level IP geolocation algorithms based on fine-grained landmarks in existing IP geolocation techniques that rely on network measurements. These street-level IP geolocation algorithms achieve high accuracy by performing network measurements on landmark IPs surrounding the target to obtain probing data. They often utilize landmark nodes with relatively low latency to the target device for geographical location estimation. However, these algorithms heavily rely on the density, positional accuracy, and information accuracy of the landmarks used for geolocation. The final geolocation accuracy and error are closely related to the landmark precision. In particular, the key landmark information with low relative delay to the target device significantly determines the geolocation results of the algorithm. Therefore, when there are significant errors in the positional information of key landmarks, the geolocation will be greatly affected, resulting in large errors.

Based on this, this paper attempts to disrupt the accuracy of key landmark information by deploying constructed web landmarks in a locally concentrated manner near the protected target. This approach aims to introduce errors into the landmark information collected by unauthorized locators. When the constructed web landmarks deployed by the anti-geolocation party exhibit low relative delay to the protected target and successfully participate in the geolocation process of the unauthorized geolocation party, there is a high probability of interfering with the geolocation results, successfully countering illegal geolocation attempts.

Taking the classic SLG algorithm as an example, it discovers landmarks near the target through two rounds of landmark discoveries. Then, it analyzes the network measurement data and calculates the landmark with the minimum relative delay to the target as the "nearest landmark". Finally, utilizing the correlation between delay and distance, the algorithm outputs the position of the nearest landmark as the geolocation result. However, when we deploy constructed web landmarks around the target in a concentrated manner, once the constructed landmarks are acquired by the locator through landmark mining or other means, there is a high probability that the locator will estimate the target position as the nominal position of the constructed landmarks due to their naturally smaller relative delay to the target, resulting in significant errors.

Furthermore, considering the classic LBG algorithm, it initially measures the delay and hop count between multiple probing sources and all landmarks. Then, it determines the probability distribution obeyed by the delay and hop count between each probing source and landmark within different ranges. Subsequently, it combines the probing data with demographic information from different regions to establish a probability distribution model for geographical distances when the delay and hop count are fixed. Finally, the trained model is used to geolocate the target. This algorithm treats the delay and hop count information from the probing source to the target IP landmark as features and transforms the IP geolocation problem into a machine learning problem using a Bayesian probability model. When constructed web landmarks are deployed around the target, and once they are acquired by the locator through landmark mining or other means, the naturally smaller relative delay between the constructed landmarks and the target, combined with their similar positions in the network topology, generates similar response data during network measurements. This, in turn, affects the position prediction of the Bayesian probability model (Fig. 1).

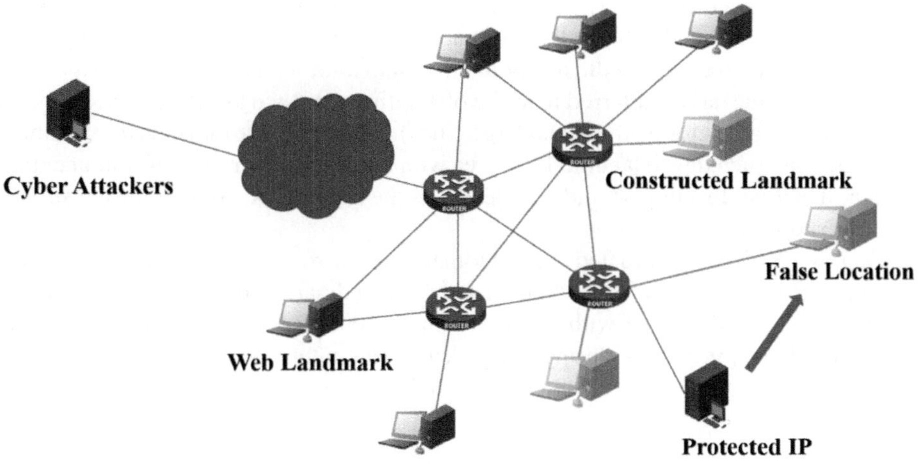

Fig. 1. The principle of the method.

3.3 Generation of Constructed Web Landmarks

The key to this anti-geolocation method lies in the generation and deployment of constructed web landmarks. To generate constructed web landmarks that meet the conditions for anti-geolocation, this paper proposes the following method for generating constructed web landmarks, which consists of five steps.

1. Select the entity to be disguised based on the geographical location of the protected target. To enhance the credibility of the constructed web landmarks, we disguise them as official webpages of real entities. To align with local industrial characteristics, we first determine the entity type of the constructed web landmark by examining the distribution of entities in the location of the protected target. For example, if there are many educational institutions or construction companies in the target area, we select a school or construction company as the entity type for the constructed web landmark. Then, to further enhance the credibility of the constructed web landmark, we screen entities of the above type that do not have official websites and disguise the constructed web landmark as the website of that entity. The screening can be done by querying online maps, local government lists, and business directories.
2. Crawl similar websites as templates to create constructed web landmark webpages. After determining the type of entity to be disguised, we crawl similar websites as templates for building the constructed web landmark website, making the webpages more aligned with the actual industry websites and further enhancing credibility.
3. Determine the deployment location of the constructed web landmark. To ensure that the constructed web landmark successfully influences the geolocation results of illegal localizers, it should have a small communication delay with the target, i.e., a small "distance" from the target in the network topology. Therefore, when deploying the constructed web landmark, we choose to deploy it under the same direct route as the target device or its adjacent routes.
4. Determine the nominal position. The nominal position is the most important information for a web landmark. To successfully interfere with the geolocation results of illegal localizers and achieve the basic anti-geolocation effect, the nominal position of the constructed web landmark should maintain a sufficient distance from the actual position of the target (referred to as the offset distance, such as 20 km, since 20 km is a common radius for medium and large cities). Meanwhile, to enhance the credibility of the constructed web landmark, an area with a high concentration of similar entities near the target location should be selected as the nominal position of the constructed web landmark.
5. Deploy multiple constructed web landmarks to corroborate each other. To further enhance the credibility of the constructed web landmarks, multiple constructed web landmarks are deployed with similar nominal positions. Additionally, they exhibit similar detection results during network measurements, achieving mutual corroboration among multiple constructed web landmarks and further enhancing their credibility.

4 Evaluation

To validate the anti-geolocation effectiveness of our proposed method in a real-world network environment, we selected several landmarks in Shanghai, China, as the protected targets. We performed multiple network measurements on the targets and surrounding landmarks using multiple probing sources to obtain probing data. Then, we utilized the classical fine-grained geolocation algorithm, SLG, to locate the protected targets and compared the changes in geolocation errors before and after applying our anti-geolocation method.

Initially, we localized 156 landmarks in Shanghai, and the results showed that the mean error was 5.951 km, and the median error was 3.779 km, as shown in the figure below. The relatively small median error indicates that a considerable number of network devices can be precisely located, even without disclosing their geographical locations or using remote positioning technologies (such as GPS or the BeiDou Navigation Satellite System). This demonstrates that their street-level locations can still be grasped by illegal localizers, thereby exposing their geographical location privacy (Fig. 2).

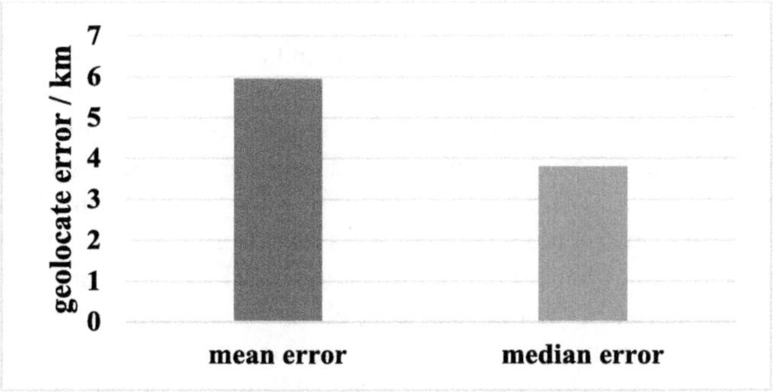

Fig. 2. Non-confronted IP geolocation results.

Subsequently, we followed the steps mentioned earlier to generate constructed web landmarks, deploying them under routers directly connected to the targets, and setting the offset distance to 20 km. By geolocating each of the 156 targets individually, calculating the mean, median, and maximum errors for each round of geolocation, and repeating the process six times, we obtained the following results (Fig. 3).

In the six experimental runs, we deployed the constructed web landmarks on different servers separately. Specifically, we used servers relatively close to the target's directly connected router twice (corresponding to the first and second experiments), servers further away from the router twice (corresponding to the third and fourth experiments), and servers on the same server as the target (corresponding to the fifth and sixth experiments).

Based on the experimental results, we observed that when the constructed web landmarks were deployed on servers far from the target's directly connected router, there was only a minimal increase in the mean and median geolocation errors, and even a decrease in the maximum error. However, when the constructed web landmarks were deployed on servers closer to the target's directly connected router, the anti-geolocation effect

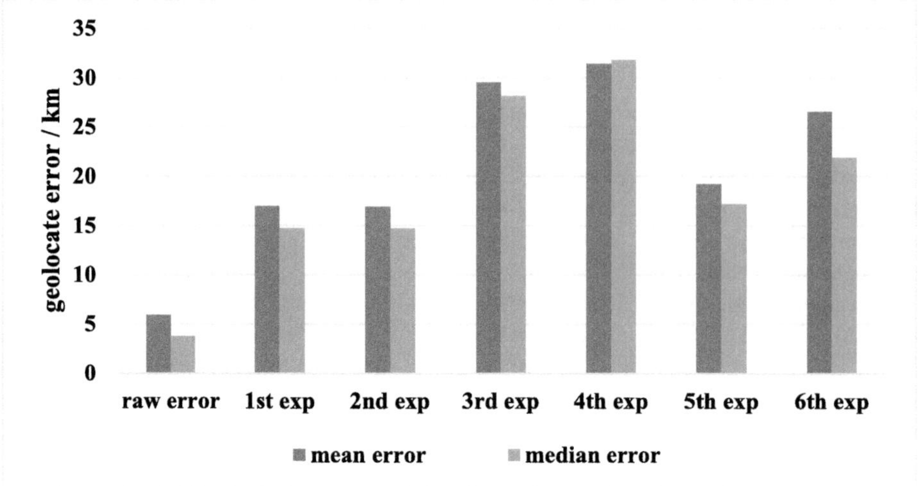

Fig. 3. The raw geolocation errors and results from 6 experimental rounds.

was more significant, with significant improvements in the mean, median, and maximum errors. When the constructed web landmarks were deployed on the same server as the target, the anti-geolocation effect was moderate. After analysis, we believe that IP geolocation algorithms based on fine-grained landmarks primarily utilize landmarks with relatively low latency compared to the target for geolocation. Therefore, when we choose to deploy constructed web landmarks on different servers, we are essentially altering the relative latency between the constructed web landmarks and the target. When the relative latency between the constructed web landmarks and the target is too large, the geolocation algorithm may resort to using other landmarks instead of the constructed web landmarks to estimate the target's location, leading to a failure in anti-geolocation (Table 1).

Table 1. The P-values and mean errors for each experimental round

Experimental rounds	Select probability (%)	Mean error
1st	11.54	16.963
2nd	9.97	16.922
3rd	72.44	29.552
4th	76.92	31.421
5th	54.28	19.237
6th	62.13	26.597

To validate our hypothesis, we calculated the selection probability P of the constructed web landmarks for each of the six experiments. We define the selection probability P as the percentage of times the geolocation algorithm used the geographical location of the constructed web landmarks as the primary geolocation data during the geolocation process for all targets. For the SLG algorithm, the selection probability P is equivalent to the percentage of targets whose estimated location in the geolocation results is based on the nominal location of the constructed web landmarks. After calculation, we obtained the following selection probabilities P:

By correlating the selection probability P with the geolocation results of each experimental round, we observed that when the constructed web landmarks have the same offset distance, the anti-geolocation effect is significantly more pronounced in experimental rounds with a higher selection probability P. There is a positive correlation between the magnitude of selection probability P and the effectiveness of anti-geolocation. In the first two experimental rounds, we deployed the constructed web landmarks on servers far from the target's directly connected router, increasing the relative latency between the constructed web landmarks and the target, which reduced the selection probability P and resulted in poor anti-geolocation performance. Conversely, in the third and fourth experimental rounds, due to a higher selection probability P, the anti-geolocation effect was significantly improved. In the last two experimental rounds, since the constructed web landmarks were deployed on the same server as the target, the relative latency between them was moderate compared to the previous two scenarios. The results are as shown in the figure below (Fig. 4).

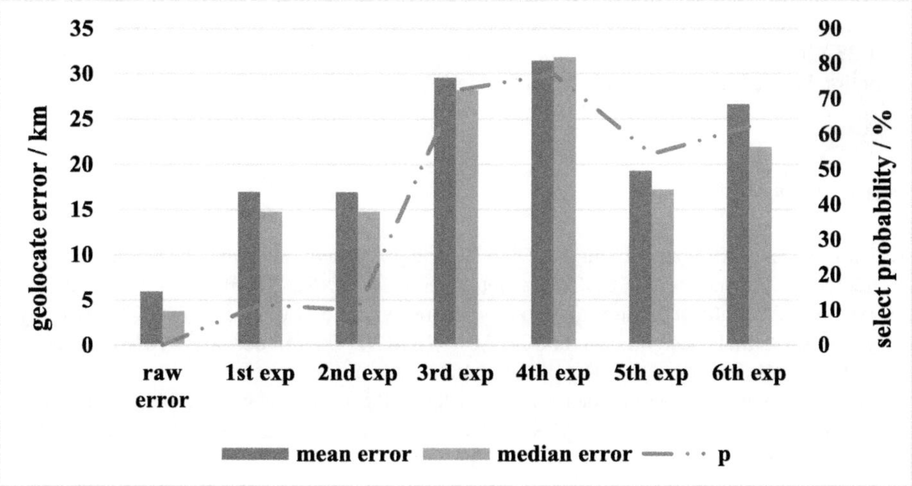

Fig. 4. The P-values of each experimental round and their corresponding mean, median, and maximum errors

5 Conclusion and Perspectives

The existing fine-grained IP geolocation techniques based on network measurements bring convenience to people, but they also pose a threat to their geographical privacy security. To address this issue, this paper proposes an IP anti-geolocation method based on the deployment of constructed web landmarks. This method achieves anti-geolocation by generating and deploying constructed web landmarks, primarily targeting street-level IP geolocation algorithms based on fine-grained landmarks. Unlike other existing anti-geolocation methods, this approach focuses on protecting fixed devices with known national or provincial geographical locations, primarily resisting street-level geolocation of targets by illegal localizers, causing significant errors in their geolocation results at the street level. In experiments conducted on 156 landmarks in Shanghai, China, with a constructed web landmark offset distance of 20 km, the average geolocation error could be increased from 5.6 km to 31.4 km, and the median error could be increased from 3.8 km to 31.8 km, demonstrating a significant anti-geolocation effect and have protected the fine-grained geographical privacy of critical network devices of important enterprises.

In this paper, we assume that the cyber attacker is unaware that we have protected the target IP beforehand, and that most existing measurement-based IP geolocation technology does not consider adversarial IP anti-targeting methods. In the following research, we will further optimize the IP anti-geolocation method and propose an IP anti-geolocation framework to make it more difficult for cyber attackers to detect that we have implemented IP anti-geolocation on the protected IP.

Acknowledgment. This work was supported by National Key R&D Program of China (Grant No. 2022YFB3102904), the National Natural Science Foundation of China (Grant No. U23A20305,62302521,62172435), and Henan Province Key Research, Development and Promotion Project on Tackling Key Scientific Problems (232102211052).

References

1. Ding, S., Luo, X., Wang, J., Fu, X.: GNN-Geo: a graph neural network-based fine-grained IP geolocation framework. IEEE Trans. Netw. Sci. Eng. (TNSE) **10**(6), 3543–3560 (2023)
2. Wenxin, T., et al.: TrustGeo: uncertainty-aware dynamic graph learning for trustworthy IP geolocation. In: Proceedings of the 29th ACM SIGKDD Conference on Knowledge Discovery and Data Mining (KDD 2023), pp. 4862–4871 (2023)
3. Wang, Z., et al.: Connecting the hosts: street-level IP geolocation with graph neural networks. In: Proceedings of the 28th ACM SIGKDD Conference on Knowledge Discovery and Data Mining (KDD 2022), pp. 4121–4131 (2022)
4. Li, Q., et al.: GeoCAM: an IP-based geolocation service through fine-grained and stable webcam landmarks. IEEE/ACM Trans Netw. (TON) **29**(4), 1798–1812 (2021)
5. Rye, E C., Beverly, R.: IPvSeeYou: exploiting leaked identifiers in IPv6 for street-level geolocation. In: IEEE Symposium on Security and Privacy (S&P 2023), pp. 3129–3145 (2023)
6. Ding, S., Zhao, F., Luo, X.: A street-level IP geolocation method based on delay-distance correlation and multilayered common routers. Secur. Commun. Netw. **2021**(1), 6658642 (2021)

7. Zhang, F., Yin, M., Liu, F., Luo, X.: IP2vec: an IP node representation model for IP geolocation Front. Comput. Sci. (FCS) **18**(6), 186506 (2024)
8. Yang, K., et al.: Exploring self-explainable street-level IP geolocation with graph information bottleneck. In: IEEE International Conference on Acoustics, Speech and Signal Processing (ICASSP 2024), pp. 7270–7274 (2024)
9. Dan, O., Parikh, V., Davison, B.D.: IP Geolocation through Geographic Clicks. ACM Trans. Spatial Algorithms Syst. (TSAS) **8**(1), 1–22 (2022)
10. Tai, W., Chen, B., Zhong, T., Wang, Y., Chen, K., Zhou, F.: RIPGeo: robust street-level IP geolocation. In: 2023 24th IEEE International Conference on Mobile Data Management (MDM 2023), pp. 138–147 (2023)
11. Abdou, A M.: Internet location verification: challenges and solutions. arXiv preprint (2018). arXiv:1802.05169
12. Abdou, A M., Matrawy, A., van Oorschot, P.C.: On the evasion of delay-based IP geolocation. Technical report, Carleton University TR-14–03 (2014)
13. Nur, A.Y.: Accuracy and coverage analysis of IP geolocation databases. In: 2023 International Balkan Conference on Communications and Networking (BalkanCom 2023), pp. 1–6 (2023)
14. Poese, I., Uhlig, S., Kaafar, M.A., Donnet, B., Gueye, B.: IP geolocation databases: unreliable? ACM SIGCOMM Comput. Commun. Rev. **41**(2), 53–56 (2011)
15. Shavitt, Y., Zilberman, N.: A geolocation databases study. IEEE J. Sel. Areas Commun. **29**(10), 2044–2056 (2011)
16. Guo, C., Liu, Y., Shen, W., Wang, H.J, Yu, Q., Zhang, Y.: Mining the web and the internet for accurate IP address geolocations. In: IEEE INFOCOM 2009-IEEE Conference on Computer Communications (INFOCOM 2009), pp. 2841–2845 (2009)
17. Liu, H., Zhang, Y., Zhou, Y., Zhang, D., Fu, X., Ramakrishnan, K.K.: Mining checkins from location-sharing services for client-independent IP geolocation. In: IEEE INFOCOM 2014-IEEE Conference on Computer Communications (INFOCOM 2014), pp. 619–627 (2014)
18. Dan, O., Parikh, V., Davison, B.D.: Improving IP geolocation using query logs. In: Proceedings of the 9th ACM International Conference on Web Search and Data Mining (WSDM 2016), pp. 347–356 (2016)
19. Huffaker, B., Fomenkov, M., Claffy, K.C.: DRoP: DNS-based router positioning. ACM SIGCOMM Comput. Commun. Rev. **44**(3), 5–13 (2014)
20. Dan, O., Parikh, V., Davison, B.D.: Distributed reverse DNS geolocation. In: 2018 IEEE International Conference on Big Data (Big Data 2018), pp. 1581–1586 (2018)
21. Scheitle, Q., Gasser, O., Sattler, P., Carle, G.: HLOC: hints-based geolocation leveraging multiple measurement frameworks. In: 2017 Network Traffic Measurement and Analysis Conference (TMA 2017), pp. 1–9 (2017)
22. Eriksson, B., Barford, P., Sommers, J., Nowak, R.: A learning-based approach for IP geolocation. In: 11th International Conference, Passive and Active Measurement (PAM 2010), pp. 171–180 (2010)
23. Gueye, B., Ziviani, A., Crovella, M., Fdida, S.: Constraint-based geolocation of internet hosts. In: Proceedings of the 4th ACM SIGCOMM Conference on Internet Measurement (SIGCOMM 2004), pp 288–293 (2004)
24. Eriksson, B., Barford, P., Maggs, B., Nowak, R.: Posit: a lightweight approach for IP geolocation. ACM SIGMETRICS Perform. Eval. Rev. **40**(2), 2–11 (2012)
25. Arif, M.J., Karunasekera, S., Kulkarni, S.: GeoWeight: internet host geolocation based on a probability model for latency measurements. In: Australasian Computer Science Conference 2010, pp. 89–98 (2010)
26. Laki, S., Mátray, P., Hága, P., Sebők, T., Csabai, I., Vattay, G.: Spotter: a model based active geolocation service. In: 2011 Proceedings IEEE INFOCOM, pp. 3173–3181 (2011)

27. Wong, B., Stoyanov, I., Sirer, E.G.: Octant: a comprehensive framework for the geolocalization of internet hosts. In: Symposium on Networked Systems Design and Implementation (NSDI 2007), pp. 23–23 (2007)
28. Wang, Y., Burgener, D., Flores, M., Kuzmanovic, A., Huang, C.: Towards street-level client-independent IP geolocation. In: 8th USENIX Symposium on Networked Systems Design and Implementation (NSDI 2011), pp. 365–379 (2011)
29. QQWry [DB/OL]. https://www.cz88.net/
30. Padmanabhan, V.N., Subramanian, L.: An investigation of geographic mapping techniques for internet hosts. In: Proceedings of the 2001 Conference on Applications, Technologies, Architectures, and Protocols for Computer Communications, pp. 173–185 (2001)
31. Katz-Bassett, E., John, J.P., Krishnamurthy, A., Wetherall, D., Anderson, T., Chawathe, Y.: Towards IP geolocation using delay and topology measurements. In: Proceedings of the 6th ACM SIGCOMM Conference on Internet Measurement (SIGCOMM 2006), pp 71–84 (2006)
32. Wang, Z., Chen, Y., Wen, H., Zhao, L., Sun, L.: Discovering routers as secondary landmarks for accurate IP geolocation. In: 2017 IEEE 86th Vehicular Technology Conference (VTC2017-Fall), pp. 1–5 (2017)
33. Kido, H., Yanagisawa, Y., Satoh, T.: Protection of location privacy using dummies for location-based services. In: 21st International Conference on Data Engineering Workshops (ICDEW 2005), pp. 1248–1248 (2005)
34. Wang, G., He, J., Shi, X., Pan, J., Shen, S.: Analyzing and evaluating efficient privacy-preserving localization for pervasive computing. IEEE Internet Things J. (IoT-J 2017) **5**(4), 2993–3007 (2017)
35. Chow, C.Y., Mokbel, M., Liu X.: A peer-to-peer spatial cloaking algorithm for anonymous location-based service. In: Proceedings of the 14th Annual ACM International Symposium on Advances in Geographic Information Systems, pp. 171–178 (2006)
36. Liu, X., Liu, K., Guo, L., Li, X., Fang, Y.: A game-theoretic approach for achieving k-anonymity in location based services. In: 2013 Proceedings IEEE INFOCOM, pp. 2985–2993 (2013)
37. Li, X.Y., Jung, T.: Search me if you can: privacy-preserving location query service. In: 2013 Proceedings IEEE INFOCOM, pp. 2760–2768 (2013)
38. Castelluccia, C., Kaafar, M.A., Manils, P., Perito, D.: Geolocalization of proxied services and its application to fast-flux hidden servers. In: Proceedings of the 9th ACM SIGCOMM Conference on Internet Measurement (SIGCOMM 2009), pp. 184–189 (2009)
39. Beresford, A.R., Stajano, F.: Location privacy in pervasive computing. IEEE Pervasive Comput. **2**(1), 46–55 (2003)
40. Skyhook [DB/OL]. https://www.skyhook.com/
41. Geobytes [DB/OL]. http://geobytes.com/iplocator/
42. DB-IP [DB/OL]. https://db-ip.com/
43. Gill, P., Ganjali, Y., Wong, B., Lie, D.: Dude, where's that IP? Circumventing measurement-based IP geolocation. In: 19th USENIX Security Symposium (USENIX Security 2010) (2010)
44. Abdou, A.M., van Oorschot, P.C.: Secure client and server geolocation over the internet. arXiv preprint (2019). arXiv:1906.11288
45. WHOIS [DB/OL]. https://www.whois.com/
46. IPcn [DB/OL]. http://www.ipcn.co.uk/zh/home-zh/
47. IP138 [DB/OL]. https://www.ip138.com/
48. MaxMind [DB/OL]. https://www.maxmind.com/en/home/
49. Quova [DB/OL]. https://www.home.neustar/security-intelligence/
50. IP2Location [DB/OL]. https://www.ip2location.com/

Burst Sequence Based Graph Neural Network for Video Traffic Identification

Jian Xiong[1], YingShuo Bao[1], ShengBao Li[3,4], Kun Zhao[5], and LiZhi Peng[1,2(✉)]

[1] Shandong Provincial Key Laboratory of Network Based Intelligent Computing, University of Jinan, Jinan 250022, China
plz@ujn.edu.com

[2] Quancheng Laboratory, Jinan, China

[3] School of Cyber Security, University of Chinese Academy of Sciences, Beijing, China

[4] Shandong Branch of National Computer Network Emergency Response Technical Team/Coordination Center of China, Jinan, China

[5] Inspur Computer Technology Co., Ltd., Jinan, China

Abstract. With the vigorous development of video applications and the comprehensive upgrade of encryption protocols, video content review is becoming increasingly difficult. As a practical solution, video traffic identification has attracted more and more attention in recent years. In order to achieve more refined video traffic recognition, a primary problem to be solved is that the extracted traffic features lack higher-level semantic information to reflect changes in video content. Fortunately, under the same network conditions, similar types of video clips or traffic data generated by live video often have the same traffic change pattern, which allows different types of video traffic to be distinguished. Therefore, this paper extracts burst sequences from video traffic to represent video changes and constructs a graph structure based on burst sequences to extract high-level semantic information. With the powerful performance of a graph neural network, we transform video traffic classification into a graph classification problem and introduce GraphBurst, a model based on burst sequences and graph neural networks. We collected real-world traffic data from different network environments with five video types, including on-demand live streaming, with more than one hundred thousand streams. We launch a set of comparing experiments on the dataset, and compared with the existing methods, the experimental results show that our method has higher accuracy and interpretability.

Keywords: Video traffic identification · Deep Learning · Encrypted Traffic Classification · Graph neural network

1 Introduction

Video traffic, which includes data transmitted across networks and constitutes a significant portion of internet data types, witnessed a 23% growth in global internet traffic from 2021 to 2023. During this period, video traffic's share escalated

J. Xiong and Y.S. Bao—Contribute equally to this work.

S. Goel et al. (Eds.): ICDF2C 2024, LNICST 614, pp. 207–226, 2025.
https://doi.org/10.1007/978-3-031-89360-5_13

to 62.93%, marking a 24% increase from the first half of 2021 [1]. The diversity and quantity of video applications such as video on demand, live streaming, conferencing, and gaming have surged, consuming a substantial amount of network bandwidth and presenting numerous challenges to network management and security. For instance, scenarios requiring high-quality user experiences, like gaming live streams, compel video websites and operators to identify specific stream types to optimize bandwidth allocation for enhanced economic efficiency [2]. In addition, The quality of video content is highly variable, and certain content, such as some gaming videos, may include harmful elements like violence or explicit materials that could affect minors [3]. Consequently, video stream identification has emerged as a crucial area of research in network security and management.

However, identifying video traffic is fraught with challenges. Advances in encryption protocols, including HTTPS, TLS, and QUIC, have rendered traditional content analysis or port number identification methods ineffective [4]. Current identification techniques primarily depend on extracting various fingerprints from encrypted traffic and matching them with known video titles. These methods typically employ statistical flow features [5], bytes per second (BPS) [2], or burst patterns [6] as identifiers, utilizing machine learning or deep learning for classification or matching. Nevertheless, these approaches often fall short as they lack the ability to capture higher-level semantic information necessary for nuanced video content differentiation [7], and they require maintaining a large, frequently updated database of fingerprints, which significantly increases the overhead in terms of time and space [8].

To address these shortcomings, we propose a novel graph neural network (GNN) model GraphBurst based on burst sequences for video traffic identification. We believe that under identical network conditions, similar video segments or live streams generate traffic with comparable burst sequence patterns, enabling the distinction between different types of video traffic [9]. GraphBurst leverages burst sequences extracted from traffic to depict video content changes and constructs a graph structure from these sequences to mine high-level semantic information. By harnessing the robust capabilities of GNNs, we transform the video traffic classification challenge into a graph classification task, allowing the GNN to discern hidden relationships and dependencies within the graph structure.

In this paper, our key contributions are as follows.

1. We introduce a fine-grained burst sequence extraction algorithm that divides complete bursts into rising and falling bursts, characterizing rapid increases and decreases in data changes.
2. We propose a graph-based structural representation method for video traffic data, termed **V**ideo traffic **I**nteraction **G**raph (VIG), where each node corresponds to a burst in the traffic, and the edges encapsulate the relationships between bursts.
3. We have developed GraphBurst, a robust classifier based on graph neural networks (GNNs) that derives VIG from raw traffic without the need for

manually crafted features, learning the feature representations of each node in VIG for effective and accurate classification.

4. We collected two real-world video traffic datasets from different network environments, including five types of videos, with over one hundred thousand streams. Experiments on our datasets demonstrate that GraphBurst outperforms existing methods, offering significant advantages in interpretability, scalability, and robustness.

The remainder of this paper is organized as follows: Sect. 2 reviews related work on video traffic recognition; Sect. 3 describes the GraphBurst model in detail; Sect. 4 presents our experimental results and analysis; Sect. 5 concludes the paper and discusses future work.

2 Related Work

Video traffic identification is a technique that extracts effective features from encrypted traffic to identify different types of videos and their related information. Video traffic identification has important applications in network management, video service quality assessment, and copyright protection. Existing video traffic identification methods can be divided into three categories:

2.1 Methods Based on Statistical Flow Features

These methods use statistical features such as packet header information or packet length information to estimate or predict the service quality (QoE) or semantic information of video traffic. These methods usually use traditional machine learning classifiers, such as support vector machines (SVM) or k-nearest neighbors (k-NN). For example, Mangla et al. [10] proposed a method called eMIMIC, which estimates video QoE indicators by using packet header information of network traffic. Wassermann et al. [11] introduced ViCrypt, a system based on online machine learning that predicts the QoE of YouTube videos, using 208 statistical flow features.

2.2 Methods Based on Bytes Per Second (BPS)

These methods extract BPS from raw traffic as an important feature for video traffic identification, to capture the fluctuations generated by video encoding and transmission processes. These methods usually use deep neural networks, such as convolutional neural networks (CNN) or long short-term memory (LSTM). For example, Saponas et al. [12] converted traffic traces into BPS time series per 100 milliseconds and applied sliding window discrete Fourier transform to match the closest signal. Khan et al. [13] extracted BPS from video streams with different resolutions and used them as features for training different machine learning models, including support vector machines and convolutional neural networks (CNN).

2.3 Methods Based on Burst Patterns or Video Chunks

These methods use the characteristics of video streaming to extract burst patterns or video chunks from traffic as fingerprints, to achieve more fine-grained video identification. These methods usually use customized algorithms or models to match or recover video fingerprints. For example, Schuster et al. [9] analyzed the burst ON-OFF cycles presented in encrypted video traffic and found that the root cause was the different sizes of video segments produced by VBR encoding. Therefore, the authors proposed that the burst pattern of video streams can be used as a unique fingerprint and that CNN classifiers can accurately identify the burst pattern of video streams in coarse network measurements. Reed et al. [14] developed a system for identifying encrypted Netflix videos using graph neural networks. The system uses video description information obtained by an intermediate proxy to build a plaintext fingerprint database. When identifying encrypted video traffic, it uses Application Data Unit (ADU) features extracted by adudump to build video transmission fingerprints. Wu et al. [15] used HTTP headers and TLS segment features as ADU length fitting features, and proposed an accurate recovery method to identify encrypted ADU fingerprints, and applied it to encrypted video identification.

Overall, the main goal of current research is to use machine learning algorithms to extract various fingerprints from encrypted video traffic and match them with known video titles to complete video identification. In this paper, we are more inclined to directly infer fine-grained live scene categories from the traffic level rather than specific titles. We believe that such a task is more challenging and practical, because different live scenes may have different requirements and impacts on network resources and service quality. To achieve this goal, we propose a video traffic identification method based on graph neural networks (GNN), which can effectively capture the structure and dynamic information in traffic, and adapt to different traffic scales and distributions.

3 Method

In this section, we present our model GraphBurst in details, whose basic workflow is shown in Fig. 1. GraphBurst comprises three primary stages: the video flow identification stage, the burst sequence extraction stage, and the graph representation learning stage. We firstly identify video flows from row traffic, and further extract burst sequence from identified video traffic to describe the variation of video content. Then, to more accurately exploit higher level semantics of video traffic, we use a graph structure to express the temporal and spatial relationship. Afterward, we use a powerful graph neural network to achieve the classification of different live-streaming scenarios.

3.1 Video Flow Identification

Video flow identification is the first part to pick out video flows from other different hybrid traffic caused by video sessions. Among raw traffic, video flow has

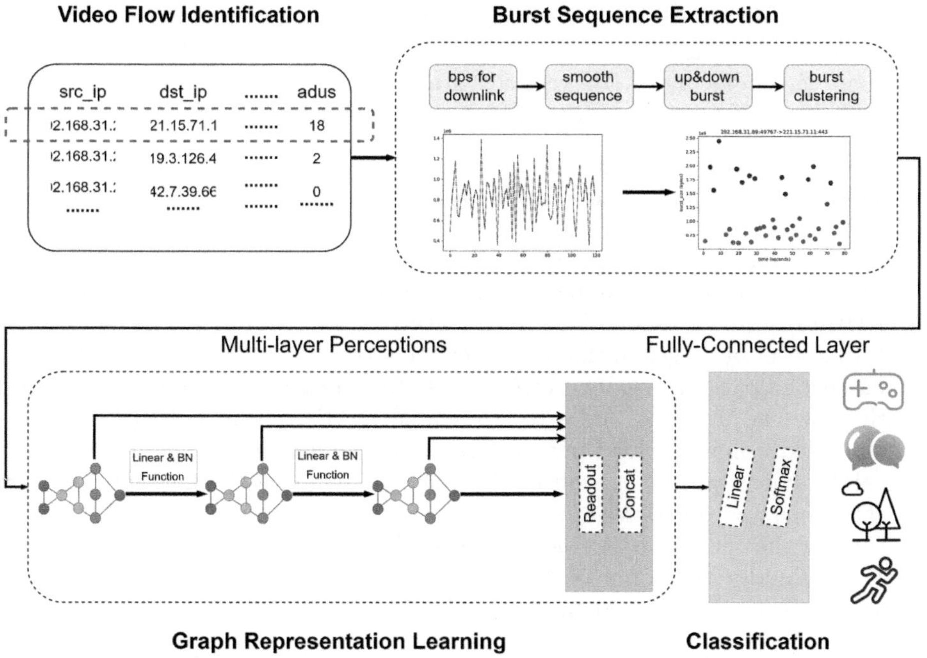

Fig. 1. The overall framework of entire method for Burst Sequence Based Graph Neural Network for Video Traffic Identification.

a special transmission pattern for transmitting massive high payload packets of video content. Therefore, we can use proper feature threshold to fit video flow, and these features can be basically divide into ADU features and statistic features. Consequently, we employ the video traffic identification threshold method within the video traffic identification module of GraphBurst. Based on the intrinsic properties of video transmission, the identification thresholds for video streams are set empirically as Table 1 shows. The identification procedure is illustrated in Algorithm 1.

Table 1. The details of threshold conditions

Thresh.	Description	Defaults
T_v	segment length threshold for video ADU	100 KB
R_v	rate threshold for video	300 Kb/s
R_a	rate threshold for non-video	192 Kb/s
L_v	pkt length threshold for video	900 B
L_a	pkt length threshold for non-video	450 B
S_v	segment for Live ADU	3
σ	time interval for Live ADU	2 sec.
ϵ	fixed uplink payload for Live ADU	89 B

Identification Conditions Setting: Table 1 shows a series of feature thresholds of video flow identification, which can be divided into rate threshold, packet payload threshold and ADU related threshold. Based the combination of the above feature thresholds, we design the algorithm as the pseudo-code displayed.

1. Rate Threshold: This threshold pertains to the transmission rate of the flow. This rate is evaluated whether is greater than a certain value, R_v, to determine if the flow is a video stream.
2. Packet Payload Threshold: If the average packet size within a flow is greater than or equal to L_v, it indicates that the flow may be a video stream.
3. ADU Related Threshold: The ADU feature provides information about application level messages in the flow, effectively treating a video chunk as encompassing all packets over a certain period. To compute the standard ADU from the flow, we utilize σ and ϵ to segment live ADUs from both time interval and fixed uplink payload perspectives. If the uplink packets of a flow have a valid payload packet size of exactly 89B, we segment the flow into different chunks using ϵ. Otherwise, we solely uses σ for chunk segmentation. We then check if the chunk size exceeds a certain threshold, T_v, to identify a standard ADU. Finally, the count of ADUs, which should be more than S_v, serves as a critical condition for identifying video flow.

Algorithm 1. Video Flow Identification

Input: Traffic features at flow level
c: number of pkts with transport layer payload.
l: transport layer payload length of pkt p.
t_e: elapsed time from 1st pkt.
$\overline{L}$: average length of transport layer payload.
L_s: cumulative length of transport layer payload.
R: data rate of transport layer payload.
C_{adu}: The number of ADUs of flow f_{id}.
Output: Identification result
for each downlink packet p in flow id **do**
    $l \Leftarrow payload\_len(p)$
    $C_{adu} \Leftarrow C_{adu} + 1$
    $c \Leftarrow c + 1$
    $L_s \Leftarrow L_s + l$
    $\overline{L} \Leftarrow \frac{L_s}{c}$
    $R \Leftarrow \frac{L_s}{t_e}$
    if $l = 0$ **then**
        return current type(id)
    end if
    if $(R \geq R_v) \cap (\overline{L} \geq L_v) \cap (C_{adu} \geq T_v)$ **then**
        return Video
    else if $(R < R_a) \cap (\overline{L} < L_a) \cap (L_s < T_v)$ **then**
        return Nonvideo
    else
        return Maybe
    end if
end for

The video identification procedure is depicted in Algorithm 1. According to the difference in threshold matching, the algorithm outputs three types of results. The first is when the features of the flow hit three necessary conditions for video flows at the same time (L_v, R_v, S_v). It will be identified as a Video flow. The second is when the data volume of the flow is less than the minimum load T_v of an ADU, the flow rate is less than the minimum video flow rate R_a, and the average packet size is less than the minimum video flow payload L_a. It will be identified as Nonvideo. The third is when flow features between the above two conditions are identified as Maybe. Finally, we successfully identified video traffic from raw flows, laying the groundwork for the extraction of burst sequences.

3.2 Burst Sequence Extraction

Burst sequences serve as critical fingerprints for capturing changes in video content within encrypted traffic, which is typically defined as a sudden increase or spike in data transmission rate over a network in a short period of time. Many researchers have devoted to present video flows using burst features, but they had primarily focused on extracting burst events based on frequency, which often provides a coarse representation of video information. In the preceding section, we extracted video traffic from raw flows. To achieve more refined burst extraction, this section introduces an effective approach to obtain fine-grained burst sequences only from video streams, and then uses these sequences to construct a graph structure, thereby capturing this advanced semantic information. The burst sequence extraction process encompasses four key components: BPS for Downlink, Sequence Smoothing, Upward and Downward Burst Extraction, and Clustering Burst.

BPS for Downlink: In our research, we discovered that the uplink payload of video traffic contains less pertinent information. Therefore, our focus is primarily on the downlink flow of video traffic. The initial step involves extracting the Bytes Per Second (BPS) for the downlink, which encompasses all server response data. We implement a temporal window designed to slide over the flow to capture regular intervals, empirically set at 1.5 s. Within each interval, the byte size of all packets is aggregated to form a BPS sequence. This sequence provides a snapshot of traffic distribution within the designated time window. During this process, BPS elements under 20 bytes are considered 'noise' and discarded, as they likely do not represent significant video content. With these foundational BPS sequences established, our methodology is well-prepared for subsequent operations such as sequence smoothing, burst extraction, and clustering. These steps enable us to delve deeper into the complexities of video traffic patterns.

Sequence Smoothing: Based on the extracted BPS data for the downlink, we applied the moving average method to better reveal the underlying trends by effectively filtering out the small, transient fluctuations or noisy data points. This process involved calculating the average of a specific number of adjacent data points within a moving window, and replacing each data point with the average. The result is a significantly smoother sequence that emphasizes more prominent and long-term patterns. Supposed x_t represent the observation value of the BPS for downlink at the $t-th$ interval with noises. To get the smoothed value p_t, we calculate the sample moving average (SMA) with a window size of $2n+1$ $(n \geq 1)$ we sum up the value of the adjacent $2n+1$ data points and divide by $2n+1$ as follows:

$$p_t = \frac{\sum_{i=1}^{n-1}(x_{t-i} + x_{t+i}) + x_t}{2n+1} \tag{1}$$

where p_t is the simple moving average at $t-th$ interval, x_{t-i} and x_{t+i} represents the adjacent data values at the $(t-i)-th$ and the $(t+i)-th$ interval, respectively. As the description of Eq. (1), the window size n is crucial because it determines the level of smoothing. A larger n results in smoother data but may cause a lag in capturing recent changes, while a smaller n reacts more quickly to changes but may be noisier.

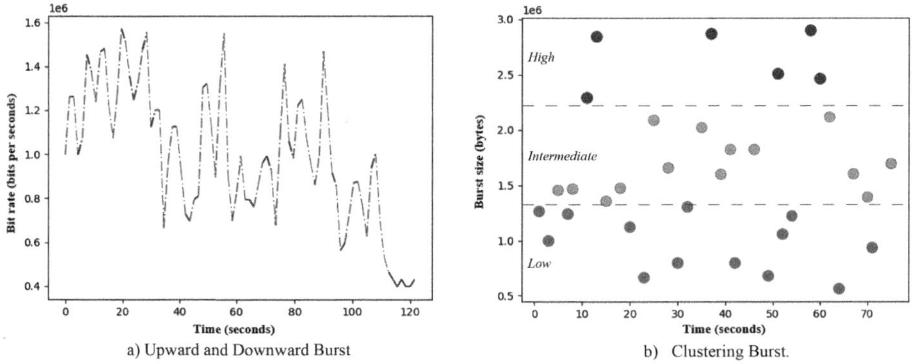

Fig. 2. The visualization of Upward and Downward Burst Extraction and Clustering Burst.

Upward and Downward Burst Extraction: Different from the concept of burst in previous work [16], the paper focuses on the more fine-grain burst information. Therefore, we divide the complete burst into up and down bursts to describe the rapid rising and falling data variation. The rate sequence is firstly extracted from the previously smoothed BPS sequence, which is as Eq. (2):

$$r_t = \frac{p_t}{\tau} \tag{2}$$

where p_t is the smoothed value after smoothing at the $t-th$ interval, τ is the value of interval ($\tau = 1.5$ seconds in our case), r_t is the calculated rate at $t-th$ interval. Based on the calculated rate sequences, we propose a burst flagging method to identify significant changes within these sequences. It involves defining thresholds based on a parameter k and comparing the rate of the current rate r_t with that of the last rate r_{t-1}. An upward burst is flagged when the current rate r_t exceeds k times the last rate r_{t-1}. As shown in the left part of Fig. 2, red dot lines represent upward bursts, green ones represents downward bursts, and blue ones represent those burst do not meet the criteria, termed as non-bursts. A downward burst is identified when the rate of the current rate r_t drops below $\frac{1}{k}$ of the last rate r_{t-1}. Equation (3) gives the formal definition of the method.

$$flag = \begin{cases} upward\ burst & r_t > k * r_{t-1} \\ downward\ burst & r_t < \frac{1}{k} * r_{t-1} \\ not\ burst & other\ situations \end{cases} \tag{3}$$

This method intuitively fits the characteristics of video streams. For example, a sudden increase in data rate may indicate scene transitions or fast-paced actions. In contrast, a rate decrease may indicate static scenes or buffering pauses.

Clustering Burst: Following the extraction of burst sequences from video traffic, we apply time series clustering techniques to categorize the burst within these sequences into various levels. This categorization assists in constructing the Video traffic Interaction Graph (VIG) and aids in identifying distinct burst behavior patterns across different types of video traffic. Due to its straightforwardness and high computational efficiency, the Euclidean k-means algorithm is particularly apt for handling large-scale network traffic data. Consequently, we employ the Euclidean k-means algorithm to cluster the burst sequences based on the burst payload size.

The Euclidean k-means clustering method for time series data is particularly suited for handling time series data. It is based on the traditional k-means clustering method and uses the Euclidean distance as a measure of similarity. The objective of k-means clustering can be expressed through the following mathematical formula Eq. (4):

$$\text{minimize} \quad J = \sum_{i=1}^{k} \sum_{\mathbf{x} \in C_i} \|\mathbf{x} - \mu_i\|^2 \tag{4}$$

where x represents the payload size of a burst within the burst sequence, C_i is the ith cluster, μ_i is the centroid of C_i, $\|\cdot\|$ denotes the Euclidean distance. Using the Euclidean distance as a measure of similarity, as shown in the right part of Fig. 2, the bursts are grouped into three clusters, effectively representing low, intermediate, and high frequency bursts, corresponding to red, green, and blue circles in the diagram, respectively. As a significant part of GraphBurst, the clustering of bursts can significantly improve the quality of the generated graph data.

3.3 Graph Representation Learning Based on Burst Sequence

Inspired by the information-rich graph structure, we represent video traffic as a Video traffic Interaction Graph (VIG) based on the fine-grained bursts extracted from video traffic. Figure 3 show an example demonstrating how to construct the VIG from the extracted fine-grained bursts. A VIG comprises vertices, edges, and a five-dimensional feature set corresponding to each vertex. Utilizing flow burst features for graph classification has demonstrated reliability and efficiency [17].

Serial Number	Burst Payload (bytes)	Burst Time (s)	Burst Duration (s)	Trend Indicator	Maximum Drop (bytes)
0	1263746.5	1.5	1.5	1	265019.0
1	998727.5	4.5	4.5	-1	456563.5
2	1455291.0	7.5	6.0	1	456563.5
3	1240131.5	10.5	6.0	-1	241819.0
...	...	...	...	...	...

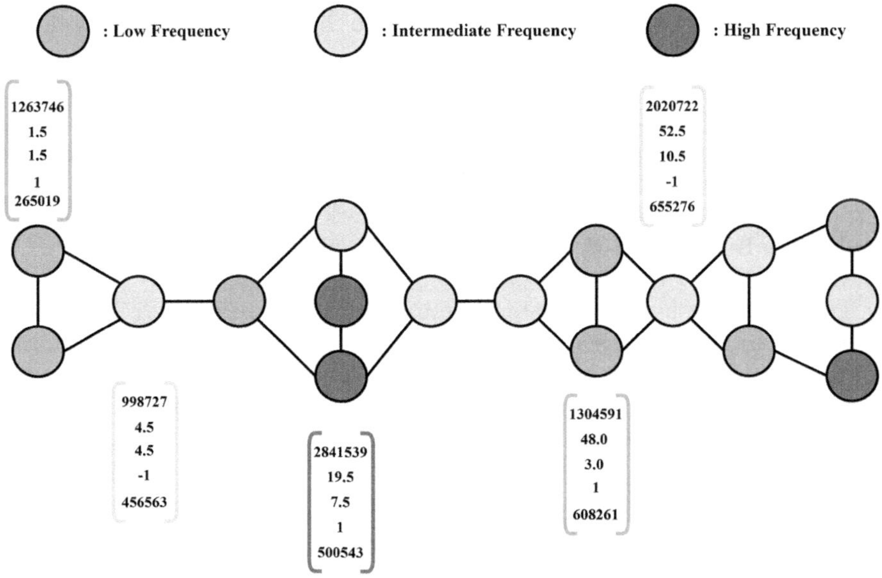

Fig. 3. Graph-based Representation of Burst Sequence.

Vertices: In a given stream, a vertex in the VIG represents a burst, encapsulating a unique characteristic or behavior of the video stream. Each vertex has 5 attributes, Burst Payload, Burst Duration, Trend Indicator, and Maximum Drop. Burst Payload is the total payload size of all packets in the burst; Burst Time, the time of the first packet's arrival, marking the onset of the burst; Burst Duration, the time difference between the last and first packets of the burst; Trend Indicator, a binary flag that denotes trend, with "1" indicating an upward trend if the burst size difference from the previous vertex is positive, and "−1" for a downward trend; and Maximum Drop, the largest difference between the current burst and previous sequences, capturing the local fluctuations in the traffic, with larger values indicating greater volatility.

Edges: The edges in the VIG encapsulate the relationships between bursts. These edges can be categorized into two types, intra-burst edges and inter-burst edges. Intra-burst edges connect vertices with the same trend, and these vertices are considered as the same layer within the VIG. Specifically, if a couple of adjacent vertexes share the same trend indicator, they are connected by an intra-burst edge and considered part of the same layer. Inter-burst edges, on the other hand, connect sequences of bursts with different trends, and vertices connected by inter-burst edges are not considered as the same layer. This cross-level linkage effectively captures the dynamic sequence and relationships between different burst levels, providing a comprehensive expression of the temporal and directional dynamics within burst data.

3.4 Graph Neural Network for Video Traffic Identification

Following the construction of the VIG, the task of video traffic classification is redefined as a graph classification challenge. GNNs demonstrate superior performance in identifying both local patterns, such as burst sequences, and global patterns spanning the entire video stream. This dual capability is crucial for an accurate and comprehensive analysis of video traffic patterns. Xu et al. [18] introduced a powerful GNN model, the Graph Isomorphism Network (GIN), which extends the Weisfeiler-Lehman (WL) test and exhibits strong graph classification capabilities. Consequently, this section leverages the core components of GIN to detail the design specifics of the classifier, GraphBurst, which is based on GIN.

GNN Architecture: The objective of the GNN model is to accurately classify each VIG, thus translating the video traffic recognition task into a graph classification problem. The architecture of the GNN model comprises Multi-Layer Perceptrons (MLP) and a fully connected layer. Here, MLP serves to extract features from VIGs, while the fully connected layer is employed to make classification decisions.

1. Multi-Layer Perceptrons: GIN employs MLP to learn representation vectors of nodes within the graph. Employing a recursive neighbor aggregation scheme, the feature vector of each node aggregates feature information from its neighbors, thereby capturing the structural relationships between adjacent nodes in the graph. Each layer of MLP comprises a linear transformation and a Batch Normalization function, ensuring consistency in the input distribution across the learning process. Subsequently, GNNs update node representations as depicted in Eq. (5):

$$h_v^k = MLP^k\left(\left(1+\epsilon^{(k)}\right)\cdot h_v^{k-1} + \sum_{u\in\mathcal{N}(v)} h_u^{(k-1)}\right) \tag{5}$$

where h_v^k denotes the feature vector of node v in the k-th layer, $N(v)$ represents the set of neighboring nodes of node v, $\epsilon^{(k)}$ represents the parameters learnable in the k-th layer, aimed at adjusting the relative importance of the node's own features and those of its neighbors.

2. Fully Connected Layer: Following the extraction of feature vectors by MLP, the fully connected layer performs linear transformations on these features to make classification decisions, employing a dropout function to mitigate overfitting. The output of the linear function is denoted as the feature representation vector H_{G_i}. To derive the final classification result, H_{G_i} is mapped to the sample label space $H_{G_i} \in \mathbb{R}^C$, where C represents the number of video traffic types to be recognized. Finally, employing the softmax function yields the predicted probability vector y_{ic}, indicating the probability of G_i belonging to the video category c, as demonstrated in Eq. (6):

$$\hat{y}_{ic} = \text{Softmax}\left(H_{G_i}\right) \tag{6}$$

3. Loss Function: Cross-entropy serves as the loss function, apt for multi-class problems. It measures the difference between predicted labels and true labels, guiding the model towards accurate classification, as defined in Eq. (7):

$$\mathcal{L} = -\frac{1}{|X|}\sum_{i=1}^{|X|}\sum_{c=1}^{C} y_{ic}\log\left(\hat{y}_{ic}\right) \tag{7}$$

where $|X|$ denotes the number of training instances, y_{ic} denotes the ground truth label, $\hat{y}_{ic}$ represents the probability predicted by the model. This loss function quantifies the disparity between model predictions and true labels.

This architectural design of the GIN model equips it to capture intricate relationships and interactions between nodes in the graph structure, furnishing a robust theoretical and empirical foundation for video traffic classification. In video traffic identification, the GraphBurst model represents one video flow instance as a VIG, harnessing the potent graph processing capabilities of GIN to discern and classify diverse types of video traffic.

4 Experiment

This section focuses on evaluating the model's effectiveness. We start by outlining the experimental setup and describing the datasets used for evaluation. Subsequently, we discuss the optimization of hyperparameters and compare the model's performance in coarse-grained classification and fine-grained Classification tasks across different datasets.

4.1 Datasets

We utilized two self-collected datasets, D1 and D2, obtained from distinct network environments, for various experimental purposes. During data collection, we employed a host running the Edge browser to stream live videos, while Wireshark was used to capture the traffic. The collected data was divided into the training and testing sets in a 9:1 ratio. The collected traffic data was first segmented into flows based on packet five-tuple (protocol, source/destination IP addresses, source/destination ports), and then, a VIG was constructed on each flow.

1. D1 Dataset: The D1 dataset was created by streaming live videos under both wired and wireless network environments using a laptop with the Edge browser, primarily consisting of IP protocol traffic. It contains video traffic data of three classes, game, online chatting, and outdoor activities.
2. D2 Dataset: The D2 dataset, collected under 4G and 5G network conditions, which expands on the D1 dataset by further refining video traffic types into finer-grained categories. It incorporates a wider range of network protocols, including mixed IPv6 (TCP, UDP) and TCP flows, providing a closer approximation to real-world conditions. Chatting videos are divided into entertainment videos and general chatting videos based on actions such as dancing in entertainment videos. Similarly, gaming videos are categorized into online and standalone games. Additionally, shopping videos are included as this type is also a popular video type. We consider the D2 dataset to be a fine-grained dataset compared to the D1 dataset, designed specifically to capture more nuanced user behavior patterns.

Both D1 and D2 datasets collected here represent raw traffic datasets, as our model has the capability to extract video traffic from raw data by eliminating noise. For detailed dataset composition, refer to Table 2.

Table 2. The Composition of the Datasets

Dataset	Class	Number of flows
D1	Game	44905
	Chat	13960
	Outdoor	24506
D2	Entertainment	13925
	Chat	7182
	Online Game	21188
	Standalone Game	21345
	Shopping	9319

4.2 Parameter Tuning

It can be seen that the performance of the GraphBurst is potentially impacted by three types of parameters, GNN hyperparameter settings, burst sequence extraction parameters, and dataset scale. Therefore, we studied the impact of these parameters on classification accuracy and training time aiming at optimal parameter settings.

Table 3. Hyperparameters Selection for GraphBurst

Hyperparameters	Search Range	Final
Optimizer	[Adam, RMSProp, SGD]	Adam
Learning Rate	[0.0001, ..., 0.02]	0.001
Training Epochs	[5, ..., 300]	200
Batch Size	[5, ..., 300]	16
Activation Functions	[Tanh, Relu, Elu]	Relu
Dropout	[0, ..., 0.6]	0.5
Number of MLP layers	[1, ..., 10]	3
Number of Hidden Units	[0, ..., 100]	16
Graph Pooling Type	[Sum, Average]	Sum
Neighbor Pooling Type	[Sum, Average, Max]	Sum
BPS Window Size	[0.5, ..., 2]	1.5
Burst Detection THR	[0.5, ..., 3]	1.1
Smoothness Window Size	[2, ..., 5]	4

GNN Hyperparameter Settings: We conduct a search within predefined ranges for GNN hyperparameters, which are shown in Table 3. Table 4 illustrates the effect of varying the number of training epochs on classifier training time (CTT), test accuracy, GraphBurst achieved its optimal performance during the 200 epoches, with a classifier training time of 140.94 s and a peak testing accuracy of 0.917. During training, each hyperparameter is modified to estimate parameter gradients and determine whether to increase or decrease them. After this process, the top value of each parameter is selected as the final optimal combination of all hyperparameters. Accuracy serves as the performance metric, defined as the proportion of correctly classified video stream instances.

Table 4. Impact of the Number of Training Epochs on Classifier Training Time (CTT), Testing Accuracy of GraphBurst

Epochs	10	20	50	100	**200**	300
CTT (s)	36.15	22.51	77.21	89.74	**140.94**	262.12
Testing Accuracy	0.667	0.708	0.833	0.875	**0.917**	0.833

Burst Sequence Extraction Parameters: Burst sequence extraction from video traffic is a pivotal component of our model, involving key hyperparameters such as BPS window size, burst detection threshold, and smoothness window size. These parameters play a critical role in ensuring that the extracted burst sequences faithfully represent the semantic content embedded within the video traffic.

Our optimal parameters for burst sequence extraction are detailed in Table 3. The BPS window size is designed to segment the flow into regular intervals. For our experiments, it is set at 1.5 seconds per interval for extracting the BPS of downlink traffic, which encompasses all server response data. The burst detection threshold, denoted as parameter k in Eq. (2), is calibrated to effectively identify significant bursts, setting the stage for subsequent burst graph construction. In our setup, this threshold is established at 1.1. The smoothness window size, represented as parameter n in Eq. (1), dictates the level of smoothing applied. We have chosen a window size of $n = 4$ in our experiments to facilitate precise local adjustments and prevent excessive smoothing.

Table 5. Impact of Dataset Scale on Feature Extraction Time (FET), Classifier Training Time (CTT) and Accuracy of GraphBurst

Proportion (%)	20	40	**50**	80	100
FET (s)	52.31	53.13	**52.50**	53.19	54.31
CTT (s)	134.57	137.16	**136.58**	138.59	140.94
Accuracy	0.80	0.60	**0.875**	0.842	0.917

Dataset Scale Adjustments: To investigate the impact of dataset scale on the performance of GraphBurst, we varied the proportion of the original dataset to ensure robustness under different network conditions and to more accurately simulate real-world scenarios. We used the D1 dataset as our experimental dataset. Given a proportion value, for instance, 20%, we randomly selected 20% of the traffic from the D1 dataset to form a new dataset. Table 5 summarizes the impact of dataset scale on Feature Extraction Time (FET), Classifier Training Time (CTT), and the accuracy of GraphBurst. Remarkably, our model achieves an accuracy of 0.875 using only 50% of the training samples, with FET and CTT requiring only 52.5 s and 136.58 s, respectively. This indicates that it can learn sufficient graph representations from limited training data.

4.3 Comparison Experiment

To comprehensively evaluate the performance of GraphBurst, we employed seven typical methods for comparison, including traditional models based on statistical feature methods such as APPS and RandomForest, as well as deep learning methods like DFmaster, 2d-CNN, Lenet, Mobilenet, and Mobilenetv2. Each method was fine-tuned to achieve optimal accuracy on the evaluation dataset. As stated in the introduction, most research works of video traffic analysis focus on the identification of video titles. That is to say they concern on the specific identification of video traffic, but not the type classification. Therefore, there is no public video traffic type classification data set as far as we know, resulting that we have to use our data sets to test all the compared methods.

- AppScanner (APPS): Captures statistical features from packet sequences and utilizes a RandomForest classifier to identify encrypted or unencrypted traffic from mobile applications [19].
- Randomforest: Combine the video flow classification component of GraphBurst with the traditional machine learning model, Random Forest. This integration will enable the extraction of video traffic from mixed traffic streams and capture their statistical features. Finally, Random Forest will be used to classify the extracted video traffic.
- DFmaster: Simplifies network traffic traces into packet direction sequences and inputs them into a Convolutional Neural Network (CNN) for traffic classification [20].
- 2d-CNN: Transforms the first 1024 bytes of each packet into a 32x32 pixel grayscale image, facilitating intuitive traffic data classification using 2d-CNNs. [21]
- Lenet: Similar to the above method, converts packet data into a 28x28 pixel grayscale image and utilizes Lenet for classification [22] [23].
- Mobilenet: Converts the first 1024 bytes of each packet into a 224x224 pixel grayscale image and employs the lightweight convolutional neural network architecture Mobilenet for classification, optimized for mobile and embedded devices [24] [25].
- Mobilenetv2: Similar to Mobilenet, but with improvements such as the introduction of inverted residual structures for enhanced efficiency and performance optimization [26].

Table 6. Accuracy of Coarse-grained Classification

Method	APPS	RF	DF	2d-CNN	Lenet	Mobilenet	Mobilenetv2	**GraphBurst**
Accuracy	0.28	0.54	0.866	0.698	0.898	0.876	0.877	**0.917**

Table 7. Accuracy of Fine-grained Classification

Method	Lenet	Mobilenet	Mobilenetv2	**GraphBurst**
Accuracy	0.708	0.737	0.655	**0.75**

Two experiments were conducted to evaluate the performance of all the compared methods, using accuracy as the metric. The three-class task is considered coarse-grained, while the five-class task is viewed as finer-grained.**1) Coarse-grained Classification Model Comparison Experiment:** We employed ten-fold cross validation to train and test on the D1 dataset, comparing our model against statistical feature-based models such as AppScanner and RandomForest, along with deep learning models DF-master, 2d-CNN, lente, mobilenet, mobilenetv2. The experimental results can be seen in Table 6 and Fig. 4. **2) Fine-Grained Classification Model Comparison Experiment:** Building on Experiment 1, to enhance the finer-grained classification capabilities of GraphBurst, we implemented ten-fold cross-validation on the D2 dataset, extending the classification from three to five classes. This expansion enables a more detailed analysis of video user behavior. Furthermore, models such as DF, Apps, RM, and 2d-CNN showed less than optimal results in this five-class setup, hence, we employed advanced deep neural network-based models, including Lenet, Mobilenet, and Mobilenetv2. These models have exhibited superior performance in the classification of encrypted traffic. This experiment compared the five-class classification abilities of GraphBurst on the D2 dataset to identify more detailed user behaviors. Results of this experiment are presented in Table 7 and Fig. 4. From the experimental results, we can see some significant points as follows.

1. In the coarse-grained experiment, our model significantly outperformed all baseline models. The results demonstrate the superiority of using the VIG to represent traffic and transforming the traffic classification challenge into a graph classification problem. This capability has proven particularly useful for accurately classifying dynamic content such as video games and live streams, which often experience sudden bursts of data.
2. In the fine-grained classification comparison experiment, our model surpassed those based on deep learning, validating its effectiveness in tasks requiring finer-grained classification to better analyze video user behavior.
3. The superior performance of the GNN model in these experiments can be attributed to its graph-based approach, which naturally adapts better to network data structures than traditional methods. By converting traffic data into graph structures and utilizing Graph Neural Networks, we are able to leverage relational information between different data packets, an aspect often overlooked by traditional models. Compared to baseline models, our model displayed satisfactory performance in comparative experiments conducted on various datasets, confirming the robustness and effectiveness of our model in video traffic identification tasks across different network conditions.

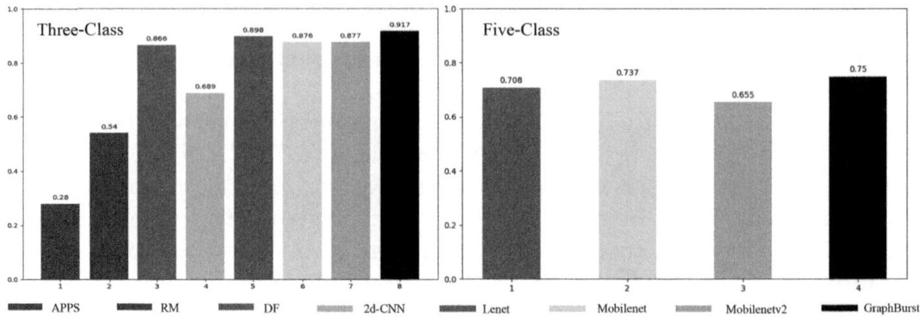

Fig. 4. The comparison of experimental accuracy in coarse-grained and fine-grained classification.

5 Conclusion

In this paper, we propose GraphBurst, a model based on burst sequences and graph neural networks. And effectively utilizes burst sequences to construct the VIG, thereby transforming video traffic identification into a graph classification challenge. We leverage Multi-Layer Perceptrons to develop a classifier based on Graph Neural Networks (GNNs). Our methodology is tested on real-world traffic data from diverse network environments, encompassing five types of video content, including on-demand live streaming, with over one hundred thousand streams. The experimental results show that: **1)**GraphBurst significantly outperformed baseline models in coarse-grained classification tasks, achieving 91.7% accuracy on the D1 dataset.**2)**The model demonstrated exceptional capability in fine-grained classification tasks, outperforming deep learning-based models in the five-class comparison experiment. **3)**GraphBurst displayed consistent performance across various network settings and video types, establishing its reliability and adaptability in real-world scenarios.

These results confirm the GraphBurst model's potential as an effective tool for network security, particularly adept at managing encrypted video traffic. In future work, we plan to extend the application of GraphBurst to encrypted video monitoring and user behavior identification. Additionally, we aim to broaden this approach to encompass other types of network traffic and further enhance its accuracy and interpretability.

Acknowledgements. This research was partially supported by Shandong Provincial Natural Science Foundation, China under Grant (No. ZR2021LZH002), Jinan Scientific Research Leader Studio, China under Grant (No.202228114), Shandong Provincial Key Projects of Basic Research, China under Grant (No. ZR-2022ZD01), Key Research Project of Quancheng Laboratory, China under Grant (No. QCLZD202303), and Research Project of Provincial Laboratory of Shandong, China under Grant (No. SYS202201).

References

1. Sandvine. Sandvine global internet phenomena report (2023)
2. Jiaxi, G., Wang, J., Zhiwen, Yu., Shen, K.: Traffic-based side-channel attack in video streaming. IEEE/ACM Trans. Networking **27**(3), 972–985 (2019)
3. Scheuerman, M.K., Jiang, J.A., Fiesler, C., Brubaker, J.R.: A framework of severity for harmful content online. Proc. ACM Hum.-Comput. Interact. **5**(CSCW2), 1–33 (2021)
4. Karagiannis, T., Papagiannaki, K., Faloutsos, M.: BLINC: multilevel traffic classification in the dark. In: Proceedings of the 2005 Conference on Applications, Technologies, Architectures, and Protocols for Computer Communications, pp. 229–240 (2005)
5. Li, H., He, Y., Sun, L., Cheng, X., Yu, J.: Side-channel information leakage of encrypted video stream in video surveillance systems. In: IEEE INFOCOM 2016-The 35th Annual IEEE International Conference on Computer Communications, pp. 1–9. IEEE (2016)
6. Dubin, R., Dvir, A., Pele, O., Hadar, O.: I know what you saw last minute-encrypted http adaptive video streaming title classification. IEEE Trans. Inf. Forensics Secur. **12**(12), 3039–3049 (2017)
7. Lin, X., Xiong, G., Gou, G., Li, Z., Shi, J., Jing, Yu.: ET-BERT: a contextualized datagram representation with pre-training transformers for encrypted traffic classification. In: Proceedings of the ACM Web Conference 2022, pp. 633–642 (2022)
8. Nasr, M., Houmansadr, A., Mazumdar, A.: Compressive traffic analysis: a new paradigm for scalable traffic analysis. In: Proceedings of the 2017 ACM SIGSAC Conference on Computer and Communications Security, pp. 2053–2069 (2017)
9. Schuster, R., Shmatikov, V., Tromer, E.: Beauty and the burst: remote identification of encrypted video streams. In: 26th USENIX Security Symposium (USENIX Security 2017), pp. 1357–1374 (2017)
10. Mangla, T., Halepovic, E., Ammar, M., Zegura, E.: Using session modeling to estimate http-based video QOE metrics from encrypted network traffic. IEEE Trans. Netw. Serv. Manage. **16**(3), 1086–1099 (2019)
11. Wassermann, S., Seufert, M., Casas, P., Gang, L., Li, K.: Let me decrypt your beauty: real-time prediction of video resolution and bitrate for encrypted video streaming. In: 2019 Network Traffic Measurement and Analysis Conference (TMA), pp. 199–200. IEEE (2019)
12. Saponas, T.S., Lester, J., Hartung, C., Agarwal, S., Kohno, T., et al.: Devices that tell on you: privacy trends in consumer ubiquitous computing. In: USENIX Security Symposium, pp. 55–70 (2007)
13. Khan, M.U.S., Bukhari, S.M.A.H., Khan, S.A., Maqsood, T.: ISP can identify youtube videos that you just watched. In: 2021 International Conference on Frontiers of Information Technology (FIT), pp. 1–6. IEEE (2021)
14. Reed, A., Kranch, M.: Identifying https-protected netflix videos in real-time. In: Proceedings of the Seventh ACM on Conference on Data and Application Security and Privacy, pp. 361–368 (2017)
15. Wu, H., Yu, Z., Cheng, G., Guo, S.: Identification of encrypted video streaming based on differential fingerprints. In: IEEE INFOCOM 2020-IEEE Conference on Computer Communications Workshops (INFOCOM WKSHPS), pp. 74–79. IEEE (2020)
16. Al-Naami, K., et al.: Adaptive encrypted traffic fingerprinting with bi-directional dependence. In: Proceedings of the 32nd Annual Conference on Computer Security Applications, pp. 177–188 (2016)

17. Li, Z., Chen, J., Ma, X., Du, M., Zhang, Z., Liu, Q.: A robust and accurate encrypted video traffic identification method via graph neural network. In: 2023 26th International Conference on Computer Supported Cooperative Work in Design (CSCWD), pp. 867–872. IEEE (2023)
18. Xu, K., Hu, W., Leskovec, J., Jegelka, S.: How powerful are graph neural networks? arXiv preprint arXiv:1810.00826 (2018)
19. Taylor, V.F., Spolaor, R., Conti, M., Martinovic, I.: Appscanner: automatic fingerprinting of smartphone apps from encrypted network traffic. In: 2016 IEEE European Symposium on Security and Privacy (EuroS&P), pp. 439–454. IEEE (2016)
20. Sirinam, P., Imani, M., Juarez, M., Wright, M.: Deep fingerprinting: undermining website fingerprinting defenses with deep learning. In: Proceedings of the 2018 ACM SIGSAC Conference on Computer and Communications Security, pp. 1928–1943 (2018)
21. Wang, W., Zhu, M., Wang, J., Zeng, X., Yang, Z.: End-to-end encrypted traffic classification with one-dimensional convolution neural networks. In: 2017 IEEE International Conference on Intelligence and Security Informatics (ISI), pp. 43–48. IEEE (2017)
22. Zhou, H., Wang, Y., Lei, X., Liu, Y.: A method of improved CNN traffic classification. In: 2017 13th International Conference on Computational Intelligence and Security (CIS), pp. 177–181. IEEE (2017)
23. LeCun, Y., Bottou, L., Bengio, Y., Haffner, P.: Gradient-based learning applied to document recognition. Proc. IEEE **86**(11), 2278–2324 (1998)
24. Wang, X., et al.: Evolutionary algorithm-based and network architecture search-enabled multiobjective traffic classification. IEEE Access **9**, 52310–52325 (2021)
25. Masum, M., Shahriar, H.: A transfer learning with deep neural network approach for network intrusion detection. Int. J. Intell. Comput. Res. **12**(1) (2021)
26. Sandler, M., Howard, A., Zhu, M., Zhmoginov, A., Chen, L.-C.: Mobilenetv2: inverted residuals and linear bottlenecks. In: Proceedings of the IEEE Conference on Computer Vision and Pattern Recognition, pp. 4510–4520 (2018)

KP-WF: Cross-Domain Few-Shot Website Fingerprinting

Lin Liu, Ziling Wei(✉), Shuhui Chen, Jinshu Su, and Yong Yuan

National University of Defense Technology, Changsha, China
{liulin18,weiziling,shchen,sjs,yuanyong}@nudt.edu.cn

Abstract. Website fingerprinting is emerging as a technique capable of compromising anonymous communication (such as Tor), which provides a way for forensic investigation of illegal activities in anonymous networks. However, current research makes critical assumptions about data collection, where the digital investigator needs to collect extensive user traffic data, and the data are required in the same domain.

In this paper, we propose a cross-domain few-shot method **KP-WF**, a **K**nowledge Fusion-based Two-Branch **P**rototypical Network **W**ebsite **F**ingerprinting method, to realize accurate website fingerprinting in a realistic scenario. With the proposed method, we reduce the digital investigators' dependence on auxiliary and target datasets through a prototypical network, addressing its inherent limitations in cross-domain scenarios by designing a novel knowledge fusion-based two-branch architecture. Additionally, the knowledge fusion module in the sub-branch empowers investigators to establish an advantage in targeted tasks. We conduct extensive experiments on 14 datasets to demonstrate the superiority of the proposed method in different scenarios. Experimental results show that in the most challenging 1-shot scenario, KP-WF achieves an accuracy improvement of more than 10% compared to the state-of-the-art method in the closed-world setting, and an improvement of 13% in open-world evaluation metrics. In addition, in the case of cross-dual-domain, KP-WF also shows the best performance.

Keywords: Website fingerprinting · Cross-domain · Few-shot · Prototypical network

1 Introduction

The dark web serves as a significant conduit for criminal activities, leveraging the Tor network [1] to provide a high degree of anonymity, which renders traditional digital forensic methods less effective [2]. However, when it comes to uncovering criminal activity on the dark web, forensics of illegal transactions and browsing of sensitive websites by criminals is essential. Investigators urgently need technology that can assist with forensics. Therefore, website fingerprinting (WF)

This work was supported by the National Natural Science Foundation of China under Grant No. 62202486, U22B2005, and 12102468.

S. Goel et al. (Eds.): ICDF2C 2024, LNICST 614, pp. 227–245, 2025.
https://doi.org/10.1007/978-3-031-89360-5_14

shows a particular value in this environment. Despite Tor being designed to counter traffic analysis, WF identifies specific websites visited by users by analyzing non-content features such as packet sizes and transmission directions. This technology does not decrypt data but identifies communicative behaviours through feature matching [3], thus enabling effective monitoring and forensics of the dark web without infringing on privacy. Consequently, researchers have formalized WF as a multi-class classification problem and have refined the machine learning algorithms used, achieving an accuracy rate exceeding 98% [4–9].

Unfortunately, existing effective WF methods suffer from two fatal flaws [4, 10,11]. (i) Data collection typically requires hundreds of days. However, in most website fingerprinting (WF) methods, it is imperative that the data be fresh, as using outdated data can lead to a significant decrease in accuracy, a phenomenon known as concept drift. (ii) When the investigator adds interested websites to the monitoring list, a considerable amount of time is required to re-collect data and retrain the model. It severely impacts the flexibility of the model. To address these issues, the few-shot WF method, which only requires a few data samples to train a new model, has been proposed.

In the context of few-shot WF methods, models are typically trained using auxiliary datasets in order to develop an effective feature extractor. Consequently, investigators only require a very small target dataset (1–20 samples) in order to fine-tune the feature extractor for monitoring a specific target website. It should be noted that the auxiliary datasets can be unrelated to the target monitoring websites. This enables investigators to switch target websites while only requiring a minimal number of samples from the new target dataset. However, most existing few-shot WF methods (for example, [11–13]) overlook two key problems that limit their usability. (i) In few-shot WF works, the datasets are referred to as cross-domain when the auxiliary and target datasets are collected under different domains (such as on different days or using different Tor browser bundles). In these circumstances, there is a noticeable reduction in the accuracy of the model [14]. However, such scenarios are common in real network environments. For example, in situations involving multiple users, investigators cannot expect the auxiliary dataset to match the environmental settings of each user. (ii) There is a significant demand for large-scale auxiliary datasets in many existing methods [12,13]. Updating the auxiliary dataset can reduce the decay in accuracy, so efforts should be made to minimize the size of the auxiliary dataset. Otherwise, it contradicts the original purpose of the few-shot WF method. Therefore, it holds significant relevance for digital forensics in real network environments to propose a WF method capable of effectively identifying users' web browsing behavior using a small auxiliary dataset and an extremely limited target dataset in cross-domain scenarios.

Our Work. To achieve this goal, we propose a new cross-domain few-shot WF method, KP-WF. The core of KP-WF can be summarized into three key ideas. *(i) We enhance few-shot learning capabilities using a prototypical network architecture* [15] *under the condition of using a small to medium-scale auxiliary dataset. This is the first attempt to use a prototypical network in the field of*

WF. (ii) We propose a knowledge fusion module that incorporates variable expert knowledge into the model, enhancing the flexibility of KP-WF. (iii) We design a novel knowledge fusion-based two-branch network architecture to mitigate the simplicity bias issue of the prototypical network in cross-domain scenarios. To demonstrate the effectiveness of KP-WF, we conduct extensive experiments on 14 datasets in different scenarios. All experiments consistently demonstrate the superiority of KP-WF over state-of-the-art methods.

The contributions of our work are three-fold:

1. We develop KP-WF, a novel WF method specifically designed for the cross-domain few-shot scenario with a small to medium-scale auxiliary dataset.
2. KP-WF utilizes a knowledge fusion-based two-branch prototypical network architecture, enabling its functionality in real-world few-shot scenarios where auxiliary and target datasets can be cross-domain. Moreover, KP-WF exhibits superior few-shot capabilities compared to existing methods, showing great performance even in the 1-shot scenario.
3. Extensive experiments demonstrate the superiority of KP-WF in various scenarios, including closed-world and open-world settings. Particularly in the 1-shot scenario, KP-WF outperforms the state-of-the-art method with up to a 10% increase in accuracy for closed-world experiments. In open-world experiments, there is an improvement of 13% in open-world evaluation metrics for KP-WF compared to the best baseline method. In addition, under the case of cross-dual-domain, KP-WF also shows the best performance.

2 Related Work

2.1 Traditional WF Methods

The fingerprint of a website represents a combination of its network traffic patterns (e.g., packet size) during the loading of the website's resources. Even with encrypted traffic, the fingerprints formed by these traffic patterns are unique. WF leverages the fingerprint of the target monitored website to identify whether a user accesses the target website by some anonymous communication tools (e.g. Tor) [3].

WF can be treated as a multi-classification problem, and consequently, numerous investigations have been conducted using machine learning (ML) [16–24]. Although ML-based WF methods have achieved high accuracy (over 90%) using 90 instances, all of these methods are based on manual feature engineering. In this case, the methods require a large amount of expert knowledge, and thus, they can lead to poor generalization due to biased feature selection. With the development of deep learning algorithms, researchers have introduced them into WF to address the limitations of ML-based WF methods. By automatically mining deep features, deep learning-based WF methods have achieved remarkably high accuracy (over 98%) [4–9] in the same scenarios and demonstrated the capability to effectively bypass the existing WTF-PAD defense [25]. However, DL-based WF methods encounter two challenges: relying on large-scale training data and inflexibility when changing the monitored websites. Relying on large-scale training data implies that the investigator needs to spend a long time collecting data. Meanwhile, limited by the problem of concept drift, the investigator must update the data from time to time to maintain the performance of the model, and it is unrealistic to continuously collect a large number of data. [4]). Furthermore, when the investigator tries to adjust the target website, significant time is required to re-collect data and retrain the model. In this case, the few-shot WF method has received much research attention.

2.2 Few-Shot WF Methods

To address the issues mentioned above, Sirinam et al. introduced the Triplet Network (TF), achieving accuracy rates ranging from 79.4% to 94.5% with only 1–20 training samples [11]. TF is based on the Few-Shot Learning (FSL) technique, which trains a highly adaptive feature extractor using an auxiliary dataset. When faced with different target websites, only a small number of samples are required to fine-tune the feature extractor, achieving high recognition accuracy. The few-shot WF method increases the flexibility of WF methods. In recent years, researchers have proposed various few-shot WF methods (FS-WF) such as HDA [26], MBL [12], WFBDC [14]. However, for HDA, Chen [12] has demonstrated that without knowledge transfer from other websites, it is only reasonably effective when a substantial number of training examples or shots (e.g. 10) are available. Meanwhile, MBL requires a large-scale auxiliary dataset. As shown in Zou's work [14], even for few-shot WF methods, a significant mismatch between the auxiliary and target datasets leads to a significant decrease in effectiveness. Therefore, in real-world applications, continuous updating and collection of the auxiliary dataset are necessary. However, it is impractical to collect large-scale auxiliary datasets frequently, and there is a need to consider the cross-domain few-shot WF method (CDFS-WF) to reduce the frequency of collecting auxiliary datasets. In summary, it is imperative to simultaneously minimize the sizes of both the auxiliary and target datasets in FS-WF. In this context, TF [11] and WFBDC [14] have been proposed. For TF, it is representative of FS-WF due to its low cost and high efficiency. As for WFBDC, it is the only research work targeting CDFS-WF and has achieved excellent results. TF and WFBDC represent the state-of-the-art (SOTA) methods.

3 Threat Model

The threat model is illustrated in Fig. 1. In the threat model, users access websites through the Tor network to realize anonymity. The investigator tries to monitor the browsing behaviour of the website by the WF. The investigators' position to collect the client's encrypted network traffic can be anywhere between the user's client and the Tor entry node (e.g., a compromised router or Internet server provider). Additionally, the investigator may need to target multiple users, reflecting the possibility of users employing different environmental settings, such as the Tor browser bundle (TBB). The investigator can only use the network traffic to infer whether they are accessing a specific website, without the capability to actively delay or discard network traffic. It ensures that the process of digital forensics remains covert. Simultaneously, to ensure the availability of the forensics, in our threat model, the investigator only collects a small to medium-scale auxiliary dataset in advance. In addition, the website samples of the auxiliary dataset do not need to be the same as the target websites. The investigator collects only 1–3 samples for each target website during forensics. It is necessary to note that this auxiliary dataset can be collected in advance and needs to target different users, making it potentially cross-domain with the target dataset.

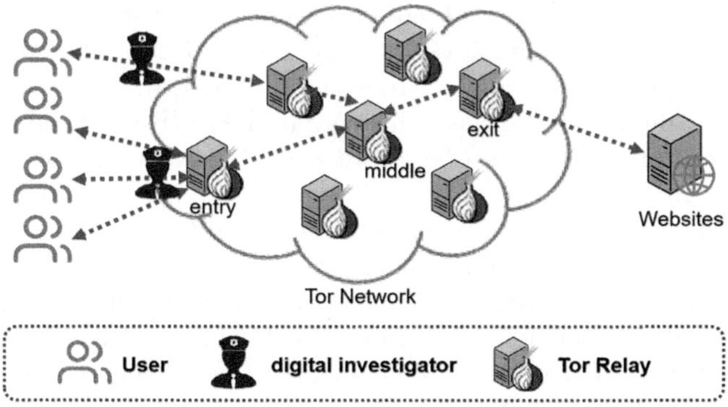

Fig. 1. The threat model of Website Fingerprinting

Our threat model is more challenging than the existing few-shot WF models [11–13], which relax some critical assumptions about data collection, making it more representative of real-world scenarios. This is primarily reflected in the following three aspects. (i) *Limited use of a small to medium-scale auxiliary dataset.* Considering the hardware constraints typically faced by ordinary investigators, it can facilitate the collection and updating of datasets. (ii) *Potential cross-domain nature of auxiliary and target datasets.* Since the investigator deals with multiple users and the process of data collection is not instantaneous, this setting is pervasive, allowing a more realistic representation of the scenario. (iii) *Collection of only 1 to 3 samples for each target website.* Considering the timeliness of the target dataset, the requirement for the number of samples should be extremely low. In other words, this setting allows forensics to be easily performed in a real network. However, this makes the adjustment of the feature extractor more challenging.

Similarly to the existing literature [4,6,11,14,27], we consider both open-world and closed-world scenarios. The closed-world scenario represents a situation where the investigator has prior knowledge of all websites that users might access, while the open-world scenario involves users potentially accessing websites unknown to the investigator. Obviously, the open-world setting is more realistic [10], but the closed-world setting remains an important indicator to evaluate the effectiveness of the method. Therefore, we will carry out experiments in both scenarios.

4 Design of KP-WF

4.1 Overview

As discussed in Sects. 1 and 2, the effectiveness of previous WF methods is limited by some issues such as inflexibility in changes of monitored websites, large-scale data requirements, and weak cross-domain capabilities, which limits their practical deployment. To address these issues, we propose KP-WF.

As illustrated in Fig. 2, KP-WF trains a powerful feature extractor to address these challenges. KP-WF employs an episode-based training approach (meta training), aiming to enable the feature extractor to "learn" how to handle similar tasks in data-hungry scenarios. This enables KP-WF to quickly adapt to the changes of monitored websites (details in Sect. 4.2). During each episode, KP-WF randomly samples the support and query sets from the auxiliary datasets. Considering the diverse prior knowledge present in different real-world scenarios, the query set will be augmented with expert knowledge through a modular tailored traffic augmentation module (details in Sect. 4.3). The support and query sets' samples will be input into the prototypical network (ProtoNet) for extracting high-dimensional features. KP-WF utilizes the augmented set to establish an additional sub-branch network, addressing the simplicity bias issue of the ProtoNet to enhance the performance under cross-domain scenarios (details in Sect. 4.4). The loss design is crucial to constrain the main branch using the sub-branch (details in Sect. 4.5). KP-WF optimizes the feature extractor of the main branch by computing the loss based on the features of the query set, the augmented set, and the prototypes. The sub-branch is optimized through Exponential Moving Average (EMA).

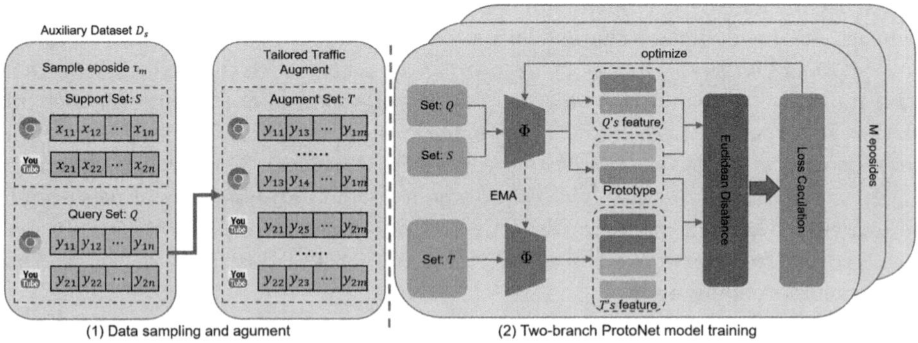

Fig. 2. The overview of Knowledge-fusion Two-branch ProtoNet WF model training

4.2 Data Organization

The WF can be regarded as a multi-classification problem. We input a traffic trace (x) and predict the output, indicating which website fingerprint (W) can be matched with the trace. For most privacy-enhancing technologies, the WF can leverage information such as packet size and direction as the input. However, when using Tor for network browsing, all packets are fixed-sized cells. Therefore, we only consider the direction information of the packets as input. To formalize the input, we use $+1$ to represent an outgoing packet and -1 to represent an incoming packet. The length of each trace is fixed to 5000, following the setup of previous works [4,6]. Traces exceeding this length are truncated, and those less than 5000 are padded with zeros at the end. Therefore, the final input is a sequence of length 5000, for example ($x = [+1, -1, ..., 0, 0]_{5000}$).

To address the challenges of dependency on large-scale datasets and inflexibility in adapting to the changes of monitored websites, KP-WF employs Few-Shot Learning (FSL) techniques as a solution.

As we can see in Fig. 3, it is necessary to utilize both auxiliary dataset D_s and target dataset D_t to achieve this goal. The auxiliary dataset is randomly sampled into M classification episodes. The episode is based on a concept called N-way k-shot, meaning that the classification task in this episode involves N websites, and each website has k training samples. Therefore, the samples in τ_m will be further divided into the support set S_m and the query set Q_m. S_m is used to train the feature extractor Φ, while Q_m is used to evaluate the effectiveness of this classification task. Through large numbers of episodes M, Φ is tuned to perform well on each randomly selected classification task. Formally, it can be defined as follows:

$$S_m = \{(x_i, n_i) \mid n_i \in [0, N)\}_{i=1}^{N*k} \quad (1)$$

$$Q_m = \{(x_i, n_i) \mid n_i \in [0, N)\}_{i=1}^{N*q} \quad (2)$$

$$S_m \cup Q_m = \tau_m, S_m \cap Q_m = \phi \quad (3)$$

$$m \in [1, M], \tau_m \in D_s. \quad (4)$$

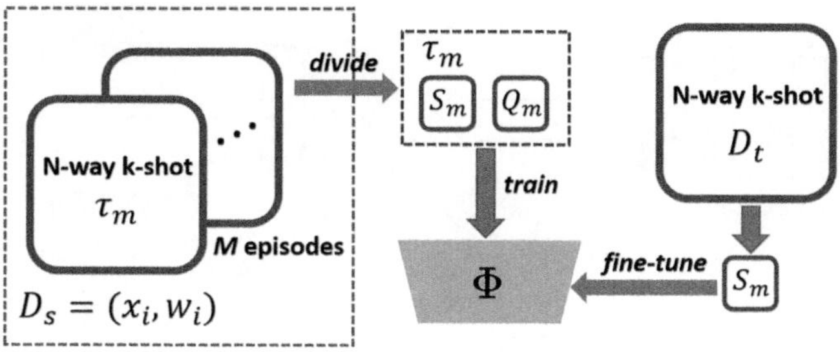

Fig. 3. Basic frame diagram for few-shot WF methods

After meta training, Φ can quickly adapt to new tasks with a small number of samples from the support set. Therefore, when an investigator collects the target dataset, it only needs to collect k traces for each website. Note that the website between D_s and D_t can be disjoint. Furthermore, when D_s and D_t are in different environments, it is referred to as the cross-domain few-shot website fingerprinting (CDFS-WF).

4.3 Tailored Traffic Augmentation

Unlike typical FSL technologies, KP-WF incorporates an additional augmented set alongside the support set and query set, based on the following two key observations. (i) In real-world scenarios, additional prior knowledge is available. Investigators often possess more specific prior knowledge than was considered during the design of the method. In such cases, the modular tailored traffic augmentation module can incorporate expert knowledge into the training of the feature extractor in the form of enhancement strategies, thus enhancing the performance of KP-WF. (ii) Neural networks in WF methods latch to the simplest feature in few-shot scenarios. A newly proposed defense method, FRONT [28], summarized that some of the most effective WF methods [19,22] primarily focus on the features of the FRONT part of each trace. By obtaining crops from the query set, the feature extractor is forced to extract effective features even without the FRONT part of the trace. Therefore, in this module, KP-WF will crop the traces from the query set and simulate variations on these crops according to a specific strategy (named knowledge fusion).

After several rounds of adjustments, we crop each trace into six crops, with three of them undergoing additional adjustments using specific strategies. The length of each crop is fixed at 1500. However, for comparative experiments, we only use the strategy with traffic variations induced by the Transmission Control Protocol (TCP) reliable transmission as shown in Fig. 4 to avoid undue influence of prior knowledge on experimental fairness.

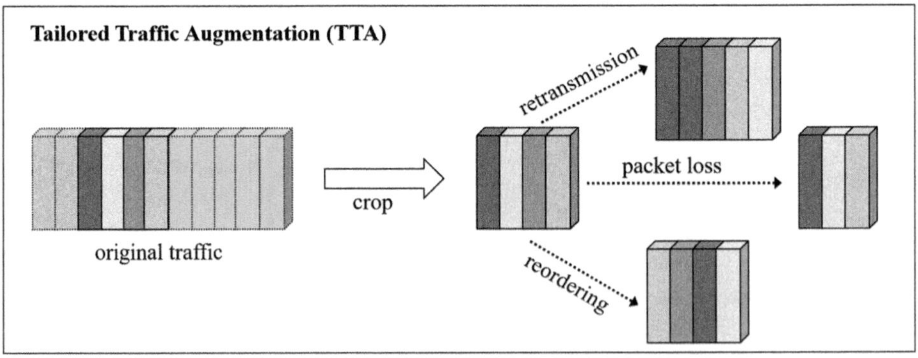

Fig. 4. The strategy of the TCP reliable transmission

4.4 Two-Branch Architecture Building

Aiming to learn few-shot classification capabilities from a small to medium-scale auxiliary dataset, ProtoNet [15] is introduced in KP-WF. The core idea is to achieve FSL by learning prototypes for each class. Given traces from a support set, KP-WF will feed them into the feature extractor to calculate the high-dimensional features. Based on these features, prototypes c_n for each class are computed. Then, the Euclidean distance D_i between the query set's features and these prototypes will be calculated, which is used for the classification and loss computation. Formally, prototypes are defined as follows:

$$c_n = \frac{1}{k}\sum_{i=1}^{k} \Phi(x_i) \quad where\ (x_i, n_i) \in S_m, n_i \in [0, N) \tag{5}$$

$$D_i = \sqrt{\sum_{j=1}^{d} (x_{ij}, c_{ij})^2} \quad where (x_i, n_i) \in Q_m \tag{6}$$

However, ProtoNet is not suitable for CDFS-WF tasks directly. It has been shown that its performance degrades significantly when faced with tasks in a new domain. This is attributed to its susceptibility to the problem of simplicity bias. In other words, it tends to rely on certain simple features that are sufficient to discriminate a small number of classes in the meta training task within a source domain, while ignoring complex semantic features [29–32]. To alleviate this issue, establishing a sub-branch containing crops from the original sample to constrain the main branch can be effective [29].

Therefore, the knowledge fusion-based two-branch architecture is proposed in KP-WF. As shown in Fig. 2(2), a main branch is established to extract global features from traces, while a sub-branch is set up to learn local features from the augmented set. Note that the samples in the augment set are cropped from traces in the query set and contain only a portion of a trace. In addition, these local crops do not necessarily contain certain biased abbreviation features. By optimizing the loss between the augment set, the query set, and prototypes, the feature extractor is prevented from focusing only on certain local features of a trace. By treating the original trace as the primary feature and local crops as constraints, KP-WF can embed richer semantic information into the final global feature representation. This approach has been shown to be more domain-invariant [33–36].

4.5 Loss Design

In order to extract meaningful information from both the main branch and the sub-branch in the network architecture, the loss computation is crucial. Our goal is to constrain the network with sub-sequences while preserving the original sequence's features and incorporating expert knowledge from the sub-sequences. Therefore, the first step is to compute the loss between the original traces and the labels, which is used as the primary loss. It ensures the semantic correctness of our original traces' features. We use a cross-entropy-based approach, following the ProtoNet paradigm, to compute the global loss.

$$Loss_{orig} = \sum_{i=1}^{N*q} H(D_i, n_i) \tag{7}$$

where H means the cross-entropy, D_i means the Euclidean distance of the query set belongs to class i, $Loss_{orig}$ means the loss value between the original traces and labels.

It is imperative to ensure that the predictions of the crops and the original traces remain consistent in order to prevent the feature extractor from latching onto the simplest feature. Therefore, we apply the principles of cross-entropy to constrain the high-dimensional feature distance between the original traces and the crops. However, due to the possible extreme numerical values during the softmax computation in high-dimensional feature space, we adjust it using the temperature coefficient as follows.

$$Loss_{crop} = -\sum_{i=1}^{N*q} \frac{1}{L} \sum_{l=1}^{L} \sigma\left(\frac{D_{i,l}}{T}\right)^{-\sigma\left(\frac{D_i}{T}\right)} \tag{8}$$

where σ is the softmax function, $D_{i,l}$ means the Euclidean distance of the l-th crop, $Loss_{crop}$ means the loss value between the local crops and original traces.

In [29,37], it has been pointed out that enforcing consistency only between original traces and their corresponding sub-sequences can lead to the model collapse. Therefore, it is also necessary to constrain the distance between the crops and other original traces within the same category. This is essential for extracting semantic information across samples.

$$Loss_{diff} = -\sum_{i=1}^{N*q} \frac{1}{L} \sum_{l=1}^{L} \sigma\left(\frac{D_{i,l}}{T}\right)^{-\sigma\left(\frac{D_j}{T}\right)}, i \neq j \tag{9}$$

where $Loss_{diff}$ means the loss value between crops and other traces of the same category.

To enable the feature extractor to learn more domain-transferable semantic features, we jointly optimize the feature extractor using these three loss values.

$$Loss_{kp} = Loss_{orig} + \alpha \cdot Loss_{crop} + \beta \cdot Loss_{diff} \tag{10}$$

$Loss_{kp}$ refers to the final loss used for optimizing the feature extractor, α and β are the hyperparameters.

In summary, during the meta training, we use $Loss_{kp}$ to tune the feature extractor in the main branch and use EMA to tune the parameters in the sub-branch. Once training is complete, there is no need for further fine-tuning in the target domain.

5 Experimental Setup

5.1 Datasets

To evaluate the effectiveness of KP-WF, we conduct extensive experiments on several publicly available datasets. The details are as follows:

DS-19 datasets [28]: The DS-19 dataset was collected by Gong et al. in 2019 during experiments on the FRONT defense method. It is the most recent available dataset to date. The dataset consists of traces from 100 visits to the home pages of the Alexa Top 100 websites collected using the TBB v8.5a7. In addition, the authors provided the method to deploy the FRONT defense method on this dataset, from which we generated the DS-19-FRONT dataset. Therefore, for the DS-19 dataset, we used the following categories of data:

- **DS-19$_{\mathbf{100}}$:** 100 Websites * 100 Instances
- **DS-19$_{\mathbf{100,FRONT}}$:** 100 Websites * 100 Instances with FRONT defense method

AWF datasets [4]: The AWF dataset was collected by Rimmer et al. in 2017 during the Automated Website Fingerprinting (AWF) experiments. This is the largest dataset currently available. It includes traces from monitored and unmonitored websites, collected using TBB v6.5. This dataset has two subsets, namely AWF_{900} and AWF_{400K}. In AWF_{900}, Rimmer et al. performed thousands of visits to the top 1200 Alexa websites, ultimately selecting 900 effective websites. Each website was subjected to 2500 full visits. Considering our previous setting that auxiliary datasets should be limited to a small to medium scale, we utilize only 100 instances for each website. In addition, to assess the performance of the method at different sampling time intervals, the authors revisited 200 sites from the AWF_{900} dataset after 3 days, 10 days, 14 days, 28 days, and 42 days, creating five additional datasets, AWF_{200_3d}, AWF_{200_10d}, AWF_{200_14d}, AWF_{200_28d}, and AWF_{200_42d}. AWF_{400K} is the dataset utilized to evaluate performance in an open-world scenario, representing a single network visit from 400,000 websites.

- **$\mathbf{AWF_{900}}$:** 900 Websites * 100 Instances
- **$\mathbf{AWF_{400k}}$:** 400000 Websites * 1 Instance
- **$\mathbf{AWF_{200\_n}}$:** 200 Websites * 100 Instances for n days after AWF_{900}

Wang$_{100}$ datasets [19]: The $Wang_{100}$ dataset was collected by Wang et al. in 2013 during experiments for Wa-KNN [19]. Wang et al. used TBB v3.5 to make 90 visits to the home pages of 100 websites. We use the $Wang_{100}$ dataset exclusively for the cross-domain experimental validation.

A brief summary of the datasets is given in Table 1.

Table 1. All datasets used for evaluation

Dataset	Categories	Instances	Raw Dataset	Provider
DS-19_{100}	100	100	DS-19	[28]
DS-$19_{100,FRONT}$	100	100	DS-19	[28]
AWF_{900}	900	100	AWF_{900}	[4]
AWF_{200_3d}	200	100	AWF_{900}	[4]
AWF_{200_10d}	200	100	AWF_{900}	[4]
AWF_{200_14d}	200	100	AWF_{900}	[4]
AWF_{200_28d}	200	100	AWF_{900}	[4]
AWF_{200_42d}	200	100	AWF_{900}	[4]
$Wang_{100}$	100	90	$Wang_{100}$	[19]
AWF_{9k}	9000	1	AWF_{400k}	[4]
AWF_{50k}	50000	1	AWF_{400k}	[4]
AWF_{100k}	100000	1	AWF_{400k}	[4]
AWF_{200k}	200000	1	AWF_{400k}	[4]
AWF_{400k}	400000	1	AWF_{400k}	[4]

5.2 Implementation Details

Meta Training: In the setting of the meta training, we train the network for 200 epochs. Each epoch during the meta training involved sampling for 50 episodes. For the AWF dataset, we set the number of classes to 100, as it has a sufficient number of website categories. However, for dataset DS-19_{100} and $Wang_{100}$, we use 20 classes for training. During the meta training, we use 5 samples for the support set of each website and set the number of samples of the query set to 15.

Evaluation: Similarly, during the evaluation phase, we use 100 classes for the AWF dataset and 20 classes for DS-19_{100} and $Wang_{100}$. To adjust the feature extractor, we only use 1–3 samples per website and evaluate using 15 samples. This means that KP-WF only needs 1–3 samples for classification in the target domain. We perform 30 evaluation rounds in each experiment and average the results for the final evaluation.

Baseline: In the evaluation, we take TF [11] and WFBDC [14] as the baseline. TF is known for its classic nature and outstanding performance on the FS-WF task. The WFBDC is designed for the CDFS-WF task. These two methods are the SOTA approaches according to the defined threat model.

6 Evaluation

In the evaluation of the closed-world scenario, we will conduct experiments in the following settings, including few-shot scenario, cross-time-domain few-shot scenario, cross time and Tor browser bundle domain (cross-dual-domain) few-shot scenario, and few-shot scenario with defense deployment.

6.1 Closed-World Few-Shot Website Fingerprinting

To evaluate the performance under the few-shot case in the closed-word environment, we conduct experiments using the AWF_{900} dataset. We evaluate it in two different scenarios. (i) *Category overlap and sample disjoint.* It means that both training and testing included all categories in AWF_{900}, but with different samples. In this scenario, during the meta training, each category has 60 samples, and during testing, 40 samples per category are used. (ii) *Category disjoint and sample disjoint.* This means that the test categories are new categories that were not seen during the meta training. We also use the AWF_{900} dataset, with 80% of the categories used for meta training and the remaining 20% used for testing. In this scenario, both training and testing involve 100 samples.

Result. As shown in Table 2, regardless of the used method, results are poor in the case of non-overlapping categories. This means that the difficulty of classification increases when the categories are disjoint. Similarly, as the number of support samples in the target domain increases, the accuracy of the methods improves significantly. However, KP-WF consistently outperforms the baseline methods. In the 1-shot scenario, KP-WF achieves a significant improvement of 10.5% and 9% accuracy over WFBDC in two separate experiments. In both the sample overlap and disjoint scenarios, KP-WF achieves over 90% accuracy in the 1-shot setting.

Table 2. Comparison of the accuracy for few-shot WF methods in closed world scenario with AWF_{900} datasets

Setting	Category overlap			Category disjoint		
Method	KP-WF	WFBDC	TF	KP-WF	WFBDC	TF
1-shot	**94.86**	84.52	79.56	**90.77**	81.01	71.30
2-shot	**96.57**	90.41	86.52	**93.14**	88.92	81.07
3-shot	**96.68**	93.41	90.53	**94.07**	91.51	85.21

6.2 Closed-World Few-Shot Website Fingerprinting with Cross-Time-Domain

Cross-time-domain means a time gap between the collection of the auxiliary and target datasets, which better reflects real-world settings. The AWF_{200} dataset provides an ideal testing condition for this scenario. However, unlike other works [12–14], we do not restrict our training to the 200 categories included in the AWF_{200}. Instead, we use 900 categories from AWF_{900} for training. Hence,

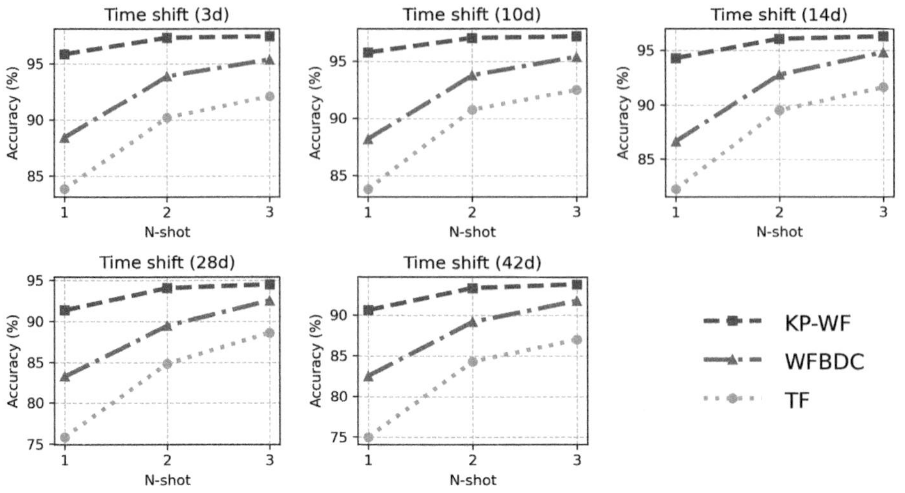

Fig. 5. Comparison of the accuracy for cross-time-domain few-shot WF methods in closed world scenario with AWF_{900} and AWF_{200_n}

the model must learn the classification ability for the other 700 classes. Obviously, this scenario is more stringent.

Result. The experimental results are presented in Fig. 5. It can be observed that KP-WF consistently outperforms the other two baseline methods in all scenarios, with sampling intervals ranging from 3 days to 42 days. In the 1-shot scenario, KP-WF achieves 8% to 10% higher accuracy than WFBDC. In addition, as shown in Fig. 5, as the time intervals increase, the performance of all methods decreases slightly, but KP-WF consistently maintains an accuracy above 90%.

6.3 Closed-World Few-Shot Website Fingerprinting with Cross-Dual-Domain

In [14], it has considered the cross-dual-domain scenario and proposed an approach called WFBDC. The cross-dual-domain scenario is more suitable for the real network but comes with increased difficulty in website identification. In this case, there may be a time gap of several years between the auxiliary and target datasets. In addition, the browser bundle used during data collection could also be different. Adhering to this setup, we conduct experiments using three datasets, DS-19_{100}, AWF_{900}, and $Wang_{100}$.

In our experiments, we use AWF900 as an auxiliary dataset and perform evaluations on DS-19_{100} and $Wang_{100}$. The collection of $Wang_{100}$ predates AWF_{900}, while DS-19_{100} was collected after AWF_{900}.

Result. The experimental results, as shown in Fig. 6, show that the performance of KP-WF consistently surpasses that of TF, which is only designed for few-shot

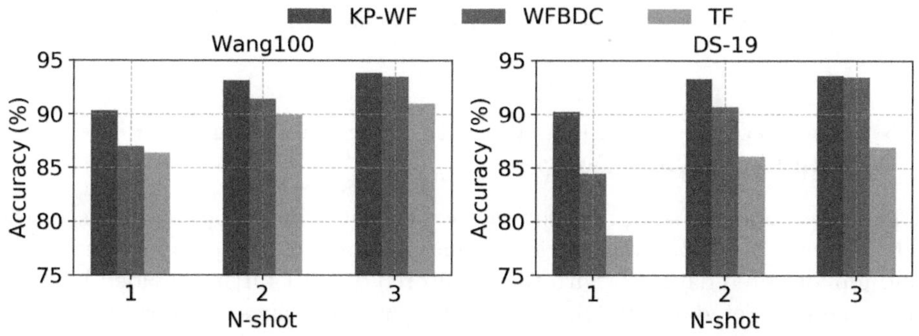

Fig. 6. Comparison of the accuracy for cross-dual-domain few-shot WF methods in closed world scenario with AWF_{900}, $Wang_{100}$ and DS-19_{100}

scenarios. There is a noticeable improvement in identification accuracy. Even for WFBDC, which is designed for cross-domain scenarios, only approaches the performance of KP-WF in the 3-shot setting, while it falls 5% below KP-WF in the 1-shot scenario. It is essential to note that KP-WF does not incorporate expert knowledge specifically for the cross-dual-domain scenario.

6.4 Closed-World Few-Shot Website Fingerprinting Against Defense

The FRONT defense method is the latest and most reliable defense approach in the field of WF [28]. Therefore, we utilize the official implementation of FRONT and generate DS-$19_{100,FRONT}$ based on DS-19_{100}. We conduct experiments using 80% of the samples as the auxiliary dataset and 20% as the target dataset.

Table 3. Comparison of the accuracy for few-shot WF methods in closed world defended scenario with DS-$19_{100,FRONT}$

Metrics	Accuracy			F1 score		
Method	KP-WF	WFBDC	TF	KP-WF	WFBDC	TF
1-shot	**82.53**	76.85	77.23	**0.8207**	0.7490	0.7622
2-shot	**87.58**	85.23	85.89	**0.8756**	0.8448	0.8579
3-shot	**88.80**	87.84	87.90	**0.8880**	0.8742	0.8765

Result. The experimental results, as shown in Table 3, show that KP-WF outperforms the other two methods in all scenarios, particularly in the 1-shot scenario where there is a notable improvement of 4.5%. Compared to experiments in which the method is not deployed, the performance of the methods decreases by more than 10%. Thus, it can be inferred that the FRONT defense method is effective. However, even under the FRONT defense, KP-WF remains the most effective.

6.5 Open-World Few-Shot Website Fingerprinting with Cross-Time-Domain

Following the above setup, we conduct experiments in the open-world scenario. The dataset used for open-world evaluation must be divided into monitored and unmonitored datasets, with the monitored dataset further divided into auxiliary and target datasets. In this experiment, we choose a more demanding configuration than other few-shot methods in open-world evaluation [11–14]. We use AWF_{900} as the auxiliary dataset, AWF_{200_42d} as the target dataset and AWF_{400k} as the unmonitored dataset. Wang reveals that concept drift leads to more severe performance degradation in an open-world setting [9]. In addition, using AWF_{900} as the auxiliary dataset requires a feature extractor with stronger generalization capabilities compared to using AWF_{200_0d}. At the same time, for the unmonitored dataset, we evaluate the KP-WF method using subsets provided by the official dataset, including AWF_{9k}, AWF_{50k}, AWF_{100k}, AWF_{200k}, and AWF_{400k}, assessing the variation in the performance of KP-WF under the dynamic growth of the unmonitored dataset.

Table 4. Comparison of the AUC_2 and AUC_m for cross-time-domain few-shot WF methods in open world scenario with AWF_{900}, AWF_{200_42d} and AWF_{400k}

#	Method	1-shot		2-shot		3-shot	
		AUC_2	AUC_m	AUC_2	AUC_m	AUC_2	AUC_m
9k	KP-WF	**0.931**	**0.862**	**0.935**	**0.891**	**0.940**	**0.904**
	WFBDC	0.856	0.756	0.902	0.839	0.918	0.869
	TF	0.500	0.005	0.816	0.736	0.850	0.778
50k	KP-WF	**0.933**	**0.868**	**0.936**	**0.894**	**0.934**	**0.896**
	WFBDC	0.839	0.732	0.895	0.831	0.925	0.871
	TF	0.500	0.005	0.807	0.719	0.842	0.771
100k	KP-WF	**0.931**	**0.864**	**0.938**	**0.899**	**0.939**	**0.904**
	WFBDC	0.829	0.732	0.895	0.831	0.925	0.871
	TF	0.500	0.005	0.812	0.723	0.854	0.779
200k	KP-WF	**0.931**	**0.860**	**0.934**	**0.891**	**0.936**	**0.895**
	WFBDC	0.841	0.739	0.897	0.832	0.920	0.865
	TF	0.500	0.005	0.811	0.727	0.851	0.774
400k	KP-WF	**0.930**	**0.864**	**0.935**	**0.888**	**0.936**	**0.897**
	WFBDC	0.848	0.767	0.906	0.838	0.922	0.869
	TF	0.500	0.005	0.802	0.711	0.847	0.767

Result. The experimental results are presented in Table 4. From the comparison of the data, we can draw the following conclusions.

1. KP-WF is significantly better than TF and WFBDC in all experimental evaluations in all settings.
2. In all experimental settings, KP-WF consistently achieved AUC_2 scores of 0.93 or higher and AUC_m scores exceeding 0.86.
3. In the 1-shot experimental settings, KP-WF and WFBDC do not have the effect of crashing. Meanwhile, the AUC_m score of KP-WF is improved by more than 0.1 compared to WFBDC, and the AUC_2 score is improved by 0.05–0.10, no matter the size of the unmonitored dataset is.
4. The performance of KP-WF is similar in unmonitored datasets of different sizes, which shows that it is also applicable to real networks where the category of the unmonitored class is uncontrollable.

7 Conclusion

In this paper, we focus on the more realistic scenario of cross-domain few-shot website fingerprint methods with small to medium-scale auxiliary datasets and propose an effective method, KP-WF. KP-WF mitigates the assumptions associated with data collection and eliminates the unrealistic requirement that auxiliary and target datasets must belong to the same domain. Through the meta learning, our method allows the investigator to quickly adapt the monitoring of websites in practice. The accuracy in cross-domain few-shot scenarios can be improved by utilizing a knowledge fusion-based two-branch prototypical network architecture. We conduct extensive experiments using several publicly available datasets. All experimental results show that KP-WF performs better than SOTA methods, with a significant improvement observed in the 1-shot experiments. In the future, we plan to extend the few-shot work to the multi-tab domain, aiming to achieve website fingerprinting methods under complex background traffic by performing multi-object detection on traces.

References

1. Dingledine, R., Mathewson, N., Syverson, P.F.: Tor: the second-generation onion router. In: USENIX Security Symposium, vol. 4, pp. 303–320 (2004)
2. Moore, D., Rid, T.: Cryptopolitik and the darknet. Survival **58**(1), 7–38 (2016)
3. Wagner, D., Schneier, B., et al.: Analysis of the SSL 3.0 protocol. In: The Second USENIX Workshop on Electronic Commerce Proceedings, vol. 1, pp. 29–40 (1996)
4. Rimmer, V., Preuveneers, D., Juarez, M., Van Goethem, T., Joosen, W.: Automated website fingerprinting through deep learning. In: Network and Distributed System Security Symposium (2017)
5. Abe, K., Goto, S.: Fingerprinting attack on tor anonymity using deep learning (2016)

6. Sirinam, P., Imani, M., Juarez, M., Wright, M.: Deep fingerprinting: undermining website fingerprinting defenses with deep learning. In: Proceedings of the 2018 ACM SIGSAC Conference on Computer and Communications Security, pp. 1928–1943 (2018)
7. Rahman, M.S., Sirinam, P., Mathews, N., Gangadhara, K.G., Wright, M.K.: Tik-tok: the utility of packet timing in website fingerprinting attacks. Proc. Priv. Enhancing Technol. **2020**, 5–24 (2019)
8. Bhat, S., David, L., Kwon, A., Devadas, S.: Var-CNN: a data-efficient website fingerprinting attack based on deep learning. Proc. Priv. Enhancing Technol. **292–310**, 2018 (2019)
9. Wang, Y., Haitao, X., Guo, Z., Qin, Z., Ren, K.: snWF: website fingerprinting attack by ensembling the snapshot of deep learning. IEEE Trans. Inf. Forensics Secur. **17**, 1214–1226 (2022)
10. Juarez, M., Afroz, S., Acar, G., Diaz, C., Greenstadt, R.: A critical evaluation of website fingerprinting attacks. In: Proceedings of the 2014 ACM SIGSAC Conference on Computer and Communications Security (2014)
11. Sirinam, P., Mathews, N., Rahman, M.S., Wright, M.K.: Triplet fingerprinting: more practical and portable website fingerprinting with n-shot learning. In: Proceedings of the 2019 ACM SIGSAC Conference on Computer and Communications Security (2019)
12. Chen, M., Wang, Y., Zhu, X.: Few-shot website fingerprinting attack with meta-bias learning. Pattern Recognit. **130**, 108739 (2022)
13. Zhou, Q., Wang, L., Zhu, H., Tong, L.: Few-shot website fingerprinting attack with cluster adaptation. Comput. Netw. **229**, 109780 (2023)
14. Zou, H., Su, J., Wei, Z., Chen, S., Zhao, B.: An efficient cross-domain few-shot website fingerprinting attack with brownian distance covariance. Comput. Netw. **219**, 109461 (2022)
15. Snell, J., Swersky, K., Zemel, R.: Prototypical networks for few-shot learning. In: Advances in Neural Information Processing Systems, vol. 30 (2017)
16. Dyer, K.P., Coull, S.E., Ristenpart, T., Shrimpton, T.: Peek-a-boo, i still see you: why efficient traffic analysis countermeasures fail. IEEE (2012)
17. Cai, X., Zhang, X.C., Joshi, B., Johnson, R.: Touching from a distance: website fingerprinting attacks and defenses. In: Computer and Communications Security (2012)
18. Wang, T., Goldberg, I.: Improved website fingerprinting on tor. In: Workshop on Privacy in the Electronic Society (2013)
19. Wang, T., Cai, X., Nithyanand, R., Johnson, R., Goldberg, I.: Effective attacks and provable defenses for website fingerprinting. In: USENIX Security Symposium (2014)
20. Feghhi, S., Leith, D.J.: A web traffic analysis attack using only timing information. IEEE Trans. Inf. Forensics Secur. **11**(8), 1747–1759 (2016)
21. He, G., Yang, M., Gu, X., Luo, J., Ma, Y.: A novel active website fingerprinting attack against tor anonymous system. In: Proceedings of the 2014 IEEE 18th International Conference on Computer Supported Cooperative Work in Design (CSCWD), pp. 112–117 (2014)
22. Hayes, J., Danezis, G.: k-fingerprinting: a robust scalable website fingerprinting technique. In: USENIX Security Symposium (2015)
23. Jahani, H., Jalili, S.: A novel passive website fingerprinting attack on tor using fast fourier transform. Comput. Commun. **96**, 43–51 (2016)
24. Panchenko, A., et al.: Website fingerprinting at internet scale. In: Network and Distributed System Security Symposium (2016)

25. Juárez, M., Imani, M., Perry, M., Dıaz, C., Wright, M.: WTF-PAD: toward an efficient website fingerprinting defense for tor. CoRR, abs/1512.00524 (2015)
26. Chen, M., Wang, Y., Qin, Z., Zhu, X.: Few-shot website fingerprinting attack with data augmentation. Secur. Commun. Netw. 1–13 (2021)
27. Deng, X., et al.: Robust multi-tab website fingerprinting attacks in the wild. In: 2023 IEEE Symposium on Security and Privacy (SP), pp. 1005–1022. IEEE Computer Society (2023)
28. Gong, J., Wang, T.: Zero-delay lightweight defenses against website fingerprinting. In: 29th USENIX Security Symposium (USENIX Security 2020), pp. 717–734 (2020)
29. Zhou, F., Wang, P., Zhang, L., Wei, W., Zhang, Y.: Revisiting prototypical network for cross domain few-shot learning. In: Proceedings of the IEEE/CVF Conference on Computer Vision and Pattern Recognition, pp. 20061–20070 (2023)
30. Shah, H., Tamuly, K., Raghunathan, A., Jain, P., Netrapalli, P.: The pitfalls of simplicity bias in neural networks. Adv. Neural. Inf. Process. Syst. **33**, 9573–9585 (2020)
31. Teney, D., Abbasnejad, E., Lucey, S., Van den Hengel, A.: Evading the simplicity bias: training a diverse set of models discovers solutions with superior OOD generalization. In: Proceedings of the IEEE/CVF Conference on Computer Vision and Pattern Recognition, pp. 16761–16772 (2022)
32. Lyu, K., Li, Z., Wang, R., Arora, S.: Gradient descent on two-layer nets: margin maximization and simplicity bias. Adv. Neural. Inf. Process. Syst. **34**, 12978–12991 (2021)
33. Bardes, A., Ponce, J., LeCun, Y.: Vicregl: self-supervised learning of local visual features. Adv. Neural. Inf. Process. Syst. **35**, 8799–8810 (2022)
34. Caron, M., Misra, I., Mairal, J., Goyal, P., Bojanowski, P., Joulin, A.: Unsupervised learning of visual features by contrasting cluster assignments. Adv. Neural. Inf. Process. Syst. **33**, 9912–9924 (2020)
35. Van Gansbeke, W., Vandenhende, S., Georgoulis, S., Gool, L.V.: Revisiting contrastive methods for unsupervised learning of visual representations. In: Advances in Neural Information Processing Systems, vol. 34, pp. 16238–16250 (2021)
36. Huynh, T., Kornblith, S., Walter, M.R., Maire, M., Khademi, M.: Boosting contrastive self-supervised learning with false negative cancellation. In: Proceedings of the IEEE/CVF Winter Conference on Applications of Computer Vision, pp. 2785–2795 (2022)
37. Srivastava, A., Valkov, L., Russell, C., Gutmann, M.U., Sutton, C.: Veegan: reducing mode collapse in GANs using implicit variational learning. In: Advances in Neural Information Processing Systems, vol. 30 (2017)

Generative AI, Emerging Threats

Pixel-Level Face Correction Task for More Generalized Deepfake Detection

Xiang Li, Weike You(✉), Qingran Lin, and Linna Zhou

Beijing University of Posts and Telecommunications, Beijing, China
{xli,ywk,linqingran,zhoulinna}@bupt.edu.cn

Abstract. Deepfake detectors nowadays have achieved impressive performance on intra-dataset evaluation, where training and testing images are collected from the same dataset. However, their detection results decrease when dealing with deepfake samples from unknown data collection. This paper introduces a novel Pixel-level Face Correction (PFC) task that involves pre-training with authentic facial data. Specifically, PFC generates pixel-level discrepancy by constructing a multi-scale facial pyramid and applying pixel-level resolution blending technique, then leverages masked image modeling framework to correct the subtle difference and learn facial representations that can be transferred to unseen deepfake detections. Extensive experimental results show that the proposed method obtains robust facial reconstruction ability and improves the model generalization to unknown manipulations.

Keywords: Deepfake detection · Multimedia forensics · Masked image modeling

1 Introduction

Deepfakes, multimedia content manipulated using artificial intelligence techniques to create highly realistic yet false portrayals of events or individuals, presents a growing challenge as their sophistication increases [27]. This escalating sophistication blurs the lines between genuine and counterfeit media, posing substantial risks such as the propagation of fake news, disinformation campaigns, and propaganda.

In the field of deepfake detection, the primary task is to determine the authenticity of a video, often treated as a binary classification problem. Early research focused on crafting hand-engineered features for detection, such as eye-blink frequency [28], artifact identification [8], and inconsistencies in information [2]. However, recent deepfake-generation methods can produce highly realistic content without easily detectable anomalies. Consequently, the field has shifted towards leveraging deep learning methods to reveal hidden features [13, 31, 38, 40]

X. Li, W. You and Q. Lin—Equal contribution.

S. Goel et al. (Eds.): ICDF2C 2024, LNICST 614, pp. 249–262, 2025.
https://doi.org/10.1007/978-3-031-89360-5_15

[35]. Although these deep learning models have shown promising detection performance with deepfake-generation methods seen during training, they suffer a significant decline while generalizing to other unseen forgery datasets.

To combat this, we aspire to propose a generalizable strategy to identify subtle manipulation indicators. This paper proposes a Pixel-level Face Correction (PFC) task. This self-supervised pre-training strategy introduces a unique approach to simulate the pixel-level manipulation common in Deepfakes and challenges the model to correct such manipulation. Through a facial image pyramid with varying resolutions, the PFC task aims to rectify inconsistencies arising from fine-grained manipulations. Through this approach, models can inherently capture the intricate patterns and underlying multiscale structures that define authentic facial characteristics. Subsequently, these pre-learned representations serve as the foundation for our deepfake detector, needing fewer resources for fine-tuning via binary deepfake supervised learning.

The notion of leveraging extensive genuine facial data for deepfake detection isn't novel [7,9,21,22], building upon the foundation of transfer learning. Transfer learning enables models to enhance performance in specific tasks or domains by leveraging additional knowledge. Reconstruction results in the experiment part show the effectiveness of our PFC task in capturing human facial attributes with improved fidelity. By integrating relevant facial domain knowledge, PFC infuses the model with a preemptive understanding of facial intricacies, thus aligning its input domain to accommodate diverse facial features and facilitate deepfake detection.

In summary, our contributions encompass:

- Introducing the Pixel-level Face Correction (PFC) task: This novel pre-training method prepares for deepfake detection by tackling challenges related to pixel-level manipulation. Through insights from a facial image pyramid and rectification of pixel-level mixing, the PFC task improves the model's ability to identify manipulated features, streamlining subsequent deepfake detection.
- Advancing deepfake detection through a generalizable approach: Shifting focus from specific models, we develop generalizable methods that detect subtle manipulation indicators adeptly. Rooted in a profound understanding of authentic facial data, PFC reaches better generalization results with less fine-tuning consumption.
- Experimental validation and performance evaluation: We validate the efficacy of the proposed PFC task through extensive experiments. Using benchmark deepfake datasets, we demonstrate the superiority of the PFC task in enhancing deepfake detection.

2 Related Works

2.1 Deepfake Detection Methods

The deepfake detection task is typically framed as a binary classification problem, aiming to discern whether a video is authentic or fake. In earlier research,

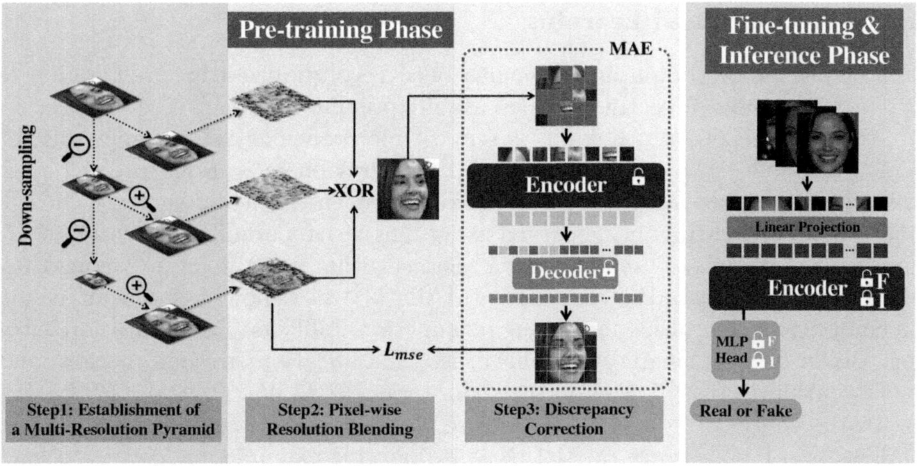

Fig. 1. PFC Overview. In the pre-training phase, we employ pixel-wise resolution blending to generate synthetic images from a multi-resolution pyramid, which serve as inputs for subsequent discrepancy correction. During the Fine-tuning(F)/Inference(I) Phase, the model performs face forgery classification by fine-tuning the capabilities of the pre-trained encoder. The state of the lock sign means whether we fix the parameters during the process.

considerable emphasis was placed on devising hand-crafted features for detection, encompassing characteristics like the frequency of eye blinking [28,30], identification of artifacts [8,31,36], and information inconsistencies [1,2,44,48]. However, with the rapid advancement of deepfake techniques, many forgery methods now produce highly realistic outputs that exhibit no discernible abnormal features. Consequently, the field has witnessed a shift towards adopting deep learning methods, enabling models to uncover latent features [13,31,40]. These deep learning models have demonstrated promising performance across diverse datasets, showcasing their effectiveness in detecting deepfakes.

More recently, F^3-Net [38] takes frequency details into account and proposes a frequency-aware model. Local-relation, also known as LRL [10], creates a robust and generalized similarity pattern and fuses RGB and frequency domain information to enhance local feature representation and reliability. Finfer [26] learns referenced representations from current and future frames and devises a novel loss function to enhance discriminability between real and fake videos. Moreover, certain deep-learning approaches utilize genuine data to bolster the model's ability to learn authentic facial representations. For instance, similar to our objectives, RECCE [7] leverages a reconstruction network to mine the representations of real faces from forgery ones. Hence, we will include these methods mentioned above for comparison in our experimental section.

2.2 Self-supervised Learning

The landscape of computer vision has been revolutionized by pre-training on extensive datasets. A recent and increasingly popular approach is self-supervised pre-training [11,24], which exhibits remarkable proficiency in learning valuable representations even without labeled data. Previously, various pretext tasks [20,37] were utilized for representation learning in the pre-training stage. Masked image modeling (MIM) has emerged as an innovative paradigm [3,12,23,46,47], empowering models to predict unseen regions within input images. Among these MIM methods, masked autoencoder (MAE) [23] has shown significant results on computer vision tasks, indicating its superior ability for representation learning. Based on that, many works have used modifications to yield performance improvements across diverse downstream tasks [19,43,45].

In the context of deepfake detection, MAE has also been employed in several studies. For instance, MARLIN [5], a notable example, endeavors to learn universal facial embeddings by reconstructing the spatiotemporal details of the face from the densely masked facial regions.

3 Methodology

Our approach comprises two core components, which we clarify in this section. We initiate by introducing the concept of Pixel-level Face Correction (PFC). Subsequently, we outline how the PFC pre-trained model can be harnessed to effectively carry out the deepfake detection task. Figure 1 provides an overview of the general workflow with detailed two-phase technical insights.

3.1 Pre-training Phase: Pixel-Level Face Correction

The fundamental aim of the PFC process is to enhance the model's capability to acquire intricate pixel-level knowledge of facials, thus preparing it for adept deepfake detection. This objective is achieved through a multi-step strategy:

Establishment of a Multi-resolution Pyramid. In the initial stage, we construct a pyramid of facial images at various resolutions by down-sampling the original image multiple times, yielding a collection of images. The ensuing goal is to generate pixel-level discrepancy and rectify them back to single-resolution facial images via following steps.

Pixel-Wise Resolution Blending. We then employ the Dirichlet distribution to randomly generate a mixing ratio:

$$f(x_1, ..., x_k; \alpha_1, ..., \alpha_k) = \frac{1}{B(\alpha)} \prod_{i=1}^{k} x_i^{\alpha_i - 1}, \tag{1}$$

where $\{x_i\}_{i=1}^{i=k}$ belong to the standard $K-1$ simplex and $B(\alpha)$ denotes the multivariate beta function. The generated ratio is subject to maintaining the proportion of a specific resolution above some percentage, and we achieve that by controlling the concentration of the distribution. Notably, the reconstruction signal in the subsequent "Discrepancy Correction" step is sourced from the pyramid layer with the highest proportion in the mixing ratio. Finally, a pixel-wise resolution blending technique is employed to generate the final composite image using the derived mixing ratio and the set of down-sampled images.

Discrepancy Correction. To further enhance the model's grasp of pixel-level facial features, we leverage Masked Image Modeling (MIM) to train a representation learning model with authentic facial images, thereby training the feature encoder. The input image is partitioned into non-overlapping patches, each represented by a token embedding. Subsequently, a subset of tokens is randomly masked with a substantial masking ratio, and only the remaining tokens are fed into the transformer encoder. we mark the region of masked patches as $\tilde{m}_{[M]}$ and the unmasked patches as $\tilde{m}_{[U]}$. For the encoder F_{ϕ_E}, it is applied only on unmasked patches $\tilde{m}_{[U]}$ and output the unmasked tokens $F_{\phi_E}(\tilde{m}_{[U]})$. Finally, a shallow decoder is superimposed on the visible tokens from the encoder, *i.e.*, $F_{\phi_E}(\tilde{m}_{[U]})$, along with learnable mask tokens that occupy the position embeddings of $\tilde{m}_{[M]}$, to reconstruct the image. Following the MAE model, the loss function involves mean squared error (MSE) between the normalized masked tokens and their reconstructed counterparts in pixel space. It needs to be clarified that the loss is computed between the corrected patches $\tilde{t}_{[M]}$ and the original patches $\tilde{y}_{r_{[M]}}$ from image $y_{r=max\_index}$, whose pixels take the vast majority in the pixel-wise blended image. The loss function can be formulated as:

$$L_{mse} = \frac{1}{N}\sum_{i=1}^{N} \|\tilde{m}_{[M]}^{(i)} - \tilde{m}_{[M]}^{p(i)}\|_2^2, \tag{2}$$

where N is the number of masked patches, $\tilde{m}_{[M]}$ and $\tilde{m}_{[M]}^{p}$ refers to the original masked patches and the predicted masked patches. By mastering the reconstruction of masked regions and addressing pixel-level disparities, the model acquires the competence to capture and preserve intricate facial structure details.

3.2 Fine-Tuning and Inference Phase: Accomplish the Deepfake Detection Task

Upon successfully establishing the multi-resolution pyramid and executing pixel-wise resolution blending and discrepancy correction, we anticipate the model to be suitably equipped to execute the deepfake detection task effectively. We fine-tune the encoder F_{ϕ_E} obtained from the preceding steps as a binary classifier. We employ cross-entropy loss L_{cls} to identify the discrepancy between reals and fakes. The formula is as follows:

$$L_{CE} = -\frac{1}{N}\sum_{i=1}^{N} y_i \log p_i + (1-y_i)\log(1-p_i), \tag{3}$$

where N is the batch size, y_i is the label of the i-th sample, and p_i represents the probability that the i-th sample is predicted to be a positive class. We only use the original deepfake samples in this phase, and we train the classifier for fewer iterations than other supervised methods. Further insights into the specifics of this training process will be provided in the forthcoming experimental section. Finally, we freeze the parameter of F_{ϕ_E} in the inference phase to complete the entire deepfake detection task.

4 Experiments

4.1 Datasets

We use real images of the ForgeryNet [25] for our PFC task. It contains over 5,400 subjects collected from four other datasets [6,14,18,34], with diversified dimensions of shooting conditions, expressions, and subject identity.

We evaluate our model on FaceForensics++(FF++) [39], DFDC-preview [16] and Celeb-DF(v2) [32] datasets. The FF++ dataset contains 1,000 unique videos with a split strategy: 720 videos for training, 140 for validation, and 140 for testing. Each video is forged using one of the four deepfake techniques: Deepfakes (DF) [15], Face2Face (F2F) [42], NeuralTextures (NT) [41] and FaceSwap (FS) [29]. We collect the number of real images four times the number of each manipulation method to solve the data imbalance of FF++ during the fine-tuning phase. 270 frames are sampled from each video for training and 100 for testing, following the setting as in the original paper. The Celeb-DF(v2) [32] contains 590 original videos taken from YouTube and 5,639 corresponding synthesized videos forged by a more sophisticated deepfake approach. DFDC-preview [16] is a dataset for Facebook DeepFake Detection, containing 855 real videos and 3,618 fake videos manipulated by selecting pairs of similar appearance. Training and testing sets are divided according to the official split lists for all three datasets.

4.2 Implementation Details

During the pre-training phase, we adopt the base version of Masked Autoencoder (MAE) [23] to perform our PFC task on the real face dataset. We downsampled the input images at rates of 1, 1/4, and 1/8 to establish the multi-resolution pyramid and apply pixel-wise resolution blending at a rate of 80%. We adopt AdamW optimizer [35] with an initial learning rate of 1e-5, a momentum of 0.9, and a weight decay of 0.05. We train the entire PFC task for 100 epochs with a batch size of 256. Following MAE, we simply use cropping operations for data augmentation. For simplicity, we refer to the model obtained after PFC task pre-training as **PFC-MAE**.

For fine-tuning, we exclusively leverage the encoder component of the PFC-MAE model, specifically the ViT-Base-16 model [17]. We adopt the AdamW with an initial rate of 1e-3 for optimization. We train our fine-tuning network for 20 epochs without additional data augmentations. All experiments in the pre-training and fine-tuning phases were implemented in PyTorch with two NVIDIA V100 GPUs.

4.3 State-of-the-Art Comparison

In this subsection, we compare our proposed method with current representative state-of-the-art approaches [4, 7, 13, 26, 31, 33, 38, 40].

Table 1. Intra-dataset evaluation AUC (%) comparisons with current state-of-the-art approaches on three popular benchmarks. The best results are in **bold**.

Method	FF++(HQ)	Celeb-DF	DFDCP
DSP-FWA	80.10	60.16	72.97
Xception	96.30	89.75	81.58
FInfer	95.67	93.30	82.88
F^3-Net	98.65	99.49	92.13
RECCE	**99.32**	99.94	-
PFC-MAE (Ours)	98.70	**99.95**	**94.52**

Intra-Dataset Evaluation. We evaluate our method on lightly compressed FaceForensics++(HQ), CelebDF and DFDC-preview. As shown in Table 1, for Celeb-DF and DFDC-preview, our method achieves improvements and gets the best results in both datasets. Especially on the DFDC-preview, PFC outperforms previous best results F^3-Net 2.39% in AUC scores. Moreover, on the FF++(HQ) dataset, our method achieves an accuracy of 98.70%, exhibiting a difference of just 0.62% compared to the best-performing RECCE.

Furthermore, we rigorously evaluate our method under conditions of heavy video compression (FF++ (LQ)). Since few existing arts report AUC scores on FF++(LQ), we use ACC for a fair comparison. Based on the data presented in Table 2, It is evident that the proposed PFC outperforms other methods for detecting the majority of deepfake techniques (DF, F2F, and FS), even when subjected to heavy video compression. However, it is essential to acknowledge that our method displays a noticeable disadvantage in detecting NT samples, which just slightly tampered with lip area, signifying the existence of certain constraints of detecting local manipulations. Despite this, when considering the overall performance, our PFC-MAE approach best results regarding average comprehensive accuracy.

These results collectively underscore the competitiveness and robustness of our approach in detecting a wide range of deepfake techniques and in scenarios involving heavy video compression.

Table 2. Overall ACC (%) performances on four manipulation methods of FF++(LQ).

Methods	DF	F2F	FS	NT	Avg
Xception	95.15	83.48	92.09	**77.87**	87.15
F^3-Net	97.78	91.30	95.38	76.22	90.17
SPSL	93.48	86.02	92.26	76.78	87.14
ADD+ResNet50	95.50	85.42	92.49	68.53	85.49
PFC-MAE (Ours)	**98.05**	**91.41**	**95.68**	76.47	**90.40**

Cross-Dataset Generalization. To evaluate the generalization ability of PFC on unseen manipulation methods, we conduct the cross-dataset experiment by training our model on the FF++(HQ) dataset and evaluating its performance on the Celeb-DF and DFDC-preview test sets. The results are summarized in Table 3. Our method exhibits exceptional performance on the DFDC-preview dataset, achieving an impressive AUC of 79.46%. This achievement notably surpasses the previous leading method by a significant margin. Furthermore, our method outperforms most existing techniques on Celeb-DF, which can be attributed to the stable and comprehensive understanding of facial intricacies gained during the PFC pre-training phase.

Table 3. Cross-dataset generalisation. AUC scores (%) on CelebDF-v2, DeepFake Detection Challenge preview datasets after training on FF++.

Method	Celeb-DF	DFDCP
DSP-FWA	64.60	-
Xception	65.90	64.29
EfficientNet-b4	68.67	64.61
F^3-Net	67.47	68.33
RECCE	68.71	-
FInfer	70.60	70.39
SPSL	76.88	-
PFC-MAE (Ours)	**78.05**	**79.46**

4.4 Ablation Study and Visualizations

To evaluate the effectiveness of our approach and visually illustrate the discrepancy-aware embeddings learned by the proposed method, we conduct ablation experiments and present reconstruction results.

Table 4. PFC task ablation. Analysis on effectiveness of PFC on Celeb-DF(v2) and DFDCP by training on FF++.

Method	Celeb-DF		DFDCP	
	ACC(%)	AUC(%)	ACC(%)	AUC(%)
MAE	72.95	76.07	68.35	76.86
PFC-MAE	**73.69**	**78.05**	**69.82**	**79.46**

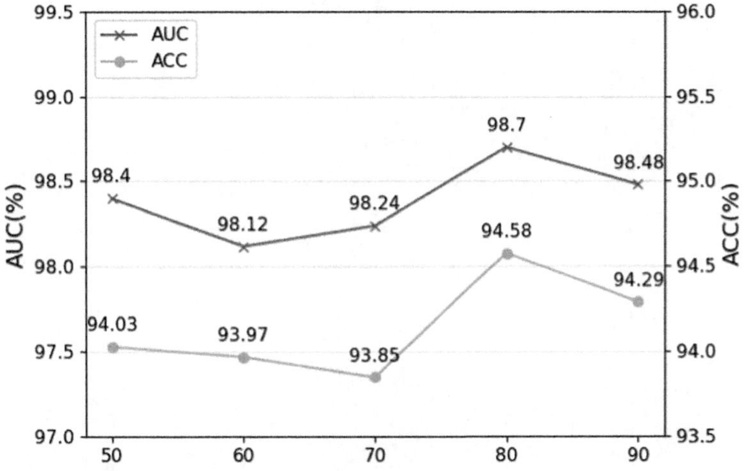

Fig. 2. Mixing ratio ablation. A high proportion (80%) of certain resolution works well for PFC pre-training. The y-axes are AUC (%) and ACC(%) of FF++ validation set.

PFC Task. To evaluate the effectiveness of the proposed PFC task, we conduct cross-dataset experiments on Celeb-DF(v2) and DFDCP datasets, employing training on the FF++(HQ) dataset with and without PFC. Specifically, we compared the performance of our PFC-MAE model against the original MAE model. The results presented in Table 4 reveal that our method outperforms the original MAE model regarding both ACC and AUC scores for both Celeb-DF(v2) and DFDCP datasets.

Mixing Ratio. Figure 2 illustrates the impact of the predominant ratio of a specific resolution during Pixel-wise Resolution Blending in PFC. The ratio of 80% demonstrates both favorable AUC and ACC scores. From this, we deduce that maintaining a substantial proportion of one particular resolution during Pixel-wise Resolution Blending ensures the preservation of ample corrective information. This observation highlights the significance of achieving a balanced harmony between preserving and replacing information, a crucial factor for enhancing PFC task results.

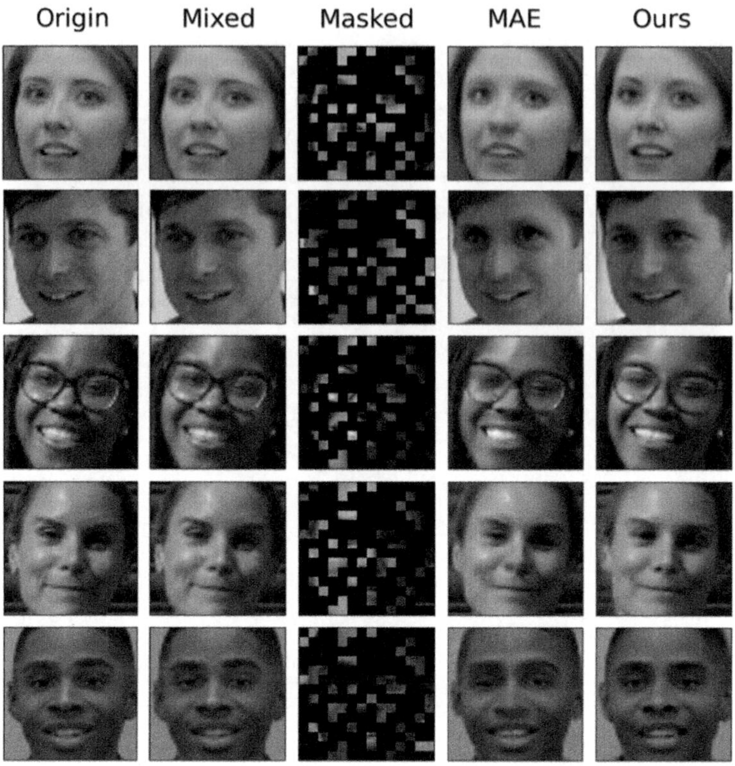

Fig. 3. Example results of the reconstructed faces of MAE and PFC-MAE. For each quintuplet, we show the ground-truth (leftmost), the mixed image of PFC-MAE (second from the left), the masked image of MAE (middle), the MAE reconstruction (second from the right), our PFC-MAE reconstruction (rightmost). The similarity between PFC-MAE reconstructions and the ground-truth images is notably higher, surpassing the corresponding MAE reconstructions, especially in intricate facial details.

Reconstruction Result. We have also presented the visualization of reconstructed faces in Fig. 3, ensuring fairness by maintaining a fixed position for the random MAE mask solely for this specific experiment. As evident from the comparison in the fourth and fifth columns, it becomes apparent that PFC-MAE surpasses the original MAE in effectively reconstructing intricate facial details. For example, in the first and second rows, PFC-MAE reconstructions remarkably preserve the fine details of the eyes. Similarly, in the fifth row, the PFC-MAE reconstruction demonstrates a more faithful replication of the distribution of facial features. This observation implies a superior capability of PFC-MAE in capturing subtle facial features, thus enhancing its potential for subsequent deepfake detection tasks.

5 Conclusions

In this paper, we introduce the Pixel-level Face Correction (PFC) task, involving the pre-training of models through a multi-scale authentic facial reconstruction objective, thus enabling a profound comprehension of intricate human facial knowledge. Extensive experiments prove the effectiveness of our method for general face forgery detection. General models (in our case, MAE), empowered by PFC, seamlessly navigate subsequent deepfake detection tasks, showcasing commendable efficiency and practicality. Furthermore, visualizations demonstrate the great capabilities of our proposed method of learning discrepancy-aware representations that enhance subsequent deepfake detection.

Acknowledgements. Research was supported by the National Natural Science Foundation of China (No. 62172053), the National Key Research and Development Program of China (No. 2021YFC3340700, No. 2022YFC3303300, No. 2021YFC3340600, No. 2022YFC3300800), the Fundamental Research Funds for the Central Universities (No. 2023RC30), and Shanghai Key Laboratory of Forensic Medicine and Key Laboratory of Forensic Science, Ministry of Justice (KF202420).

References

1. Agarwal, S., Farid, H., Fried, O., Agrawala, M.: Detecting deep-fake videos from phoneme-viseme mismatches. In: CVPR Workshops, pp. 2814–2822 (2020)
2. Amerini, I., Caldelli, R.: Exploiting prediction error inconsistencies through LSTM-based classifiers to detect deepfake videos. In: IH&MMSec, pp. 97–102. ACM (2020)
3. Bao, H., Dong, L., Piao, S., Wei, F.: Beit: BERT pre-training of image transformers. In: Proceedings of International Conference on Learning Representations (ICLR) (2022)
4. Binh, L.M., Woo, S.S.: ADD: frequency attention and multi-view based knowledge distillation to detect low-quality compressed deepfake images. In: AAAI, pp. 122–130 (2022)
5. Cai, Z., et al.: Marlin: masked autoencoder for facial video representation learning. In: Proceedings of the IEEE/CVF Conference on Computer Vision and Pattern Recognition (CVPR), pp. 1493–1504 (2023)
6. Cao, H., Cooper, D.G., Keutmann, M.K., Gur, R.C., Nenkova, A., Verma, R.: CREMA-D: crowd-sourced emotional multimodal actors dataset. IEEE Trans. Affect. Comput. **5**(4), 377–390 (2014)
7. Cao, J., Ma, C., Yao, T., Chen, S., Ding, S., Yang, X.: End-to-end reconstruction-classification learning for face forgery detection. In: Proceedings of the IEEE/CVF Conference on Computer Vision and Pattern Recognition (CVPR), pp. 4103–4112 (2022)
8. Chen, H., Li, Y., Lin, D., Li, B., Wu, J.: Watching the big artifacts: exposing deepfake videos via bi-granularity artifacts. Pattern Recognit. **135**, 109179 (2023)

9. Chen, H., Lin, Y., Li, B., Tan, S.: Learning features of intra-consistency and inter-diversity: keys toward generalizable deepfake detection. IEEE Trans. Circuits Syst. Video Technol. **33**(3), 1468–1480 (2023)
10. Chen, S., Yao, T., Chen, Y., Ding, S., Li, J., Ji, R.: Local relation learning for face forgery detection. In: AAAI, pp. 1081–1088 (2021)
11. Chen, T., Kornblith, S., Norouzi, M., Hinton, G.E.: A simple framework for contrastive learning of visual representations. In: Proceedings of the International Conference on Machine Learning (ICML), pp. 1597–1607 (2020)
12. Chen, Y., Liu, Y., Jiang, D., Zhang, X., Dai, W., Xiong, H., Tian, Q.: SdAE: self-distillated masked autoencoder. In: Proceedings of the European Conference on Computer Vision (ECCV), vol. 13690, pp. 108–124 (2022)
13. Chollet, F.: Xception: deep learning with depthwise separable convolutions. In: Proceedings of the IEEE/CVF Conference on Computer Vision and Pattern Recognition (CVPR), pp. 1800–1807 (2017)
14. Chung, J.S., Nagrani, A., Zisserman, A.: Voxceleb2: deep speaker recognition. In: INTERSPEECH, pp. 1086–1090 (2018)
15. Deepfakes: Faceswap: Deepfakes Software. https://github.com/deepfakes/faceswap/. Accessed 2023
16. Dolhansky, B., Howes, R., Pflaum, B., Baram, N., Canton-Ferrer, C.: The deepfake detection challenge (DFDC) preview dataset. CoRR abs/1910.08854 (2019)
17. Dosovitskiy, A., et al.: An image is worth 16x16 words: transformers for image recognition at scale. In: Proceedings of International Conference on Learning Representations (ICLR) (2021)
18. Ephrat, A., et al.: Looking to listen at the cocktail party: a speaker-independent audio-visual model for speech separation. ACM Trans. Graph. **37**(4), 112 (2018)
19. Feichtenhofer, C., Fan, H., Li, Y., He, K.: Masked autoencoders as spatiotemporal learners. In: NeurIPS (2022)
20. Gidaris, S., Singh, P., Komodakis, N.: Unsupervised representation learning by predicting image rotations. In: ICLR (2018)
21. Haliassos, A., Mira, R., Petridis, S., Pantic, M.: Leveraging real talking faces via self-supervision for robust forgery detection. In: Proceedings of the IEEE/CVF Conference on Computer Vision and Pattern Recognition (CVPR), pp. 14930–14942 (2022)
22. Haliassos, A., Vougioukas, K., Petridis, S., Pantic, M.: Lips don't lie: a generalisable and robust approach to face forgery detection. In: Proceedings of the IEEE/CVF Conference on Computer Vision and Pattern Recognition (CVPR), pp. 5039–5049 (2021)
23. He, K., Chen, X., Xie, S., Li, Y., Dollár, P., Girshick, R.B.: Masked autoencoders are scalable vision learners. In: Proceedings of the IEEE/CVF Conference on Computer Vision and Pattern Recognition (CVPR), pp. 15979–15988 (2022)
24. He, K., Fan, H., Wu, Y., Xie, S., Girshick, R.B.: Momentum contrast for unsupervised visual representation learning. In: Proceedings of the IEEE/CVF International Conference on Computer Vision (CVPR), pp. 9726–9735 (2020)
25. He, Y., et al.: Forgerynet: a versatile benchmark for comprehensive forgery analysis. In: Proceedings of the IEEE/CVF Conference on Computer Vision and Pattern Recognition (CVPR), pp. 4360–4369 (2021)
26. Hu, J., Liao, X., Liang, J., Zhou, W., Qin, Z.: Finfer: frame inference-based deepfake detection for high-visual-quality videos. In: AAAI, pp. 951–959 (2022)
27. Juefei-Xu, F., Wang, R., Huang, Y., Guo, Q., Ma, L., Liu, Y.: Countering malicious deepfakes: survey, battleground, and horizon. Int. J. Comput. Vis. **130**(7), 1678–1734 (2022)

28. Jung, T., Kim, S., Kim, K.: Deepvision: deepfakes detection using human eye blinking pattern. IEEE Access **8**, 83144–83154 (2020)
29. Kowalski, M.: FaceSwap: Deep Learning for Face Swapping. https://github.com/MarekKowalski/FaceSwap. Accessed 2023
30. Li, Y., Chang, M., Lyu, S.: In ictu oculi: exposing AI created fake videos by detecting eye blinking. In: WIFS, pp. 1–7 (2018)
31. Li, Y., Lyu, S.: Exposing deepfake videos by detecting face warping artifacts. In: CVPR Workshops, pp. 46–52 (2019)
32. Li, Y., Yang, X., Sun, P., Qi, H., Lyu, S.: Celeb-DF: a large-scale challenging dataset for deepfake forensics. In: Proceedings of the IEEE/CVF Conference on Computer Vision and Pattern Recognition (CVPR), pp. 3204–3213 (2020)
33. Liu, H., et al.: Spatial-phase shallow learning: rethinking face forgery detection in frequency domain. In: Proceedings of the IEEE/CVF Conference on Computer Vision and Pattern Recognition (CVPR), pp. 772–781 (2021)
34. Livingstone, S.R., Russo, F.A.: The ryerson audio-visual database of emotional speech and song (RAVDESS): a dynamic, multimodal set of facial and vocal expressions in North American English. PLoS ONE **13**(5), 1–35 (2018)
35. Loshchilov, I., Hutter, F.: Decoupled weight decay regularization. In: Proceedings of International Conference on Learning Representations (ICLR) (2019)
36. Matern, F., Riess, C., Stamminger, M.: Exploiting visual artifacts to expose deepfakes and face manipulations. In: WACV Workshops, pp. 83–92 (2019)
37. Noroozi, M., Favaro, P.: Unsupervised learning of visual representations by solving jigsaw puzzles. In: Leibe, B., Matas, J., Sebe, N., Welling, M. (eds.) ECCV 2016. LNCS, vol. 9910, pp. 69–84. Springer, Cham (2016). https://doi.org/10.1007/978-3-319-46466-4_5
38. Qian, Y., Yin, G., Sheng, L., Chen, Z., Shao, J.: Thinking in frequency: face forgery detection by mining frequency-aware clues. In: Proceedings of the European Conference on Computer Vision (ECCV), pp. 86–103 (2020)
39. Rössler, A., Cozzolino, D., Verdoliva, L., Riess, C., Thies, J., Nießner, M.: Faceforensics++: learning to detect manipulated facial images. In: Proceedings of the IEEE/CVF International Conference on Computer Vision (ICCV), pp. 1–11 (2019)
40. Tan, M., Le, Q.V.: Efficientnet: rethinking model scaling for convolutional neural networks. In: Proceedings of the International Conference on Machine Learning (ICML), vol. 97, pp. 6105–6114 (2019)
41. Thies, J., Zollhöfer, M., Nießner, M.: Deferred neural rendering: image synthesis using neural textures. ACM Trans. Graph. **38**(4), 66:1–66:12 (2019)
42. Thies, J., Zollhöfer, M., Stamminger, M., Theobalt, C., Nießner, M.: Face2face: real-time face capture and reenactment of RGB videos. In: Proceedings of the IEEE/CVF Conference on Computer Vision and Pattern Recognition (CVPR), pp. 2387–2395 (2016)
43. Tong, Z., Song, Y., Wang, J., Wang, L.: Videomae: masked autoencoders are data-efficient learners for self-supervised video pre-training. In: NeurIPS (2022)
44. Tursman, E., George, M., Kamara, S., Tompkin, J.: Towards untrusted social video verification to combat deepfakes via face geometry consistency. In: CVPR Workshops, pp. 2784–2793 (2020)
45. Wang, Y., Wang, J., Chen, B., Zeng, Z., Xia, S.: Contrastive masked autoencoders for self-supervised video hashing. In: AAAI, pp. 2733–2741 (2023)
46. Wei, C., Fan, H., Xie, S., Wu, C., Yuille, A.L., Feichtenhofer, C.: Masked feature prediction for self-supervised visual pre-training. In: Proceedings of the IEEE/CVF International Conference on Computer Vision (CVPR), pp. 14648–14658 (2022)

47. Xie, Z., et al.: Simmim: a simple framework for masked image modeling. In: Proceedings of the IEEE/CVF Conference on Computer Vision and Pattern Recognition (CVPR), pp. 9643–9653 (2022)
48. Yang, X., Li, Y., Lyu, S.: Exposing deep fakes using inconsistent head poses. In: Proceedings of International Conference on Acoustics, Speech and Signal Processing (ICASSP), pp. 8261–8265 (2019)

Evaluating and Extending Techniques for Fine-Grained Text-Topic Prediction for Digital Forensic Data

Khan Mohammad Al Farabi[1](✉), Gagan Agrawal[1], Gokila Dorai[2], Rajon Bardhan[2], Hoda Maleki[2], and Thomas E. Kadri[1]

[1] University of Georgia, Athens, USA
{kma27987,gagrawal,tek}@uga.edu
[2] Augusta University, Augusta, GA, USA
{gdorai,rbardhan,hmaleki}@augusta.edu

Abstract. In digital forensics, the search of personal devices by the police is constrained by judicial warrants and must adhere to constitutional privacy rights as prescribed by the Fourth Amendment. Determining which documents align closely with the topics specified in a warrant becomes challenging when a judge attempts to limit the search's scope based on the content of extracted data. This paper focuses on identifying, evaluating, and extending topic classification techniques for this end application, to which computer/data scientists have not yet received attention. After analyzing the requirements of this domain and considering applicable techniques, we focus on a class of techniques known as zero-shot classifiers. To improve their effectiveness, we propose a method that essentially involves clustering the candidate topics and the documents. A detailed comparison of two datasets shows the effectiveness of combining clustering with zero-shot classifiers. This combined method outperforms supervised methods requiring training data for specific topic inference.

Keywords: Digital Evidence · Privacy · Unstructured Data · Zero-Shot Classifier

1 Introduction

The work here is driven by a data-analytic problem arising in the context of digital forensics. As legal proceedings increasingly rely on data as proof, police will seek to draw from "big data" as evidence of human activity. This eagerness, however, creates tensions between the public's interest in effective criminal investigations and constitutional privacy rights. People will suffer privacy harm if police have free rein to search their devices for evidence of a suspected crime. Under the Fourth Amendment to the U.S. Constitution, judges can try to curb this discretion through warrants that limit device searches to specific data relevant to the investigation. However, this approach is complicated because diverse

S. Goel et al. (Eds.): ICDF2C 2024, LNICST 614, pp. 263–278, 2025.
https://doi.org/10.1007/978-3-031-89360-5_16

data are often intermixed in a single device. These legal and technical dynamics present unique challenges when courts seek to protect people's privacy by restricting the authority of police to gather digital evidence.

This scenario motivates an interesting "big data" problem: Can documents that are within the scope of a permissible search be identified with a high degree of accuracy? While this might sound like an application of the well-known approach of topic classification [19], a distinct challenge arises here for the following reasons. Because of the variety of topics that can be covered in a judge's warrant, it is unlikely that a model would be available pre-trained on that specific topic. Training a new model, on the other hand, requires sufficient training data with appropriate class labels, which is unlikely or at least a complex human effort. At the same time, topic modeling methods [8,28] are not likely to be helpful either because they are not designed to determine all contextually relevant topics from a given document.

Building on the outlined context, this paper offers the following four contributions: 1) We define a Machine Learning (ML) problem centered on the challenges of digital forensics and its associated legal issues; 2) We evaluate existing solutions relevant to this problem, concluding that the zero-shot approach is most fitting; 3) We describe a method to enhance the effectiveness of zero-shot classifiers by clustering both topics and documents; and 4) We propose new evaluation metrics tailored for this problem and conduct a thorough evaluation.

To elaborate on these contributions, after a careful review of existing techniques, we pick the zero-shot model and, more specifically, its Hugging Face zero-shot implementation [29] as the most promising technique. However, we further improve its applicability with a *clustering-based approach* that pre-processes the input data. We have compared the zero-shot approach with other ML-supervised techniques [3] like Support Vector Machine (SVM), Naive Bayes (NB), Random Forest (RF), and Decision Tree (DT). We have shown that the zero-shot outperforms these methods. We have also shown that our cluster-based approach improves the performance of the zero-shot model concerning prediction accuracy.

2 Detailed Motivation: Digital Forensics and the Legal Context

Digital forensics is a branch of forensic science that encompasses the recovery and investigation of data found in digital devices [2,24,30]. There are five fundamental stages in the digital forensic process: (1) identification, (2) preservation, (3) collection, (4) analysis, and (5) reporting. The first stage involves identifying potential sources of evidence and information, as well as the individual(s) associated with the device. The second stage entails preserving relevant electronically stored information (ESI), capturing visual images of the scene, and documenting pertinent information about the evidence and its acquisition. During the third stage, investigators collect digital information pertinent to the case, which includes imaging and copying the contents. In the fourth stage, investigators conduct a meticulous examination of the evidence related to the incident, culminating in its analysis and drawing conclusions. The final stage, reporting, involves generating reports based on established techniques and methodologies, as outlined in the NIST guidelines [11].

Based on the request of police or a prosecutor, a magistrate judge may issue a warrant to search or seize property to uncover evidence of criminal activity. The warrant's scope and specificity may depend on the nature of the alleged crime, the type of digital evidence, and the particulars of the court's jurisdiction. As a result, forensic software must adapt to varying search perimeters. Unlike searches of physical evidence like weapons or drugs, searching data presents complications because relevant and irrelevant evidence is interwoven within multiple files and folders [10,12,18].

The relevant legal considerations go beyond questions of technical feasibility. As James Grimmelmann has observed, searching digital devices presents contentious "evidentiary" concerns because "[t]he police are looking to gather evidence that can be used against a defendant at trial," while "the defendant is looking either to keep the police from getting access to the evidence, or to keep the prosecutors from presenting it to the jury" [6]. In the United States, the basic legal limitations often come from the Fourth Amendment of the Constitution, which provides that *"The right of the people to be secure in their persons, houses, papers, and effects, against unreasonable searches and seizures, shall not be violated, and no warrants shall issue, but upon probable cause, supported by oath or affirmation, and particularly describing the place to be searched, and the persons or things to be seized"*. If the police violate a person's constitutional right to privacy during their investigation, the evidence they gather will usually be inadmissible. Even if the proof they uncover is undeniable, prosecutors cannot use it to make their case.

The Fourth Amendment's application to digital devices has been a hot topic in recent years. As a threshold matter, a Fourth Amendment "search" occurs when the government gathers evidence by violating a person's "reasonable expectation of privacy"[1] or by physically trespassing on your personal property[2], while a "seizure" happens when the government engages in "some meaningful interference with [your] possessory interest"[3]. Gathering evidence from a device falls comfortably within the Fourth Amendment's scope, but that is just the start of the legal analysis. The Fourth Amendment, after all, prohibits only those searches and seizures that are *unreasonable.* This key point has been at the heart of high-profile court decisions in recent years.

3 Application Needs and Existing Methods

Techniques based on natural language processing (NLP) could provide one way to approach the challenges explored in the previous section. For this approach to be viable, these techniques would need to classify documents as sufficiently

[1] Katz v. United States, 389 U.S. 347 (1967).

[2] United States v. Jones, 132 S. Ct. 945 (2012).

[3] United States v. Jacobsen, 466 U.S. 109 (1984).

matching a given topic listed in a warrant. We examine the literature for suitable techniques.

Supervised Learning for Document Classification: Typically, the existing ML [19] algorithms can classify the texts after training ML models with labeled data. More specifically, a trained model can predict a topic of the text if that topic and similar texts are present in the training phase and not otherwise. This limitation presents a challenge for using these techniques in the context of digital forensics because every new warrant may involve new (and even multiple) topics, not allowing us to train the model separately for a specific set of topics.

Zero-Shot Classifier: The approach to zero-shot learning (ZSL) [20,25] is similar to how humans can detect topics or images without seeing them earlier. For example, if a child knows what a tiger looks like and we then give the child the description of a panther, the child can recognize a panther without seeing it first. In contrast, in most Artificial Intelligence (AI) approaches, the models can recognize the objects only if they have already seen them or similar patterns. The zero-shot classifier is based on the concept of ZSL. The zero-shot classifier [4] can figure out the most relevant topic of a text without any human annotation and training and thus is robust to the unseen (i.e., not part of the training phase) data and unseen class labels. The zero-shot classifier takes the text and the list of candidate labels as the input. It proceeds by finding the most similar texts and labels from its pre-training phase and detecting the most relevant classes based on contextual similarity. Finally, the model returns the ranked list of the class labels along with the probability scores. This probability score is computed using the softmax activation function [27]. If we enable multi-class prediction, the zero-shot classifier independently computes the probability score for each class between 0 and 1.

Exploration of Relevant Techniques: The forensics context poses two critical requirements. First, we aim to find all documents related to topics that sufficiently match the topic listed in a warrant while recognizing that these documents might also match other topics. For example, the relevant warrant topic might be "harassment," and while a document might match "co-worker" and "restaurants" (even more closely), it may be sufficiently related to harassment and needs to be identified as such. Second, given the range of topics that could be listed in a warrant, it is not feasible to train a model specifically for every topic because such training would require many documents matching the topic in hand, as well as other topics. Collecting such a corpus seems unlikely after receiving a warrant. Thus, unlike the other techniques discussed above, the zero-shot classification model appears the most suitable. However, it remains to be seen exactly how well it can perform or if other steps are needed to improve its applicability.

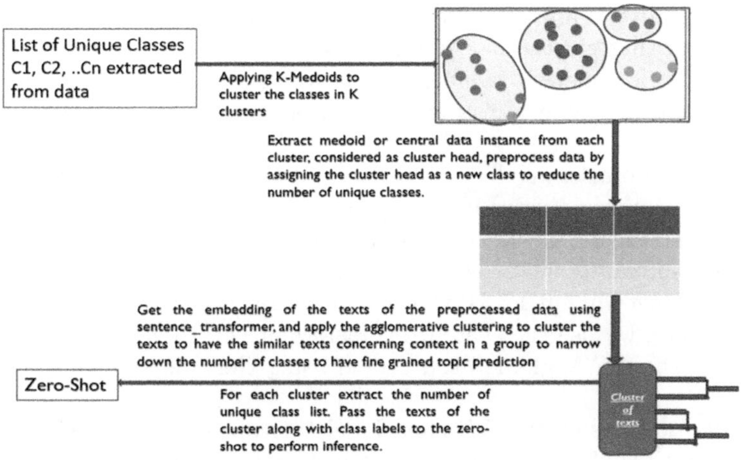

Fig. 1. A schematic illustration of our cluster-based approach

4 Enhancing Zero-Shot Classifier Predictions

To evaluate and improve methods for applying zero-shot classifiers to digital forensics, we consider the following problem. We are given a set of N documents, D_1, D_2, ... D_n. Each of these documents is associated with a set of topics or labels—let LB (comprising T_1, T_2, ..., T_m) denote the corpus of topics and let the topics associated with the document D_i be T_{i1}, (optionally) T_{i2}, and so on. We evaluate various techniques (and in one case, an enhanced version, described below) by focusing on how well they can, in an unsupervised fashion, predict (probabilities associated with) these actual topics. More concretely, we used Reuters dataset with ninety labels ($|LB| = 90$) and Yahoo-Answers-Topic data with 10 labels ($|LB| = 10$). Besides evaluating existing techniques, we also improve the pre-trained classifier model [29] by prepossessing labels and documents using clustering. In Fig. 1 we have represented our approach in a schematic form. To elaborate, we have applied the cluster-based approach [16] in two phases. In the first phase, we cluster the class labels and associate the documents with new labels (cluster head of the cluster). The goal of this step is to have the classifier deal with a smaller number of (mutually dissimilar) labels, as compared to a larger set of topics, many of which can be similar to each other. Then, in the second phase, we cluster the documents, to provide the classifier with similar documents together.

To elaborate, we have used K-Medoids (KMD) [21,26] to cluster the set of labels in the corpus LB. K-medoids cluster the texts based on contextual similarity. We have used this method because, unlike K-Means, it is robust to outliers and noise and it provides medoids of documents instead of the position. After clustering the labels, we consider the medoids of a cluster as a *cluster head*. For each text, if any of its original labels appear in a cluster, we assign the cluster head of that cluster as the new class for the text. As a result, the entire dataset (set of documents) is labeled with fewer classes. As stated previously, the overall goal of this exercise is to focus on labels that are clearly distinct from each other.

In the second phase, we cluster the documents after assigning them with new class labels through a cluster head approach. After re-labeling the documents, we now cluster the set of documents themselves. The purpose is to group the contextually similar texts together. To this end, we have used Agglomerative Hierarchical Clustering [9,17,31] that uses the distance threshold to perform the clustering. Here, we use the sentence transformer [23] to get the embeddings of the texts. We fit the Agglomerative model using the embeddings to cluster the texts.

Formally, we cluster the LB class labels or topics into K_1, K_2, K_3, ... K_k clusters using K-Medoids. For each of these clusters, we select cluster medoids as cluster head H_1, H_2, H_3, ..., and H_k respectively. a Let T_1a, T_1b, ... T_1z be the set of classes of the document, D_1. If the label T_1a appears in a K_1 cluster of classes, we reassign the H_1 as the new class for the document, D_1. Thus we reduce the number of unique labels. Then we assign the embeddings, Em to each of the n pre-processed documents using sentence transformer, st. We fit the embeddings, Em into hierarchical agglomerative clustering, AG, and generate Q_1, Q_2, Q_3 ... Q_z clusters of documents based on the contextual similarity. From the clusters of documents, let us say in cluster Q_1, we count the number of unique labels, Lb_1, and for each document, D_{1a} in Q_1, we now perform the inference, I using the zero-shot classifier.

5 Experiments

We conducted a series of experiments with the following goals: i) to assess the overall performance of the zero-shot classifier with respect to two metrics we introduce, which are the accuracy for multi-label prediction and average probability scores for the original class labels; ii) to compare zero-shot with several supervised machine learning models when the objective is binary classification; and iii) to examine the improvements in the performance of the zero-shot classifier through the cluster-based approach on the labels and documents we have introduced. We used the most widely used pre-trained classification model, "bart-large-mnli" [29], as the zero-shot model.

5.1 Datasets

We conducted two distinct sets of experiments. In the first set, we evaluated the performance of all methodologies using two standard benchmarks: the Reuters News-Group [15] and the Yahoo-Answers-Topic [14] datasets. For the Reuters dataset, we selected documents with more than one but no more than three class labels. For the Yahoo-Answers-Topic dataset, nearly every document has

Table 1. Datasets Used

Dataset	Total Texts	Texts used in Expt.	Sample Classes	Selection Rationale
Reuters Data	8762	900	Money-supply, earn etc.	Each text has more than one class label
Yahoo-Answers Topic	300 M	3 M	Politics and Government, Science and Mathematics etc.	Each text has more than one class label

multiple class labels, often combined as compound labels like "Society and Culture" or "Science and Mathematics." In total, the Yahoo-Answers-Topic dataset contains ten unique compound class pairings. We have summarized the primary details of these two datasets in Table 1.

In our second set of experiments, detailed in Sect. 5.5, we utilized a practical applications-based forensic dataset we developed. To create this dataset, we began by extracting texts from an Android mobile device using the Magnet Axiom Process/Examine commercial digital forensics tool. From this device, we gathered text data from the Gmail, Facebook, and Twitter applications. Specifically, we extracted 58 texts from the Gmail application, 28 from the Facebook application, and 26 tweets from the Twitter application. These texts from Gmail, Facebook, and Twitter served as the basis for this experiment.

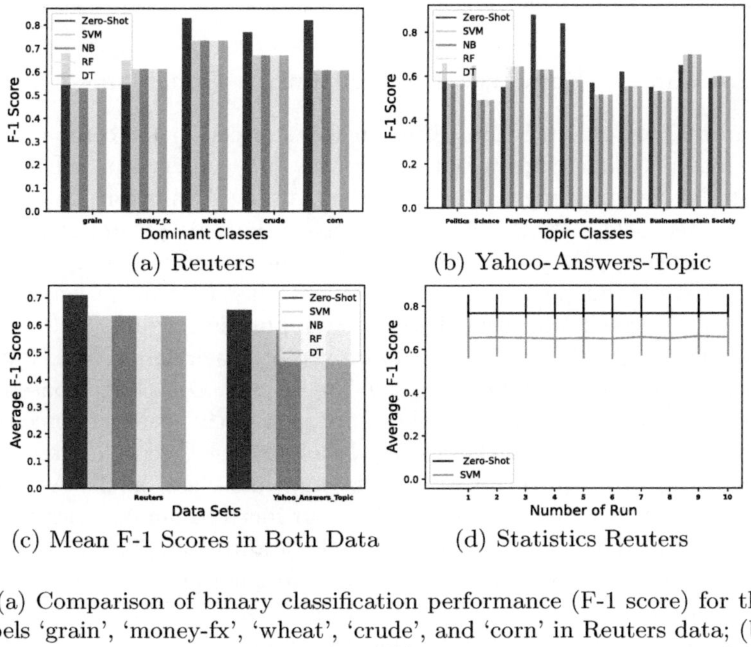

(a) Reuters (b) Yahoo-Answers-Topic

(c) Mean F-1 Scores in Both Data (d) Statistics Reuters

Fig. 2. (a) Comparison of binary classification performance (F-1 score) for the dominant labels 'grain', 'money-fx', 'wheat', 'crude', and 'corn' in Reuters data; (b) same comparison for Yahoo-Answers-Topic data, (c) averages F-1 scores across all labels for both data, (d) comparison between the zero-shot, and SVM for Reuters data concerning mean F-1 score and standard deviation.

5.2 Methods Evaluated and Metrics

We have evaluated all methods using two metrics that we deemed critical. The first metric is *labels prediction accuracy*, and the second is the *probability scores* of the labels. For the first metric, we computed the Top-K (K = 1, 2, 3) prediction accuracy. In this context, Top-K refers to the top K classes predicted by the classifier (based on highest probability) and how these predictions align with the original labels. To ensure consistency when computing label prediction accuracy, we maintained the same size for both the *prediction class window* and the *original class window*.

To illustrate, let's assume a document originally has two labels, c_1 and c_2. Let the classifier's top two predicted labels (based on highest probability) be p_1 and p_2. For a Top-1 prediction, we select the highest predicted class, p_1, and compare it with the first original label, c_1. For a Top-2 comparison, we assess if any predicted label from the set p_1, p_2 matches any label from the original set c_1, c_2. This method of computing prediction accuracy is applied across multi-class predictions.

For the second metric, as previously mentioned, the zero-shot classifier yields probability scores for the predicted labels, ranging between 0 and 1. We calculate the average probability score for the original labels and contrast it with the average probability score for the Top-3 non-original labels of a specific document. A notable difference indicates that the original labels receive higher probability scores, while other labels get lower scores.

5.3 Zero-Shot vs. Supervised Algorithms: A Constrained Evaluation

Experiment Design and Training: In this subsection, we compare the zero-shot approach against supervised algorithms [3]. Supervised ML algorithms necessitate labeled training data. While the training details for our experiments are enumerated below, it's crucial to emphasize that such training isn't feasible for our intended application. Given that leading supervised text classification methods often exhibit peak accuracy in binary classification tasks, our focus is primarily on this task, and we subsequently report F-1 scores [22]. We utilized four supervised algorithms [1,13]: Support Vector Machine (SVM), Naive Bayes (NB), Random Forest (RF), and Decision Trees (DT). Our cluster-based method was not incorporated into the zero-shot approach in this context since the inference pertains to only two labels, making label reduction redundant.

In the Reuters Data, documents carry multiple class labels. As previously noted, there are 90 distinct labels. To pivot our focus to binary classification, we pre-processed the dataset using the One-Vs-Rest approach [7]. We also identified the *dominant labels*, those that appear most frequently in the dataset. Specifically, we selected the top five labels: "grain", "money-fx", "wheat", "crude", and "corn". From a total of 900 documents, we filtered out 600 that bore these dominant labels. For each of these five predominant labels, we curated a sample of 100 documents: 50 labeled explicitly with that label and 50 labeled otherwise. This approach ensured a balanced data set of 100 documents per dominant label, striving to prevent biased outcomes. Each dominant label thus had two associated class labels.

Subsequently, we carried out inference for each dominant label using zero-shot, SVM, NB, RF, and DT methods. After training, these models were applied to the test data for further inference. For each dominant label, we computed the F-1 scores to gauge the performance of the SVM, NB, RF, and DT models.

As mentioned earlier, the zero-shot model returns a ranked list of the predicted classes. For binary inference, we feed the document and the two class labels to the zero-shot model. Take, for instance, the 100 balanced documents we previously generated for the "corn" category. We input each document into the model along with the candidate class labels, [*"corn"*, *"noncorn"*], to execute the inference. The class predicted with the higher probability is selected for the document, after which we compute the F-1 score.

For the Yahoo-Answers-Topic dataset, we selected 1,000 documents. This dataset features ten distinct compound class pairs. Just as we did with the Reuters data, we produced 100 balanced datasets for each of these ten unique compound class pairs. We conducted the binary class inference using the One-Vs-Rest approach with the zero-shot model. F-1 scores were computed for both the zero-shot and supervised models as previously outlined.

Inference Results

From Fig. 2 (a), it's evident that the zero-shot model yields notably better F-1 scores than the supervised algorithms in every instance. In Fig. 2 (b), which displays results for the Yahoo-Answers-Topic dataset, the zero-shot model surpasses supervised algorithms in F-1 scores for seven out of ten labels: "politics", "science", "computers", "sports", "education", "health", and "business".

As shown in Fig. 2 (c) for the Reuters Data, we calculated the average F-1 scores for dominant labels between the zero-shot classifiers and supervised algorithms. The findings clearly indicate the zero-shot classifier's superior performance in terms of average F-1 scores. A similar trend is observed for the Yahoo-Answers-Topic dataset when evaluating average F-1 scores across all class labels.

Table 2. Comparison of the statistics of the zero-shot model, before and after clustering for two datasets

Approach	Method	Mean-Acc	Peak-Acc	Std-Dev
Before Clustering (Yahoo)	zero-shot	0.54	0.65	0.12
After Clustering (Yahoo)	zero-shot	0.94	0.977	0.04
Before Clustering (Reuters)	zero-shot	0.59	0.80	0.30
After Clustering (Reuters)	zero-shot	0.88	0.99	0.15

In a further analysis, we evaluated the F-1 scores of the zero-shot and SVM models using Reuters data over 10 experimental runs. For each run, F-1 scores

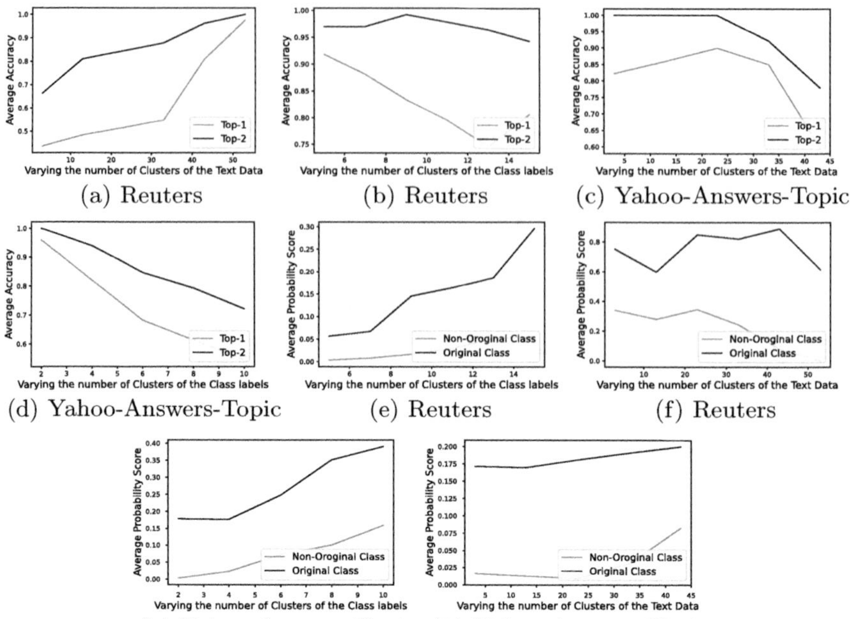

(a) Reuters (b) Reuters (c) Yahoo-Answers-Topic
(d) Yahoo-Answers-Topic (e) Reuters (f) Reuters
(g) Yahoo-Answers-Topic (h) Yahoo-Answers-Topic

Fig. 3. (a) and (c): comparison of the Top-K (K = 1, 2) average prediction accuracy by varying the clusters of the documents; (b) and (d): Top-K (K = 1, 2) average prediction accuracy of zero-shot classifier while varying the clusters of the class labels; (e), and (g): comparison of the average probability scores of the original labels and non-original labels while varying the clusters of the labels; (f) and (h): comparison of the average probability score while varying the clusters of the documents.

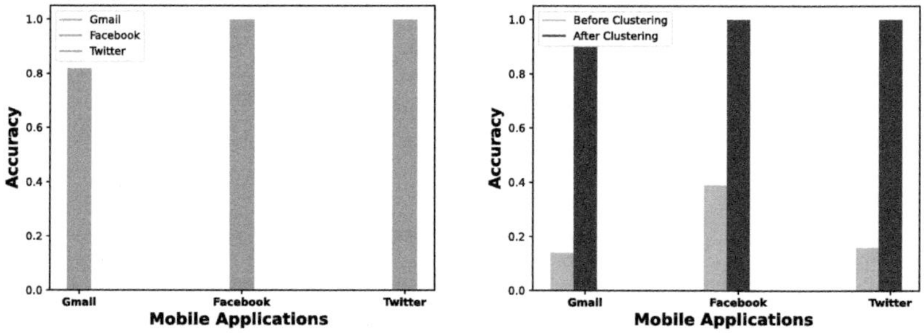

(a) SVM trained on Hate-Speech as ground truth
(b) SVM trained on Reuters as ground truth

Fig. 4. Performance of zero-shot for real forensic data, (a) classification on 2 classes, (b) classification on 10 classes before and cluster clustering.

were computed for dominant classes, including "grain," "money-fx," "wheat," "crude," and "corn," for both zero-shot and SVM. Subsequently, we calculated the mean and standard deviation of these F-1 scores for each run.

In Fig. 2 (d), we present a comparison of mean F-1 scores and standard deviations between zero-shot and SVM over the 10 runs. The maximum standard deviations observed were 0.08 for zero-shot and 0.09 for SVM. The average F-1 score across the runs was 0.76 for the zero-shot and 0.65 for the SVM. In comparisons with other supervised algorithms like NB, RF, and DT, the results were analogous to those of SVM, with the zero-shot consistently outperforming them in both mean F-1 score and standard deviation.

Although the supervised algorithms are trained with the data and corresponding labels, the zero-shot performs much better than the supervised algorithms in most cases without any training phase.

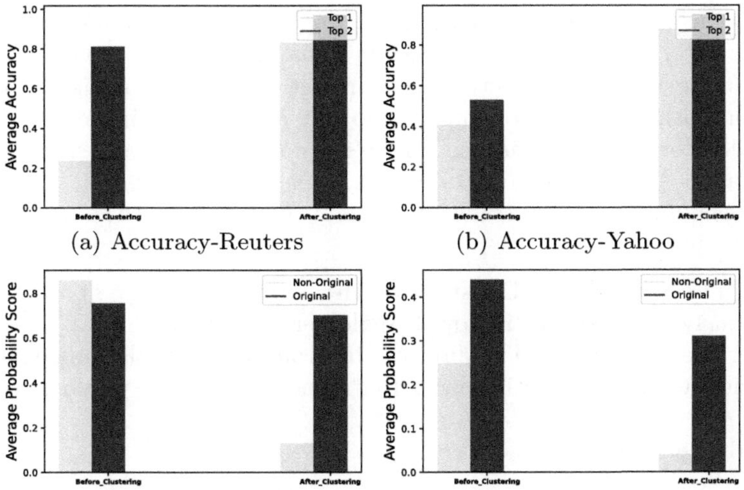

(a) Accuracy-Reuters (b) Accuracy-Yahoo

(c) Probability-Score Reuters (d) Probability-Score Yahoo

Fig. 5. (a) and (b): Average accuracy (Top-K = 1, 2) of original and non-original class labels before clustering and after clustering for two datasets; (c) and (d): average probability scores of original and non-original class labels before clustering and after clustering for two datasets

5.4 Improvements from Cluster-Based Method

We have implemented the cluster-based approach in two ways. First, we have varied the number of clusters of the labels and kept the number of document clusters fixed. Second, we have varied the number of clusters of the documents, keeping fixed the number of clusters of the labels.

Varying the number of Clusters of the Class Labels
The performance of the zero-shot model is influenced by the number of class labels. We noticed that the model's efficacy diminishes when faced with a very

high number of unseen labels. To address this, we clustered the class labels, aiming to reduce their count.

In the experiments for the Reuters data, we varied the number of class label clusters, experimenting with configurations of 5, 7, 9, 11, 13, and 15 clusters. Throughout these tests, the document cluster size remained consistent at 40. We then gauged the average Top-K (K = 1, 2) prediction accuracy for each configuration using our previously outlined method.

For the Yahoo-Answers-Topic dataset, we adjusted the number of class label clusters to 2, 4, 6, 8, and 10. Here, the document cluster size was set to 44. Again, we calculated the average Top-K (K = 1, 2) prediction accuracy for each setup.

In Fig. 3 (b) and (d), we present a comparison of the Top-K (K = 1, 2) prediction accuracy for the zero-shot model using the Reuters and Yahoo-Answers-Topic datasets, respectively. These results reveal that even with a relatively large number of clusters, we get better class prediction accuracy using the zero-shot model for both datasets as compared to not using clustering of labels at all. Specifically, for Top-1 predictions, there's a notable improvement in accuracy. In the Yahoo-Answers-Topic dataset, a clearer trend emerges: accuracy diminishes as the number of clusters increases, likely influenced by the original presence of only ten initial labels.

Varying the number of Clusters of the Documents
As previously detailed, we employed Agglomerative Hierarchical Clustering [31] to cluster the documents. The aim was to group contextually analogous documents within a cluster, anticipating that these documents would have similar class labels.
For the Reuters dataset:

- We adjusted the number of document clusters, ranging from 3 to 50.
- We modified the distance threshold in the agglomerative model, setting it between 1 and 6.
- We consistently set the class label cluster size at 5.

For the Yahoo-Answers-Topic dataset:

- We varied the number of document clusters between 3 and 45.
- The distance threshold in the agglomerative model was adjusted from 4 to 8.
- The class label cluster size was maintained at 5.

We have also computed the average Top-K (1, 2) prediction accuracy for both data. In Fig. 3 (a), and (c), we have shown a comparison of the Top-K (K = 1, 2) prediction accuracy of the zero-shot method for the Reuters and Yahoo-Answers-Topic data, respectively. The prediction accuracy increases along with the number of clusters of documents increasing in Fig. 3(a) for the Reuters data. Here, the accuracy values are also declining for Yahoo-Answers-Topic because the number of clusters containing documents with multiple labels increases, and it deteriorates the accuracy values generated by the zero-shot model. Although the accuracy values decrease along with the increase in the number of clusters of documents, the accuracy values improve significantly after clustering. Specifically, here we also observe that Top-1 accuracy improves significantly in both Reuters and Yahoo-Answers-Topic data.

In Fig. 3 (e), (f), (g), and (h), for both Reuters and Yahoo-Answers-Data, we have compared the average probability scores of the original and non-original labels. The original labels here are the newly assigned labels. It is clear from the results that the original labels' average probability scores are much better than that of the top three non-original labels after applying our cluster-based approach (in both variation cases, clustering labels, and clustering documents) in most of the cases. This finding implies that, after applying the clustering, the zero-shot model is more likely to positively identify actual labels, and not identify the documents as being associated with other labels.

In Fig. 5 we have shown the influence of our cluster-based approach with respect to the prediction accuracy and the probability scores. We observe in Figures (a) and (b) of Fig. 5 that the cluster-based approach improves the performance of the zero-shot model significantly concerning prediction accuracy for both Reuters and Yahoo-Answers-Topic data, respectively. In Figures (c) and (d) we have shown the comparison between the original labels and the non-original labels concerning the probability scores for both the Reuters and Yahoo-Answers-Topic data, respectively. The results depict that our clustering approach increases the difference in the probability scores between the original and non-original labels significantly. Here, we also compute the average probability scores of the top three non-original labels. This implies that the zero-shot model truly predicts the original labels as the top labels in most cases after clustering and the prediction accuracy increases significantly.

To further investigate the results, in Table 2 we have shown the comparison of the statistics for the zero-shot before and after clustering. We have computed mean accuracy, peak accuracy, and standard deviation before and after clustering for both the Reuters and Yahoo-Answers-Topic data. We computed the statistics before clustering for a random case where we selected 100 documents randomly. We run this experiment up to 10 times and compute the Top-K (K = 1, 2, 3) prediction accuracy each time. We have computed average prediction accuracy for Top-1, Top-2, and Top-3, respectively. Then we compute the mean values of these average prediction accuracy values of Top-1, Top-2, and Top-3 predictions and consider it as a mean accuracy value in our table. We have picked the maximum average prediction accuracy values of Top-1, Top-2, and Top-3, as the peak accuracy value. We have computed the standard deviation of the mean accuracy values of Top-1, Top-2, and Top-3 predictions. Similarly, we have computed the mean, peak, and standard deviation after clustering. From Table 2 it is clear that, for both of the data, the difference between the mean and peak values is at least 0.10 or above, and the standard deviation is high before clustering. After applying our cluster-based approach, the difference between the mean and peak values reduces significantly and the standard deviation also declines. We observe that, after applying the clustering, the mean prediction accuracy values improve significantly for both data.

5.5 Experiments with Applications-Based Forensic Dataset

We present our findings from experiments conducted on the practical applications-based dataset. The specific challenge here is that no labels are available. We used a supervised algorithm, SVM [3], to provide the topic labels of these unlabelled texts. SVM was trained separately using one of the datasets used in our experiments and a Hate-Speech data [5] dataset. In using the latter, we have used ten thousand texts with two classes, "nohate", and "hate". After such training, SVM model is used to predict the topic labels of the texts (either "hate" or "nohate") of Gmail, Twitter, and Facebook datasets and the prediction obtained is considered the ground truth. Next, we evaluate the accuracy of the zero-shot. In Fig. 4 (a), we observe that the accuracy is quite high across the data obtained from the three applications.

Next, SVM is trained using Reuters data, we have used 696 texts which are labeled with ten topics. For our evaluation, we apply the zero-shot model to infer the topic labels among these 10. We observe that the performance of the zero-shot, as compared to the "ground truth" obtained, is not good. Next, we have applied our cluster-based approach to reduce the number of topics from to 10 to 3, and associate each topic in the training dataset with one of the 3 topics. We again train the SVM model with these updated topics, generate new ground truths, and then apply the zero-shot model. As seen in Fig. 4 (b), the prediction accuracy surged post-clustering, reinforcing observations from our prior experiments.

Data and code are available at: https://github.com/anonimoustt/code

6 Limitations

This paper explores zero-shot classifiers in digital forensics within the context of the Fourth Amendment, acknowledging specific limitations. Using datasets like Reuters News-Group and Yahoo-Answers-Topic, which feature multiple ground-truth labels, we conduct a thorough analysis emphasizing binary classification, while recognizing the potential for broader, multi-label experiments. Real-time short texts from social media, due to privacy concerns and limited availability, were not used. Our empirical analysis underscores the zero-shot model's efficacy in inferring multiple topics from new documents without retraining, unlike typical machine learning algorithms. Despite producing high probability scores for irrelevant topics when analyzing numerous topics, our approach clusters documents based on context using sentence transformer embeddings, improving topic prediction accuracy. Novel metrics tailored to digital forensics were introduced, and our method does not require training data. The potential bias in inference, due to the zero-shot model's reliance on a static knowledge base from the MNLI [29] dataset, points to future work where fine-tuning methods will be developed to address this issue. This study's significant contributions include context-based document clustering, enhanced topic prediction accuracy, and the introduction of new performance metrics specific to digital forensics.

7 Conclusion and Future Work

In this paper, we formulated and tackled a problem rooted in the domain of digital forensics and its intertwined legal implications. Our approach hinged on the application of a zero-shot classifier, enhanced with the strategic clustering of topics and texts to improve accuracy. Our findings underscore that the zero-shot classifier outpaces supervised algorithms in topic prediction, and the integration of our clustering techniques further augments this performance. While our current endeavors have been centered around documents, future avenues include branching out to topic predictions for chat and conversation threads on social media platforms. Exploring the incorporation of context, such as information about conversational partners, may offer additional layers of accuracy enhancement.

References

1. Aggarwal, C.C., Zhai, C.: A survey of text classification algorithms. In: Mining Text Data, pp. 163–222. Springer, Heidelberg (2012). https://doi.org/10.1007/978-1-4614-3223-4_6
2. Carrier, B., et al.: Defining digital forensic examination and analysis tools using abstraction layers. Int. J. Digital Evid. **1**(4), 1–12 (2003)
3. Caruana, R., Niculescu-Mizil, A.: An empirical comparison of supervised learning algorithms. In: Proceedings of the 23rd International Conference on Machine Learning, pp. 161–168 (2006)
4. Feng, Z., et al.: Codebert: a pre-trained model for programming and natural languages. arXiv preprint arXiv:2002.08155 (2020)
5. de Gibert, O., Perez, N., García-Pablos, A., Cuadros, M.: Hate speech dataset from a white supremacy forum. In: Proceedings of the 2nd Workshop on Abusive Language Online (ALW2), pp. 11–20. Association for Computational Linguistics, Brussels (2018). https://doi.org/10.18653/v1/W18-5102. https://www.aclweb.org/anthology/W18-5102
6. Grimmelmann, J.: Internet law: Cases and problems. Semaphore Press (2017)
7. Hong, J.H., Cho, S.B.: A probabilistic multi-class strategy of one-vs.-rest support vector machines for cancer classification. Neurocomputing **71**(16–18), 3275–3281 (2008)
8. Hu, Y., Boyd-Graber, J., Satinoff, B., Smith, A.: Interactive topic modeling. Mach. Learn. **95**(3), 423–469 (2014)
9. Johnson, S.C.: Hierarchical clustering schemes. Psychometrika **32**(3), 241–254 (1967)
10. Judish, N.: Searching and seizing computers and obtaining electronic evidence in criminal investigations. Office of Legal Education, Executive Office for United States Attorneys (2009)
11. Kent, K., Chevalier, S., Grance, T., Dang, H.: Sp 800-86. Guide to integrating forensic techniques into incident response (2006)
12. Kerr, O.S.: Ex ante regulation of computer search and seizure. Va. L. Rev. **96**, 1241 (2010)
13. Kowsari, K., Jafari Meimandi, K., Heidarysafa, M., Mendu, S., Barnes, L., Brown, D.: Text classification algorithms: a survey. Information **10**(4), 150 (2019)

14. Kucuktunc, O., Cambazoglu, B.B., Weber, I., Ferhatosmanoglu, H.: A large-scale sentiment analysis for yahoo! answers. In: Proceedings of the Fifth ACM International Conference on Web Search and Data Mining, pp. 633–642 (2012)
15. Lhoest, Q., et al.: Datasets: a community library for natural language processing. In: Proceedings of the 2021 Conference on Empirical Methods in Natural Language Processing: System Demonstrations, pp. 175–184. Association for Computational Linguistics (2021). https://aclanthology.org/2021.emnlp-demo.21
16. Likas, A., Vlassis, N., Verbeek, J.J.: The global k-means clustering algorithm. Pattern Recogn. **36**(2), 451–461 (2003)
17. Nielsen, F.: Hierarchical clustering. In: Introduction to HPC with MPI for Data Science. UTCS, pp. 195–211. Springer, Cham (2016). https://doi.org/10.1007/978-3-319-21903-5_8
18. Ohm, P.: Massive hard drives, general warrants, and the power of magistrate judges. Va. L. Rev. Brief **97**, 1 (2011)
19. Osisanwo, F., Akinsola, J., Awodele, O., Hinmikaiye, J., Olakanmi, O., Akinjobi, J.: Supervised machine learning algorithms: classification and comparison. Int. J. Comput. Trends Technol. (IJCTT) **48**(3), 128–138 (2017)
20. Palatucci, M., Pomerleau, D., Hinton, G.E., Mitchell, T.M.: Zero-shot learning with semantic output codes. Adv. Neural Inf. Process. Syst. **22** (2009)
21. Park, H.S., Jun, C.H.: A simple and fast algorithm for k-medoids clustering. Expert Syst. Appl. **36**(2), 3336–3341 (2009)
22. Pedregosa, F., et al.: Scikit-learn: machine learning in python. J. Mach. Learn. Res. **12**, 2825–2830 (2011)
23. Reimers, N., Gurevych, I.: Sentence-bert: sentence embeddings using siamese bert-networks. arXiv preprint arXiv:1908.10084 (2019)
24. Reith, M., Carr, C., Gunsch, G.: An examination of digital forensic models. Int. J. Dig. Evid. **1**(3), 1–12 (2002)
25. Romera-Paredes, B., Torr, P.: An embarrassingly simple approach to zero-shot learning. In: International Conference on Machine Learning, pp. 2152–2161. PMLR (2015)
26. Schubert, E., Rousseeuw, P.: Faster k-medoids clustering: improving the pam. CLARA, and CLARANS Algorithms, Cornell University, Ithaca, NY (2018)
27. Tang, Y.: Deep learning using linear support vector machines. arXiv preprint arXiv:1306.0239 (2013)
28. Vayansky, I., Kumar, S.A.: A review of topic modeling methods. Inf. Syst. **94**, 101582 (2020)
29. Yin, W., Hay, J., Roth, D.: Benchmarking zero-shot text classification: datasets, evaluation and entailment approach. arXiv preprint arXiv:1909.00161 (2019)
30. Zatyko, K.: Commentary: defining digital forensics. Forensic Maga. **20** (2007)
31. Zhang, W., Zhao, D., Wang, X.: Agglomerative clustering via maximum incremental path integral. Pattern Recogn. **46**(11), 3056–3065 (2013)

Driven to Evidence: The Digital Forensic Trail of Vehicles

Catherine McKay(✉) and Nhien-An Le-Khac

School of Computer Science, University College Dublin, Dublin, Ireland
mckayforensics@gmail.com, an.lekhac@ucd.ie

Abstract. Digital forensic investigations are constantly growing in both the volume and variety of available data sources. Today, many vehicles possess an in-vehicle infotainment system (IVI), providing communication capabilities and entertainment. These features, such as the ability to send messages, place and receive phone calls, access emails and browse the internet, are user driven, however, IVIs can also obtain information that is not user controlled, such as the location and mapping data of where the vehicle was driven, and further data such as when car doors were open and closed and lights turned on and off. Vehicle forensics is the area of digital forensics that involves the acquisition and analysis of this data stored on various computer electronic systems within a vehicle and is becoming increasingly more prevalent as technology evolves. Vehicle forensics can be especially useful when it comes to a wide variety of investigations, including but not limited to law enforcement cases, insurance fraud, and accident reconstruction. Throughout literature, there is a focus on 'dead-box' forensic approaches and few of them also focus on the network infrastructures within vehicles and the associated investigative opportunities. The current research is further missing the analysis and comparison of artifacts between connected devices, such as mobiles, and the data residing on an IVI system. This paper presents a new approach of vehicle forensics with the acquisition and analysis of not only artifacts from internal storage in the IVI system, but also artifacts that can be recovered off mobile devices connected to the infotainment unit, and additionally what data can be retrieved from a live network capture. The objective of this research is to determine further available avenues for vehicle forensics investigations. This approach is validated with a case study of analyzing Ford Explorer systems with both iOS and Android devices.

Keywords: Digital Forensics · Vehicle Forensics · iOS Forensics · Android Forensics · Mobile Forensics · Live Data Forensics · IVI System Analysis. Network Interception

1 Introduction

Today, vehicles store significant amounts of information, and a single vehicle can contain over a hundred computer systems, 300 million lines of code and 25 GB of data generated per hour [1]. This extensive amount of data can be generated from sensor data, scanning

S. Goel et al. (Eds.): ICDF2C 2024, LNICST 614, pp. 279–295, 2025.
https://doi.org/10.1007/978-3-031-89360-5_17

the environmental surrounding conditions, telemetry data, collating performance metrics and communicating with devices, other vehicles, and infrastructure.

Infotainment, or IVI, systems are integrated into modern vehicles with the purpose of improving the user experience, through audio and video interfaces with touch screen displays and controls, button panel and voice commands. IVI systems have the ability for mobile device integration and allow for user entertainment such as live media streaming and smart technology. The Internet of Things (IoT) encompasses a network of interconnected devices gathering data, and in the context of vehicles, means vehicles turn from transportation tools, into smart devices with enhanced capabilities.

Vehicle Forensics is an area that is constantly evolving and growing in interest in digital forensics, incident response and cybercrime fields. IVI systems are complex embedded computer systems, therefore act in a consistent likeness to computers systems, which in turn provide the capability to circulate a large amount of data and retain volatile and non-volatile artifacts. A vast amount of data has proven to be recoverable from vehicle systems due to their many capabilities and features, across the telemetric data and vehicle IVI systems. However, in literature, vehicle forensics is often approached by way of a traditional 'dead-box' forensics method. While there is research conducted into what artifacts can be obtained from mobile device extractions showing traces of connections to a vehicle and associated activities, this has not yet been compared to whether the same data also resides on an IVI system. This is important as it provides a rounded approach to vehicle-related investigations, navigating through different methods as to where information or potential evidence could be stored. For example, if an IVI system acquisition has been completed and does not contain any data of interest, could this data further be stored on a synced mobile device and obtained through a forensic extraction (or vice versa). There is further no research in the vehicle forensic area of exploring a live network traffic intercept on a mobile device when connected to an IVI system and whether this yields any further data of interest. There is potential opportunity to determine what artifacts may be left behind or recovered through live data capture of a paired mobile device to an IVI system that was not obtained through the first two phases and methods. This research and comparative analysis underscore the importance of leveraging a variety of forensic methodologies when it comes to digital forensic investigations. Previous studies in the realm of vehicle forensics have focused on one primary approach of data acquisition from the IVI, whereas this research complements these previous approaches by introducing the methodology of live network interceptions. Instead of reliance on one acquisition, this research discusses forensic opportunities across multiple. Live network interceptions, mobile device extractions and IVI data retrieval each offer unique advantages and face their own technical challenges. By integrating these approaches, this provides the enhanced ability to gather comprehensive, reliable and contextually in-depth evidence.

The contribution of this paper can be listed as follows: (i) demonstrate that mobile device extractions from synced devices to the IVI are crucial for comparison in not only providing further artifacts and evidence but providing attribution to artifacts located on an IVI system; (ii) network interception of connected mobile devices to IVI systems can yield further insight and results to corroborate findings from a mobile device extraction.

2 Related Work

Various research has been undertaken in the vehicle forensics space, reviewing different use cases, possibilities, integrated networks and storage of data. This has commonly been case studies relating to specific vehicle types and what information can be obtained.

A paper published by Lacroix et al. (2016) [2] vehicular ad-hoc networks, security, interconnectivity, and privacy aspects of vehicles. Vehicular Ad-Hoc Network (VANET) infrastructure has the ability to communicate with other vehicles through peer-to-peer communication (or Vehicle-to-Vehicle communications), Vehicle-to-Infrastructure and Infrastructure-to-Vehicle communications (V2I and I2V). This research established findings that vehicles can generate a significant number of logs and therefore may be able to be accessed in real time. Research was completed on a Ford F-150 truck SYNC infotainment file system and the content and files analyzed reflecting that it is possible to gather a large amount of data. This research also determine that Ford SYNC models were often found to be Windows CE operating system and its base form can be straightforward to exploit.

Research by Moos et al. (2016) [3] addresses the variety in which different vehicles require different forensic methods to extract data successfully. This paper makes mention of facing constant barriers when attempting to acquire data. Some of these barriers include the potential to encounter ATA passwords. This was identified on a BMW 4 Series vehicle, however this password was easily bypassed at acquisition using common forensic tools, such as a PC3000 [4]. It was noted that the ATA password on the specific unit was likely made up of unique IDs, which would provide an avenue for examiners should they not have access to specialized forensic equipment such as aforementioned tool 'PC3000' that can assist with this issue.

Further to this, Magnet, Davies (2021) presents research regarding CMD42 locks and bypassing embedded system security for forensic data acquisition specifically relating to vehicle security [5] and the topic of CMD42 locks is discussed. CMD42 locks are found on eMMC chips which work in a similar way to ATA locks. These may be encountered built into vehicle systems and may continue to pose an issue in the future. CMD42 locks are commonly used in mobile and internet of things devices, to protect user data and specific to vehicle infotainment units, to block access to their proprietary firmware. These eMMC chips are made up of the controller and a raw NAND flash memory chip. The CMD42 is found in the controller of the chip, therefore, to access the data stored on the NAND flash memory chip, the controller needs to be bypassed. The NAND flash memory chip consists of scrambled data and the controller required to structure it in order to be in a readable format. Using a JTAG method and direct connection using tool 'ruSolut Visual Nand Reconstructor', [6] it was possible to get a data extraction by reading the chip directly to a NAND flash protocol, bypass the controller chip and dump the data out as a bin file.

Researchers found Henry (2017) [7], identifies the importance of differentiating between vehicle infotainment systems and telematics systems and that these are vastly different from crash data records (CDR) or event data recorders (EDR). CDR possesses safety sensor information, including but not limited to brake position, speed, steering wheel position, and airbag deployment. This information is recorded only for a few seconds prior to a crash occurring. This is vastly different than infotainment systems and telematics system data that is obtained from components that are not directly safety related (i.e., GPS data). This information indicates CDR data is the best for establishing direct crash diagnostics, however may not be the most beneficial for sources of more user generated forensic data.

Edwards et al.'s (2019) [8] research presented only certain applications can be used with Apple CarPlay. It is also noted that some of the data gathered from mobile devices can only be extracted with a mobile Full File System extraction, typically achieved through jailbroken devices, or advanced extraction tools including GrayShifts GrayKey and Cellebrite's Premium. This provided valuable insight in relation to further research for this paper's focus and lead to developing a forensic methodology in the research questions, and scope that a full file system extraction would be used.

Researchers Sladović et al. (2019) [9] found that a large amount of data can be recovered from vehicle forensics, including security logs of a vehicle moment before an accident occurs. The research further reflected a plethora of data can be gathered from vehicles infotainment units, including logs and what devices the IVI has been connected to. This paper does not look to verify the data located across multiple forensic interpretation software tools.

Research assessed in Mekki et al. (2019) [10] focused on the topic of driver identification and finger printing, its application for enhanced driver profiling and car security in connected cars. A cross-validation technique was used to provide results that could be reconstructed on unpredictable data for a driver identification model.

A paper written by Kopencova et al. (2020) [11] describes the challenges faced such as the storage of vehicle data, as it may be across different devices, in different data formats, and is often not standardized. Forensic tools used to analyze this wide variety of data are not standardized in the EU. This research further goes on to comment on the sources, classification, and characteristics of vehicle data, concluding that in the future there will be a need for affordable, sufficiently general and certified forensic technologies to approach vehicle forensics.

Research in the paper from Le-Khac et al. (2020) [12] explores the recoverable data from vehicle manufacturers, specifically models of Audi, VW, and BMW. Recovering data off these models and their electronic modules and places such as memory chips of the RNS device, was successful. This research further discusses the increasing challenge in obtaining information about the design of the vehicle digital components and their interactions.

Journal article Dobromirov et al. (2017) [13] explores the requirements and need for findings in the field of vehicle forensics to be determined by an expert witness in the framework of their professional knowledge, system analysis and scientific approach. This paper describes a method to determine an expert witness aiming to increase the degree of objectiveness when inspecting the technical state of vehicles and the procedure and rules. While research in the field of vehicle forensics tends to focus on the infotainment system and modules themselves, a key part is to begin to cross reference and look at data obtainable from a synced mobile device. Due to the continuously evolving field of technology and mobile devices and their ever-growing features and storage, many people store more information and personal information on their mobile devices than a computer [14].

In summary from the literature identified, it is clear that whilst vehicle forensics is a newer area of digital evidence, it is growing in both capability, awareness and utility when it comes to both investigations and data collection. The research provides groundwork approaches for data extraction and possible data that can be recovered from vehicles. It can also be learnt from the research, the intricacies of the on-board network and data storage functionality. However, the research is missing the analysis and comparison of artifacts between connected devices such as mobiles, and live capture of data.

3 Forensic Approach

3.1 Research Objectives

Vehicles store data as it is collected and processed by the vehicles system. This paper aims to investigate if there is data that is obtainable through not only the IVI acquisition, but further through a mobile device that had been connected to IVI and if similar data resides on both. Additionally, this research looks at the live interception data of a connected mobile device that may not be recoverable through acquiring the IVI system. By comparing these approaches, any inconsistencies in the data can be identified.

Vehicles contain a rich source of evidential data obtained across a wide variety of sources. It is also considered to be a newer area of digital forensics, with commercial tools in constant development to be able to support a wide range of vehicles, the associated vehicle data, and parse it accurately. It is imperative the data is validated to allow for the best assessment of evidence and forensic integrity.

Areas that remain unexplored include the live capture of data when a mobile is synced to an infotainment system. If the capture of this data were to be compared with the traditional dead-box forensics acquisitions, it may yield further artifacts of interest that were previously unobtainable. This provides additional avenues and approaches to explore for investigations.

This presents an opportunity for comparison between sources that may store valuable vehicle data. Vehicle data can be recovered from infotainment systems, through connected mobile devices and the mobile devices network traffic capture. There is potential for data to exist on one extraction method and not on the other.

There is a wide variety of vehicle systems created by manufacturers which means different data may be obtained in some but not others. It is of value to the wider forensic community to explore and test various models of devices.

Based on the described forensic approach, the research questions addressed in this paper are as follows: (i) will forensic extractions of synced mobile devices to the IVI systems yield more data and artifacts than the IVI system, and do some of these artifacts appear on both and; (ii) will live network interception of mobile devices, when synced to a vehicle, yield more information unavailable through the previous two acquisition methods.

3.2 Forensic Methodology

The adopted approach will be managed systematically, focusing on each forensic area of IVI systems, i.e. (i) internal storage in the IVI system; (ii) internal storage in the mobile device; (iii) wireless communication between the IVI and mobile device.

Internal Storage in the IVI System. The data will be acquired from vehicle infotainment units, with the focus on obtaining physical extractions and validating the data through parsing the acquired data structure through commercial tools, manual interpretation and further comparing the results to extractions from attached mobile devices. The IVI vehicles selected are two Ford Explorer models, one released 2015 and one in 2019. Data acquisition in the field of vehicle forensics can vary, with multiple open source and commercial tools existing to obtain this physical image from IVI's. Methods for data acquisition include reading the flash memory through Universal Asynchronous Receiver-Transmitter (UART), Join Test Action Group (JTAG), In-System-Programming (ISP), or completing a chip-off to acquire a physical image, or bit by bit copy of the flash memory. JTAG has become increasingly important as a way to bypass security [15]. JTAG methodology has been selected for this testing for the IVI acquisition. This is a physically invasive process that requires disassembly of the IVI in order to obtain access to the circuit board. This method was selected due to providing the ability to obtain a physical extraction of the devices data. Physical extractions provide a complete image of all data stored on the IVI, ensuring access to system data and allow for the ability to recover deleted files. This provides the research with the most comprehensive number of artifacts able to be obtained from the IVI system.

Tools selected for parsing and validation as they automate the interpretation of data, are as follows: Cellebrite Physical Analyser, X-Ways Forensics and further manual and open-source database viewers.

Artifacts of interest are as follows: User generated information including call logs, contact information, messaging content, third party application data e.g. Telegram, and Internet browsing and related artifacts.

Data that may further be available from vehicles include: (i) Application data, (ii) Connections through Bluetooth, (iii) Wi-Fi, (iv) cable connection and unique identifiers, (v) Contacts, (vi) Call logs, (vii) SMS, (viii) Media Files, (ix) System metadata and (x) Event data such as Blue tooth connections, Door opening/closing, Gear shifts, Light status, Media, Odometer Readings, Engine start/stop times, System information, USB connections, Wi-Fi connections, Hard braking and acceleration, Traction Events, Driver distraction, Apple CarPlay/Android Auto enabled,Voice command, Web browser history, Seatbelts, Ignition Key, Navigation, Emergency Assistance, Indicators, Navigation, Tracklogs, Location, Route. The infotainment system and user data connected to a synced mobile device will be the focus of this paper, although further aforementioned data is also likely to be available.

Internal Storage in the Mobile Device. The most extensive level of mobile device extraction possible at time of writing will be performed on the mobile devices attached and synced to the IVI system. The devices selected will be one each of Android and Apple operating systems, allowing for a comparison across different features that interface with a vehicle that may be used, such as Apple CarPlay and Android Auto. These makes of devices were selected due to their prevalence in the mobile device industry, as there was estimated to be over 6 billion smartphones in use globally in 2021, with half of those being Apple or Samsung devices [16]. The extracted data relevant to the vehicle and specified timeframe will be examined and compared to the direct infotainment system extraction. The two test devices will be used to interact with each other through calling and messaging, for the creation of test data and artifacts.

The first Samsung device is a Galaxy S9 + running Android OS 9, Model SM-G965U1. The device was named with test user profile of an online random name generator, 'Ida Evaristo' and account created was that of 'Ida.evaristo2@gmail.com' and mobile SIM card with active network connection, inserted with phone number '571 478 5440'.

The second device for testing is an Apple iPhone XR, Model A1984, running iOS 15.5. A name for the device to be applied to the user profile was also created using an online random name generator, of 'Plato Isador' with the attached email 'plato.isadore @icloud.com'. A mobile SIM card with active network connection was inserted with phone number '571 478 5516'.

Forensic tool 'Cellebrite UFED' [17] will be used for data extraction. This tool is commonly used in law enforcement agencies and private industry globally, having the capability to acquire various devices and extraction levels i.e., Logical, Filesystem, Physical and Full File System. A physical extraction will be completed on the Android mobile device as it is a bit-for-bit copy, copying all binary data from available chips on the circuit board and providing the most in-depth level of extraction. A Full File System will be done on the Apple iOS due to the iPhone architecture not allowing a Physical extraction for the selected model. These extraction types for these specific mobile devices are the most comprehensive for the respective models at the time of writing and can also be achieved with open-source tools.

Wireless Communication Between the Cloud and Mobile Device. A live network capture of transmitted data will be analyzed when testing the mobile devices connecting to the IVI. This is done through installed application 'Fiddler' on a mobile device, synced to an infotainment system. Application 'Fiddler' has been chosen for this research which is a tool that is utilized for inspecting and debugging network issues [18]. It offers capability that can inspect network browsing traffic, making it suitable for the testing goals.

The results of this captured data will be compared to the "dead-box" forensic findings of the IVI acquisition and mobile device extractions. The device will browse the internet to numerous online servers via user input search terms and navigating through web browsers.

This analysis will focus on capturing and analyzing network traffic from the mobile device's connection to the internet. Mobiles are not solely used for traditional communication methods due to their ever-developing computational power, larger screen display and increased memory, but now for a large number and variety of applications such as gaming, applications and browsing the internet. From these activities, a significant amount of network activity is generated over the internet or a Wi-Fi connection, which has the potential to provide evidential information should it be gathered. Due to the continuously increasing number of features on IVI systems, many of these contain the capabilities that allow for internet connectivity. Due to several of these applications requiring network connection, this provides a forensic opportunity for data interception.

The goal of analyzing mobile traffic data is to determine whether any further artifacts can be obtained that are not present on a forensic acquisition of the IVI system. This analysis and any learnings assume that the appropriate legal authorization has been obtained prior to any data interception, respective to any individual country and jurisdiction.

Data that is potentially available for interception includes packet capture data. These are files that contain packet data of a network and can subsequently be utilized to analyze network characteristics and determine network status. Metadata can also be obtained through live interception. Metadata can be defined as data about data.

The method chosen for capture and inspection of network traffic whilst a mobile device is connected to an infotainment unit via Bluetooth tethering, is to install a certificate directly on the mobile that will allow for a connection through a proxy and to an application that will log the required data. The approach requires direct access to the target mobile device. This method leverages the mobile devices operating system and must have granted permissions on the device it is installed on.

The focus of the live data interception is on network traffic. The HTTP/HTTPS traffic will then be captured from the mobile browser using the installed root certificate which can decrypt HTTP traffic. The browsers that will be tested include Google Chrome, Samsung browser and, on the iOS device, Safari. Live traffic can be filtered in Fiddler, for the specific IP address a mobile device is using under the established 'Client IP' column for the duration of the testing. Figure 1 depicts a connection being established between the vehicle and the testing devices (both Apple and Android). The Fiddler cert is installed on the device and then various web browsers are used to navigate online internet searching from the mobile device, generating user data. This traffic is then captured and viewable through the running application Fiddler on the connected laptop.

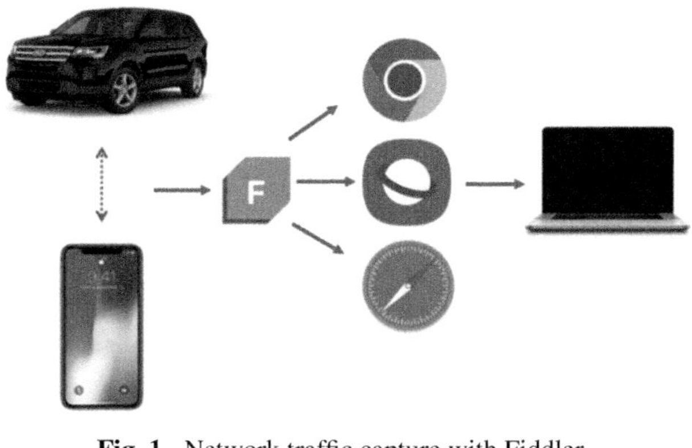

Fig. 1. Network traffic capture with Fiddler

Wireless Communication Between The IVI And Mobile Device. A function of mobile devices is their ability to interact with the vehicle infotainment system. Simultaneously capturing the network data from a connected mobile device and then imaging the IVI system, will determine what information gets stored where. There is the ability for data to be stored exclusively on the mobile device, or exclusively on the IVI system.

It is important for this analysis to be performed to determine where artifacts will be found and then further compare them to the live network capture.

4 Description of Results

4.1 Internal Storage in the IVI System

Two versions of IVI systems were selected for testing from different versions of Ford Explorer models. The first, a Ford Explorer 2015 model, found to contain a SYNC Generation 2 (Gen2) IVI system. This generation of Ford SYNC is a complete communications link for the late model Ford, Lincoln and Mercury product lines [19].

The second model chosen was a 2019 Ford Explorer containing a SYNC Generation 3 (Gen3) IVI system. A Physical image was acquired from both vehicles IVI's and the data examined. The IVI's varied greatly between each other, largely due to the respective operating systems (OS) they were running.

The acquired physical images were ingested into Cellebrite Physical Analyser v 7.55, which interpreted them as a relational database file. Data that is not successfully parsed into Physical Analyser's visual '*Analysed Data*' workbench tab, can be located manually in this database file, collated in a SQLite format. As it is all collated in a single database, this does not reflect the native forensic acquisition of the file and folder structure of the IVI system. The physical images can further be viewed manually, to parse, analyze and view data.

Ford Explorer 2015 and 2019 IVIs. The Ford Explorer 2019 contained an IVI of a SYNC Generation 3 running Blackberry's Limited [20] QNX OS. This was found to be a significant difference from the 2015 Ford Explorer, which contains a SYNC Generation 2 Microsoft Embedded Automotive OS IVI. Cellebrite Physical Analyser was able to be utilized to load the IVI extraction. The format that is created and imported, is a relational database file, therefore all data is being interpreted through SQLite tables. The acquired physical image file that is the Blackberry QNX OS is not able to be interpreted by all forensic tools. X-Ways Forensics for example, was not able to parse the image file in its native state at time of writing.

To enable interpretation and analysis of the data, a manual examination process had to be completed. A Linux virtual machine was used. By mounting the image file, a logical extraction of the partitions could be created. The partition type can be established as QNX Neutrino Power-Safe filesystem, through the identification of '0xb1' and '0xb2'.

This allows for two partitions to be extracted to a zip file for manual logical analysis, showing the files, and can further be ingested into other forensics tools.

4.2 Internal Storage in the Mobile Device

Internet Browsing History Ford Explorer. The browsing history data was generated on the mobile devices through user input search terms and subsequent navigation to websites while connected to the vehicle. This browser data was not captured in either physical acquisitions of the IVI's, therefore could not be viewed in any forensic tool, commercial or open source. Further forensic opportunities to obtain this data reside with the attached mobile devices used for this browsing or a live network capture.

Cellebrite Physical Analyser parsing the Full File System acquisition from *'Plato's iPhone'* was able to successfully obtain and interpret the web history data, across both browsers, Google Chrome, and Safari. The extraction also captured all the user input search terms accurately, along with the correlating time and date information.

Web history and search terms were also successfully parsed from *'Ida Evaristos'* Samsung Galaxy. Tested browser types were Android Browser and Google Chrome.

4.3 Wireless Communication Between the Cloud and Mobile Device

Live network intercept testing was completed on the mobile devices at the time of being connected to the vehicles IVI systems. Data was analyzed from both connected Android and Apple devices.

A connection to Fiddler was established through the mobile devices and a cert installed to route the traffic through a proxy.

Apple iPhone Testing Connected To Ford Explorer 2019 Live Network Intercept. Encrypted traffic flows through an allocated CONNECT tunnel and as HTTPS decryption were enabled in Fiddler. Decrypted sessions running in the tunnel can be viewed and saved in the application.

Data was able to be captured as online user input searches were conducted on the device. The GET request was obtained through the device using HTTPS and whilst the mobile device used Safari to search terms, this data was captured. The user-agent string was captured within the GET request header, which correctly identified the iPhone model, running OS and what browser was used to conduct the search. The history of search terms had been successfully captured by Fiddler. All the test data was able to successfully be obtained using this method. Further, pictures were obtained from searches conducted across Google images as depicted in Fig. 2.

A comparative analysis on the full file system extraction of the mobile device did not obtain the picture files that the user would have seen at the time of testing and/or interacted with. This reflects that the live interception data has insights that may not be recovered through mobile extraction artifacts later. The specific search terms, however, were recovered, validating the results to be accurate.

This testing also showed results did not differ across browsers, as from within both Safari and Google Chrome, the network traffic was still able to be captured.

These findings have shown that if a live interception were taking place, it is possible to obtain the users online browsing activity in real time. This is dependent on gaining access to the device and a cert to be installed for the best results.

Samsung Android Testing Connected to Ford Explorer 2019 Live Network Intercept. The connection to the vehicle from the Android device was set up in the same manner as the iPhone testing, utilizing application Fiddler. It successfully collected the same information, such as user-agent string attribution data and user driven and browsed data i.e., search terms and the resulting online images.

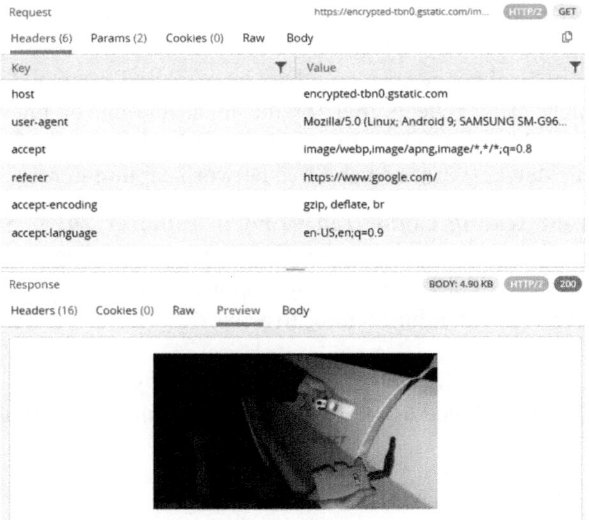

Fig. 2. Image results following 'how to hack key fobs' search query

Apple iPhone Testing Connected to Ford Explorer 2015 Similar successful results were obtained through testing the mobile traffic network interception for the devices connected to the 2015 Ford Explorer Gen2. Test search results were conducted such as the user input Google search *'how to hack cars'*. Fiddler captured the data as seen in Fig. 3.

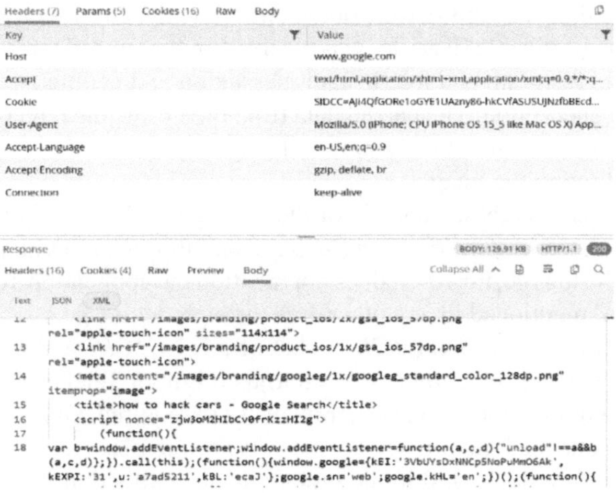

Fig. 3. Search 'how to hack cars'

This testing was also conducted across the aforementioned multiple chosen browsers and successfully obtained the search traffic and pictures. These results were able to be corroborated with the Apple iPhone mobile forensic extraction, as the key search terms were also located in the search history artifacts, however not the resulting displayed pictures.

All web history results, however, could not be extracted from the IVI system storage from either vehicle. This reflects that for the most amount of potentially evidential artifacts to be located for analysis, a combination of the three methods are required, IVI extraction, mobile device extraction and live network capture in real-time.

Samsung Android Testing Connected to Ford Explorer 2015. Similar tests were conducted on the Android Samsung device. User search terms input through the Google browsing application, Fiddler was able to capture and record this result. It further obtained the correct information relating to what device was in use in the user-agent string.

The traffic capture data did not obtain any tested navigational results; therefore, this data would need to be obtained using the prior two methods, IVI acquisition and mobile device imaging and analysis.

4.4 Wireless Communication Between the IVI and Mobile Device

Call Data Ford Explorer 2019. Call Data was extracted from the IVI. Test records from test iPhone connection 'Plato Isadore' were successfully obtained, with calls outgoing and incoming from test profiles *'Ida Evaristro'* (+1 572 478 5440). These records also contain accurate latitude and longitude information. This information was acquired directly from non-volatile data stored on the IVI, not pulled from local storage on the attached mobile device.

Calls placed natively through the iPhone calling functionality, using the mobile devices built-in calling capability were obtained and attributed correctly, however incoming call data from profile Ida Evaristo, was received and answered through mobile Application Telegram. Telegram is a free instant messaging and calling Application and utilizes end-to-end encryption. The parsed data from the IVI, while it records the call event occurring, does not attribute it to Telegram in any way, nor is *'Telegram'* mentioned in any other area through the image.

Through manual database analysis of the testing call log, the Telegram call information can be located in *'fordlogs' – pasdebug.log.1* through searching the '*RemoteID*' value (Fig. 4). The log file, however, does not mention the application Telegram by name, nor is *'Telegram'* mentioned in any other area through the image.

Further analysis of the *'RemoteID'* value of *5512815015* within the physical IVI image is unable to be specifically attributed to its origin of Telegram. To obtain further artifacts for attribution, other forensic approaches are required. One of these approaches is to analyze the attached mobile device that was used to place and receive these calls.

Parsing the information held in the mobile device extraction from 'Plato's iPhone' that was attached to the IVI, assists with the identification of the data source and further potentially providing further information of interest. The database '*CallHistory.storedata'* holds records attributing the 'RemoteID' 5512815015 to 'Ida Evaristo' and that the source is Telegram. This provides more insight to the involved parties than solely relying on one method.

```
67301 CallRemoteID::5512815015
67302 CallDisplayName::Ida Evaristo
67303 CallStatus::Ringing
67304 CallDirection::Incoming
67305 CallUUID::9E2EFDDC-D66E-47BD-A901-700B40A3C52D
67306 CallAddressBookID::
67311 07/23/2022 14:30:08.526/5108/29/NM_DioService/CPpsListener::Run/378/=Name:=> communications
67312 07/23/2022 14:30:08.526/5109/29/NM_DioService/CPpsListener::Run/424/-communications: Attr Name:=> CallAddressBookID Value:=>
67313 07/23/2022 14:30:08.526/5110/29/NM_DioService/CPpsListener::Run/424/-communications: Attr Name:=> CallDirection Value:=> Incoming
67314 07/23/2022 14:30:08.526/5111/29/NM_DioService/CPpsListener::Run/437/-communications: CallDirection = Incoming
67315 07/23/2022 14:30:08.527/5112/29/NM_DioService/CPpsListener::Run/424/-communications: Attr Name:=> CallDisplayName Value:=> Ida Evaristo
67316 07/23/2022 14:30:08.527/5113/29/NM_DioService/CPpsListener::Run/424/-communications: Attr Name:=> CallIsConferenced Value:=> 0
67317 07/23/2022 14:30:08.527/5114/29/NM_DioService/CPpsListener::Run/488/-communications: CallIsConferenced = 0
67318 07/23/2022 14:30:08.527/5115/29/NM_DioService/CPpsListener::Run/424/-communications: Attr Name:=> CallLabel Value:=>
67319 07/23/2022 14:30:08.527/5116/29/NM_DioService/CPpsListener::Run/424/-communications: Attr Name:=> CallRemoteID Value:=> 5512815015
67320 07/23/2022 14:30:08.527/5117/29/NM_DioService/CPpsListener::Run/444/-communications: Dialed Number = 5512815015
67321 07/23/2022 14:30:08.527/5118/29/NM_DioService/CPpsListener::Run/424/-communications: Attr Name:=> CallService Value:=> Unknown
67322 07/23/2022 14:30:08.527/5119/29/NM_DioService/CPpsListener::Run/424/-communications: Attr Name:=> CallStatus Value:=> Ringing
67323 07/23/2022 14:30:08.527/5120/29/NM_DioService/CPpsListener::Run/451/-communications: Call Status = Ringing
67324 07/23/2022 14:30:08.528/5121/29/NM_DioService/CPpsListener::Run/424/-communications: Attr Name:=> CallUUID Value:=> 9E2EFDDC-D66E-47BD-A901-700B40A3C52D
67325 07/23/2022 14:30:08.528/5122/29/NM_DioService/CPpsListener::Run/458/-communications: CallUUID = 9E2EFDDC-D66E-47BD-A901-700B40A3C52D
```

Fig. 4. Pasdebug.log.1

The *CallHistory.storedata* contained a record of all the further test data calls, providing the most comprehensive picture of call log activities. Cellebrite Physical Analyser was able to interpret and display this information in the database and further successfully obtain and parse the Telegram messaging history and associated contact information from the Apple iPhone mobile device extraction. This was not stored in the IVI system.

The Telegram message content was also parsed from the extraction of the Samsung Galaxy attributed to '*Ida Evaristo*'. The analysis of both mobile devices reflected a successful result of locating all tested messaging mechanisms, native message through the built-in phone features and Telegram, however the messaging was not located on the IVI. Further analysis of these devices was conducted which also captured the call logs of interest. Even if forensic tools are unable to locate these artifacts, a manual analysis of the source data can confirm the origin of the calling data, particularly in relation to a call being placed through Telegram, as it is stored in the 'cache4.db' database file created from the Telegram application.

4.5 Summary of Forensic Findings

Throughout the testing, a range of results were encountered following the forensic methodology approach taken. The file systems of the IVI systems have a great impact on forensic tool's ability to decode the data. It was found that the Ford Explorer 2015 Gen2 contained a Windows file system. However, the Gen3 contains a Blackberry QNX file system, with the latter having limitations on forensic tools abilities to interpret the data. Therefore, it is imperative a manual analysis be undertaken.

It was consistent across both IVIs that the best approach to obtain the most amount of data in the realm of vehicle forensics, would be to acquire both the IVI system, any mobile devices synced with the system, and conduct a live interception of network data from the mobile device. Artifacts were located from the synced mobile device extractions from both Apple and Android devices that were not located on the IVI system and vice versa. The live network interception was able to provide further browsing data information that was not obtained through all acquired forensic acquisitions. This provides a comprehensive approach to data recovery to corroborate events and located artifacts.

5 Evaluation and Discussion of Results

Data relating to vehicles can be recovered from vehicles in a variety of ways, whether this be from a direct imaging of the modules and infotainment units, extracted from mobile devices, or from interception data from a connected mobile device. Data from these methods can be analyzed to provide insight into the user's location history, connections, and pattern of life through behavior of the user. This research has shown that artifacts gathered from each device can vary substantially, with not all artifacts able to be obtained from any one specific approach.

This research has further shown that not only does the data obtained in the realm of vehicle forensics vary greatly, so do forensic tools in their abilities to parse data. Forensic tools should always be validated both manually, and compared with other forensic tools findings as it may yield further results.

A variety of prior research has been done in this space; however, this discusses the available data obtainable from IVI systems yet does not address using a variety of tools for interpretation to evaluate what may be missing, and for different methods to locate this. The findings of this paper can be applied to future research and analysis of vehicle forensic data and artifacts from connected devices.

Due to many common factors in an examination or laboratory setting, such as time-restraints, cost restraints and skill level, this research is practically useful to assist with determining what tools would make-up an ideal toolkit. This research has also shown that it is fundamental to have an appropriate level of understanding of how various file systems store data and how to manually parse this data out. This was discovered upon analysis of the 2019 Ford Explorer containing a SYNC Gen3 IVI system, as it had a QNX file system and OS. This file system was unable to be directly ingested into all tested forensic tools at time of writing and required manual interaction to allow for a logical analysis of the files.

The method of using forensic tools and a JTAG approach for IVI acquisition was used due to being a common approach particularly in digital forensic investigations today. However, there are other methods available to obtain data from IVI systems. These include using the OBDII (On Board Diagnostics) connector to attach directly to an IVI system and using publicly available scanning tools. This method has limitations, as it is not able to acquire a physical extraction this way and provides only limited data. A further option for data extraction is the crash data retrieval system created by Bosch, which has the ability to connect directly to the event data recorder (EDR). It also does not allow for physical extraction of data, but instead extracts the EDR data that contains information leading up to, during and following a crash event. This is data such as the vehicles velocity, braking and seatbelt deployment. While a further option of obtaining the data directly from an eMMC chip from the IVI systems circuit board to provide a physical image is available, this can potentially be an entirely destructive process.

Data that is often of interest throughout a vehicle forensic investigation has shown to be stored in either the vehicle IVI system or the synced mobile devices. Some of the user data can be found in both of these locations, for example messaging communication. This is made possible through allowing the pairing interconnectivity of these two devices.

It is possible for data to reside solely on the mobile device. The approach of extracting the mobile can be taken if there is no data of interest located on the IVI system, and that it may instead be stored on the previously connected mobile device. It can further assist with corroborating data obtained from an IVI system. For instance, the testing reflected that call data records can be obtained from the IVI system, but not attributed to what application the calls were placed through. By extracting the associated mobile device, further data was located to confirm and corroborate the application used, in this testing specifically, Telegram.

Mobile extractions to obtain information have long been used in the field of forensics. This is a common phase of digital forensic and law enforcement investigations, especially to assist in mapping the user of the mobile device's previous locations at a time of interest. This research has established that there are further avenues to explore in order to obtain this location data, than relying solely on the traditional forensic approach of extracting the mobile device. IVI systems now either simultaneously store the data from the connected mobile device that is location related, or create their own, providing a much more extensive picture of the user's location movements.

Further capturing live network data of a mobile device connected directly to a vehicles IVI system has proven to be beneficial, as this can capture user activity that is not always stored on an IVI. By intercepting data in real-time, this proved to be valuable to the overall picture and analysis of artifacts. Should only the methodology of acquiring the IVI have been undertaken, data available through network intercept, such as online activity and internet browsing, would have been unavailable.

The data interception methodology contains limitations such as gaining the necessary access to the mobile device and network to allow for the data to be captured. The results of this research were influenced by the ability to successfully establish the intercept. This methodology is unlikely to be conducted in a lab environment, therefore the appropriate legal authority and technical training is imperative and may not be possible in further cases if directly physical access to devices is not possible. This method may further yield different results should alternative models of vehicles and IVI systems be tested that may store web history. An additional challenge that persists in this area is the use of encryption. If this is present, it makes analysis of captured data, whether directly from the IVI or through captured network data, an area that requires further research.

6 Conclusion and Future Direction

Vehicle forensics has traditionally been considered to solely involve the in-vehicle infotainment system. While this may be the primary source of evidential data, further information can be obtained through other forensic methods. These methods include comparing the extraction data from a paired mobile device and further analysis of network traffic in-real time from a device connected to an in-vehicle infotainment system.

This paper shows that both data sources from in-vehicle infotainment systems and mobile devices are not mutually exclusive and when they are synced together via tethered USB, Bluetooth or Wi-Fi connection, data could be stored in either place. Data could reside solely on the in-vehicle infotainment system, the mobile device or both. This research has further shown, the results are likely to vary dependent on the models used.

It is the conclusion of this research that vehicle forensics cannot be approached from a stand-alone perspective of only analyzing the in-vehicle infotainment system. More data is obtained when approached from a multi-phase process, to include extracting forensic data from a synced mobile device to corroborate data from the in-vehicle infotainment system and provide further artifacts. By combining these methodologies each method's strengths can compensate for others' weaknesses.

The findings from this research reflect forensic best practices would be enhanced by instead of addressing vehicle forensics as dead-box forensics and solely analyzing an IVI in isolation, to look at combining this with live network interceptions and mobile device extractions. By integrating these approaches into a consistent methodology for approaching each vehicle forensic investigation, a more extensive amount of data can be gathered along with robust and reliable results. The practical implications for digital forensics practitioners based on these findings mean that a larger amount of data would need to be examined in the form of a physical IVI extraction and either a physical or full file system extraction from a mobile device, protocols developed for safely and effectively accessing IVI and mobile devices to establish network interceptions and processes implemented for capturing, filtering and analyzing network data in real-time.

Further work could be done in this area of vehicle forensics, with consideration to the potential for vehicles to follow the natural progression of technology in the privacy space and widely enable encryption. Further research into this area could be considered, as this is also relevant to the interception of live network data. Developing new practical methods for bypassing or decrypting IVI's and research in cryptographic vulnerabilities and lawful interception techniques could enhance access to critical data. There may be opportunity to take an approach such as sniffing the communication between the phone and the car to the internet or cloud activity, or a man-in-the-middle attack.

Further research could also be conducted on a larger sample size of vehicle data using this papers approach, comparing the thousands of makes and models of vehicles available on today's market to determine if their varying file systems yield the same results. By investigating how various architectures and IVI systems affect the data extraction process, this could lead to an improved methodology.

Additional future research directions could also focus on removing a large amount of the manual overhead on the validation of the data obtained by creating forensic tools that provide a streamlined experience of ingesting data form mobile device extractions, IVI's and network interceptions with the goal of presenting reliable forensic evidence in a clear and concise manner.

The field of vehicle forensics can contain data that is critical within digital forensic investigations due to the ever-increasing number of connected vehicles on the road today. This research has provided findings reflecting the various methods to obtain vehicle related forensic artifacts and with further research, the capabilities in this area can continue to grow.

References

1. Corporation, B.: Discover Vehicle Data. https://berla.co/discover. Accessed Dec 2022
2. Lacroix, J., El-Khatib, K., Akalu, R.: Vehicular digital forensics: what does my vehicle know about me? In: Proceedings of the 6th ACM Symposium on Development and Analysis of Intelligent Vehicular Networks and Applications, pp. 59–66 (2016). https://doi.org/10.1145/2989275.2989282

3. Moos, J., et al.: Digital forensics for automobile systems: the challenges and a call to arms. Int. J. Forensic Sci. **1**(1), 2016 (2016)
4. AceLabs.: PC3000 UDMA (2022). https://www.acelab.eu.com/pc3000.udma.php. Accessed 18 Aug 2022
5. Davies, G.: CMD42 Lock: Bypassing Embedded System Security for Forensic Data Acquisition A.K.A Bypassing Vehicle Infotainment Security. Magnet Forensics (2021). https://www.magnetforensics.com/resources/cmd42-lock-bypassing-embedded-system-security-for-forensic-data-acquisition-recorded-webinar-feb-25/. Accessed 18 Aug 2022
6. Resolut: Visual NAND Reconstructor (2020). https://rusolut.com/. Accessed 18 Aug 2022
7. Henry, P.: Digital forensics – automotive infotainment and telematics systems. SANS Institute of Technology (2017). https://www.sans.org/blog/digital-forensics-automotive-infotainment-and-telematics-systems/. Accessed 18 Aug 2022
8. Sarah Edwards, H.M.: They See Us Rollin, They Hatin-Forensics of iOS CarPlay and Android Auto. SANS DFIR. https://papers.put.as/papers/ios/2019/summit_archive_1564072550.pdf. Accessed 18 Aug 2022
9. Sladović, D., Topolčić, D., Hausknecht, K., Sirovatka, G.: Investigating modern cars. In: 42nd International Convention on Information and Communication Technology, Electronics and Microelectronics (MIPRO), Opatija, pp. 1159–1164 (2019). https://doi.org/10.23919/MIPRO.2019.8756732
10. Mekki, A.E., Bouhoute, A., Berrada, I.: Improving driver identification for the next-generation of in-vehicle software systems. IEEE Trans. Veh. Technol. **68**(8), 7409–7415 (2019)
11. Kopencova, D., Rak, R.: Issues of vehicle digital forensics. In: 2020 XII International Science-Technical Conference Automotive Safety, Poland (2020)
12. Le-Khac, N.-A., Jacobs, D., Nijhoff, J., Bertens, K., Choo, K.-W.R.: Smart vehicle forensics: challenges and case study. Future Gener. Comput. Syst. **109**, 500–510 (2020). https://doi.org/10.1016/j.future.2018.05.081
13. Dobromirov, V., Dotsenko, S., Verstov, V., Volkov, S.: Methods of examining vehicle electronic systems in the course of automotive forensic expert examinations. Transp. Res. Procedia **20**, 143–150 (2017). https://doi.org/10.1016/j.trpro.2017.01.037
14. Li, Y., et al.: A Blockchain-assisted intelligent transportation system promoting data services with privacy protection. Sensors **20**, 2843 (2020). https://doi.org/10.3390/s20092483
15. Hayes, D.R.: A Practical Guide to Computer Forensics Investigations, Pearson Education (2020)
16. O'Dea, S.: Number of smartphone subscriptions worldwide from 2016 to 2027. Accessed 2 July 2022
17. Cellebrite: Digital Intelligence Solution Suite (2022). https://cellebrite.com/en/product/
18. Telerik: Fiddler Everywhere (2022). https://www.telerik.com/download/fiddler-everywhere
19. l. a. Semiconductors, Ford SYNC (2nd generation) Teardown. Electronics360 (2013). https://electronics360.globalspec.com/article/3192/ford-sync-2nd-generation-teardown
20. Blackberry: Power-Safe filesystem. Blackberry (2022). https://www.qnx.com/developers/docs/7.1/index.html#com.qnx.doc.neutrino.user_guide/topic/fsystems_QNX6_filesystem.html

Autonomous Driving System Configuration Defect Detection Method Based on Fuzzing

Jinzhao Liu[1], Xiao Yu[1](✉), Li Zhang[2], Yanqiu Zhang[1], Yuanzhang Li[3], Kun Tan[4], and Yuan Tan[3]

[1] School of Computer Science and Technology, Shandong University of Technology, Zibo, China
yuxiao8907118@163.com

[2] Department of Media Engineering, Communication University of Zhejiang, Hangzhou, China

[3] School of Computer Science and Technology, Beijing Institute of Technology, Beijing, China

[4] Shandong Institute of Information Technology Industry Development, Jinan, China

Abstract. The configuration item values of each component within the autonomous driving system (ADS) are mutually constrained and complexly associated, which leads to problems such as configuration logic faults and memory overflow easily occurring during the configuration process, thus triggering the frequent occurrence of system configuration faults. This paper proposes a dynamic fuzzing method for configuration parameters based on static analysis of source code, through mapping and extracting configuration constraints within the system, realizing dynamic fuzzing for configuration parameters based on source code characterization, and completing the diagnosis of configuration defects and assistive repair functions. The experimental results show that the fuzzing method is effective in detecting and localizing configuration parameter defects under a variety of ADS anomalies, which not only dramatically improves the coverage rate of system configuration defect detection, but also achieves a configuration defect detection rate of 89.9%.

Keywords: Autonomous Driving · Fuzzing · Static Analysis · Configuration Defects

1 Introduction

With the rapid development of computer technology and the continuous improvement in computing power, the scale of modern computer software systems continues to expand. Commonly used open-source software systems have now grown to millions of lines of code. Configuration faults have become a significant cause of system anomalies, service failures, and even system crashes [1]. Researchers have found that among major services such as Google, configuration failures ranked second as the cause of failure, accounting for nearly 29% [2]. Similarly, in systems like Hadoop, configuration failures are also a primary factor leading to failures [3].

S. Goel et al. (Eds.): ICDF2C 2024, LNICST 614, pp. 296–312, 2025.
https://doi.org/10.1007/978-3-031-89360-5_18

Table 1. Root causes of bugs in ADS.

Root cause	Apollo	Autoware	$Total_{cause}$
Algorithm	74	65	139
Assignment	25	22	47
Missing condition checks	16	4	20
Incorrect conditional logic	17	13	30
Concurrency	2	4	6
Incorrect documentation	36	13	49
Misconfiguration	34	102	136
Others	39	33	72
$Total_{system}$	243	256	499

The configuration framework of the Robot Operating System (ROS) includes a large number of parameters and is susceptible to various configuration defects [4]. In domains such as ADS, which face numerous configuration items and complex constraint relationships. Misconfigurations can lead to system security issues, potentially endangering lives and causing privacy concerns [5]. Table 1 illustrates the causes of software defects in Apollo and Autoware ADS [6], where configuration flaws accounted for 27.25% of the cases, posing significant challenges to ADS security. For instance, PlanFuzz [23] identified an issue in the Apollo system where overly conservative lateral distance thresholds in lane change decision logic caused nearby vehicles to be perceived as occupying the target lane, forcing ADS vehicles to abandon lane change decisions, potentially preventing them from reaching their destinations. Fuzzing techniques have proven advantageous in identifying configuration security issues. Popular fuzzing tools like Microsoft's OneFuzz [7], Google's AFL [8], and Honggfuzz [9] primarily target testing C/C++ applications, system kernels, browsers, and network protocols, but cannot be directly applied to unmanned systems due to factors such as monitoring categories and input space. To tackle this challenge, researchers have proposed automated (or semi-automated) techniques to generate AV test cases and observing the behavior of target self-driving vehicles [10–15]. These approaches utilize methods ranging from random sampling [13] to training machine learning models [15] for test case generation, though they often overlook edge cases and require extensive time investments.

To address the above-described challenges, this study explores an approach for detecting configuration defects in ADS based on fuzzing. The proposed method integrates static analysis and fuzzing techniques to identify system defects accurately. The source code undergoes parsing and semantic analysis using static analysis to identify and extract configuration constraints precisely. Fuzzing is then employed to simulate diverse configuration scenarios that users might encounter, verifying system behavior in realistic settings to uncover potential configuration defects and abnormal behaviors.

By leveraging both techniques, the proposed method comprehensively detects potential configuration defects and verifies system stability and fault tolerance in real-world scenarios.

2 Related Work

2.1 Configuration Constraint Inference

Configuration constraint inference forms the foundation for studying software configuration defects. Researchers construct software configuration constraint models based on their understanding of configuration rules. These models can generate test cases that violate configuration constraints, thereby uncovering potential configuration defects and vulnerabilities. They can also be utilized in tools for detecting and localizing configuration defects. Current research in this field typically falls into four categories: configuration file parsing, system source code analysis, and configuration log analysis.

Some of this work analyzes software configuration items by modeling them at the software engineering level. Xiong et al. [16] modeled value ranges for multiple parameters of a system to aid in detecting and repairing misconfigurations. Huang et al. [17] implemented a prototype tool called ConfValley, which provides a simple domain specific language for cloud system operators to express configuration checking logic.

Some of the work starts from the perspectives of configuration file parsing of finished software products and source code analysis of software systems to infer constraints on the configuration items of a software system. ConfTest, a configuration testing tool proposed by Wang Li et al. [18], parses configuration files to generate structured data as a model of configuration constraints of a system. SPEX, a tool implemented by Sai Zhang et al. [19], targets the source code of the system and accurately identifies the statements and execution paths affected by configuration parameters, enabling the detection and localization of system anomalies caused by configuration defects.

Some researchers have adopted the method of self-learning configuration rules to discover the 'common pattern' of correct configuration from configuration-related data. The CODE tool, implemented by Ding Yuan et al. [20], and the Encore tool, implemented by Jiaqi Zhang et al. [21], employ a template-based learning approach to analyze and extract association constraints between configuration items. They gather extensive training data from public image files on Amazon EC2.

To address the limitations of existing software configuration constraint extraction methods in the context of ADS, this paper proposes an innovative method designed to efficiently extract configuration constraints. This method fully considers the characteristics and complexity of such systems.

2.2 Fuzzing

In recent years, researchers have continued to innovate fuzzing techniques. They have adopted new vulnerability mining methods, proposed new frameworks for vulnerability mining, and developed new tools to enhance the effectiveness of vulnerability mining techniques for software systems.

DeepFuzz [22] is an enhanced gray-box fuzzing tool using symbolic execution for initial seed generation and a statistical seed selection algorithm for balanced mutation frequency. However, symbolic execution can result in insufficiently diverse initial seeds due to the path explosion problem. PlanFuzz [23] attempts to discover denial-of-service vulnerabilities in the planning layer by introducing physical objects, but this can increase system complexity and difficulty in scenario generation. DriveFuzz [24] is a feedback-guided fuzzing framework guiding variant generation to trigger safety-critical misbehavior through driving quality metrics.

To address the problems of excessive input space, inconsistent fault determination conditions, and incomplete coverage, this paper proposes a dynamic fuzzing method for ADS configuration parameters. This method aims to discover potential configuration defects and abnormal behaviors.

3 Design and Technical Implementation

Based on an investigation of existing work, this paper proposes and implements a configuration defect detection method for ADS by analyzing configuration-related source code features. The overall architecture is depicted in Fig. 1.

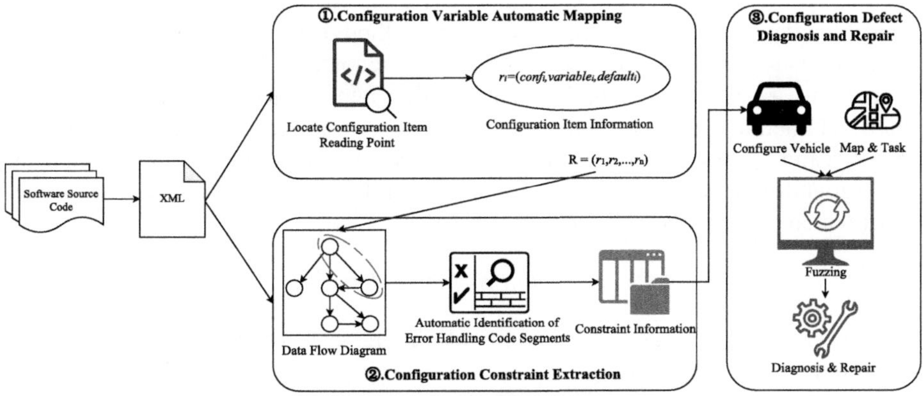

Fig. 1. System architecture diagram.

The system is divided into three parts:

1. Configuration variable automatic mapping. This section implements automatic mapping of configuration item variables through source code features, establishing mapping relationships from software configuration items to corresponding hidden configuration variable names in program source code.
2. Configuration constraint extraction. This section focuses on extracting relevant constraints of configuration variables from branch processing statements, including type constraints, value range constraints, and control constraints between multiple configuration items. Reasonable constraints are extracted by automatically recognizing the semantics of branch processing statements and determining whether they are normal functional logic code segments or error handling code segments.

3. Configuration defect diagnosis and repair. This section is based on extracted constraints. A configuration defect diagnosis and assisted repair tool is designed and implemented using fuzzing. Leveraging an automated fuzzing framework, the tool enables rapid diagnosis and assisted repair of configuration faults by continuously changing configuration items, repeatedly testing the ADS in real driving scenarios, and monitoring vehicle operation status in real-time.

3.1 Configuration Variables Automatic Mapping

To map configuration items to program variables in source code, it's necessary to identify and locate them in the software system. In the ADS, configuration files exist as Launch text files, from which information can be extracted by parsing. The system stores and shares data through a parameter server, involving three roles: ROS Master, Talker, and Listener. The Talker defines configuration items in the Launch file, which the ROS Master loads into ROS space upon launch. The Listener then uses Param and GetParam methods to read the loaded items from ROS space and assign them to corresponding configuration variables. These variables affect the runtime system's behavior.

Based on the above code analysis, the automatic mapping method of configuration variables designed in this paper is as follows: preprocess the source code file and convert it into an abstract syntax tree as well as an XML format document. XPath syntax is used to locate the call locations of Param and GetParam methods in the XML file and extract their parameter lists. The final parameter list found is denoted as the set $R = (r_1, r_2, \ldots, r_n)$. r_i represents a vector consisting of configuration item names, configuration variable names, and default values of configuration items, denoted as Eq. (1). For instance, in the A* search algorithm of the planning module, the configuration information that can be found is default values default values as follows: ("longitudinal_goal_range", "longitudinal_goal_range_", 2.0).

$$r_i = (conf_i, variable_i, default_i) \tag{1}$$

Algorithm 1 provides an overview of the process of automatic mapping of configuration item variables.

Algorithm 1. Automatic mapping of configuration variables

Auxiliary Functions:

XMLDocUtils(): Parse XML documents to generate tree models.

isMatch(): Determine whether the current node is the calling node of the Param or GetParam method

TextContent(): Convert node information to text content.

getvalue(): Get node parameter information.

Input: XML file of system source code *XML_file*.

Output: Mapping list of configuration items *R*.

```
R ← ∅
Processed_nodes ← ∅
NodeDocument ⇐ XMLDocUtils(XML_file)
for each node in NodeDocument do
   if isMatch(node) then
      NodeContent ⇐ TextContent(node)
      conf, variable, default ⇐ NodeContent.getvalue()
      if (conf, variable, default) not in Processed_nodes then
         R ← conf, variable, default
         Processed_nodes.add((conf, variable, default))
   end if
end for
return R
```

3.2 Configuration Constraint Extraction

Once the automatic mapping of configuration item variables is completed, analyzing program variable usage and extracting configuration variable-related constraints from the source code becomes necessary. This process involves acquiring configuration variable types and extracting branching constraints associated with them. Basic types of configuration variables are obtained from the abstract syntax tree, while semantic types are derived from the name and value features of the configuration items. The branching conditions of configuration variables are analyzed and recorded, facilitating the extraction of valid configuration constraints through automated recognition of error handling code segments based on source code features.

Obtain Configuration Variable Type. Software configuration items are external variables required during software runtime and belong to specific types. For example, “use_sukf” is a Bool type, “update_rate” is an Integer type. There are more complex types like “output_file”, which is a String type that requires a valid file path, and “port”, which is an Integer type that requires a value between 0 and 65535. These complex types contain specific semantic information and must meet specific formats or requirements, differing from common basic types. The focus of this section is to obtain the basic types and semantic types of configuration variables.

Obtain the Basic Type of Configuration Variables. To obtain the basic type of configuration variables, it is mainly implemented based on the abstract syntax tree (AST) when these variables are declared and used. The specific implementation extracts the semantic information of configuration variables from AST to determine their basic types.

For example, for the configuration variable "_leaf_size" shown in Fig. 2, its corresponding AST information is depicted in the identification position in Fig. 3. It is evident from this depiction that the basic type of "_leaf_size" is floating point.

autoware.ai-1.14 -
lidar_euclidean_cluster_detect.cpp

```
103 static bool _pose_estimation;
104 static double _leaf_size;
105 static int _cluster_size_min;
```

Fig. 2. Configuration variable basic type code example.

```
|-VarDecl 0x55c6928b2bf8 <line:103:1, col:13> col:13 _pose_esti
|-VarDecl 0x55c6928b2c88 <line:104:1, col:15> col:15 _leaf_size
|-VarDecl 0x55c6928b2d18 <line:105:1, col:12> col:12 _cluster_s
```

Fig. 3. Configuration variable basic type AST example.

Acquisition of Semantic Types of Configuration Variables. The semantic type of configuration variables refers to categorizing configuration items based on specific meanings in their values. Research on configuration files of open-source software classified common semantic types into file types, IP types, network ports, and more. The naming of certain configuration items and their corresponding variables usually follows specific conventions. For example, "calibration_file" indicates the path to the sensor calibration file, and "port" indicates the system's port number. This paper designed rules to obtain semantic types based on names and default values, as shown in Table 2.

Based on the rules in Table 2, the semantic types of certain configuration items can be extracted through string matching for configuration item names or regular expression matching for configuration item values.

Configuration Variable Branch Constraint Extraction. Through analysis, this paper finds that there are a large number of branching statement modules in the software source code, which allow the software to process configuration items based on different conditional restrictions.

Figure 4 shows the branching condition checks whether the configuration variable "declaration_source" is less than 1 or greater than 3. If so, the system triggers an error and reassigns the value. This implies the value range of "declaration_source" is [1, 3]. Figure 5 illustrates a branching statement extracts inter-configuration value constraints. The comment preceding the branch and the subsequent code indicate the configuration variable "iteration_threshold_warning_" must be smaller than "iteration_threshold_stop_".

Table 2. Configuration extraction rules for semantic types.

Semantic Type	Name Characteristics	Value Characteristics	Example
File type	*_file_*	?+(/+)*	/tmp/ mxnet-network.json
Directory type	None	/?+(/+)*/?	/detection/ fusion_tools/objects
IP type	None	\b(?:[0-9a-fA-F]{1,4}:){7}[0-9a-fA-F]{1,4}\b	192.168.1.1
Network address	None	https?://+(.+)*.+|+(.+)*.+	https://github.com/ ANYbotics/kindr.git

autoware.ai-1.14 - microstrain.cpp

```
private_nh.param("declination_source",declination_source,2);
if (declination_source < 1 || declination_source > 3) {
    ROS_WARN("declination_source can't be %#04X. Setting to 2.", declination_source);
    declination_source = 2;
}
```

Configuration parameter correction.

Reasonable constraints should be the inversion of logical judgment conditions.

Fig. 4. Examples of configuration variable value range constraints.

autoware.ai-1.14 - ndt_matching_monitor.cpp

```
//swap values in case of error
if (iteration_threshold_warning_ > iteration_threshold_stop_) {
    auto aux = iteration_threshold_stop_;
    iteration_threshold_stop_ = iteration_threshold_warning-warning;
    iteration_threshold_warning_ = aux;
}
```

Fig. 5. Examples of numerical constraints between multiple configurations.

For the above constraints that can be extracted by branching statements, this paper considers two common branching structures: If control statements and Switch selection statements. These are utilized for extracting configuration variable constraints based on the XML file generated from the source code.

In this process of branch constraint extraction, the established mapping relationship between configuration items and configuration variables is used to locate branch statements and value-passing calls of configuration variables in the XML file. It determines whether there is a logical judgment related to the configuration variable in the branch statement; whether there is a branch statement with a formal parameter corresponding to the configuration variable in the value passing call. If such conditions are met, the branch statement and its subsequent code block are recorded.

Algorithm 2 shows an overview of branch constraint extraction.

Algorithm 2. Configuration item constraint extraction without function call

Auxiliary Functions:

XMLDocUtils(): Parse XML documents to generate tree models.

TextContent(): Convert node information to text content.

isConditionMatch(): Determine whether the current node is an if or switch conditional judgment node.

isHasBranchStatements(): Determine the existence of branch statements in the current function

getConditionvalue(): Get the logical judgment and structure information of the current node.

getFunctionvalue(): Get the node information, function name, and corresponding formal parameters for calling the value of the current configuration parameter.

getParam(): Analyze variables for logical judgment.

Input: XML file of system source code *XML_file*; mapping list of configuration items *R*.

Output: Configuration variable logical judgment list *ConfList*.

```
ConfList ←∅
NodeDocument ⇐ XMLDocUtils(XML_file)
for each node in NodeDocument do
  if isConditionMatch(node) then
    LogicJudgment, Structure ⇐ node.getConditionvalue()
    for variable in R do
      if getParam(LogicJudgment) == variable do
        ConfList ← LogicJudgment, Structure
      end if
    end for
  end if
end for
for variable in R do
  node, FunctionName, FormalParameter ← getFunctionvalue(variable)
  if isHasBranchStatements(FunctionName, FormalParameter) then
    LogicJudgment, Structure ⇐ node.getConditionvalue()
    ConfList ← LogicJudgment, Structure
  end if
end for
return ConfList
```

This paper implements automatic identification of error handing modules based on source code features to obtain legitimate configuration variable constraints. After initial steps, branching statement conditions are analyzed and documented. Semantic information of branching statement conditions is analyzed to determine whether they represent normal functional logic or error handing code segments. Branching conditions are then evaluated to determine if they need to be changed based on identification results.

Automatic Identification of Error Handling Code Segments. Error handling code segment features are diverse, and error handling code segments in different software systems many different features. Through manual analysis, this section summarizes the features of error handling code segments, which include three categories: error handling function naming features, error message keyword features, and reassignment of values to configuration variables.

By analyzing the above three features, this paper designs and implements an automatic identification method for error handling code segments. This method is used to determine whether the branch statement containing the configuration variable is classified as an error handling code segment. If it is, the judgment logic of the branch condition needs to be inverted to obtain the final legitimate branch constraint of the configuration variable.

3.3 Configuration Defect Diagnosis and Repair

In this study, a dynamic fuzzing method is proposed for driverless vehicles using the results of configuration constraint extraction. The method parses the extracted configuration constraint into a seed file, processes the seed file to generate multiple sets of configuration parameter test cases through mutation policies, and uploads them to the ADS. The effectiveness of the fuzzing process is evaluated by calculating the code coverage rate, function coverage rate, and fault rate. In case of abnormal behaviors, the system reports the violated constraints and assists in configuration repair. The detailed system diagram is shown in Fig. 6.

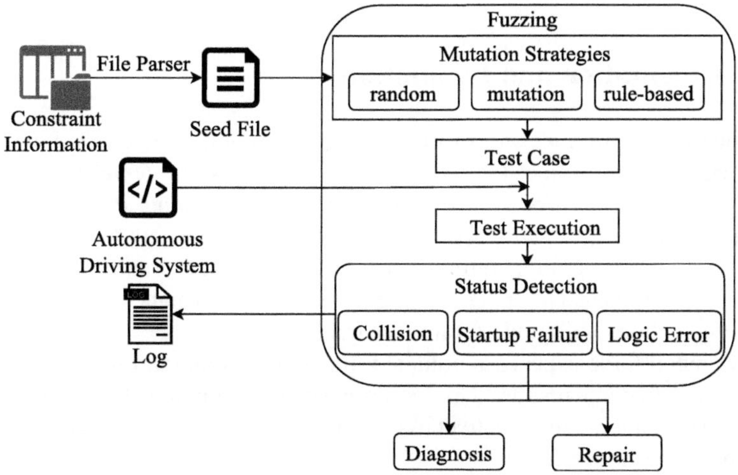

Fig. 6. Fuzzing architecture diagram.

Mutation Strategies. This paper employs various configuration term mutation strategies: random, mutation, and rule-based methods, to evaluate system performance under different configurations. The random method generates test cases within legal configuration constraints, the mutation method generates configuration errors by violating parameter specifications, and the rule-based method mutates given values according to predefined rules.

Combining these strategies enables a more comprehensive assessment of the system's adaptability to different configuration conditions.

State Detection. Configuration test cases generated after fuzzing may lead to various issues in the operation of the autonomous driving vehicle, making the judgment the ADS state crucial for error detection. In this paper, we assess the specific state of the ADS by defining the state categories and analyzing real-time data flow such as speed, acceleration, sensor information, etc., through the simulator. The specific state categories are detailed in Table 3.

Table 3. Autonomous vehicle status categories.

ADS Status	Meaning
Collision	The ADS vehicle has a collision problem during operation
Startup Failure	The ADS vehicle fails to start if there is an abnormality in a configuration item
Logic Error	The unmanned vehicle can start normally, but cannot reach the set end point properly

4 Experimentation and Evaluation

To evaluate the performance and validity of our experiments, we utilized the Autoware open-source software project for ADS vehicles as the experimental target. Autoware includes settings for sensors, control parameters, path planning, obstacle recognition, and more, encompassing many critical configuration parameters for ADS safety. We assessed automated mapping, configuration variable constraint extraction, and fuzzing results. This comprehensive understanding of system performance and effectiveness in practical applications will guide future research.

We evaluated three aspects: automated mapping, configuration variable constraint extraction, and fuzzing results. This comprehensive evaluation helps understand the system's performance and effectiveness in practical applications, providing valuable insights for future research.

4.1 Automatic Mapping of Configuration Item Variables

Experiments were designed to evaluate an automated mapping tool. The following indicators were assessed:

- Accuracy of configuration item variable mapping;
- Efficiency of configuration item variable mapping;

To validate the effectiveness of the mapping method proposed in this paper, it was compared with a conventional text matching method. As shown in Table 4, when only the improved text matching method is used, the recognition rate for some software systems is relatively low. However, after applying the method proposed in this paper, the number of mappings increased significantly, achieving 100% recognition accuracy. This indicates the method outperforms the text matching method in terms of mapping results.

Table 4. Configuration item automatic mapping results.

Module	Automatic mapping results	Text matching results
common	74	21
core-perception	366	197
core-planning	557	359
utilities	67	7
simulation	47	12
visualization	35	18
drivers	96	66
Total	1242	680

Finally, this paper evaluates the mapping efficiency. The analysis time required for targeting the Autoware system is only 10.871 s, which falls well within the acceptable range. This further validates the efficiency and feasibility of the methodology in this paper.

4.2 Configuration Variable Constraint Extraction

Based on the automatic identification of error handling code segments, this subsection conducts an experimental evaluation of configuration variable constraint extraction. By testing each Autoware module, specific experimental results are shown in Table 5. In total, 721 configuration constraints of various types were extracted. Automated analysis and validation based on source code semantics and references such as user manuals resulted in a 91.8% accuracy rate for configuration variable constraint extraction.

As seen from the table, the core-perception and core-planning modules extract relatively more constraints, a phenomenon closely related to the importance of these two modules in the system. This paper conducts an in-depth analysis of configuration items that are not extracted with constraints, focusing on a detailed study at the source code level. Although these configuration items are used in the source code, their values are not rigorously checked. This is not an isolated case. If the value of a configuration term is modified through some loophole, the lack of necessary security checks on the subsequent use of the configuration term by the system could lead to potential system problems caused by misconfiguration, with vulnerabilities to configuration defects. This finding highlights a possible security issue in automated driving systems that requires further attention and resolution.

Table 5. Configuration variable constraint extraction quantity.

Module	Single Configuration Item Constraint				Multiple Configuration Item	Type Constraint
	Boolean Type	Enum Type	Numeric Type	Other		
common	7	2	0	2	0	36
core-perception	38	4	5	3	4	157
core-planning	47	14	2	4	6	182
simulation	8	2	1	0	0	31
utilities	5	0	1	2	2	51
visualization	1	0	0	0	0	31
drivers	11	0	3	2	0	57
#Total	117	22	12	13	12	545

4.3 Experiment and Evaluation of Fuzzing Method

Experimental Evaluation Indicators. In this paper, we consider two fuzzing metrics: failure rate and coverage rate, which are important indicators of the quality of test cases generated by fuzzing. Failure rate represents the ratio of configuration parameters that can lead to abnormal behaviors of the ADS to the total number of parameters. A higher failure rate indicates a higher likelihood of discovering vulnerabilities. Coverage rate represents the ratio of executed statements, functions, and methods during testing. In this study, line and branch coverage of the core-planning and core-perception modules in the Autoware system are assessed to evaluate the effectiveness of fuzzing.

Analysis of Experimental Results. For the failure rate, based on the results of configuration constraint extraction, this paper selects enum type, boolean type, and numerical type, totaling 151 configuration parameters. It generates a total of 1,000 groups of configuration parameter test cases using random, mutation, and rule method. These cases are statistically analyzed to count the occurrence and percentage of various states in the ADS. The specific results of these percentage are shown in Fig. 7.

From Fig. 7, it can be observed that among the configuration parameter test cases generated by fuzzing, 89.9% of the cases can lead to abnormal behaviors of the ADS vehicle. This indicates that the fuzzing method designed in this paper effectively detects a high number of configuration faults. Details of some configuration settings and software operation statuses are shown in Table 6.

The experiments demonstrate that software configuration failures occur when settings don't meet configuration constraints. Once the configuration is adjusted to align with constraints, the software operates normally. The proposed configuration constraint extraction method is effective in diagnosing configuration faults.

In addition, when generating test cases with configuration parameters randomly within the legal configuration constraints using the random method, 40 software configuration defects were successfully detected. These defects involved multiple software

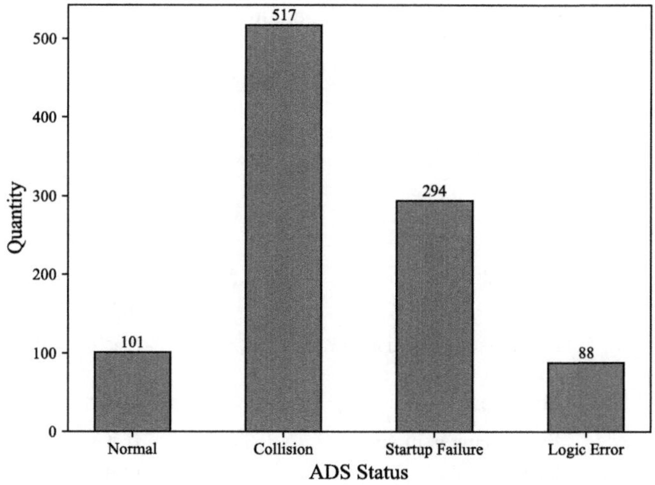

Fig. 7. The number and proportion of various states of ADS.

Table 6. Software configuration settings that partially violate constraints.

Configuration Items	Constraints	Values	Status	Mutation Strategy
overwrite_vmax_mode	true/false	faLse	Collision	Rule-Based
temporal_waypoints_size	[0,150]	151	Collision	Random
concentric_divider_ distance	[0,1]	0.5846	Normal	Random
velocity_min	[0,10]	10.26	Collision	Random
replanning_mode	true/false	1.2	Startup Failure	Mutation
stop_distance_obstacle	[0,50]	True	Startup Failure	Mutation
local_max_slope	[1,25]	None	Logic Error	Rule-Based
reclass_distance_threshold	[0.01,1]	1.0448312	Logic Error	Rule-Based

configurations of planning module, control module, and sensors. Some of these results are shown in Table 7.

For the coverage rate, this paper calculates the line coverage and function coverage of the ADS system and two key modules (core-planning and core-perception) using Lcov and Gcov tools. We compare the coverage results with DriveFuzz to verify the effectiveness of fuzzing. DriveFuzz [24] is a feedback-driven fuzzing framework for testing autonomous driving systems end-to-end, which automatically generates safety critical driving scenarios where an autonomous driving system misbehaves.

We demonstrate this in Table 8, which shows the code coverage measured using the Gcov coverage test program during fuzzing. From the table, the proposed fuzzing method maintains more than 38% in both code coverage rate and branch coverage rate, which is much higher than that of DriveFuzz method, which is about 32%. The line coverage of

Table 7. Examples of configuration security defects.

Configuration Items	Function Description	Configure	Software Configuration Defects
velocity_max	maximum speed limit	[0.1,100.0]	If the value is 97.6860579, the speed will exceed the map speed limit, causing a collision
radial_divider_ angle	define divider angle of the radar	[0.01,5]	If the value is 0.844832132, the vehicle will collide
stop_distance_ obstacle	define stopping distance for obstacles	[0,50]	If it's a floating point number, the vehicle won't start
velocity_ change_limit	limit changes in vehicle speed	[5,40]	If it's a floating point number, the vehicle won't start

two key modules, core-planning and core-perception, is more than 60%, and the function coverage is more than 61%. This comparison result highlights the significant advantage of this system in terms of coverage rate.

Table 8. Results of coverage rate compared with DriveFuzz.

	All System	Core-planning Modules	Core-perception Modules	DriveFuzz
Line coverage	38.6%	60.35%	67.95%	Around 32%
Function coverage	44.6%	61.77%	73.46%	–

However, some code was not fully covered due to constraints on test case configurations to ensure safety within the Autoware system. This prevented testing of code dealing with out-of-bounds cases. In addition, the code includes modules that were not used in Autoware, such as visualizations, GUI, and so on, which are irrelevant to the operation of Autoware. The results of the fuzzing did not cover these modules due to their performance impact.

5 Conclusion

In actual production environment, user misconfiguration leading to system failure has become a common problem. To address this issue, this paper proposes a dynamic fuzzing method for configuration parameters based on static analysis of source code. The method utilizes static analysis techniques for automatic mapping and constraint extraction of configuration variables, while applying dynamic fuzzing methods to configuration parameters to induce the ADS into multiple anomalous states and detect specific configuration parameter defects. Experimental results demonstrate that the method performs well in detecting configuration defects.

References

1. Zhou, S.: Research on Configuration Fault Diagnosis Techniques for Software Evolution. National University of Defense Science and Technology (2016)
2. Barroso, L.A., Hölzle, U., Ranganathan, P.: The Datacenter as a Computer: Designing Warehouse-Scale Machines. Springer Nature, Cham (2019). https://doi.org/10.1007/978-3-031-01761-2
3. Rabkin, A., Katz, R.H.: How hadoop clusters break. IEEE Softw. **30**(4), 88–94 (2013)
4. Liu, B.: Cloud service system and face recognition application based on ROS and OpenCV. Sci. Technol. Plaza (11), 40–43 (2016). https://doi.org/10.13838/j.cnki.kjgc.2016.11.010
5. Gou, C.: Research on Authentication and Privacy Protection Scheme for Vehicular Self-Organizing Networks. Xihua University (2019)
6. Garcia, J., Feng, Y., Shen, J., Almanee, S., Xia, Y., Chen, A.: A comprehensive study of autonomous vehicle bugs. In: Proceedings of the ACM/IEEE 42nd International Conference on Software Engineering, pp. 385–396(2020). https://doi.org/10.1145/3377811.3380397
7. OneFuzz: A self-hosted Fuzzing-As-A-Service platform. https://github.com/microsoft/onefuzz. Accessed 10 Oct 2023
8. American Fuzzy Lop. https://lcamtuf.coredump.cx/afl/. Accessed 04 Nov 2017
9. Honggfuzz. https://honggfuzz.dev/. Accessed 25 Nov 2023
10. Fremont, D.J., Dreossi, T., Ghosh, S., Yue, X., Sangiovanni-Vincentelli, A.L., Seshia, S.A.: Scenic: a language for scenario specification and scene generation. In: Proceedings of the 40th ACM SIGPLAN Conference on Programming Language Design and Implementation, pp. 63–78. Association for Computing Machinery, Phoenix (2019). https://doi.org/10.1145/3314221.3314633
11. Madrigal, A.C.: Inside waymo's secret world for training self-driving cars. The Atlantic, vol. 23 (2017)
12. Lee, R., et al.: Adaptive stress testing: finding failure events with reinforcement learning. arXiv preprint (2018). https://doi.org/10.48550/arXiv.1811.02188
13. Koren, M., Alsaif, S., Lee, R., Kochenderfer, M.J.: Adaptive stress testing for autonomous vehicles. In: 2018 IEEE Intelligent Vehicles Symposium, Changshu, China, pp. 1–7 (2018). https://doi.org/10.1109/IVS.2018.8500400
14. Abeysirigoonawardena, Y., Shkurti, F. Dudek, G.: Generating adversarial driving scenarios in high-fidelity simulators. In: 2019 International Conference on Robotics and Automation (ICRA), Montreal, QC, Canada, pp. 8271–8277 (2019). https://doi.org/10.1109/ICRA.2019.8793740
15. Corso, A., Du, P., Driggs-Campbell, K., Kochenderfer, M.J.: Adaptive stress testing with reward augmentation for autonomous vehicle validatio. In: 2019 IEEE Intelligent Transportation Systems Conference (ITSC), Auckland, New Zealand, pp. 163–168 (2019). https://doi.org/10.1109/ITSC.2019.8917242
16. Xiong, Y., Hubaux, A., She, S., Czarnecki, K.: Generating range fixes for software configuration. In: 34th International Conference on Software Engineering (ICSE), Zurich, Switzerland, pp. 58–68 (2012). https://doi.org/10.1109/ICSE.2012.6227206
17. Huang, P., Bolosky, W.J., Singh, A., Zhou, Y.: KungfuValley: a systematic configuration validation framework for cloud services. In: Proceedings of the 10th ACM European Conference in Computer Systems (EuroSys'15), pp. 1–16. Association for Computing Machinery, New York (2015). https://doi.org/10.1145/2741948.2741963

18. Li, W., Li, S., Liao, X., Xu, X., Zhou, S., Jia, Z.: ConfTest: generating comprehensive misconfiguration for system reaction ability evaluation. In: Proceedings of the 21st International Conference on Evaluation and Assessment in Software Engineering (EASE'19), pp. 88–97. Association for Computing Machinery, Karlskrona (2017). https://doi.org/10.1145/3084226.3084244
19. Zhang, S., Ernst, M.D.: Automated diagnosis of software configuration errors. In: 35th International Conference on Software Engineering (ICSE), San Francisco, CA, USA, pp. 312–321 (2013). https://doi.org/10.1109/ICSE.2013.6606577
20. Yuan, D., Xie, Y., Panigrahy, R., Yang, J., Verbowski, C., Kumar, A.: Context-based online configuration error detection. In: Proceedings of USENIX Annual Technical Conference (USENIX ATC'19), p. 28. USENIX Association, Portland (2011)
21. Zhang, J., et al.: EnCore: exploiting system environment and correlation information for misconfiguration detection. SIGARCH Comput. Archit. News **42**(1), 687–700 (2014)
22. Liang, J., et al.: Deepfuzzer: accelerated deep greybox fuzzing. IEEE Trans. Depend. Secure Comput. **18**(6), 2675–2688 (2019)
23. Wan, Z., Shen, J., Chuang, J., Xia, X., Garcia, J., Ma, J., Chen, Q.A.: Too afraid to drive: systematic discovery of semantic DoS vulnerability in autonomous driving planning under physical-world attacks. arXiv preprint (2022). https://doi.org/10.48550/arXiv.2201.04610
24. Kim, S., Liu, M., Rhee, J.J., Jeon, Y., Kwon, Y., Kim, C.H.: DriveFuzz: discovering autonomous driving bugs through driving quality-guided fuzzing. In: Proceedings of the 2022 ACM SIGSAC Conference on Computer and Communications Security, pp. 1753–1767. Association for Computing Machinery, New York (2022). https://doi.org/10.1145/3548606.3560558

Research on Minimum Receptive Field of Convolutional Neural Networks for Energy Analysis Attack

Jifang Jin[1], Ziran Nie[1], Yuting Wang[1], Bingqi Xie[1], Xiaobing Huang[2], and Xiaoyi Duan[1(✉)]

[1] Beijing Electronic Science and Technology Institute, Beijing, China
Xiaoyi_duan@sina.com

[2] Qianghua Times (Chengdu) Technology Co., Ltd., Chengdu, China

Abstract. Energy analysis attack secret information of cryptographic devices by analyzing the energy leaked during the operation of cryptographic devices. In recent years, CNN-based energy analysis attack is a hot research topic in recent years due to the excellent performance of deep learning convolutional neural networks in processing complex data. In previous CNN-based energy analysis attacks, attackers usually use techniques such as lattice search, random search and Bayesian optimization to carry out the parameter optimization process of convolutional neural networks, and this process consumes a relatively large amount of time. In order to solve this problem, this paper studies the energy cycle characteristics of cryptographic chip, the structural characteristics of convolutional neural network, the optimal convolutional neural network feeling field based on the feeling field, and proposes the minimum feeling field model of convolutional neural network for energy analysis attack, which can derive the minimum feeling field suitable for CNN according to the highest operating frequency of the cryptographic chip, the actual operating frequency, and the collection frequency, from the point of view of the feeling field, and only when the CNN has the minimum feeling field, can it be optimized. The model can be trained successfully only when the CNN's receptive field is larger than this value, thus reducing the search range of the CNN model parameters, and verified on the internationally public ASCAD dataset, and the experiments are consistent with the expected results of the proposed scheme in this paper.

Keywords: Power analysis attack · Receptive Field · Machine Learning · Convolutional Neural Networks

1 Introduction

Side Channel Attack (SCA) is an attack to obtain the secret information of a cryptographic device by analyzing the power consumption, operation time, electromagnetic radiation and other side-channel leakages during the operation of the cryptographic

This pater is supported by "the Fundamental Research Funds for the Central Universities" (Grant Number:20240042Z0114

S. Goel et al. (Eds.): ICDF2C 2024, LNICST 614, pp. 313–331, 2025.
https://doi.org/10.1007/978-3-031-89360-5_19

device [1]. Side channel attacks can be classified into two classes. (1)Non-Profiled Attacks, typical Non-Profiled Attacks is Differential Power Analysis (DPA) [1], Correlation Power Analysis (CPA) [2], or Mutual Information Analysis (MIA) [3]. (2)Profiling Attacks are the most threatening of the Side channel attacks, including Template attacks [4] (TA), Stochastic models [5].

In recent years, due to the powerful performance and extraordinary potential of machine learning, some scholars have begun to combine it with side channel research, such as support vector machines [6, 7], random forests [8], deep learning networks [9, 10], and K-nearest neighbor algorithms [11]. These studies have shown that machine learning works better than classical energy analysis attack methods in dealing with masking countermeasures. Deep learning Convolutional Neutral Network (CNN) [12] performs well in dealing with complex data, and shows great potential in energy analysis attack tasks [9], and even improves the performance of TA [10], so energy analysis attacks based on CNNs are a hot research topic in recent years.

In 2018, Benadjila in [11] proposed a CNN-best convolutional neural network implementation based on the classical image processing convolutional neural network VGG-16 structure for attacking ASCAD datasets.2020, Perin [9] introduced an energy analysis attack based on integration learning, through which this scheme, by integrating more than one, can solve the problem of using deep learning big models when it is difficult to obtain hyperparameters.2021, [12] lu achieved good results using End-to-End Convolutional Neural Network to attack non-synchronized ASCAD datasets; in the same year 2021, Jorai et al. [13] used reinforcement learning to tune the hyperparameters of convolutional neural network hyperparameters.In 2022, Luo et al. proposed data enhancement based on SpecAugment scheme and then attacked using convolutional neural network to solve the problem of small training data [14]. In 2023, Zhu Xiaocheng combined parametric lattice traversal optimization method to propose a lightweight convolutional neural network model and achieved good results [15].

Previously, in the process of constructing convolutional neural network models for energy analysis attacks against different attack objects, techniques such as Grid Search (GS) [16], Random Search (RS) [17], and Bayesian Optimization (BO) [18] are usually used for the convolutional parameter optimization process of neural networks, this experimental approach usually requires a lot of time and arithmetic power, especially when the network structure is complex, the problem becomes more prominent.

In order to solve this problem, this paper studies the energy cycle characteristics of cryptographic chip, the structural characteristics of convolutional neural network, the optimal feeling field of convolutional neural network based on the feeling field, and proposes the minimum feeling field model of convolutional neural network oriented to the energy analysis attack. From the perspective of the receptive field, the model can derive the minimum receptive field suitable for the CNN based on the highest operating frequency of the cryptographic chip, the actual operating frequency, and the acquisition frequency, and the model can be trained successfully only when the receptive field of the CNN is larger than this value, thus reducing the search range of the parameters of the CNN model, and verified in the internationally published ASCAD side channel dataset, and the experiments are consistent with the scheme proposed in this paper. The experiments are consistent with the expected results of the proposed scheme in this paper.

1.1 Our Contribution

(1) The structure of CMOS logic gate circuits in cryptographic chips and their dynamic power consumption characteristics are studied, and then the energy cycle characteristics of D flip-flops are investigated, so as to obtain the relationship between the power consumption of cryptographic chips and their cycle characteristics.
(2) The minimum sensory field model of convolutional neural network for energy analysis attack is proposed. According to the characteristics of the maximum operating frequency, actual operating frequency, acquisition frequency and power consumption of the cryptographic chip, a model between the maximum operating frequency, actual operating frequency, acquisition frequency and the optimal sensory field of the cryptographic chip is established, and the sensory field of the CNN model targeting the energy analysis attack has to be larger than the minimum sensory field model for the training to be successful.
(3) Verification program realization. The proposed model is validated on the internationally publicized ASCAD dataset, and the feasibility of this model is proved by comparing various evaluation indexes, such as the success rate, loss rate, and guessing entropy of the model.

1.2 Structure of the Paper

The structure of the article is as follows. The first chapter introduction mainly introduces the research background and the current status of domestic and international research. The second chapter introduces the related background knowledge. Sect. 3 in introduces the optimal sensory field calculation method of convolutional neural network for energy analysis attack. In Sect. 4, the experimental validation of the proposed scheme in this paper is carried out through the ASCAD dataset. The paper concludes with a summary and outlook.

2 Background

2.1 CNN

In recent years, deep learning has achieved technological breakthroughs in many fields, especially in key areas such as image recognition, speech recognition, and natural language processing. Among the many deep neural network architectures, convolutional neural networks have attracted much attention and have demonstrated their effectiveness in areas such as side-channel attacks and energy analysis, and have become a powerful tool for breaking complex cryptographic algorithms. A convolutional neural network is a feed-forward neural network specifically designed to process data with a distinct grid structure (e.g., images). It consists of a series of neurons optimized for learning, and is able to automatically extract useful features from data without relying on traditional manual feature extraction techniques. CNN's application range goes far beyond two-dimensional image processing, and its usage scenario has been extended to one-dimensional and multi-dimensional data, such as time series analysis and text processing.

(1) Local connectivity. In CNN architectures (Fig. 1), neurons are connected to only some of the neurons in the previous layer, and this sparse connection strategy plays a key role in reducing the number of model parameters and accelerating convergence. In addition, convolutional neural networks utilize convolutional kernels to operate on the local receptive fields of the input data, allowing each convolutional kernel to focus on capturing a particular feature.
(2) Weight Sharing. The weight sharing mechanism allows the same convolutional kernel to slide over the entire input data and use the same weights, reducing model complexity while maintaining the ability to recognize features.
(3) Down sampling Dimensionality Reduction. The pooling layer performs down sampling operations on the input feature maps, which not only helps to extract and retain key information in the image, but also further reduces the model parameters by cutting down irrelevant details.

These designs greatly improve the performance and generalization ability of convolutional neural networks when processing high-dimensional data, making them one of the most representative algorithms in the field of deep learning.

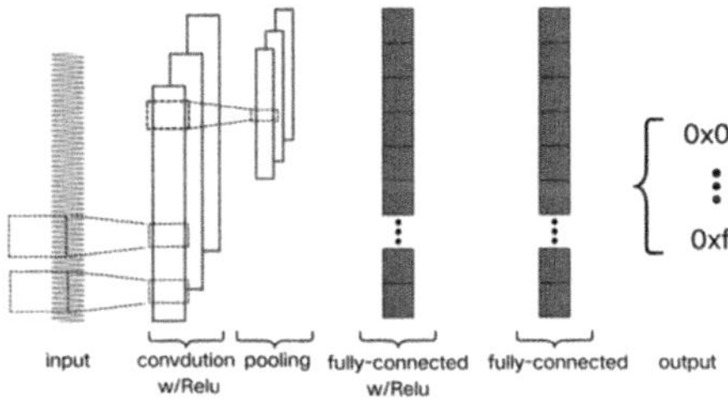

Fig. 1. A simple CNN architecture

2.2 AES Cipher Algorithm

AES (Advanced Encryption Standard) [19] represents the Advanced Encryption Standard (AES), an encryption algorithm that follows the principle of symmetric key, which is widely used worldwide and has become an important tool for securing the transmission and storage of sensitive information.The core of the AES algorithm is a series of round functions, each of which consists of four operations: Sub Bytes, Shift Rows, Mix Columns, and Add Round Key. (Mix Columns) and Add Round Key (Add Round Key). The combination of these operations creates multiple rounds of encryption, each involving the expansion and transformation of the key.

The AES algorithm uses a fixed packet length of 128 to process 128 bits of data at a time. It uses keys of the same length for encryption and decryption operations. The AES algorithm supports multiple key lengths, including 128-bit, 192-bit, and 256-bit, which correspond to the three versions of AES-128, AES-192, and AES-256, respectively. The security of the AES algorithm lies in the complexity of the design of the key lengths and the rounds function. The longer the key length, the more difficult it is to use the exhaustive method for brute-force cracking. Meanwhile, the wheel function design of AES incorporates the operation of nonlinear transformation and diffusion, which makes the algorithm more resistant to various attacks.

3 Minimum Receptive Field Study of CNN for Energy Analysis Attacks

3.1 Characterization of Power Consumption of Cryptographic Chips

Power Consumption Characterization of CMOS Logic Gate Circuits. Microprocessors used in embedded cryptosystems are generally implemented using a static complementary CMOS process, which makes circuits that have a certain correlation between the power consumption generated while performing computational tasks and the data they process, which is a key prerequisite for attacking cryptosystems using energy analysis techniques. Complementary Metal Oxide Semiconductor(CMOS) [23] is a gate circuit commonly used in integrated circuits.

The power consumption of gate circuits is mainly categorized into two parts: dynamic power consumption and static power consumption, and dynamic power consumption includes switching power consumption and short circuit power consumption.

When attacking the crypto chip, it is usually the CMOS inside that is attacked, especially using the relationship between its dynamic power consumption and the data it handles, by capturing the power consumption and analyzing the characteristics of the power consumption, so as to obtain the data handled in the crypto chip [2].

CMOS Cycle Characterization Study. CMOS tube in the circuit due to the internal junction or the circuit itself, the input and output effects of its real power consumption than the power consumption of the above composition to be more complex. CMOS tube composed of chip operation has a cyclic nature, so in the study of CMOS tube power consumption needs to consider its periodicity, a CLK clock cycle is divided into dynamic time TD and static time TS two parts, dynamic power consumption value is higher than the static power consumption value of 50% of the point Q as the cut-off point between the two parts of the time shown in Fig. 2. The dynamic power consumption value is higher than the static power consumption value of 50% of the point Q as the dividing point of the two parts of the time, as shown in Fig. 2.

Power Consumption Characterization of Master-Slave D Flip-Flops. D Flip-Flop (DFF) [20], as an edge-triggered memory unit, is a basic flip-flop commonly used in digital circuits and is one of the most used units in timing logic circuits, D flip-flop consists of the simplest CMOS logic gate circuit. In practice, the power consumption generated by the operation of cryptographic system is manifested as the flip-flop state of the internal flip-flop of the register, so the study of the power consumption characteristics of D flip-flop plays an important role in the study of the energy profile cycle characteristics of cryptographic chips.

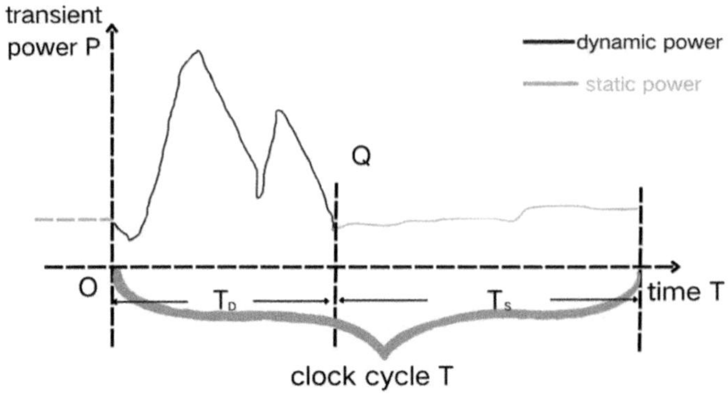

Fig. 2. Instantaneous power consumption of a single cycle of a CMOS tube

(1) Structure of a D-trigger

The Master-Slave D flip-flop consists of six and non-gates and two non-gates (as shown in Fig. 2), with an internal master-slave structure, one of which is known as the Master Flip-Flop, and the other as the Slave Flip-Flop. The main circuit structure of the D flip-flop is shown in Fig. 3, and consists of two inputs: the data input D and the clock input CLK, and two outputs: the master output Q and its complement output Q'. It consists of two inputs: data input D and clock input CLK, and two outputs: master output Q and its complement output Q'.

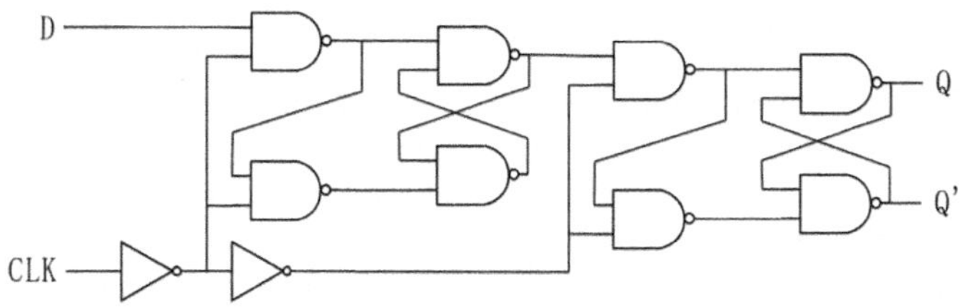

Fig. 3. D flip-flop circuit structure diagram (rising edge triggering)

The master flip-flop consists of two main inputs, data input D1 and clock input CLK1, as well as an output Q1. When the clock input CLK1 is low, the master flip-flop enable signal becomes high, and its circuit structure is shown in Fig. 4. The slave flip-flop also includes two main inputs: data input D2 and clock input CLK2, as well as an output Q2, whose circuit structure is shown in Fig. 5.

Master-Slave D-Flip-Flop Cycle Characterization. When the clock frequency is equal to the maximum operating frequency of the chip, the master flip-flop's dynamic time TD and static time TS are equal to the clock's half cycle length, while the slave flip-flop will keep the same state at the falling edge of the clock. At this time, the master-slave D flip-flop cycle waveform shown in Fig. 6, when the clock frequency is less than the maximum operating frequency, D flip-flop master flip-flop dynamic time TD and

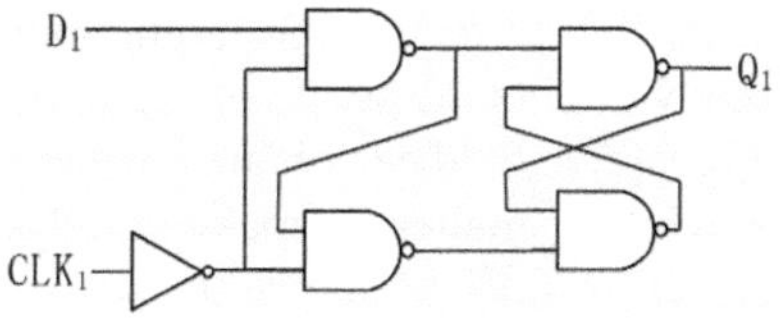

Fig. 4. Main Trigger Circuit Diagram

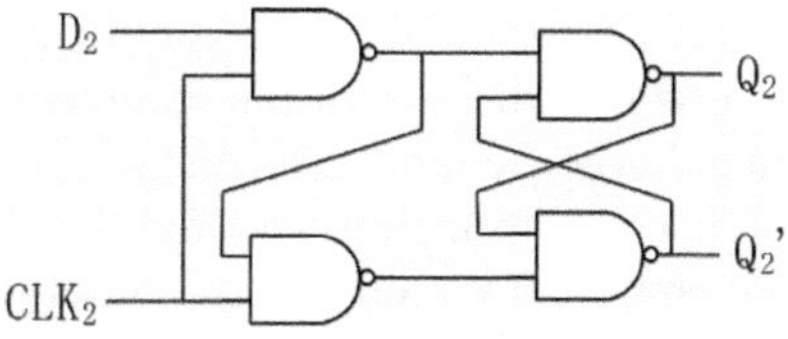

Fig. 5. Slave Trigger Circuit Diagram

static time TS is less than half a cycle length of the clock, the specific percentage of the clock frequency and the maximum operating frequency by the relationship between the decision, at the same time, the slave flip-flop in the falling edge of the clock to maintain the same state. The cycle waveform of the master-slave D flip-flop is shown in Fig. 7.

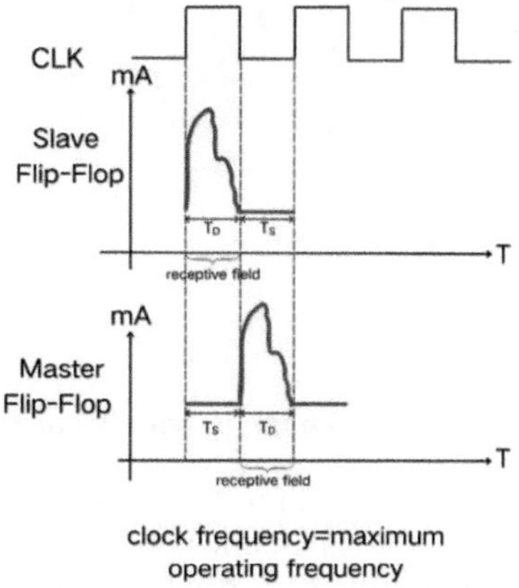

Fig. 6. D-flip-flop cycle waveform when the clock frequency is equal to the maximum operating frequency

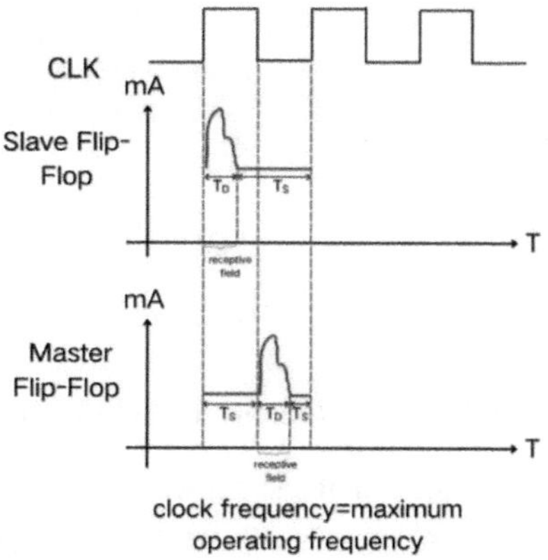

Fig. 7. D-flip-flop cycle waveform when the clock frequency is equal to the maximum operating frequency

3.2 Receptive Field Studies

In the field of machine learning, a deep neural network usually consists of multiple layers, each of which contains a number of neurons used to process part of the data in the previous layer, a process similar to the propagation of light signals in biology. In the convolutional neural network (CNN) studied in this paper, each neuron is connected to a neighboring feature region in the previous layer, and such a neighboring region is called the Receptive Field (RF) of this neuron in the previous layer [21]. Specifically, the Receptive Field is the size of the region where each feature point on the Feature Map (FM) [22] output by each layer of the convolutional neural network is mapped to the original data, representing the size of the influence of a particular layer by the original data. Thus, this concept of feeling field can build a correlation between the raw data and the neural network structure.

The model structure descriptive properties of the receptive field can be used to adjust the range of features extracted from the input data by the convolutional neural network, and the size of the receptive field can be set according to the design requirements of the network. The size of the receptive field directly affects the scope of the network's perception of the input information, and a larger receptive field can obtain a wider range of semantic information and high-level features, while a smaller receptive field focuses more on the extraction of local details and low-level features, as shown in Fig. 8.

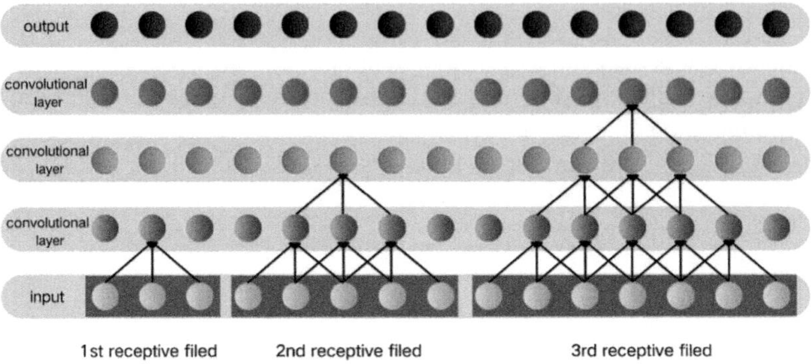

Fig. 8. Schematic diagram of Receptive Field

3.3 Minimum Receptive Field Calculation for Energy Analysis Attacks of CNN

The previous analysis shows that the size of the receptive field of the CNN model has an important impact on the performance and computational complexity of the model. Therefore, a relationship model between the highest operating frequency of the chip, the actual operating frequency of the chip, the energy harvesting frequency and the receptive field can be constructed, which is used to obtain the optimal receptive field to guide the construction of the model.

The optimal neural network model selection method based on the characteristics of the chip is shown in Fig. 9, in which the highest operating frequency, the actual operating frequency and the sampling frequency during the attack of the attacked chip are taken as input parameters, and these parameters are inputted into the optimal network selection model, which outputs the optimal sensory field of the neural network for this chip.

Receptive Field and Dynamic Power Consumption. According to the power cycle characteristics of the master-slave D flip-flop in Sect. 3.1, it can be seen that its dynamic power consumption has the following characteristics:

1. dynamic power consumption is related to the maximum operating frequency.
2. dynamic power consumption has clock cycle characteristics, in the clock high level and low level, the master flip-flop and slave flip-flop respectively produce power consumption.

And in the energy analysis attack, the main thing is to analyze its dynamic power consumption, so in order to achieve this goal, the selected feeling field needs to be able

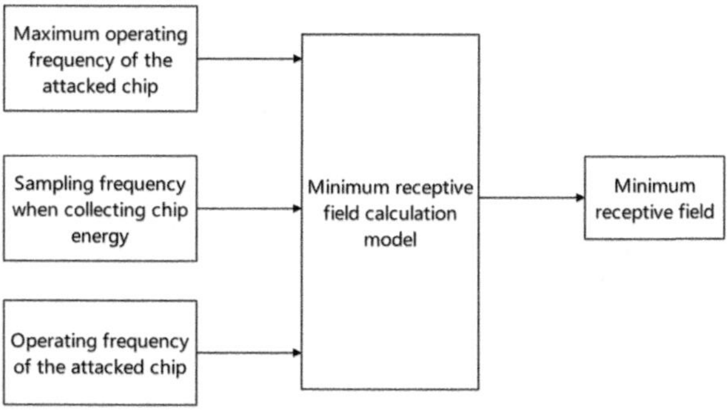

Fig. 9. Mininum Neural Network Model Selection Method Based on Chip Characteristics

to cover its dynamic power consumption. When the actual operating frequency (clock frequency) of the attacked chip is equal to the maximum operating frequency of the chip, its sense field needs to include all the dynamic power consumption of the master or slave flip-flop, as shown in Fig. 10. When the attacked chip's operating frequency (clock frequency) is less than the chip's maximum operating frequency, its sense field needs to include all the dynamic power consumption of the master or slave flip-flop, as shown in Fig. 11.

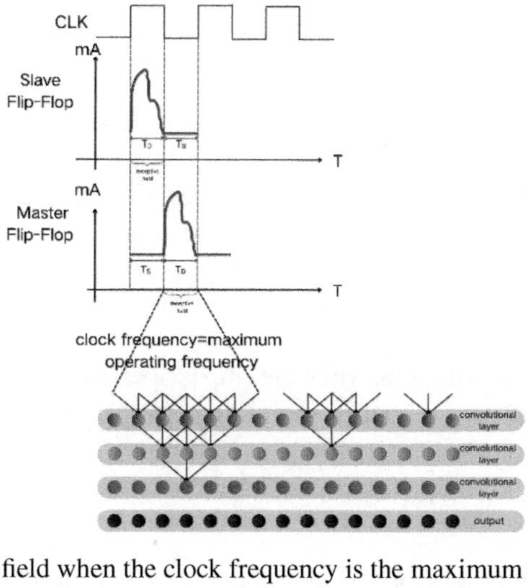

Fig. 10. Receptive field when the clock frequency is the maximum operating frequency

Minimum Sensory Field Formula. According to the above research, it can be special that, in the energy analysis attack on cryptographic chip, its information leakage is mainly through the dynamic power consumption to leak, so in the CNN model modeling, the minimum sensory field should include the dynamic power consumption, and we can get the relationship between the minimum neural network selection sensory field and the chip

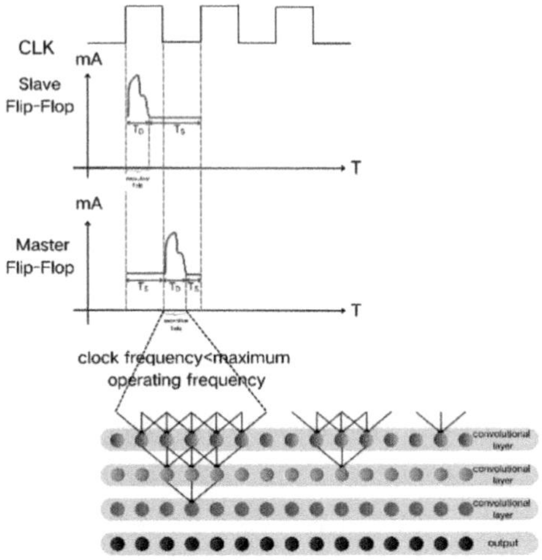

Fig. 11. Clock frequency is less than the maximum operating frequency of the feeler field

operating frequency, the maximum operating frequency and the Operating frequency is as follows:

RF: the size of the sensory field of the output.
f_{max}: Maximum operating frequency of the attacked object.
$f_{operation}$: The actual operating frequency of the attacked object when it is actually operating.
f_{sample}: Operating frequency during energy profile acquisition

In the optimal neural network selection model formula, the output is the size of the sensing field of the optimal network, and the inputs are the maximum operating frequency of the attacked chip is f_{max}, the actual operating frequency at the time of the attack is $f_{operation}$ and the sampling frequency at the time of the attack on the chip is f_{sample}.

From the previous introduction, when the chip is operating at the operating frequency, the chip is acquired and the number of sampling points in a cycle is:

$$\frac{f_{sample}}{f_{operation}} \tag{1}$$

And since in cryptographic chips, the main thing that ultimately stores the data is the register, and in today's chips, the commonly used master-slave D flip-flop as shown in 3.1, the power consumption is characterized by the fact that the power consumption generated by the first half cycle and the second half cycle is equal in a complete clock cycle. That is, depending on the data being processed, the same power consumption is consumed in the first and second half cycles, respectively, so that only half a cycle needs to be analyzed when performing energy analysis. Based on this characteristic, the size of the sensing field only needs to be half a cycle when the network fully connected operation is performed. In this case, the expression of the sensing field is as follows:

$$RF = \frac{f_{sample}}{2 \times f_{operation}} \tag{2}$$

However, since the chip's actual operating frequency may not be the highest operating frequency when it is attacked, there will be a certain amount of dynamic power consumption and static power consumption, so it is only necessary to obtain this part of the sampling point. When using the operating frequency for sampling, the effective point of dynamic power consumption, it is necessary to use the result in Eq. (2) divided by $\frac{f_{max}}{f_{operation}}$, and the final feeler field calculation formula is.

$$RF = \frac{f_{sample}}{2 \times f_{operation} \times \frac{f_{max}}{f_{operation}}} = \frac{f_{sample}}{2 \times f_{max}} \tag{3}$$

With this calculation method, only the highest operating frequency and sampling rate of the attacked object are known, and the corresponding size of the sensory field can be calculated, thus guiding the design of convolutional neural network models。

4 Experimental Validation and Evaluation

In order to verify the optimal receptive field for energy analysis attacks proposed in Sect. 3 and to guide the effectiveness of convolutional neural networks, Formula 8 will be used for experimental verification on the ASCAD dataset [14] widely used in international energy analysis attack research in recent years. The purpose is to verify the effectiveness of the given formula and conduct relevant analysis.

4.1 Experimental Platforms

In order to improve the effectiveness of the experiment, this study chose a high-performance GPU as a gas pedal for convolutional neural networks, and the experimental platform is shown in Table 1:

4.2 Datasheet

This article uses the ASCAD public dataset proposed by Benadjila et al. [14]; This dataset is based on the AES encryption standard and runs on the ATMega8515 microcontroller, collecting data by monitoring electromagnetic radiation.

ASCAD Datasheet. The ASCAD dataset is one of the most commonly used datasets for side channel analysis benchmark testing. As an important resource for research on side channel attacks, it includes performance analysis data, attack data, and metadata, providing a solid foundation for side channel attack research. The dataset contains the side channel information of the AES-128 algorithm implemented on the ATMega8515 microcontroller unit (MCU). The AES cryptographic algorithm is written in assembly language, and defense techniques such as masking and scrambling are applied during the implementation process.

Table 1. Experimental platform hardware and software configuration table

Item		environment
Hardware	CPU	i5-13600k
	GPU	NVIDIA GeForce RTX 3060 GPU
	Memory	32GB
	GPU Memory	6GB
software	Operation	Windows11
	Programming Language	Python3.8
	Anaconda	3.9.12
	Tensorflow-gpu	2.6.0
	Keras	2.6.0
	CUDA	11.2
	Cudnn	8.1.0
	Numpy	1.19.5

During the collection process of the ASCAD dataset, the captured data is the electromagnetic radiation leaked by the ATMeag8515 microcontroller during encryption operations. The specific process is to place the electromagnetic probe on the attacked cryptographic chip to capture the electromagnetic waves generated during operation, and transfer the collected energy curve to the computer for storage through an oscilloscope. During the acquisition process, the sampling frequency of the oscilloscope is 2GHz. This dataset contains a total of 60000 waveforms, of which 50000 are used for analysis and training, and the remaining 10000 are used for testing. The ASCAD variable dataset was added in 2019 under the same implementation conditions as ASCAD fix. The training subset was encrypted using a random key, with a total of 200000 waveforms. The attack subset was encrypted using a fixed key, with a total of 100000 waveforms.

Working Characteristics of the Collection Object ATMega8515 in the ASCAD Dataset. The maximum operating frequency of the ATMega8515 CPU is 16 MHz, but during ASCAD data collection, its actual operating frequency is 4 MHz, which has not reached the maximum operating frequency.

4.3 Experimentation

Minimum Receptive Field Calculation. As known from Sect. 3.3, the maximum operating frequency of the attacked ATmega8515 microcontroller is 16 MHz, and the sampling frequency of the oscilloscope is 2 GHz. Substituting the above parameters into formula 8, the calculation process is as follows:

$$RF = \frac{f_{sample}}{2 \times f_{f\,\max}} = \frac{2G}{2 \times 16} = \frac{2000}{2 \times 16} = 62.5$$

The minimum receptive field obtained is 62.5, which means that when the receptive field of the convolutional neural network is greater than 62.5 sampling points, the optimal network architecture can be obtained. When the number of sampling points is less than 62.5, the optimal network architecture cannot be obtained, resulting in unsatisfactory model training results. Therefore, the following experiment verifies the training effect when the receptive field is below 62.5 and above 62.5.

Selection of Experimental Model Parameters. In order to study the effectiveness of the minimum receptive field and its characteristics unaffected by network structure, convolutional neural networks with different convolutional layers and kernels were selected for validation in the experiment.

In the experiment, 5 levels of receptive fields were designed, and 16, 32, 64,125,250 sampling points were taken from the ASCAD dataset for model training and validation. Due to the calculated minimum receptive field being 62.5, this article uses a rounding method to select 63 points; And 31 and 16 are 1/2 and 1/4 of the minimum receptive field, respectively. The goal of selecting these two sets of data is to verify that the training effect of the model is not good when the receptive field is less than 63 data points; 126252 is twice and four times the minimum receptive field, respectively. The purpose of selecting these two data is to verify that the training effect of the model is good when the receptive field is greater than 63 data points.

The number of filters in the first stage of the experiment is 64, the second stage uses 128 filters, the third stage uses 256 filters, the fourth stage uses 512 filters, and the final fifth stage uses 1024 filters. Convolutional layers in the same level have exactly the same configuration to maintain global invariance. After each convolutional layer, ReLU activation function was used to introduce nonlinearity.

In addition, after each iteration, a max pooling layer is included and average pooling is used. The entire network is equipped with three fully connected layers, with the first two layers using ReLU activation function and the last fully connected layer using softmax activation function. During the model training process, set the number of iterations to 75 and the batch size to 200.

The Influence of Different Convolutional Layers Under the Minimum Receptive Field. When the minimum receptive field is 63, set the convolution kernel size of the model to 9 and the step size to 1. By fixing the convolution kernel and step size parameters, adjust the number of convolutional layers for the following experiments: one is to adjust the number of convolutional layers within the range below the minimum receptive field (<62.5), and finally set the number of convolutional layers to 1 and 2, respectively; Another approach is to adjust the number of convolutional layers above the minimum receptive field (>62.5), with the final convolutional layers set to 3, 4, and 5, respectively. The selected model parameters at this time are shown in Table 2. By introducing the ASCAD dataset into these five models separately, the accuracy, loss rate, key ranking, and guessing entropy of the models under these five receptive fields can be verified, thereby studying the impact of receptive fields on training and attack results under different convolutional layers, and verifying whether the theoretical predicted results are consistent with the experimental results.

Table 2. Design schemes for receptive field under different convolutional layers

Datassheet	The proportion of receptive field to chip cycle	sampling points in the field	CNN model parameters			
			receptive field	Convolutional Layer	Convolutional kernel size	step
ASCAD	1/32	16	10	1	9	1
	1/16	31	28	2	9	1
	1/8	63	64	3	9	1
	1/4	126	136	4	9	1
	1/2	252	280	5	9	1

For the ASCAD dataset, Fig. 15 shows the success rate and loss rate of training CNN using energy analysis models with different receptive fields at different convolution layers on the left and right, respectively.

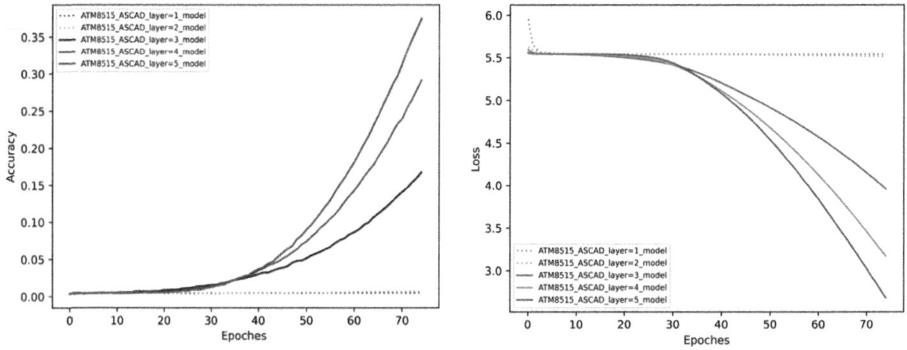

Fig. 12. Success rate (left) and loss rate (right) of CNN model training on ASCAD dataset with different convolutional layers

From Fig. 12, it can be concluded that when the selected CNN template receptive field is greater than the minimum receptive field obtained in Formula 8 (62.5 here), i.e., the receptive field is 63128250, all three models can be trained successfully. However, when the receptive field of the model is less than 62.5, the model training fails.

In order to further verify the effectiveness of formula 8, this paper conducted further experiments by guessing entropy, and the experimental results are shown in Fig. 13. From the figure, it can be seen that when the selected CNN template receptive field is greater than the minimum receptive field obtained in formula 862.5 here), the key ranking can quickly converge to 0 within 250 curves, achieving a successful attack. On the other hand, the ranking values of keys with receptive fields of 10 and 28 are almost garbled and have not achieved convergence within 2000 curves. This further proves the effectiveness of formula 8. It also proves that under formula 8, different convolutional layers have no effect, as long as the minimum receptive field formula in formula 8 is met, the attack can be successful.

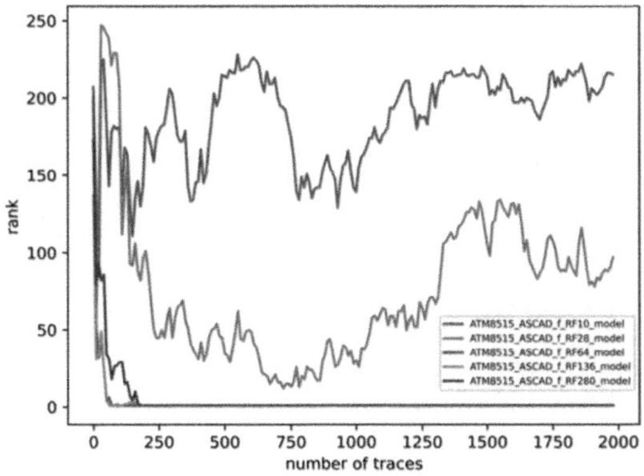

Fig. 13. Guessing entropy under different receptive fields

The Influence of Different Convolutional Kernels Under the Minimum Receptive Field. In order to study the relationship between the minimum receptive field and model performance under different convolutional kernels, this paper designed validation experiments for different convolutional kernel models. When the minimum receptive field is 63, the number of convolution layers is 3 and the step size is 1. By fixing the parameters of convolution layers and step size, the size of the convolution kernel is adjusted for the following experiments: one is to adjust the size of the convolution kernel within the range below the minimum receptive field (<62.5), and the final convolution kernels are set to 1 and 3, respectively; Another approach is to adjust the convolution kernel within a range higher than the minimum receptive field (>62.5), with the final convolution kernels set to 9, 17, and 35, respectively. Finally, five models were obtained as shown in Table 3, and the ASCAD dataset was introduced into each of these models to verify the accuracy, loss rate, key ranking, and guessing entropy of the models under these five receptive fields. This was done to investigate the impact of receptive fields on training and attack results under different convolution kernels, and to verify whether the theoretical predicted results were consistent with the experimental results.

By comparing the model performance under different convolutional kernels using the ASCAD dataset, the impact of kernel size on model training and attack processes can be studied. Figure 14 shows the success rate and loss rate of training CNN using energy analysis models with different receptive fields under different convolution kernel sizes on the left and right, respectively.

From Fig. 14, it can be seen that regardless of the size of the convolutional kernel, as long as the receptive field satisfies the minimum receptive field size in formula 8, which is 62.4, the model can be trained successfully, otherwise it will fail.

From Fig. 15, it can be seen that from the perspective of guessing entropy, as long as the receptive field meets the requirements of Formula 8, the trained model mentioned above will attack successfully and have good guessing entropy.

Table 3. Design schemes for receptive fields under different convolutional kernels

Datasheet	The proportion of receptive field to chip cycle	sampling points in the field	CNN model parameters			
			receptive field	Convolutional Layer	Convolutional kernel size	step
ASCAD	1/32	16	8	3	1	1
	1/16	31	22	3	3	1
	1/8	63	64	3	9	1
	1/4	125	120	3	17	1
	1/2	250	246	3	35	1

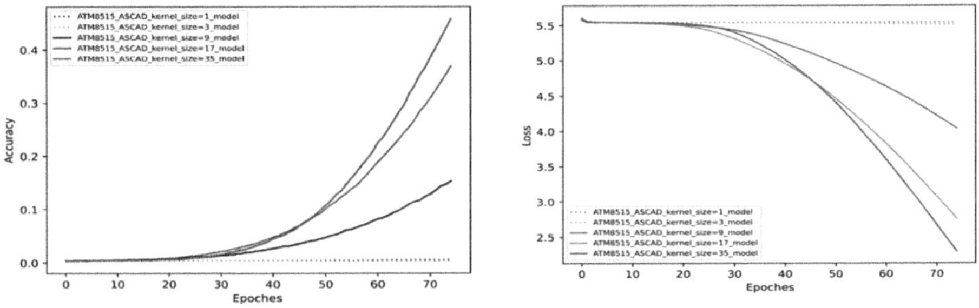

Fig. 14. The success rate (left) and loss rate (right) of CNN model training on ASCAD dataset with different kernel sizes

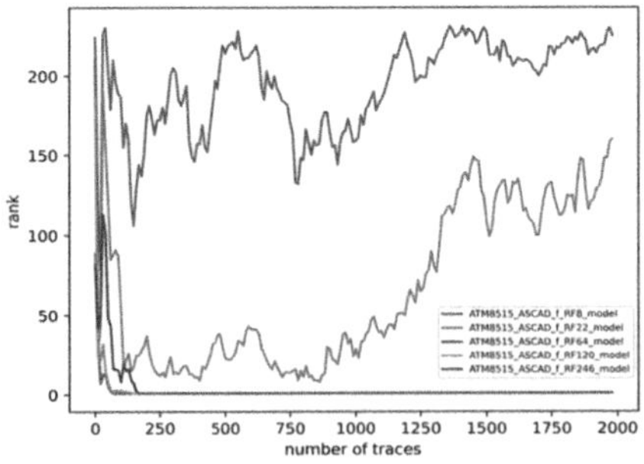

Fig. 15. Guessing Entropy under Different Convolutional Kernel Sizes

From Figs. 14 and 15, it can be seen that as long as the model satisfies the minimum receptive field in Formula 8 and does not recognize the total kernel size of the model, the model can be trained and attacked successfully. Otherwise, it fails.

The Time Superiority of this Plan. Under the guidance of no minimum receptive field, when training CNN models, it is necessary to search for model references through hyperparameter search. When conducting hyperparameter search, the parameters start from the minimum value, that is, the very small receptive field, and slowly search above the minimum receptive field described in formula 8, that is, the receptive field that can be trained successfully. When using the formula for calculating the minimum receptive field in this article (Formula 8), the range of search parameters can be reduced, and training can be started directly from the parameters that meet Formula 8. So as to reduce the parameter search time.

From the table, it can be seen that under this scheme, the parameter search time of at least 4235S can be reduced (Table 4).

Table 4. Training time of models under different receptive fields

Datasheet	The proportion of receptive field to chip cycle	sampling points in the field	Time (s)	Time of every epoch (ms)	Total time (s)
ASCAD	1/32	10	1978	104	14620
	1/16	28	2257	119	
	1/8	64	2766	142	
	1/4	136	3462	189	
	1/2	280	4157	221	

5 Conclusion

This article focuses on the energy analysis attack technology based on receptive fields, studying the power consumption characteristics of D triggers during operation, the receptive field characteristics in convolutional neural networks, the relationship between D triggers and receptive fields, proposing a calculation model between the highest operating frequency of the chip, the acquisition frequency, and the minimum receptive field of the convolutional neural network during energy analysis attacks, and applying this method to the internationally available ASCAD dataset for verification. The results show that the energy analysis attack scheme based on receptive fields can establish a theoretical system for the model architecture. Only when the minimum receptive field of the model meets the publicity proposed in this article can the model be trained successfully, otherwise it will fail. And the method proposed in this article can guide the hyperparameter search of the model, thereby reducing the parameter search time of the model.

References

1. Kocher, P., Jaffe, J., Jun, B.: Differential power analysis. In: Wiener, M. (ed.) Advances in Cryptology: Proceedings of CRYPTO 1999, nO. 1666 in Lecture Notes in Computer Science, pp. 388–397. Springer-Verlag, Berlin (2016)

2. Brier, E., Clavier, C., Olivier, F.: Correlation power analysis with a leakage model. In: 6th International Workshop on Cryptographic Hardware and Embedded Systems, pp.16–29. Springer, Berlin (2004)
3. Batina, L., Gierlichs, B., Prouff, E., Rivain, M., Standaert, F.-X., VeyratCharvillon, N.: Mutual information analysis: a comprehensive study. J. Cryptol. **24**(2), 269–291 (2011)
4. Chari, S., Rao, J.R., Rohatgi, P.: Template attacks. In: International Workshop on Cryptographic Hardware and Embedded Systems. pp. 13–28. Springer, Heidelberg (2002)
5. Gierlichs, B., Lemke2Rust, K., Paar, C.: Templates vs. stochastic methods. In: Proceedings of the Workshop on Cryptographic Hardware and Embedded Systems (CHES'06), Yokohama, vol. 15229 (2006)
6. Hospodar, G., Minder, E.D., Gierlichs, B., Hospodar, G., et al.: Least squares support vector machines for side-channel analysis. Center for Advanced Security Research Darmstadt, Darmstadt, pp. 99–104 (2011)
7. Bartkewitz, T., Lemke-Rust, K.: Efficient template attacks based on probabilistic multiclass support vector machines. In: Smart Card Research and Advanced Applications: 11th International Conference, CARDIS 2012, Revised Selected Papers 11. Springer, Heidelberg (2013)
8. Lerman, L., Bontempi, G., Markowitch, O.: Power analysis attack: an approach based on machine learning. Int. J. Appl. Cryptogr. **3**(2), 97–115 (2014)
9. Perin, G., Chmielewski, L., Picek, S.: Strength in numbers: improving generalization with ensembles in machine learning-based profiled side-channel analysis. IACR Trans. Cryptogr. Hardw. Embed. Syst., 337–364 (2020)
10. Asvija, B., Eswari, R., Bijoy, M.B.: Template attacks on ECC implementations using performance counters in CPU. Microelectron. J. **106**, 104935 (2020). ISSN 0026–2692. https://doi.org/10.1016/j.mejo.2020.104935
11. Benadjila, R., et al.: Deep learning for side-channel analysis and introduction to ASCAD database. J. Cryptogr. Eng. **10**(Feb) (2019)
12. Lu, X., Zhang, C., Cao, P., et al.: Pay attention to raw traces: a deep learning architecture for end-to-end profiling attacks (2021)
13. Rijsdijk, J., Wu, L., Perin, G., et al.: Reinforcement learning for hyperparameter tuning in deep learning-based side-channel analysis. IACR Trans. Cryptogr. Hardw. Embed. Syst. **2021**(3), 677–707 (2021)
14. Luo, Z.: Application of Data Enhancement Technology in Deep Learning Based Side Channel Modeling Attacks. University of Science and Technology of China (2022). https://doi.org/10.27517/d.cnki.gzkju.2022.001519
15. Cheng, Z.X.: Research On Side Channel Attack Based On Convolutional Neural Net Work. Beijing University of Posts and Telecommunications (2023). https://doi.org/10.26969/d.cnki.gbydu.2023.003161
16. Lavalle, S.M.: On the relationship between classical grid search and probabilistic roadmaps. Int. J. Rob. Res. **23**(7–8), 673–692 (2004). https://doi.org/10.1177/0278364904045481
17. Bergstra, J., Bengio, Y.: Random search for hyper-parameter optimization. J. Mach. Learn. Res. **13**(1), 281–305 (2012). https://doi.org/10.1016/j.chemolab.2011.12.002
18. Shahriari, B., Swersky, K., Wang, Z., et al.: Taking the human out of the loop: a review of bayesian optimization. Proc. IEEE **104**(1), 148–175 (2015). https://doi.org/10.1109/JPROC.2015.2494218
19. Buchholz, J.O.J.: Advanced encryption standard. In: International Workshop on Fast Software Encryption (1997). https://doi.org/10.1007/BFb0052336
20. Yeo, Y.C., King, T.J., Hu, C.: Metal-dielectric band alignment and its implications for metal gate complementary metal-oxide-semiconductor technology. J. Appl. Phys. **92**(12), 7266–7271 (2002). https://doi.org/10.1063/1.1521517

21. Chang, B., Park, J., Kim, W.: A 1.2 GHz CMOS dual-modulus prescaler using new dynamic D-type flip-flops. IEEE J. Solid-State Circuits **31**(5), 749–752 (1996). https://doi.org/10.1109/4.509860
22. Kohonen, T.: Self-Organized Formation of Topologically Correct Feature Maps. MIT Press, Cambridge (1988)

Heaker: Exfiltrating Data from Air-Gapped Computers via Thermal Signals

Jifang Jin, Yonghua Su, Zunyang Wang, Pengyu Li, Zhan Huang, and Xiaoyi Duan(✉)

Beijing Electronic Science and Technology Institute, Beijing, China
Xiaoyi_duan@sina.com

Abstract. As a high-level cybersecurity measure, air-gapped networks are employed in secure environments to physically isolate secure computer networks from unsecured ones, such as the public internet. However, recent studies have shown that these systems are not impervious to breaches. This paper introduces an attack method, Heaker, which targets air-gapped networks by manipulating the thermal emissions of a compromised computer's CPU and GPU. By controlling the workload on these components, the computer's exhaust temperature is modulated with encoded data. An attacker, positioned remotely, can observe these thermal variations using thermal imaging equipment and decode the transmitted information from these temperature fluctuations. We further explore signal encoding methods suitable for the thermal channel and examine factors impacting the attack's efficacy. Our experiments demonstrate the viability of this attack method within a 4-m range and a data transfer rate exceeding 60 bits per hour. This research offers insight into the potential risks of thermal-based side-channel attacks on air-gapped systems and discusses preventive and detection strategies against such threats.

Keywords: air-gap · thermal signals · cybersecurity · data exfiltration · side-channel attacks

1 Introduction

Physical isolation is an effective means of protection for securing computers. The principle is to prevent the protected computer from using WiFi, Bluetooth, and to physically isolate the computer system from external electromagnetic waves with devices such as metal shielding covers. Isolated computers cannot be physically connected to other devices, cutting off their connection to external networks. At the same time, the transfer of information between physically isolated computers and other devices can only be conducted under manual control, thus avoiding the risk of computer intrusion or information leakage [1]. Computer physical isolation is mainly applied in government sectors such as intelligence [2, 3], military [3–5], and non-government sectors such as finance [4].

This pater is supported by "the Fundamental Research Funds for the Central Universities" (Grant Number:20240042Z0114).

S. Goel et al. (Eds.): ICDF2C 2024, LNICST 614, pp. 332–355, 2025.
https://doi.org/10.1007/978-3-031-89360-5_20

However, physically isolated computers are not absolutely safe. Attackers can inject malicious software into physically isolated computers through physical media infection [6], supply chain contamination [7], strong electromagnetic irradiation [8], laser injection [9], etc., to obtain sensitive information within the physically isolated computer. Then, by using covert channel technologies such as electromagnetic, acoustic, optical, thermal, and electric power, they can transmit information from the physically isolated computer, thereby breaking through the physical isolation constraints [2].

Electromagnetic covert channels: By using computer components such as graphics cards, memory buses, USB cables, or GPIO pins as transmitters, attacks can be carried out with electromagnetic signals, with ordinary devices such as smartphones, GSM phones, or software-defined radio devices acting as receivers. This method covers a wide frequency range and can achieve relatively high data transmission rates [3, 4]. It is also possible to use the characteristic of low-frequency magnetic fields that can penetrate electrostatic shields and metal casings, using the built-in magnetic sensors of smartphones as receivers to obtain the low-frequency electromagnetic signals emitted by physically isolated computers [5–10]. This method has a low data transfer rate and short transmission distance, making it only suitable for small sensitive data such as passwords or encryption keys. They also require precise alignment and synchronization between the transmitter and the receiver.

Acoustic covert channels: By using inaudible sound waves (such as ultrasound or noise), data is transferred from speakers, microphones, CPU fans, hard drives, or power supplies to nearby smartphones or other recording devices [11, 12]. They can bypass network-based detection and prevention mechanisms and utilize audio devices that are ubiquitous in modern environments. However, they also face some challenges, such as being affected by environmental noise, limited by low data rates and short transmission distances, and hindered by physical isolation or removal of audio devices.

Optical covert channels: Data is transmitted from computer screens, keyboards, hard drives, or router LEDs, infrared monitoring systems, scanners, or light bulbs to photodetectors, cameras, or other optical devices using visible or infrared light. Compared to other methods, they can achieve higher data transmission rates and longer transmission distances, and take advantage of the fact that the human eye cannot perceive rapid flickering or infrared signals [13, 14]. However, they also have some disadvantages, such as being dependent on the line-of-sight visibility between the transmitter and receiver, being susceptible to interference from environmental light sources or optical filters, and being easily detected by optical analysis tools.

Electric power covert channels: CPU core power consumption fluctuations are transmitted to non-invasive current detection probes using power lines [1]. They can bypass network-based detection and prevention mechanisms and utilize the electrical characteristics of modern processors. However, these methods also have limitations, such as being limited to low data transmission rates and short transmission distances within the same electrical control panel, being affected by electrical noise or power filters, and requiring the installation of malicious software on the target computer and receiving devices.

Thermal covert channels have been developed in recent years; they are methods of transmitting information by controlling the operation of the CPU or GPU through programs, thereby modulating the temperature of physically isolated computers. BitWhisper is a method that uses the built-in temperature sensors of computers to sense the temperature changes of adjacent computers, thus achieving two-way communication [15]. HOTSPOT is a method that uses the temperature sensors in smartphones to sense the temperature changes of the attacked computer, thus achieving one-way communication [16]. Its advantage is that it can use universally available smartphones as receivers without professional equipment. HVACKer is a method that uses air conditioning systems as a bridge to send commands from an external network to an isolated network [17]. Its advantage is that it can perform remote attacks by using the temperature control of air conditioning systems to modulate signals.

Although Guri proposed two physical isolation-resistant attack methods based on thermal covert channels in [16, 17], both methods have their flaws. The BitWhisper communication rate is very low, capable of transmitting only 8 bits per hour, and the two computers must be very close to each other, no more than 40 cm apart. HOTSPOT has a lower communication rate, capable of transmitting 30–60 bits per hour, andrequires the attacker's smartphone to be very close to the attacked computer, no more than 50 cm away. Moreover, it necessitates the use of a temperature sensor on the receiving end's smartphone, which increases the difficulty of deployment and use. HVACKer requires the attacker to have access to the target network's air conditioning system and to install malicious software within the target network.

To address the issues of low transmission rates and short attack distances in existing thermal covert channels, we propose a new thermal covert channel attack method—Heaker. This method controls the workload of the CPU/GPU chip of a physical computer through malicious software, encodes the data to be transmitted, and then modulates the GPU/CPU to cause regular temperature changes, thereby controlling the temperature changes at the computer's exhaust vent and other places. Then, the attacker uses infrared thermal imaging equipment and other devices to observe these temperature changes from a distance and record them. By decoding the temperature data, the transmitted information can be recovered. In this paper, we introduce the design and implementation of Heaker, as well as experimental evaluations of its performance and feasibility. We also discuss factors affecting transmission rates and reliability, as well as potential countermeasures to prevent or detect such attacks.

1.1 Contribution of This Paper

We introduce a new thermal signal-based covert channel that can be used to leak data from air-gapped computers. We describe the steps involved in carrying out such an attack, the impact of various factors on the effectiveness of the attack, and the protective measures that can be taken.

We propose a new thermal signal reception scheme, using a thermal imager to collect the temperature of the computer's exhaust vent to obtain encoded information.

We propose a suitable thermal signal encoding scheme and protocol, which takes into account the small range and rapid changes in temperature at the computer's exhaust vent. Common encoding schemes such as non-return-to-zero coding, return-to-zero coding, and Manchester coding are not suitable for thermal channel transmission encoding. Using the encoding scheme proposed in this paper, the transmission rate can be effectively improved.

Through experimental verification, the proposed scheme can achieve an effective transmission distance within 4 m and a transmission rate of more than 60bit/h, both superior to comparative schemes. We believe that with better equipment or lower noise levels, longer distances and higher rates can be achieved.

1.2 Structure of This Paper

The rest of the paper is organized as follows: Sect. 2 introduces some relevant knowledge about covert channels and heat signatures. Section 3 describes our attack model and scenarios. Section 4 provides some technical background on computer thermal generation and thermal signaling encoding. Section 5 explains our experimental setup and data collection process. Section 6 provides a summary and outlook.

2 Technical Background

2.1 Sources of Heat in Computers During Operation

The heat produced by a computer during operation mainly originates from its various integrated circuits, especially the high-speed processors such as the Central Processing Unit (CPU) and Graphics Processing Unit (GPU) [18]. These components consume energy while processing information and performing computational tasks, with a portion of this energy being released in the form of heat. Below are the primary sources of heat in computers:

(1) CPU: The Central Processing Unit (CPU) is the core component of a computer, responsible for interpreting the instructions of computer programs and processing data. Heat generation in the CPU primarily stems from the switching action of its internal transistors. When transistors switch from an off state to an on state, or from an on state to an off state, electrical charges flow, generating heat. As the frequency of the CPU increases, meaning more switching actions per second, the heat produced also increases. Moreover, when the CPU executes complex instructions or operates under a high-load condition, more transistors are working simultaneously, resulting in greater heat generation.
(2) GPU: The Graphics Processing Unit (GPU) is a processor designed specifically for complex graphics and image computations. Similar to the CPU, the GPU contains tens of thousands of transistors, which generate a significant amount of heat when processing graphics and image data. The GPU produces particularly high amounts of heat when rendering high-resolution and high-frame-rate images or carrying out large-scale data computations.
(3) Power Supply Components: The power supply section on a laptop's motherboard primarily converts the direct current voltage provided by the battery or adapter into different voltage levels required by various components. This process relies on the interaction of power management chips, MOSFETs (Metal-Oxide-Semiconductor Field-Effect Transistors), inductors, capacitors, and other components. Due to inefficiencies in converting electrical energy, these components generate heat during operation.

(4) Hard Disk Drives (HDD) and Solid State Drives (SSD): Traditional mechanical hard disk drives generate heat during data read and write operations due to the mechanical movement of their spinning platters and read/write heads. Although solid-state drives lack mechanical moving parts, their internal storage cells also produce heat during the data storage and retrieval process.
(5) RAM and Other Motherboard Components: Random Access Memory (RAM) also generates heat when storing and retrieving data. Compared to the CPU and GPU, the heat generated by RAM is less significant. Other components such as sound cards and network cards also produce a small amount of heat during operation.

2.2 Computer Cooling Systems

From the introduction above, we know that the primary heat-generating components in laptops are the CPU and GPU chips. To prevent overheating and damage, modern laptops, particularly high-performance ones, require efficient cooling systems, as shown in Fig. 1. The main components of a cooling system include:

Thermal Paste: Thermal paste is a type of thermal interface material applied to the surface of CPUs and GPUs to fill any microscopic surface irregularities and enhance thermal transfer. Direct metal-to-metal contact may have gaps that reduce the efficiency of heat transfer. Thermal paste fills these tiny gaps to ensure the heat generated by the CPU and GPU is efficiently transferred to the heat spreader [19].

Heat Spreader: The heat spreader is usually made of high thermal conductivity materials such as copper or aluminum, firmly attached to the surface of the CPU and GPU coated with thermal paste. Its main function is to receive heat from the chips and distribute it evenly across a larger surface area to provide a broader contact area for the heat pipes.

Heat Pipes: Heat pipes are hollow tubes filled with a working fluid. When the fluid inside the pipes is heated, it vaporizes into gas and moves to the cooler end of the radiator, where it condenses back into a liquid. This process effectively removes heat from the CPU and GPU.

Heatsink Fins: Heatsink fins are typically made of aluminum due to its good thermal conductivity and lightweight characteristics. The cold end of the heat pipes is usually connected to a series of aluminum fins, which provide.

The heat from the heat spreader is distributed into the air through the fins, dissipating the thermal energy.

Fans: Fans are a key part of the cooling system; they accelerate the airflow between the heatsink fins, carrying away the heat produced by the CPU and GPU. The fan speed is generally adjusted automatically based on the temperature of the CPU and GPU to maximize cooling efficiency while minimizing noise. When the computer is under a high workload, the fan speed increases to provide more cool air passing through the heatsink fins, removing more heat.

When the workload of the CPU or GPU increases, heat is generated by the chip's activity. The computer's BIOS detection increase in chip temperature through temperature sensors within the chip and subsequently controls the fan speed to accelerate cooling. The heat generated is initially conducted through the thermal paste applied to the chip surface, which serves to fill the gaps in the microscopic surface irregularities and

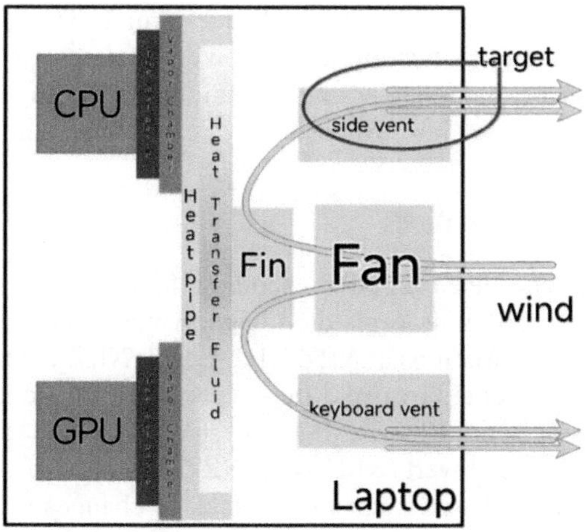

Fig. 1. Laptop Cooling System a large surface area for air to flow through and remove heat.

enhances thermal conductivity. The heat is then conducted to the copper heat spreader directly attached to the chip. The heat spreader has a large surface area, which helps to disperse the heat. The aluminum heatsink fins, connected to the heat spreader, provide an even larger surface area. The heat on the heat spreader is conducted through the heat pipes connected to it. As the working fluid inside the heat pipes absorbs the heat, it vaporizes into a gaseous state and flows to the end of the heatsink fins, where it releases heat and condenses. Thus, the heat pipe achieves the transfer of heat from the heat spreader end to the heatsink fin end. When the fan blows in cold air from the outside, it forces air cooling on the heatsink fins. The heat on the fins is carried away, achieving the cooling effect, maintaining the chip temperature within the normal operating temperature range, and ensuring the stability and performance of the computer.

In summary, changes in computer chip load can cause variations in the temperature at the laptop's exhaust. By malicious software, the load of the computer chip can be changed periodically, which can cause regular variations in the temperature at the laptop's exhaust. Attackers can observe these changes from a distance, thereby realizing information leakage.

2.3 Principles and Characteristics of Thermal Imaging Devices

Thermal imaging devices utilize infrared thermal imaging technology to measure the infrared radiation from target objects. Through photoelectric conversion, signal processing, and other means, they convert the thermal distribution data of the target object into video images. The principle of thermal imaging devices is to receive the infrared radiation energy from the target through an optical imaging system, then apply it to the photosensitive element of the infrared detector, and obtain infrared thermal images after subsequent circuit and signal processing. Essentially, the device images the energy in the infrared band and then, through pseudo-color processing, different colors represent different temperatures, allowing for a visual representation of the temperature distribution on the surface of the object [20].

The characteristics of thermal imaging devices are: 1. They are passive and non-contact for detection and identification, with good concealment. 2. They are not limited by light conditions and can operate normally both during the day and at night. 3. They have high measurement precision, with accuracy controllable within ±0.2 °C.

2.4 Common Encoding Methods

(1) Non-Return-to-Zero (NRZ): In NRZ encoding, logical states (such as 1 and 0) are represented by two different levels of voltage, which remain constant over a clock cycle. There are two variations of NRZ:NRZ-Level (NRZ-L): In this variant, logical "1" and "0" are represented by two different constant voltage levels. For example, a high level may represent "1" and a low level may represent "0", as indicated by the blue line in Fig. 2.NRZ-Invert (NRZ-I): In NRZ-I, instead of voltage levels directly representing the logical states, changes or lack of changes in voltage level signify the bit information. For instance, if the current bit is the same as the previous, the voltage level remains the same; if the current bit is different from the previous, the voltage level flips. The advantage of NRZ encoding is its simplicity and high data transmission efficiency because each bit requires only one clock cycle. The downside is the absence of clock information, making it difficult for the receiver to determine bit boundaries, and the receiver needs to recover the synchronization clock.

(2) Return-to-Zero (RZ): In RZ encoding, the signal returns to zero voltage level midway through each bit, meaning a logical "1" or "0" might be represented by a voltage jumping from zero to some positive or negative value, then back to zero, rather than maintaining a constant value throughout the bit period. A logical "1" is usually represented by a voltage jumping to a high level then back to zero, while a logical "0" by a voltage jumping to a low level then back to zero, as indicated by the yellow line in Fig. 2. The advantage of RZ coding is the self-restoring clock function, allowing the receiver to recover the clock and resynchronize through signal transitions. Since each bit returns to zero, RZ coding requires more bandwidth to transmit the same amount of data compared to NRZ.

(3) Manchester Encoding: In Manchester encoding, each bit period is divided in half, with a voltage transition occurring at the midpoint of each bit. For example, a transition from high to low voltage represents a 1, and from low to high represents a 0, as shown by the green line in Fig. 2. This transition provides a mechanism for clock synchronization to the receiving device because each data bit contains a distinct edge that can be used for timing synchronization. The advantage of Manchester encoding is that it allows for self-clock recovery and resynchronization within the signal; the downside is that each data bit requires two voltage changes for encoding, reducing the efficiency of data bandwidth.

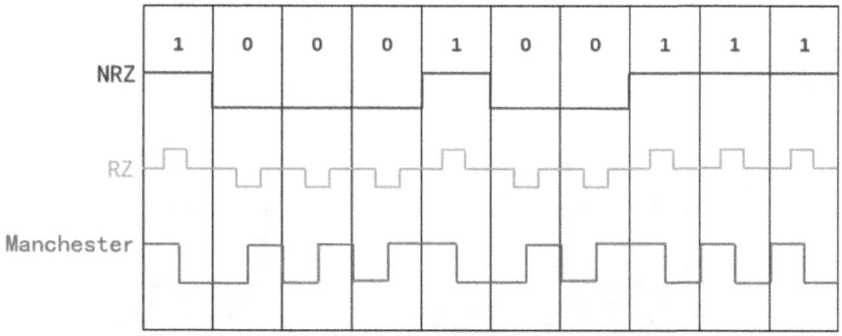

Fig. 2. Illustration of Common Encoding Methods

3 Heaker: An Efficient Scheme Against Physically Isolated Computers

To achieve long-distance, covert, and rapid communication from physically isolated computers, transmitting information out of the physically isolated computers, we designed a Heaker scheme (as shown in Fig. 3). This scheme operates by running a program within the physically isolated computer, causing the CPU/GPU to generate heat, thus leading to temperature changes at the notebook's exhaust ports. The sensitive information to be transmitted is modulated onto the exhaust port temperature to carry out the sensitive information transfer; then, using a remote thermal imager, the temperature of the physically isolated computer's exhaust port is collected, and by decoding the temperature, the sensitive information is demodulated from the temperature data.

3.1 Attack Scenario

In our study, the attack target is a notebook computer that has implemented various security measures, including physical disconnection from the public internet and strict restrictions on the use of external storage devices such as USB. Although this notebook computer has taken the aforementioned security measures, it still stores sensitive information, such as encryption keys, which are of great value to attackers.

The primary step in the attack is to deploy malicious software on the target computer stealthily. The main function of this malware is to collect and filter out high-value information, such as encryption keys and other short yet critical data, from the target system. Once the required information is collected, the malicious software will transmit the data via carefully designed thermal signals.

For covert transmission of information, the malicious software will control the notebook computer's CPU and GPU workload, modulating the temperature near the exhaust fan outlet. These subtle temperature changes are almost imperceptible to ordinary users, but for attackers equipped with thermal imaging devices, they are an effective means of data transmission.

Attackers may choose to carry out the attack when the user is absent, such as during night hours, to reduce the risk of detection. Additionally, the attack can be performed while the user is operating the computer, taking advantage of the heat generated by user operations as cover. The attacker would use a thermal imager to observe and record the temperature changes of the target computer from an appropriate distance.

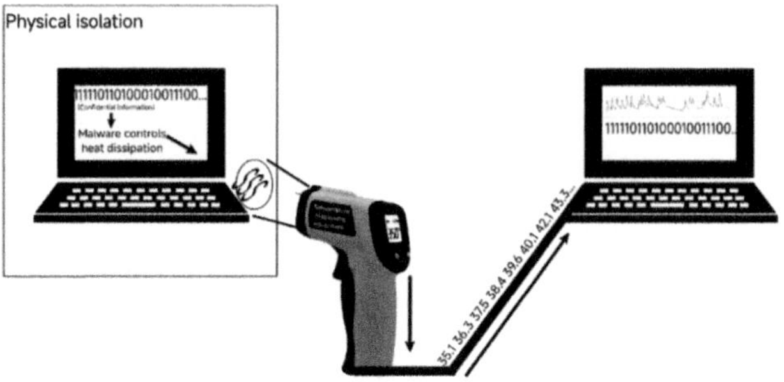

Fig. 3. Heaker method

These records are then analyzed and decoded to recover the original binary information. Our attack method faces the following challenges and limitations:

(1) Environmental factors: Thermal signals are easily affected by environmental temperature, computer workload, and observation distance. Therefore, attackers must adjust transmission parameters according to current environmental conditions to ensure the effective transmission of thermal signals.
(2) Transmission efficiency issues: Compared to electromagnetic or optical signals, thermal signals change more slowly and are more susceptible to environmental interference, limiting transmission speed and effective distance. To overcome this obstacle, attackers need to use efficient encoding schemes and communication protocols to ensure the reliability of data transmission.
(3) Challenges of concealment: Although thermal signals are covert to some extent in the process of modulating thermal signals, the target notebook computer may produce abnormal fan noise or surface temperature changes. These phenomena could attract the user's attention, thereby increasing the risk of the attack being discovered.

In summary, our attack scenario demonstrates the possibility and challenges of secretly extracting information from physically isolated secure computers. In the implementation process, attackers need to carefully plan and consider multiple factors to ensure the successful execution of the attack and minimize the risk of detection.

3.2 Communication Protocol Design

In order to implement the Heaker attack, it is necessary to design a communication protocol between the sender and receiver to achieve reliable transmission of information. Due to the thermal signal's characteristic of slow change—that is, the propagation of temperature changes do not complete instantaneously like electrical signals, and a thermal signal's change requires some time to stabilize. Besides, thermal signals are highly susceptible to environmental influences and interferences. These physical characteristics determine that our communication protocol design must possess sufficient reliability to ensure that the receiving end can accurately detect and decode the signal.

To facilitate recognition and synchronization by the receiving end, we introduced start and end flag bits, which contain specific patterns. In this paper, we define the start flag as "10101010" and the end flag as "11111111". Such flag bits can help the receiving end determine the beginning and end of a data frame. In addition, we included checksum bits to increase transmission reliability, as well as a retransmission mechanism to cope with the unidirectional nature and unreliability of the thermal channel.

Table 1. Communication Protocol

Start Flag	Data	CRC-16 Checksum	End Flag
10101010	32bit	16bit	11111111

The frame structure specifically includes the following parts, as shown in Table 1. Our communication protocol consists of the following components:

(1) Start Flag: To enable the receiver to recognize the start of transmission, the sender sends a fixed synchronization code before each transmission. In this scheme, it is "10101010," which is used to identify the start of transmission and to recognize the sending clock cycle.
(2) Data Bits: Data bits are used to transmit the actual data. The number of data bits can be adjusted as needed. In this scheme, 32 bits are packaged into one frame for transmission. The sender modulates the binary data to be transmitted according to the coding scheme of this paper, that is, within one clock cycle, if a temperature rise followed by a fall exceeding a certain threshold is detected, it is recognized as bit1. Conversely, if no significant temperature fluctuation is detected within a clock cycle—that is, if there is no significant change or a temperature drop—then it is recognized as bit0.
(3) Checksum Bits: To ensure the reliability of transmission, this paper adds a 16-bit CRC check field at the end of the data frame. Before sending each data frame, the sender calculates the CRC-16 check value corresponding to the content of the data frame and places the computed CRC value in the CRC field. After receiving a data frame, the receiver also calculates the CRC-16 check value based on the content of the received data frame. The receiver compares the CRC value it calculated with the CRC field in the data frame. If the two are the same, it indicates that there were no errors in the data frame during transmission, and the verification is passed. If the two are different, it indicates that errors have occurred in the data frame during transmission.
(4) End Bit: To enable the receiver to recognize the end of transmission, the sender sends a fixed end code after each transmission. In this scheme, it is "11111111," used to identify the end of transmission.
(5) Retransmission Mechanism: Since the thermal channel is unidirectional, the receiver cannot send acknowledgment signals directly. Reliability can only be achieved

through retransmission by the sender. For example, the sender repeatedly transmits the same frame of data 3–5 times. The receiver starts receiving when it is appropriate, and after obtaining multiple frames, extracts the correct frame through comparison. A majority voting mechanism can be used, choosing the frame that agrees with the majority as the correct data.

(6) Transmission Rate: Considering that the temperature at the exhaust port needs some time to rise and for the heat to dissipate, the sender waits for a certain time before sending the next bit, ensuring that the temperature sufficiently falls.

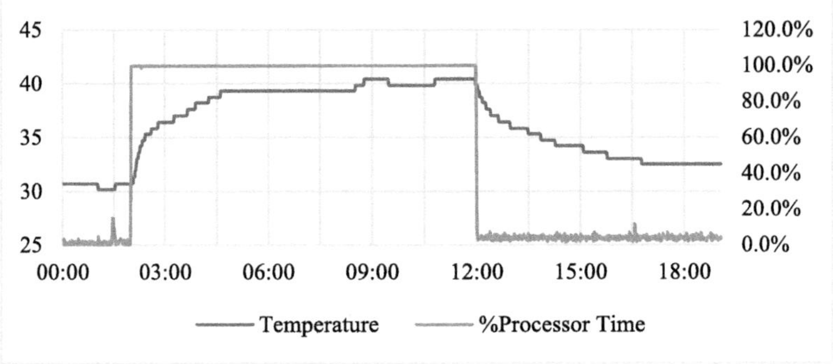

Fig. 4. Temperature changes in laptop air outlet

This paper selects a 60-s bit period, equivalent to transmitting 60 bits per hour, to achieve a lower error rate.

3.3 Design of Encoding Scheme

Common encoding methods such as non-return-to-zero (NRZ) and return-to-zero (RZ) are based on electrical or optical signals that can change rapidly (jumping from 0 to 1 or from 1 to 0) and maintain stable states (sustain a 1 or a 0 over time).

In the Heaker attack scenario, the physical layer consists of thermal signals propagated through the air. Due to the physical characteristics of thermal channels, the temperature signals at the computer's exhaust ports (rising and falling) change slowly. As shown in Fig. 4, at the 2-min mark, both the CPU and GPU are under full load, followed by a rise in temperature at the exhaust port, peaking at 4:40. Afterward, the load on the CPU and GPU continues until the 12th minute when they are released, and the computer reverts to an idle state, leading to a temperature drop at the notebook's exhaust. At the 17-min mark, the temperature drops to a valley and then stabilizes. It is evident that it takes over 150 s from the onset of full chip thermal load to reach the peak temperature. From cessation of heating in idle state to reaching the valley temperature, it takes about 5 min. It is clear that the change in thermal signals is slow and cannot achieve the rapid transitions like electrical signals. Additionally, due to the characteristics of physically isolated computers, the designed communication is simplex and handshake-free. Therefore, traditional encoding schemes for electrical or optical signals are not applicable for thermal channels, necessitating a specialized encoding method for thermal signals.

Considering the characteristics of thermal channels, this paper designs a novel binary information encoding scheme called ThermoCode. In ThermoCode, we define a clock cycle and determine the binary bit value based on the temperature change pattern within that cycle. Specifically, if an increase and subsequent decrease in temperature are observed within a clock cycle, and this change exceeds a predetermined threshold, we consider a bit1 to have been transmitted. Conversely, if there is no significant temperature rise or fall within a clock cycle, or if a temperature drop is observed, then we decide that a bit0 has been sent. The ideal situation of the ThermoCode encoding scheme is illustrated in Fig. 5.

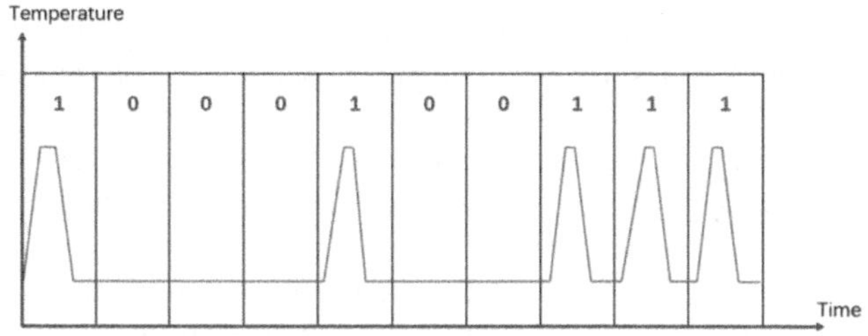

Fig. 5. ThermoCode Ideal scenario diagram

The advantages of this encoding scheme are:

(1) Low System Resource Utilization and Stealth: As the heating duration within a clock cycle is short, system resource utilization is minimized, reducing heat and fan noise, enhancing the stealth of the attack, making it difficult for users to detect abnormalities.
(2) Few Signal Flips: By reducing the number of signal transitions, the encoding method increases the amount of information carried by each signal state, improving transmission efficiency. Furthermore, according to different working environments, the sender can adjust the temperature change cycle, such as choosing 30 or 60 s as a cycle, to enhance the channel's resistance to adverse conditions.

In order to compare the performance of the coding method proposed in this paper with the existing common communication coding methods under a thermal channel, we selected a binary bit stream "1000100111" and recorded the changes in CPU load and the temperature of the laptop's exhaust under non-return-to-zero code, return-to-zero code, Manchester coding, and our coding method.

(1) Non-Return-to-Zero Code: According to the definition of non-return-to-zero code, during a clock cycle, maintaining a high temperature represents bit 1, while maintaining a low temperature represents bit 0. The experimental results are shown in Fig. 6. This method requires maintaining a high load state for a long period within a clock cycle, which generates a significant amount of heat, increasing the noise of the computer's fan. As this coding method occupies the CPU continuously when sending bit 1, it slows down the user's operation response and has poor concealment.

Furthermore, as the transmission proceeds, the temperature will show an overall rising trend, as the red line in Fig. 7 indicates. Moreover, the initial temperature and the maximum temperature that can be reached are also influenced by the ambient temperature, making it impossible to define a fixed low or high-temperature threshold, thus non-return-to-zero code is unsuitable for thermal channels.

(2) Return-to-Zero Code: In return-to-zero coding, a positive pulse represents 1, and a negative pulse represents 0. To implement a negative pulse in the thermal channel, it is necessary to maintain a certain load on the CPU at all times during and a short period before the transmission to maintain a baseline temperature. A full CPU load is used to generate a positive pulse when sending bit 1. To create a negative pulse for sending bit 0, the CPU usage is completely stopped, as shown in Fig. 8. Using return-to-zero code requires occupying the CPU for a long time, which has poor concealment, and besides, the negative pulse change is not significant and difficult to recognize.

(3) Manchester Coding: Due to the characteristics of the computer's cooling system, the temperature change at the computer's exhaust caused by the heating of the CPU or GPU is slow, and the dissipation of the cooling also has a certain lag. Manchester coding is a type of synchronous coding that relies on signal transitions at specific times to represent data. However, due to the time delay of thermal conduction, it is difficult to maintain synchronization with Manchester coding of thermal signals, making decoding difficult. Manchester coding needs frequent signal flips within each bit time cycle, but the thermal signal changes relatively slowly and cannot flip quickly at the precise moment. As can be seen from Fig. 9, the temperature signal rise and fall are not rapid but rather a gentle change. This causes the receiving end to be unable to accurately determine the timing of the signal flip.

(4) The Coding Scheme of This Paper Compared with return-to-zero coding, our coding method only occupies the CPU for 33% of the time, offering better concealment. As shown in Fig. 10, our coding method occupies the CPU only during the first 33% of the time when sending bit 1. Moreover, our coding method takes into full account the gradual and lagging characteristics of the thermal channel, conveying information through the overall trend of temperature changes rather than relying on precise flipping timing, and is less affected by environmental noise, therefore enabling more reliable communication.

3.4 Choice of Duty Cycle

In the Heaker attack methodology, the duty cycle is a key factor determining the quality of data transmission and the stealthiness of the attack. The duty cycle refers to the proportion of time that the CPU is utilized to generate heat signals during a ThermoCode encoding cycle. This section will discuss the choice of the duty cycle and its impact on the performance of the attack. To select an optimal duty cycle, a balance must be struck between a high recognition rate of transmitted data and good concealment (the shorter the CPU utilization time, the better the concealment).

We studied the error rate under different duty cycles at two different heat generation powers and two transmission rates of 60bit/h and 120bit/h. The experimental results of the duty cycle and error rate are shown in Table 2.

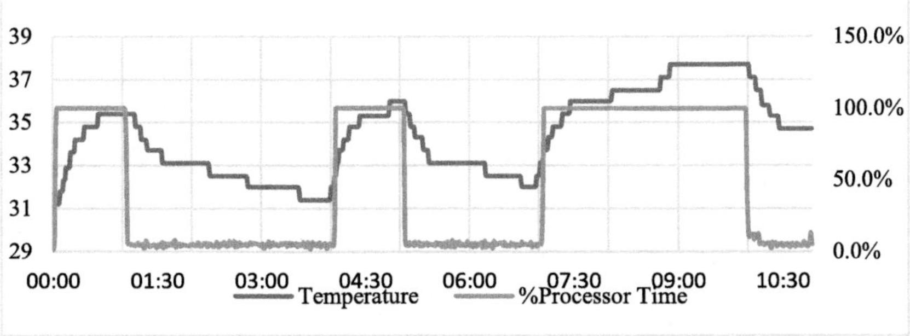

Fig. 6. Non-Return-to-Zero Code Temperature and CPU Usage

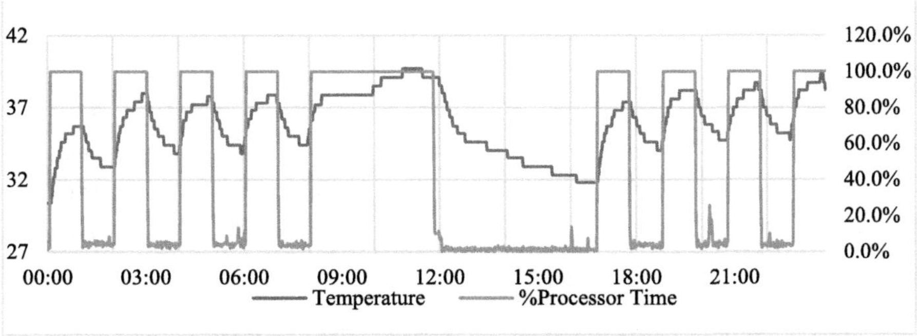

Fig. 7. Non-Return-to-Zero Code temperature trend

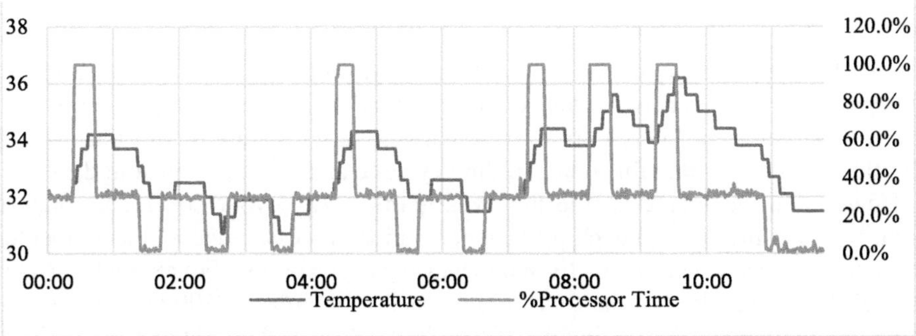

Fig. 8. Return-to-Zero Code Temperature and CPU Usage

The results demonstrate that the duty cycle plays a significant role during encoding. When set too low, for instance, at 10%, the duration of CPU workload is too short, resulting in insufficient heat generation to cause a notable temperature change at the exhaust port, making it challenging for the receiver to accurately identify the transmission of '1'. In this case, the error rate can reach as high as 100%, rendering data transmission ineffective. As the duty cycle increases, the CPU's heat generation time extends, leading

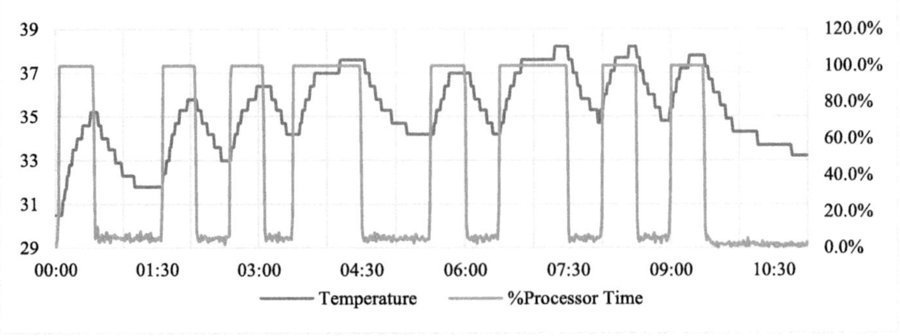

Fig. 9. Manchester Coding Temperature and CPU Usage

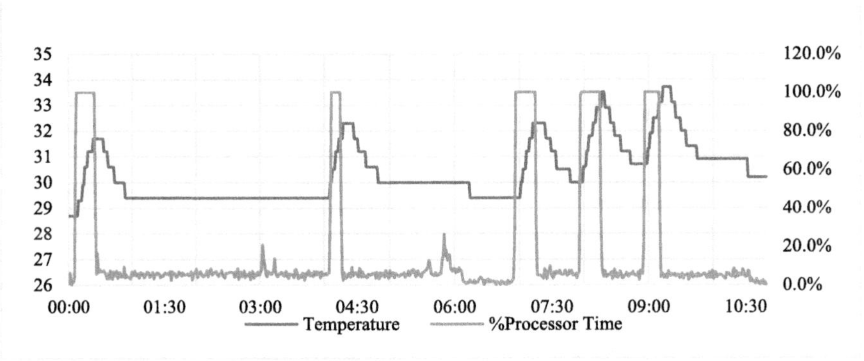

Fig. 10. The Coding Method of This Paper Temperature and CPU Usage

to more distinct temperature changes at the exhaust port, which aids in more accurate data detection by the receiving device. We observed a significant drop in error rate at a duty cycle between 33% to 66%, even reaching an error rate of 0% under certain conditions, indicating that this range of duty cycles can effectively transmit data.

However, further increasing the duty cycle, particularly beyond 66%, results in insufficient cooling time during the chip's heat generation process, reducing the temperature difference between consecutive '1's and increasing the error rate. For example, at a duty cycle of 90%, regardless of the transmission rate of 60bit/h or 120bit/h, the error rate increases significantly, suggesting that too high of a duty cycle is counterproductive for accurate data transmission.

In addition, the duty cycle directly affects the stealthiness of the attack. An increased duty cycle implies a longer time of high workload occupying the CPU, leading to louder fan noise and potentially attracting user attention, thus increasing the risk of the attack being detected. Therefore, when choosing a duty cycle, a balance must be found between signal transmission accuracy and the concealment of the attack.

Considering both the performance and stealthiness of the attack, we generally recommend a duty cycle between 30%–50%. As the experimental data indicates, this range not

Table 2. Duty Cycle Comparison Chart

Duty Cycle	Experimental Conditions	Bit Error Rate	Duty Cycle	Experimental Conditions	Bit Error Rate
10%	CPU-8 threads, 2m, 60bit/h	100.0%	10.0%	CPU + GPU, 2m, 120bit/h	100.0%
33%	CPU-8 threads, 2m, 60bit/h	0.0%	33.0%	CPU + GPU, 2m, 120bit/h	1.0%
50%	CPU-8 threads, 2m, 60bit/h	0.0%	50.0%	CPU + GPU, 2m, 120bit/h	0.0%
66%	CPU-8 threads, 2m, 60bit/h	0.0%	66.0%	CPU + GPU, 2m, 120bit/h	0.0%
80%	CPU-8 threads, 2m, 60bit/h	0.0%	80.0%	CPU + GPU, 2m, 120bit/h	3.0%
90%	CPU-8 threads, 2m, 60bit/h	2.0%	90.0%	CPU + GPU, 2m, 120bit/h	6.0%

only maintains a low error rate but also provides a degree of concealment for the attack. Additionally, different system and environmental conditions may require fine-tuning of the duty cycle to achieve optimal results.

4 Experimental Setup

This section describes how the experiments were conducted, including the experimental setup and data collection process, and outlines the environment and parameters for the experiments. Our experiments are divided into two parts: The Transmitter and The Receiver. The Transmitter sends sensitive information from the compromised computer out into the external environment via thermal signals. The Receiver captures these temperature change signals and analyzes them to reconstruct the information sent by the Transmitter.

4.1 The Transmitter

The Transmitter used in our experiments, which is the computer under attack, is the Lenovo Legion 5 Gaming Laptop. The specific configuration parameters are shown in Table 3:

To carry out our attack, it is first necessary to gain control over the target computer, in other words, to infect it with our malware. This can be achieved through supply chain attacks, social engineering, or malicious insiders. These computers typically employ a "strict-on-entry, loose-on-exit" security policy. The malware collects sensitive information within the compromised computer, such as passwords and keys, and then waits for the right moment to send this data.

Choosing the right moment to send the data is related to the current operating state of the computer, the user's activities, and the time of day. When the computer is under a

Table 3. Transmitter Computer Parameters

Parameter	Specification
Processor	AMD Ryzen 7 5800H
Graphics Card	NVIDIA GeForce RTX 3050 Ti
Memory	16 GB DDR4 3200MHz
Power Supply	230 W charger
Cooling System	4 vents, 3 heat pipes, 2 fans
Operating System	Windows 10 Pro

heavy workload, such as executing computation-intensive tasks, this leads to high CPU usage baselines. Since the attack also modifies the computer's temperature by controlling the computer's load, the heat generated by these workloads will interfere with the signal sent by the Transmitter, causing an increase in the bit error rate. User activities like office software use or web browsing usually do not interfere with the attack.

Determining the power for sending information. A higher CPU load can generate more heat, making the temperature changes at the computer's vents more noticeable and easier for the Receiver to identify, improving transmission efficiency and reducing the bit error rate. However, a higher CPU load will lead to louder fan noise and attract the user's attention, reducing the stealthiness of the attack. A lower CPU load will be quieter and not affect the user's work but may decrease the Receiver's recognition rates due to less noticeable temperature changes.

Determining the clock cycle for sending. The term "clock cycle" refers to the interval between each temperature change. The longer the clock cycle, the more sufficient the temperature change at the vent, giving the Receiver ample time to collect temperature change information. Therefore, a longer clock cycle has higher accuracy but lower transmission efficiency, as it takes more time to transmit 1 bit of information.

In our experiments, we used the AIDA64 software's System Stability Test function to control the workload of the CPU and GPU chips. The Stress FPU and Stress GPU options provided by the System Stability Test function can put the computer's CPU and GPU chips under high load, thus generating a significant amount of heat. We controlled the CPU chip load with the FurMark CPU Burner. FurMark CPU Burner allows setting the number of threads, thereby controlling the intensity of the CPU load.

To automate the process of load modulation, we developed a program that can control the mouse pointer and click the buttons of the aforementioned software. This program takes four parameters as input: 1) the coordinates for the start and stop buttons, 2) the clock cycle, 3) the duration of the full load, and 4) the binary sequence. Then, following a specific encoding scheme, the program periodically clicks the software buttons, starting and stopping the chip's work according to the binary sequence and timing parameters, thus controlling the heat dissipation.

4.2 The Receiver

The Receiver uses thermal imaging equipment to observe temperature changes in the vicinity of the vents of the attacked computer from a distance, records these temperature changes, and then analyzes the data. Reception and decoding of the data do not necessarily have to be processed in real-time, meaning the Receiver can save the temperature change data for delayed analysis.

The Receiver used in our experiments, which is the thermal imaging device that captures thermal signals, is the Uti260B model. The specific configuration parameters are shown in Table 4:

Table 4. Thermal Imaging Device Parameters

Parameter	Specification
Sensor	UFPA
Measurement resolution	0.1°C
Accuracy	±2°C/±2%(whichever is greater)
Response time	≤500 ms
Infrared spectral bandwidth	8 μm–14 μm
Field of view	56° (H) × 42° (V)
Spatial resolution (IFOV)	3.8 mrad
Thermal sensitivity	<60 mK
Frame rate	<25 Hz

As information is transmitted unidirectionally from the sender to the receiver, the two cannot engage in bidirectional negotiation. The sender is unable to know whether the receiver has successfully received the data. Therefore, a major concern is how to synchronize the signal. To address this, we propose a repeated transmission method. When the sender deems the timing appropriate, for instance when the user is away from the computer or when the computer workload is low, it begins transmitting data. The sender will continue to transmit the same data repeatedly until conditions are no longer suitable for transmission, then wait for the next opportunity to send. The receiver, when the opportunity arises, will begin receiving data, such as when there is a clear line of sight to the transmission computer. The receiver will continue receiving data until it has collected the entire data sequence. The receiver can apply error detection and correction techniques to deal with noise and interference in the thermal channel. This solution ensures the receiver eventually obtains complete data from the sender.

Industrial thermal imagers might not directly offer the function to output numerical temperature data but display the temperature values in image form. To acquire numerical temperature data, we projected the thermal imager's display onto a computer using the USB Video Class (UVC), allowing us to capture the thermal imager's display on the computer. Then, using screenshot tools, we captured the display image of the thermal imager on the computer every second, thus obtaining image format files. Some thermal imagers come equipped with an automatic screenshot function that can save picture files to a storage card within the imager, which can replace the computer screenshot step. Once we have the picture-formatted temperature data, we use OCR software to convert these pictures into text, obtaining numerical temperature data.

After acquiring numerical temperature data, it is necessary to preprocess the data since OCR conversion of original picture-formatted temperature data might introduce errors. Data is filtered and cleaned to correct non-numerical data.

In fact, attackers can manually recover the received information by carefully analyzing the temperature data. The numerical temperature data collected by the thermal imager can be plotted as a line chart, with time on the x-axis and temperature on the y-axis, and grid lines added to aid in the precise observation of temperature changes over time. To decode the transmitted binary information, the attacker needs to closely observe the temperature changes within each predefined clock cycle. A clock cycle is a fixed time interval during which the temperature change is monitored to determine the binary value being transmitted. If the temperature within a clock cycle rises significantly and then falls, exceeding a predetermined threshold, this fluctuation is interpreted as a binary '1'. Conversely, if the temperature remains relatively stable or only decreases without a preceding significant rise, it is interpreted as a binary '0'. This manual recovery process requires the attacker to pay close attention to detail, accurately understand the encoding scheme, and distinguish between normal environmental temperature variations and the deliberate temperature changes used for data encoding. This means that the attacker must repeatedly cross-reference the observed temperature data with known binary encoding patterns to ensure accurate interpretation. Although this manual method can be time-consuming and labor-intensive, it is a crucial step in validating and understanding the overall efficiency and reliability of the thermal communication channel in the Heaker scheme.

However, manual analysis is inefficient and labor-intensive when faced with large amounts of data collected over a long period. To address this, we developed a recognition program capable of automatically converting temperature data into binary information.

4.3 Implementation Details

Our experiments were conducted indoors to avoid interference caused by human movement and other heat sources or obstructions, excluding the influence of environmental temperature changes.

The thermal imager's temperature measurement display mode was set to "Key Area Temperature Measurement Mode," which can automatically track the hot spot within an area and also effectively exclude interference from other heat sources. Before the experiment began, the thermal imager was placed at a distance in line with experimental requirements, positioned to observe temperature changes at the laptop's vents.

For each experiment, a fixed 100-bit binary sequence was used as a test sample, with each set of experimental conditions repeated 5 times, and the best-performing set of data was selected for analysis.

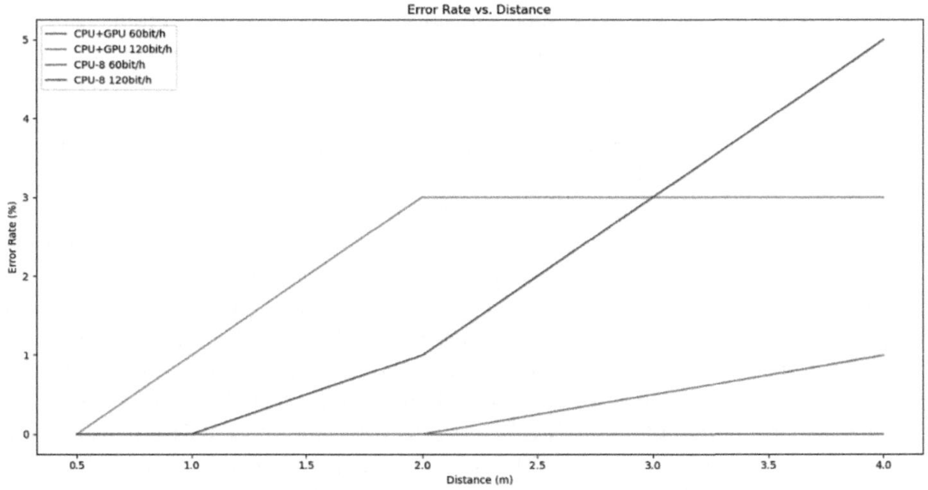

Fig. 11. Relationship between BER and Distance

5 Experimental Results

In this section, we evaluate the performance of our system based on the receiver's ability to recover information from the sender's computer, using the Bit Error Rate (BER) as a metric to assess the attack performance under different conditions, and discuss factors affecting the performance of the experiment.

(1) The Impact of Observation Distance. The farther the distance, the lower the accuracy of temperature change observation and the greater the error. We studied the relationship between BER and distance at two different transmission rates, as shown in Fig. 11. It can be seen that, under other constant conditions, as the observation distance increases, the BER increases.

(2) The Impact of Transmission Rate. The transmission rate refers to the number of bits transmitted through the thermal covert channel in a given time. A faster transmission rate means shorter intervals between sending each bit, i.e., a shorter clock cycle. Since the temperature change of the computer from heating to heat dissipation and back to the initial level takes some time, if the transmission rate is too fast and the next bit is sent before the computer surface temperature has had time to return to the initial level, this will cause the temperature data to be less distinguishable. Our experiments show that a clock cycle set to 60 s, or 60 bits per hour, can achieve better transmission performance at greater distances; a clock cycle set to 30 s, or 120 bits per hour, can achieve faster transmission speeds, but the BER increases at longer observation distances.

(3) The Impact of Ambient Temperature. Ambient temperature refers to the room temperature where the thermal imaging camera and the attacked computer are located. Changes in ambient temperature will affect the transmission of thermal signals because it affects the dissipation and propagation of heat. To assess the impact of ambient temperature on attack performance, we conducted experiments under

different conditions. The experimental results are shown in Table 5. From the experimental results, it can be seen that compared to a room temperature of 25 °C, the BER increases slightly at 30 °C. This may be due to the increase in ambient temperature causing a decrease in the efficiency of computer heat dissipation, leading to a decline in the distinctiveness of computer surface temperature changes and thus a decrease in the discrimination of thermal signals.

(4) The Impact of Other Computer Loads. In addition to executing our malware, the computer will have other programs that consume CPU resources, such as system processes, daemon processes, user processes, etc. These programs will affect the temperature changes of the CPU, thus causing interference to the transmission of thermal signals. To assess the impact of computer load on attack performance, we conducted experiments under different load conditions. The experimental results are shown in Fig. 12. It can be seen from the figure that as the CPU load increases, the BER also increases. When the CPU burner runs with 2 threads, the BER reaches close to 10% at a transmission rate of 120 bits/h, which indicates that high load reduces the distinctiveness of thermal signals and increases the difficulty of recognition by the receiver. Our experiments also found that light loads such as normal office work and web browsing have little effect on the attack. This suggests that our attack method can be carried out while the user is normally using the computer.

(5) The Impact of Heat Generation Power. The temperature change at the computer's exhaust vent is caused by changes in the load of the CPU and GPU. The higher the load, the more obvious the temperature change, and the easier it is for the receiving end to recognize the signal. However, too high a load will cause fan noise and user attention, reducing the stealthiness of the attack. We conducted experiments at a distance of 4 m under two different transmission rates to study the effect of different heat generation powers on information transmission BER. Our experimental results are shown in Fig. 13. The experimental results show that as the heat generation power increases, the BER of information transmission decreases.

Table 5. Relationship between BER and Ambient Temperature

Rate	Power Consumption	25 °C	30 °C
60bit/h	CPU + GPU Full Load	0%	1%
120bit/h	CPU + GPU Full Load	6%	8%
60bit/h	CPU Full Load	0%	2%
120bit/h	CPU Full Load	5%	16%
60bit/h	CPU-8 Threads	2%	1%
120bit/h	CPU-8 Threads	5%	9%

Our proposed method is compared with existing research as shown in Table 6. A clear limitation of existing research is the short attack distance; our experiments have achieved reliable transmission within 4 m. Furthermore, existing methods have lower

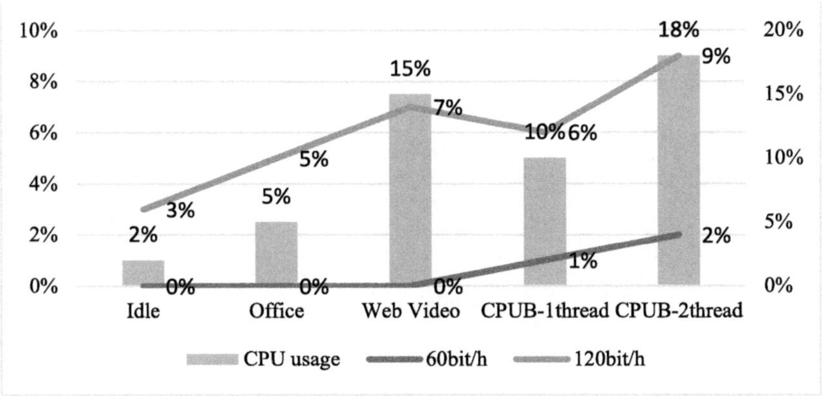

Fig. 12. Relationship between BER and Other Loads

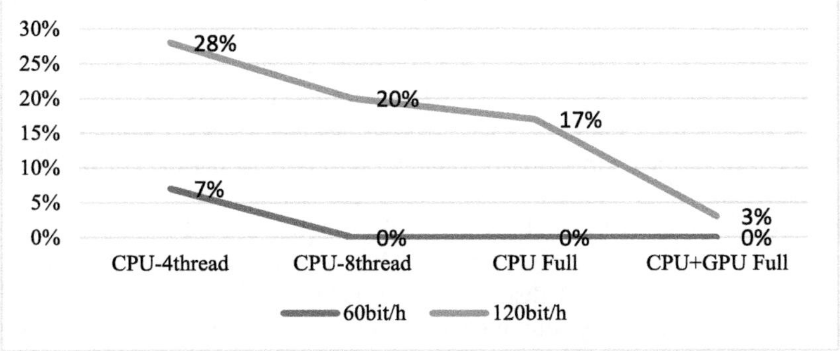

Fig. 13. Relationship between BER and Heat Generation Power

communication rates, while our method can achieve transmission of 120 bits per hour.5. Countermeasures.

In this section, we discuss some possible countermeasures to prevent or detect the covert channel attack based on thermal signals proposed in this paper.

Install firewalls, antivirus, and other security software to regularly scan for and remove malicious software. Restrict the use of storage devices such as USB drives and CDs to prevent computers from being infected with malware.

Use encryption and authentication technologies to protect the security of sensitive information and prevent malicious software from accessing or stealing data.

Employ devices like heatsinks to regulate the computer's temperature, keeping it at a stable level to minimize temperature fluctuations.

Monitor for abnormal temperature changes. Use temperature sensors or thermal imaging to detect if the computer has any unusual thermal fluctuations.

Utilize thermal noise generators or jammers to create random temperature changes around the computer, interfering with the transmission of thermal signals.

Table 6. Comparison with Existing Research

Attack Method	Emitter	Receiver	Attack Distance (m)	Effective Rate (bit/h)
This Paper's Method	Computer	Thermal Imager	4	60–120
BitWhisper	Computer	Computer	0.4	8
HVACKer	AC System	Computer	Not Provided	40
HOTSPOT	Computer	Smartphone	0.5	30–60

6 Conclusion

This paper presents a method for exfiltrating data from air-gapped computers—Heaker. The main contributions include proposing a covert information transmission method based on a thermal channel. Attackers use malware to control the load on CPU, GPU, and other chips in an air-gapped computer, thereby causing temperature changes at the computer's exhaust ports and other areas. By recording and analyzing these temperature changes with a thermal imaging device from a distance, it is possible to recover the information sent by the compromised computer through the thermal channel, achieving covert data leakage.

This paper has demonstrated that it is feasible to achieve reliable transmission within a 4-m range at a transmission rate of 60–120 bits/h. However, we believe that reliable transmission over greater attack distances can be achieved, for example, by using better-performance thermal imaging equipment or reducing the transmission rate. Furthermore, how to conduct attacks in an open environment is also worth further exploration. For instance, how to implement an attack during normal working hours with human activity. The presence of these uncertain factors may affect the quality of the signal and also make the transmission of covert channels more prone to exposure.

References

1. Guri, M., Zadov, B., Bykhovsky, D., Elovici, Y.: PowerHammer: exfiltrating data from air-gapped computers through power lines. IEEE Trans. Inf. Forensics Secur. **15**, 1879–1890 (2020). https://doi.org/10.1109/TIFS.2019.2952257
2. Guri, M.: ETHERLED: sending covert morse signals from air-gapped devices via network card (NIC) LEDs. In: 2022 IEEE International Conference on Cyber Security and Resilience (CSR), Rhodes, Greece, pp. 163–170 (2022). https://doi.org/10.1109/CSR54599.2022.9850284
3. Guri, M., Kachlon, A., Hasson, O., Kedma, G., Mirsky, Y., Elovici, Y. : Gsmem: data exfiltration from air-gapped computers over gsm frequencies. In: USENIX Security Symposium, pp. 849–864 (2015)
4. Guri, M., Monitz, M., Elovici, Y.: Usbee: air-gap covert-channel via electromagnetic emission from usb. In: 2016 14th Annual Conference on Privacy, Security and Trust (PST) , pp. 264–268. IEEE (2016)

5. Guri, M., Zadov, B., Daidakulov, A., Elovici, Y.: Odini: escaping sensitive data from faraday-caged, air-gapped computers via magnetic fields. arXiv preprint arXiv:1802.02700 (2018)
6. Vault 7: Projects (2018). https://wikileaks.org/vault7/?#Brutal%20Kangaroo
7. Glenn, G.: No Place to Hide: Edward Snowden, the NSA, and the U.S. Surveillance State. Metropolitan Books, pp. 1–10 (2014)
8. Network Centric Warfare: Appendix (2001). http://www.dodccrp.org/files/ncw_report/report/ncw_appendix.pdf
9. ACCOMPLISHMENTS (2009). http://www.selectinnovation.com/SI-accomplishments.htm
10. Guri, M., Daidakulov, A., Elovici, Y.: Magneto: covert channel between air-gapped systems and nearby smartphones via cpu-generated magnetic fields (2018). arXiv preprint arXiv:1802.02317
11. Speake(a)r: Turn speakers to microphones for fun and profit. In: 11th USENIX Workshop on Offensive Technologies (WOOT 17). USENIX Association (2017)
12. Guri, M., Solewicz, Y., Daidakulov, A., Elovici, Y.: Fansmitter: acoustic data exfiltration from (Speakerless) airgapped computers (2016). arXiv:1606.05915
13. Guri, M., Zadov, B., Elovici, Y.: LED-it-GO: leaking (a lot of) data from air-gapped computers via the (small) hard drive LED. In: Detection of Intrusions and Malware, and Vulnerability Assessment. DIMVA 2017. Lecture Notes in Computer Science, vol. 10327. Springer, Cham (2017)
14. Guri, M., Bykhovsky, D., Elovici, Y.: aIR-Jumper: covert air-gap exfiltration/infiltration via security cameras & infrared (IR) (2017). arXiv preprint arXiv:1709.05742
15. Guri, M., Monitz, M., Mirski, Y., Elovici, Y.: BitWhisper: covert signaling channel between air-gapped computers using thermal manipulations. In: 2015 IEEE 28th on Computer Security Foundations Symposium (CSF) (2015)
16. Guri, M.: HOTSPOT: crossing the air-gap between isolated PCs and Nearby smartphones using temperature. In: 2019 European Intelligence and Security Informatics Conference (EISIC), Oulu, Finland (2019)
17. Mirsky, G.M.Y., Elovici, Y.: Hvacker: bridging the air-gap by manipulating the environment temperature. In: Proceedings of DeepSec Conference, Magdeburg, Germany, vol. 2 (2016)
18. Hennessy, J.L., Patterson, D.A.: Computer Architecture: A Quantitative Approach. Elsevier, Amsterdam (2011)
19. Gwinn, J.P., Webb, R.L.: Performance and testing of thermal interface materials (2003)
20. Chuang, Y., et al.: Review of temperature measurement technology with infrared thermal imager. In: 2018 China International Conference on Electricity Distribution (CICED), Tianjin, China, pp. 1065–1067 (2018). https://doi.org/10.1109/CICED.2018.8592496

Author Index

S. Goel et al. (Eds.): ICDF2C 2024, LNICST 614, pp. 357–359, 2025.
https://doi.org/10.1007/978-3-031-89360-5

GPSR Compliance

The European Union's (EU) General Product Safety Regulation (GPSR) is a set of rules that requires consumer products to be safe and our obligations to ensure this.

If you have any concerns about our products, you can contact us on ProductSafety@springernature.com

In case Publisher is established outside the EU, the EU authorized representative is:

Springer Nature Customer Service Center GmbH
Europaplatz 3
69115 Heidelberg, Germany

Batch number: 08544862

Printed by Printforce, the Netherlands